SACRAMENT

SACRAMENT

The Language of God's Giving

David N. Power

A Herder & Herder Book
The Crossroad Publishing Company
New York

The Crossroad Publishing Company
370 Lexington Avenue, New York, N.Y. 10017

Printed in the United States of America

Library of Congress Cataloging-in-Publication Data
Power, David Noel.
   Sacrament : the language of God's giving / David N. Power.
     p. cm.
   Includes bibliographical references.
   ISBN 0-8245-1809-8 (hardcover). – ISBN 0-8245-1798-9 (pbk.)
   1. Sacraments (Liturgy) 2. Catholic Church – Liturgy. I. Title.
BX2200.P74 1999
234′.16 – dc21   98-52209

1   2   3   4   5   6   7   8   9   10   04   03   02   01   00   99

Contents

Part One
SACRAMENTAL TRADITIONS IN TRANSITION

Part Three
RENDERING AN ACCOUNT
OF SACRAMENTAL ACTION

Preface

Since this work on sacramental celebration and sacramental theology has a lengthy introduction, it does not need preface other than some words of thanks. It has come to being over several years of teaching courses on theological hermeneutics and on liturgical theology at the Catholic University of America. I wish therefore to acknowledge the insight and response received from students in those courses over the years. Without being part of a community that worships, the possibilities of a contribution that joins the work of interpretation with a knowledge of liturgical traditions might never have matured, so I am grateful to those parish and other congregations with whom I join in keeping memorial of Christ's Pasch. While no doubt some will say that the study belongs to a mature academic readership of liturgical scholars and students, it is my own persuasion that the book can find readers among all who are sensitive to the niceties of celebration and language.

Some persons have contributed to the completion of the book in such a way that their gift/ing calls for mention by name. In the first place, I wish to thank Michael Downey and Richard Fragomeni, both of whom read the entire manuscript as it was in the writing and offered encouragement for the enterprise and many helpful suggestions for its execution. David William Antonio offered the support of a persistent interest and kindly contributed the cover art for the book, as he had previously done for a work on the Eucharist, also published by Crossroad. In the final stages of preparation, I received help from Andrew Small in checking the proofs and from Peter Steiger in compiling the index. To these also I am grateful for assistance not only rendered, but pleasantly rendered.

I am on another plane indebted to my religion congregation, the Missionary Oblates of Mary Immaculate. The Provincial Superiors of the Eastern USA province have graciously afforded me the opportunity to engage in theological inquiry and teaching, and have offered continued support. The local Oblate community in Washington, and each and all of its members over a period of time, have given me a habitat truly habitable, the life-world in which the pursuit of this kind of work was possible.

Lastly, I wish to acknowledge the interest and the work of the staff of The Crossroad Publishing Company, especially James Le Grys and John Eagleson.

DAVID N. POWER, O.M.I.

Ordinary Time, 1999 c.e.
The Catholic University of America
Washington, D.C.

Introduction

Through the sacraments God gives the Church the gift of Word and Spirit, and through this gift the Church worships the giver, keeping the memorial of the Cross and Pasch of Jesus Christ. Sacramental celebrations are God's words and deeds, spoken in a plurality of tongues and forms. They are divine events, occurring among many peoples, relating to different times and different places, as the Gospel and the Church take root in different cultures and are enriched by these cultures. They are celebrations of the Church, gathered as Christ's body in his Spirit. Drawing from traditions, they are enriched by their encounter with diverse cultures.

As sacramental liturgies in many Christian Churches are today caught up in a more marked process of change and renewal, sacramental theologies have to take this into account. Where it was usual in Catholic theology to refer to sacraments as channels of grace, it is now more common to describe them as actions of the Church in which Christ and the Spirit are operative. Since they are related to the reality of the local Church, theology must advert to the fact that communities celebrate in a diversity of cultures, with liturgical adaptations that incorporate the rites and languages of different peoples. It is asked what can be appropriated from the past, and how far can present forms depart from earlier ones. The process of adaptation and inculturation is a reminder that theological explanation, sacramental catechesis, and liturgical forms are not to be too strongly distinguished. They are related to one another, and affect one another. A theology has to be a theology of celebration, not simply in the sense that it teaches us how to celebrate, or about what goes on in the soul when sacraments are celebrated, but more in the sense that theology itself is rooted in the practice of celebration. A living celebration is an interpretation of a tradition, and theology is an interpretation of celebration.

Since celebration itself is an interpretative act, recent liturgical changes have occasioned considerable strife within Christian Churches. Some members accuse their bishops of being unfaithful to the traditions of good worship or criticize the various working committees that were charged with the tasks of revision. Others find these same authorities benighted in their tendencies to revert to forms of clerical domination, giving the lie to the adage that this is the age of the laity. Bishops for their part query whether certain communities are being faithful to the apostolic and catholic teaching, either because they resist change too strongly or because they are too innovative. In relations between Churches, sometimes members of varied ecclesial allegiance happily access the Lord's table together, while others believe that this is a facile and false ecumenism. Within the Catholic Church, or within the Anglican Communion, members may refuse to worship together, being at odds with one another over such issues as the ordination of women, or priestly concelebration, or the uses of liturgical language. Some will not attend a liturgy where there is any mention of political issues; others will not frequent an assembly where such matters are not raised. Styles of worship are marked by pluralism, but it is often a militant pluralism, houses divided within themselves.

Indeed, the term *conflict of interpretations* expresses quite well the different ways in which sacramental tradition is being appropriated by different communities. The act of interpreting is inbuilt into keeping memorial, but this does not mean that a conflict of interpretations has to generate an ecclesial or intraecclesial conflict of a more divisive kind. When the framework was set and commonly accepted, there was not much attention given in sacramental catechesis or sacramental theology to the fact of being engaged in an interpretation whenever a sacrament was celebrated. The conflict was between large ecclesial bodies, not within these Churches themselves. Now, however, the pluralism of interpretation and celebration is found within particular traditions. This intraecclesial pluralism is what makes it necessary to engage consciously in the process of interpretation, doing so in a manner that begets dialogue and conversation across interpretations.

Writing a sacramental theology today, therefore, cannot be done adequately by following a systematic order of theses and the logic of assertions. As a service to the ecclesial community, theology has to arrive at a better statement of what constitutes sacramental tradition and of what it means to live from and within this tradition. This is the only way, moreover, to address present strife. What stands out is that communities are interpreting the tradition diversely, and that even without seeing it that way, they interpret even as they worship. What is intended in this book is to present an approach to sacramental worship for an interpreting Church, one that allows its members to have insight into what is going on and into how they relate to past traditions, within a present that is already passing into a future.

Historical Reconstruction

While historical reconstruction of texts and liturgies is not the intent of this work, something needs to be said, however briefly, about procedures followed in this task. In short, in reading and studying textual historical sources, a number of rules of interpretation need to be kept in mind.[1] In doing this, there is quite a mixture of texts to be kept in mind.

---

1. Paul Bradshaw, *The Search for the Origins of Christian Worship: Sources and Methods for the Study of Early Liturgy* (New York and Oxford: Oxford University Press, 1992), surveys the state of the question for the reconstruction of liturgies from early Church sources.

There are in the first place liturgical orders that provide prayers, scriptural selections, and ceremonial directives. As far as the past is concerned, frequently these elements are not found in the same book, and one does not always know, for example, what lectionary goes with what sacramentary. Hence, some historical reconstruction, such as that done by Antoine Chavasse for the Roman liturgy, is necessary.[2] In many cases, however, it is needful to ask whether a liturgical text is descriptive of what has happened, or prescriptive of what is the proper way to celebrate, or even contestatory, offering a way of celebration that is thought ideal, as opposed to what may be done in practice. Even though it has been taken as a model for some recent liturgical reforms, *The Apostolic Tradition* is a good example of a Church order whose exact nature in this regard becomes less clear the more it is subject to scrutiny.[3]

A further feature of such reconstruction is the effort to link certain liturgies with specific places of worship. This can be done to some extent for the Roman liturgy, especially for Lent and the Paschal season.[4] As another example, it can also be done for the Byzantine liturgy by relating the commentary of Germanus of Constantinople to the great Church of Hagia Sophia.[5]

A third factor to be kept in mind in reconstructing liturgical history is the effort to relate text to celebration. Some clues are found in liturgical books. The Roman *ordines*, for example, prescribe certain ritual actions which change the meaning of a more ancient text. The rubrics directing the recitation of the Roman Canon are a perfect example of this, since they interrupt the flow of the prayer by a change in the tone of voice, and highlight some parts of it, particularly the recitation of the Supper narrative and the concluding doxology. Another clue in a liturgical book is its ornamentation, since this shows how the parts adorned are being interpreted.[6] The most classic example of this is the adornment of the letter *T* in the post-Sanctus of the Roman Canon.

Besides these specifically liturgical texts, there are liturgical commentaries, such as the treatise *De Baptismo* of Tertullian, or the mystagogical catechesis of the fourth and fifth century. There are also apologetic works, such as the treatises of Justin Martyr, polemical works, such as Augustine's treatise on baptism against the Donatists, and homilies, such as those of Augustine or

---

2. See especially, Antoine Chavasse, *La liturgie de la ville de Rome du Ve au VIIe siècle* (Rome: Centro Studi S. Anselmo, 1993).

3. On this canonical and liturgical literature of early centuries, see Alexandre Faivre, *Ordonner la fraternité: Pouvoir d'innover et retour à l'ordre dans l'Église ancienne* (Paris: Éd. du Cerf, 1992), 361–94.

4. See John Baldovin, *The Urban Character of Christian Worship: The Origins, Development, and Meaning of Stational Liturgy* (Rome: Pontifical Oriental Institute, 1987), 105–66.

5. St. Germanus of Constantinople, *On the Divine Liturgy*, the Greek Text with translation, introduction, and commentary by Paul Meyendorff (Crestwood, N.Y.: St. Vladimir's Seminary Press, 1984).

6. For a good introduction, see R. Calkins, *Illuminated Books of the Middle Ages* (Ithaca, N.Y.: Cornell University Press, 1983).

John Chrysostom. These provide information both on how the liturgy was celebrated, what texts were used, and how the liturgy was being interpreted.

The interpretation of history, however, cannot be satisfied with reconstruction of texts from such sources. It needs to relate the development and variation of liturgies as much as possible to context. This context is ecclesial, political, social, and cultural.[7] Unless placed within living context, it is impossible to grasp what was going on when communities celebrated. This of course also alerts us to the fact that we now appropriate texts and liturgical orders from the past into a very different milieu, with repercussions on how these texts are now understood.

Contemporary Issues

This book, however, is not intended to be a work of historical reconstruction, nor a discussion of the hermeneutical principles employed in such work. It is more concerned with an internal hermeneutics or interpretation. That is to say, it accentuates the role of reading and interpreting text as text, following a mode of interpretation that highlights textual genres, and considers the act of appropriation that takes place in celebration. The rest is not ignored, but it plays a secondary role. It is in the eighth chapter that the critical function of attending to prejudgments, cultural values, and social ordering is taken up.

The present social and cultural context within which sacraments are celebrated and Churches draw on traditions and divergent forms of expression is of great importance. Using what have become common etiquettes, it can be said that problems over sacramental worship belong within the tensions of the time between the modern, the premodern, and the postmodern. Debates over what constitutes modernity are endless, but by and large what has disillusioned many with the developments of the last few centuries is the excessive trust in rationality, the secularization of society, and the confidence in the ability through technology and planning to guarantee a new age. There are signs all around us of the harm wrought by this brand of humanism, evidenced in the form of wars, of genocide, of the exploitation of nature, of the domination of the world by industrially and technically advanced countries, and of the growth of an economic underclass, within nations and across the relations between nations.

Somewhere near the heart of such modernity is the loss of the power of language, even as the power to communicate advances through still developing means of communication. Scientific locution, with its precision and abstractions, tended in modernity to be the ideal form of expression, invading the fields of art, architecture, literature, and religion. Hence within the vaguely defined postmodern, there is a vital interest in language and art,

---

7. Some good insights into this are found in Herman Wegman, *Christian Worship in East and West: A Study Guide to Liturgical History,* trans. Gordon W. Lathrop (New York: Pueblo, 1985).

sometimes naive, sometimes highly sophisticated, but always marked by the hope of retrieving the body, the tongue, the eye, and the domain of feeling in human interaction.

Since Christian Churches attended little in the preaching of the Gospel to the cultural realities of peoples evangelized, much needs now to be done by way of fostering a meeting between Gospel and neglected, or even maligned, cultures. Even, however, as Christians address themselves more and more to the relation between Gospel and culture, the hold on culture grows increasingly tenuous. Cultures are passing through transitions at a rapid pace, especially as the expertise of technology and global communication make marked advances across the world. We have become aware that the relation between Gospel and culture has always been problematic, and as Christians hark back to apostolic teaching to recover their roots, they have to face the pluralism of its expression. There is no ideal past on which to draw.

Once we are alerted to cultural perspectives, to the questions of the postmodern mind, and to change within the process of celebration, it is inevitable that the two words *hermeneutics* and *postmodern* come to the fore. They are words that one might like to avoid, since they are used so promiscuously. It is not intended to repeat them very often in the course of this book, where the accent is rather on what it means to interpret, and how interpretation is done, both in practice and in critical reflection. Something, however, needs to be said at the outset as to how the issues that converge under these designations are kept in mind.

Hermeneutics

Excessively simple though it may seem, it is nonetheless pertinent to note that a hermeneutical approach to a tradition and to language starts with a keen sense of listening and of being addressed. Language is not primarily an instrument that allows people and communities to accomplish something, or to produce ideas and things. Every time we hear someone speak, every time we encounter a text, every time we look at a work of art, every time we engage in a ritual action, we are addressed by some person, tradition, or reality other than ourselves. It requires attentive listening to be engaged by this, to be responsible to what is communicated. This applies even when we speak or write ourselves. Many of us in childhood were accustomed to a parental admonition, "Just listen to what you are saying." If we heeded the admonition, we came to realize that in using a language and a system of references embodied in its usage, we were saying more than we thought. Speaking or writing is a response to what has been given to us, an engagement that is attentive to being first addressed. It is in such simple, yet difficult, perceptions that hermeneutics is rooted.

Contemporary hermeneutics spells out the relation between human language and human being. It draws attention to the fact that in and through language humans are involved with that about which language is used. There is no purely objective and abstract cognition to guide thought and action, but in hearing and using language there is a radical involvement with life and with the totality of things and a world that is projected.

Hermeneutics thus means a more sharply refined appreciation of language and its polysemism and of what goes on in the course of interpreting, challenging interpretations and systems, and in appropriating, despite the variations, what is remembered and projected into life. Hermeneutics is not merely about reading codes properly, but about living within them and from what they convey or hand on. This means setting aside, or working through, attention to metaphysical constructs, to efficient activity, and to subjective consciousness so as to grasp the realities of linguistic expressions. There is need to attend to what language says to peoples of reality and to how they interpret their own language traditions and become involved as a community or as a people with what is handed on.

It is the accent on temporality that gives the edge to hermeneutics and gets its practitioners beyond the dilemma of what is objective and what subjective. Texts emerge within given circumstances, cultures, experiences, of the world. The work of human creativity is to be acknowledged, yet insight, understanding, meaning, and being do not have their origins simply in human subjectivity. The aesthetic, the artistic, the literary, express the world and human relation to it, express what comes to human persons and communities as it is worked through creativity into the realities of life within a given time. They express also the world that is beyond the immediacy of the given, of the immediately experienced, of what is most readily at hand. They invite those who see or read or hear into a communion with the fuller reality that displays its traces in what is at hand, what is shown, what is expressed. Then, since these expressions are themselves something that emerge in a culture, a time, a historical setting, a place, a space, what they offer is appropriated into another world, another time, another culture, another history.

For Christians who attend to the scriptural texts, to rituals handed on through tradition, to institutions that have taken form and offer guidance, to a history of expression and interpretation, what communicates itself is the reality of God, of God who through love enters into human facticity, into human events, into human time. The original advent, event, is one that occurred in a given time, place, people, and culture and so found its expression within this kind of given. Yet, because this communication speaks of the love of God, of a gift of God that brings humans beyond, even out of, their limited temporality, with a promise for the future, it can be appropriated into the lives of peoples in other times, places, cultures. As transposed, it takes on other historically related and culturally emerging forms and expressions. Hence the work of interpretation is to attend to what is offered in word and rite, to carefully consider the forms of expression within their temporal and cultural modality, and yet respond to what is not limited to these forms, but emerges through them. In doing this, it is not looking for human subjectivity, but for what emerges through the use of these forms in an attentive looking, listening, receiving, responding. It looks for what of the divine has opened itself up in gift, even as it works through human action and creativity to find its dwelling place on earth. What emerges in the creativity of word, of ritual, of artistic forms, expresses more than what the doers themselves see and understand, even as they are caught up in the revelation to which they seek to give expression.

A good hermeneutics has to be grounded in a good phenomenology. Much is due to the influence of Martin Heidegger in the awareness that the study of phenomena, whether of things, of human action, or of language expression, does not lead back simply to the discovery of consciousness, whether personal or collective, nor to some transcendental ego. What phenomena show is the reality and facticity of human existence and effort, and the way in which these are woven into the fabric of the world, of human interaction, and of the social. They also disclose what is offered to human being and living, to what this is directed, and to what human existence is oriented. At the same time, it is seen how humans can be so caught up in facticity and human effort that they are insensitive to, or forgetful of, what is given to them, of what comes to them that is in no way of human origin or under human control.[8] Following Heidegger, language is often referred to as the Home of Being, because in it existence and Being itself receive expression and certain kinds of language are powerful in their expression of what comes to us rather than of what comes from us.

In the hermeneutics of Hans-Georg Gadamer, what is as stake is the relation of language to a Heideggerian *Vorstehen*, poetic language being the language of participation and projection of life.[9] It refers to what it is to be immersed in reality, before any distinctions are made between subject and object, between affect and intelligence, between sensing and knowing. In the writings of Paul Ricoeur, the phenomenology of expression reveals its link to the experience of human finitude and to the intractability of measuring time, as well as to the factual experience of fault, irreducible to any plausible explanation or to any necessity inherent in human nature and will.[10] Ricoeur thus calls for attention to diverse forms of discourse which open up the possibilities of being, acting, and suffering, without having to offer metaphysical explanations. For Jean-Luc Marion, the priority of Good to Being is related to the phenomenology of perception in which he distinguishes between the idol

---

8. Heidegger's concern was with the forgetfulness of Being, but this leads to other perceptions of what it is to be forgetful of dependency and of gift, as well as of others.

9. See Hans-Georg Gadamer, *Truth and Method*, 2d rev. ed., trans. revised Joel Weinsheimer and Donald G. Marshall (New York: Continuum, 1994).

10. For the collection of essays most pertinent to this work, see Paul Ricoeur, *Figuring the Sacred: Religion, Narrative, and Imagination*, trans. David Pellauer, ed. Mark I. Wallace (Minneapolis: Fortress Press, 1995).

and the icon, bringing out the fact that if we attend properly to what it is to perceive, we note that it is what is given to us that has priority, not what we can construe and project for ourselves.[11]

The term *hermeneutics of suspicion* is much repeated of late. This means to look at the role of language in an enterprise which envisages liberation and the transformation of the human order, usually considered in some concrete way and in relation to some given set of experiences. What has to be examined within this perspective is the way in which language traditions and symbolic orders have shaped and even manipulated persons and societies, being instrumental in subjecting classes of persons or whole populations. For Rebecca Chopp, for example, the language that is given primary place is that which expresses the realities of women's experience, as this is examined in its social context and in its depth structure.[12] She asks how and why within the same tradition one can find both life-giving words and words that allow some to dominate others. This requires clear attention to linguistic and symbolic phenomena in their relation to women's experience and to the experience which all may have of a transformed society. To take another example, for the African writer Engelbert Mveng, the basic concern is with the political, cultural, and religious domination of African peoples that results from an epoch of colonialism.[13] Insight into and a close analysis of what he terms the phenomenon of Africa's "anthropological poverty" opens the door to an inculturated and evangelical language that serves to voice Jesus Christ's self-emptying of himself as a person, in behalf of the people of the African continent, where human salvation takes on this distinctive cultural expression.

Though these latter examples show it most clearly, hermeneutics is always oriented to practice (some would say praxis). This does not simply mean that a good interpretation leads to a good application or that it has an effect on behavior. What is underlined is the fact that interpretation is done in face of particular situations and in the interest of some purpose, and that it is not pure or abstract insight but a projection of what can be. For example, in the Middle Ages the liturgy was interpreted and ordered to the maintenance of a just order, in which social order was kept but divine mercy, beyond such order, was also celebrated. In these times, communities hearing the Bible proclaimed, entering into Christ's *pascha* through baptism, remembering Christ's self-gift at the table, are confronted, if so they allow themselves, by remembered genocides. The dangerous memory of Jesus Christ is thus reconstrued by them in the hope of a justice that will hold the memory of the dead and

---

11. See Jean-Luc Marion, *God without Being*, trans. Thomas A. Carlson (Chicago: University of Chicago Press, 1991).

12. Rebecca S. Chopp, *The Power to Speak: Feminism, Language, God* (New York: Crossroad, 1991).

13. Engelbert Mveng, *L'Afrique dans l'Église: Paroles d'un croyant* (Paris: Éditions L'Harmattan, 1985).

commit itself to a just reconciliation among the living. Women who celebrate the Christian memory and engage thereby in a hermeneutics of proclamation and celebration look to the inherited texts with a hermeneutic of suspicion, aware of the intrusions of patriarchy throughout the heritage, yet finding that they recover from the memory of the Jesus movement a discipleship of equals that is a movement for the freedom of the oppressed or marginalized and the possibility of a wholly transformed symbolic and social order.[14] Hermeneutics must also find its proper location. In other words, interpretation is done within a particular set of circumstances, in some place or situation where the interpreter chooses to be, this being the most appropriate positioning in which to receive what is given through words and signs. For this reason, hermeneutics, reclaiming a past and celebrating a present, is done in community. In this community action, while roles are distinguished, the normative factor is not the maintenance of hierarchical order but the reality of participation. Certainly for sacramental theology, and indeed possibly for all theology, the proper location is within sacramental celebration.[15] Even when attention to the process of interpretation distances the thinking from the act of celebration, thinking begins with celebration, is referred back to celebration, and loses itself again in the wonder of celebration.

No retrieval of tradition, however, is possible unless it is noted that the renewal of sacramental liturgy belongs in a context in which many alienations have to be overcome. There is the alienation of the inner self, between rationality and feeling. There is the alienation or estrangement between humans and the earth which they inhabit. There is the alienation of women, subjugated to patriarchal order in social action and often in the very act of liturgy. There is the alienation between races, with the subordination of other races to the white throughout the history of Christianity and the history of liturgy itself. The retrieval of the mystery of God given to believers in sacramental tradition and action must therefore be assessed through its capacity to emancipate and reconcile into fuller participation. This is why it is necessary to recognize that celebration is itself a hermeneutic, and that in the retrieval of the sacramental tradition a hermeneutics of suspicion and a hermeneutics of liberative retrieval go hand in hand.

To explain the concern in somewhat different terms, in hermeneutics one can distinguish a phenomenological moment, a philosophical one, and a properly theological one, granted that they constantly intersect. The intent of phenomenological investigation is to attend to what is expressed, not to sub-

---

14. For a concise presentation of her hermeneutical approach, see Elisabeth Schüssler Fiorenza, *Bread Not Stone: The Challenge of Feminist Biblical Interpretation* (Boston: Beacon Press, 1984).

15. For a survey of how liturgy is being integrated into fundamental theology, see A. Grillo, "L'esperienza rituale come 'dato' della teologia fondamentale: ermeneutica di un remozione e prospettive teoriche di una reintegrazione," in *Liturgia e incarnazione*, ed. Aldo Natale Terrin (Padua: Edizioni Messagero Padova, Abbazia di Santa Giustina, 1997), 167–249.

jective intention. The particular phenomenologies brought to bear on how sacrament inserts itself into life then relate sacramental interpretation and action to the given world of those whose concerns are thus expressed and opened up to understanding and allow for the Christian, imaginative, projection of a life lived in the gracious reception and appropriation of a gracious gift. Even as we seek to celebrate, understand, and appropriate what divine revelation and action give to us, it is necessary to make our own human, social, and cultural world translucent in the very anxiety to be open to the divine gift. From this there flows the importance of those phenomenological investigations which start with the factuality of a world in which people and communities belong and look for what is revealed of this world in its appearances, or in those phenomena through which lived existence, its pain, its meanings, and its possibilities are opened up if they are properly engaged. To grasp a world in its facticity is also to allow it to be opened to what gratuitously enters it.

Thus in attending to sacrament, phenomenology occurs at three levels. First, there is the consideration of the present situation in liturgy and the effort to read it from its conflictual character. Second, there has to be the phenomenology of the language of the holy, found in ritual, related to human experience. Third, is the phenomenology of the language of the Christian tradition in particular. This is the effort to isolate the modes of discourse and rite that occur in Christian sacramental parlance.

The philosophical moment is the consideration of sacramental language in its relation to the language of being and the language of the subject. The postmodern suspicion enters in to question the adequacy of these foundations to an understanding of the human, of tradition, and of the holy. Hence arises the question of positing the reference of the language of the holy outside these parameters of being and subject, so that it appear as what is "beyond being" and as that which precedes the subject in the constitution of its self-consciousness and can never be contained within it. In conjunction with this, the theological key is found in the excess of language that cannot be contained within these parameters, so that there is the effort to follow revelation's own trajectory, in its own proper discourse, to illuminate what occurs in sacrament, and how this occurs.

To sum up these points, it may be helpful to adapt Jean Grondin's distinction between a hermeneutics of suspicion, a hermeneutics of faith, and a hermeneutics of confidence.[16] The suspicion makes us alert to whatever is ideological and humanly dominating in the use and configuration of sacramental order and language. Within this, however, and beyond it, there is a hermeneutics of faith, the readiness to respond in trust to what God offers people through sacrament, demanding though it does a conversion of mind

---

16. Jean Grondin, *Introduction to Philosophical Hermeneutics*, trans. Joel Weinsheimer (New Haven and London: Yale University Press, 1994), 15.

and heart if it is to be appropriated into the life of persons, communities, and societies. The hermeneutics of confidence emerges from the trust that through Gospel and sacrament Christ and the Spirit open up believers to a world of meaning and love which they can inhabit and which will make of them a transforming presence in other human lives.

Attending to the force of language, the key words adopted in this present work are *Event*, or *Event-ing*, and *Gift*, or *Gift-ing*. In both cases, the accent is placed on the remembrance of Christ's self-emptying love, which through the sacraments enriches those who celebrate. We can write of sacrament as an economy of gift. This lays aside a metaphysical foundation and a subjective foundation to adopt instead an awareness of the Gift that precedes all worldly contours and overflows them, so that it can be contained neither in the language of being, nor in that of the human subject, nor in that of the phenomena through which it appears. In every celebration, there is a new event-ing of this Gift. When there is a "fusion of horizons" across time in the celebration of sacrament, it occurs within an openness to gift. Conjointly, texts and acts command a critical look when they obscure the transparency of gift through an instrumentalized usage of words, rites, and ordering of celebration.

In the encyclical, *Fides et Ratio*, Pope John Paul II has drawn attention to current developments in hermeneutics and the analysis of language which "can be very helpful for the understanding of faith, since they bring to light the structure of our thought and speech and the meaning which language bears."[17] He also refers to how hermeneutics can aid us in attending to the "unavoidable historical and cultural conditioning of the formulas which express" the truth about God, in studying the scriptures and the Church's living tradition.[18]

In writing of the work of theology, the pope states that "the prime commitment of theology is seen to be the understanding of God's kenosis,"[19] and elsewhere he points to the Cross, saying that "the true key point, which challenges every philosophy, is Jesus Christ's death on the cross."[20] In appealing to hermeneutical inquiry, and in pointing to the self-emptying of God revealed on the Cross, John Paul nonetheless asks for a hermeneutic "which is open to the appeal of metaphysics."[21] In the constant support given to metaphysics throughout the encyclical, the pope is concerned with the relation between meaning, reality, and ultimate truth. He does not intend to embrace any particular philosophy, but wishes that theologians address the connection between what is said, what it means, what realities it engages, and how it refers to the ultimate truth of God. While at times this work repeats the

---

17. John Paul II, "Encyclical Letter *Fides et Ratio*," no. 84, *Origins* 28 (1998): 340.
18. *Fides et Ratio*, nos. 95 and 93; ibid., 342.
19. *Fides et Ratio*, no. 93; ibid., 342.
20. *Fides et Ratio*, no. 23; ibid., 325.
21. *Fides et Ratio*, no. 95; ibid., 342.

frequently heard critique of Western metaphysics or of ontotheology, it remains deeply concerned with these relations and with the truth of divine revelation. What it does is to pursue the quest which leads from an inquiry into language and to place the mystery of the Cross at the heart of sacramental celebration, for in it are revealed to us the mystery of God's self-emptying, divine gift, and divine love.

Post[-]Modern

One can hardly address any field of human enterprise and knowledge today, be it poetry, fiction, art, architecture, philosophy, or religion, without taking the debates about the post[-]modern into account. This may be to take a stand against it, it may be to foster it, it may be to accommodate it, but ignore it, one cannot. It is not to enter a debate about the postmodern that this book on Christian sacraments has been written, though all that is signified by that term enters into the discussion. On the other hand, taken simply as a description of a current cultural reality, it cannot be passed over. The issues covered by the term *post-modern* or *postmodern* have to be placed on the table.[22]

Postmodern concerns arise principally from the loss of confidence in both holistic symbol systems and organizations, rather than directly from philosophical disaffection. Modernity's confidence in rationality is thought to be at the root of much evil, so that we are now faced with the collapse of a familiar and excessively optimistic world, which made *man* and *human progress* the center of all reality. This postmodern distrust, it is said, is modern when it accepts as given a departure from cultural forces and models of hegemony and totality. It remains modern also when it attends to the subjective conditions of knowing and to the rights and concerns of the individual person. It is postmodern in that the turn to the rational and the organizational, with supreme confidence in the power of the human to dominate the world and to create a new kind of unity, is deemed outclassed. There have been too many failures.[23] While the turn to the subject was a modern concern, postmodern is marked by doubts about the adequacy of the turn to the subject and interpersonal communication.

It is not my intention to dwell at length on the critique of ontotheology and of the ideology of presence that marks some work on the roots of postmodernity. This is not the outstanding social and shared characteristic of postmodern trends, as seen in public evidence. What is in fact to the fore is

---

22. In the encyclical, *Fides et Ratio*, after a lengthy critique of the modern, Pope John Paul states, "the currents of thought which claim to be postmodern require appropriate attention," and while giving them attention warns that they should not be pursued to the negative and destructive lengths which he finds in some such currents. See *Fides et Ratio*, no. 91; ibid., 341.

23. This applies also in the religious sphere, when there is insight into the ideological factors that are over time inbuilt into prevailing symbolic and controlling orders.

the disillusionment with modernity's confidence in reason and the inability of established orders to hold communities or societies together and to forge and foster common and shared meanings and identity. The critique of the assumption of presence or of logocentrism is the critique of the presumption of adequacy of understanding and word to reality. There follows a critique of the assumption that person, thing, power, or word may be rendered present in their being through the operation of the symbol system in which they are evoked. When this becomes a critique of ontotheology, it is a critique of theology's or philosophy's assumption to speak adequately or coherently of God in human language, so that meanings of God language may be codified and the power of God's action guaranteed through the employment of approved means. Divine presence as such need not be called into question in calling attention to those explanations which seem to make of it a kind of objective presence. No explanation is acceptable which allows humans to dispose of grace as a thing or to lay claim on the presence of mystery without attending to the factors of absence which are the very condition of properly understood presence.

Some seem to think that postmodernism indulges in referring sign to sign, without any other referent. This is not a good way to take account of the postmodern, because it dismisses it by reducing it to a play with words. How far such a point of view is verified, even in the works of Derrida or Lyotard, is a discussion that need not be engaged here. When it comes to appropriating a tradition it is more important to see postmodern evaluations as a critique of sedimentation and of imposed order. Thence one may inquire into the ability of this critique to generate meanings from the texts and to bring persons and communities into communion across a diversity of intersecting interpretations. What is held off is the design to effect unambiguous uniform meaning in favor of the effort to converse and communicate within the diversity of ways of looking at a common referent and heritage. In considering liturgical traditions, this prompts inquiry into the polysemy of rites, symbols, and texts and into the circumstances and processes of their ongoing interpretation.

For all of this systematic doubt, that in the postmodern which is most likely to effect corporate change is the attention to the other, which challenges the concern with personal development and opportunity, as well as confidence in self-sufficiency. The *other* may be texts and cultural works that are not included in the mainstream, such as women's texts, folk tales, folk art, popular religiosity. More importantly, it designates other persons, those who have been in the course of history, and in the writing of history, excluded or considered inferior, or who are presently on the outer rim of social and ecclesial life. At bottom, such postmodernism carries an almost prophetic sense of justice, because it gives voice, expression, and inclusion to those left outside or on the margins, without resorting to some grand narrative or uniform system. It does not try to escape the past, or to say that historical facts mean nothing, but it does say that it may be given voice in ways not heard, or that it may already have within it these voices to which society, or Church, has not listened.

The Hiatus of a Hyphen

When Charles Jencks distinguishes *postmodern* and *post-modern*, he affirms, positively, that the hyphen in the word marks the movement's commitment to "micro-creativity, invention within language, as well as its obligation to a local community."[24] He sees this as an effort to take in the best of the modern, but without its excessive rationality, though avoiding relapse into the premodern. Hence, in appealing to traditions or holistic symbols, as it must, it is ironic,[25] and uses double coding. Double coding means the use of an old code and a new code at one and the same time, or within the same situation, as when architecture will draw on ancient, medieval, renaissance, and baroque motifs, while also baring to view the metals and bricks inside a building. Such post-modernism is not afraid of juxtapositions that both jolt and intersect.

In this post-modern, Jencks notes three trends: (1) from few styles to many genres; (2) from purist to kaleidoscopic sensibility; (3) from exclusion to inclusion.[26] To these he seems to add elsewhere in his work the effort to be "popular," that is, for the people, while not giving up on being elitist, that is, doing what only a few can do because of their special skills.

For Jencks, and those to whom he appeals, the unhyphenated postmodern is the denial of systems and metanarratives, scepticism over meaning and standards, a war on totality. It is "agonistic," and is for Jencks the product of extreme individualism, of which he sees Jean-François Lyotard the king. Jencks does not believe that all metanarrative must disappear, as the postmodern would contend, but suggests that a new metanarrative is birthing, namely, cosmogenesis, and on this quotes Thomas Berry and Brian Swimme.[27]

Without taking a position on such disputes, which in any case have much to do with how one author interprets another (as witness the difference between Jencks and Richard Kearney in their reading of Lyotard[28]), the concern with the art of sacramental interpretation must take the following factors

---

24. Charles Jencks, *What Is Post-Modernism?* 4th and rev. ed. (London: Academy Editions, 1996). For a helpful survey and analysis of the impact of postmodernism in the fields of history, fiction, architecture, and politics, see Linda Hutcheon, *A Poetics of Postmodernism: History, Theory, Fiction* (New York and London: Routledge, 1988; repr. 1996).

25. His appeal at this point is to Umberto Eco, *Postscript to the The Name of the Rose* (New York and London: Harcourt Brace Jovanovich, 1984).

26. Ibid., 55–61.

27. Brian Swimme and Thomas Berry, *The Universe Story: From the Primordial Flaring Forth to the Erozoic Era* (San Francisco: Harper, 1992).

28. See Richard Kearney, *The Poetics of Imagining: From Husserl to Lyotard* (London: Harper-CollinsAcademic, 1991), 196–202.

of the given situation into account. They are factors which surface in the course of efforts to pin down the postmodern, or post-modern, mind-set (and heart-set), and reverberate within sacramental ritual.

1. There is abroad a strong disillusionment with modern claims to the powers of human mind and creativity, especially as they have bred involvement in catastrophes, such as war, the holocaust of midcentury, and other genocides, and have also led to the desecration and human exploitation of nature. This disillusionment and anger is the real, visceral, starting point of the post[-]modern.

2. Modes of cognition are changing with the communications blitz, which leaves practically no culture across the world intact. The use of communications skills and arts in the ordering of societies appears in ways that are hurtful and in ways that are hopeful, so that this needs to be sorted out.

3. For this twofold reason, there is doubt about whether symbolic orders can hold, as there is disgust with the linear or ordered concept of history. There is likewise perturbation in face of grand philosophical systems and traditional metanarratives, whether they are heroic, tragic, secular, or religious. The hesitation to guide cultures by metanarratives, however, does not have to mean supreme individualism, for it may go with keen attention to what is other to oneself and with the postulate to leave ample room for conversation and interaction.

4. In art, architecture, technology, and philosophy, the post[-]modern does not simply discard the modern. To some of its principles and achievements it remains attached, but it goes beyond it. This appears in the way of thinking about people/subjects, about nature and the human, about societies and economies, and in the use of materials and technical expertise. In philosophy and theology, in keeping with this trend, there is the move from metaphysics to phenomenology and hermeneutics, preferring the interpretation of language to the self-assured guidance of thoughts and ideas.

5. There is a greater sensitivity to nature and to the oneness in being with the cosmos of humanity. Some seem indeed to retreat in this sphere to an idealization of the medieval, or of the biblical, or of ecclesiastical institutions and teachings. Others simply draw attention to a better appreciation of the ways in which human being belongs with cosmic reality and look for symbols to express this that do not resort to mythical expression, unless in taking an ironic distance from it. This permits them to mine tradition in a reconstructive way.

6. The reconstructive works with the conflict of interpretations and with intertextuality, but finds ways of mining the past that are accommodating and subversive at one and the same time. This reconstructive retrieval is not allowed to gainsay the commitment to pluralism and otherness.

Sacramental theology and celebration are marked by these post[-]modern concerns. First this means a move away from metaphysical explanations of sacramental action, from explanations that focus on the transcendental human subject, and from confidence in the adequacy of sacramental representations. One has to note that this is not abstract discourse. It is not the discussion of the possibility of representation in a general way, but it is the contention that the representations claimed in sacramental action have overplayed their claim to represent. First, if the claim is made to represent past events, it is asked how we can have access to these events, how they can be represented in themselves across time. Second, if the claim is made that it is the power of God or the power of Christ which is represented and active, it is asked how this power emerges and expresses itself, by what medium it acts and how any medium adequately represents this power. If the claim is made that in representations such as the body of Christ, sacrifice, priesthood, the whole is gathered, there is a greater consciousness of those not included, of experience excluded, of creativity suppressed. If sacramental development is fostered by the turn to the subject, then it is asked how we can have access to the subject if the mediations that allow this access are incomplete and even dangerously fallible.

In keeping with the attention to the other of some critics of modernity, in sacrament also there is a new awareness of those who have been excluded or marginalized, even in Church life and liturgical celebration, and whose voices must now be heard. In its departure from modernity, this means a new search for the holy and a quest for what joins the human with other beings. Human communities need to live with greater regard for the world around them, in interdependency, instead of acting out of the assumption that humans are "stewards of creation." In sacrament, the earth is then allowed to speak. Humans live by gift, by what is always coming, adventing, eventing, being offered, not by control and instrumentality. The ethical is absolutely essential to sacramental practice, for sacramental action is intertwined with how lives are lived and with the testimony that these lives give. It is not possible to take part in liturgy without the edge of attention to, and empathy for, the other. This means an ethic rooted in the wisdom of how we live day by day in faith in God's presence and in God's coming, even amid disorder and suffering.

Against liturgical revisions that have been behavioristic and functional, the poetics of sacrament in a more recent phase of renewal explores diverse avenues to let the insight into human life, into the being of humans in the world, into the action of God's Word and Spirit, surface in language and rite. When it is not simply a retrieval of the premodern, this means attention to intertexuality, even to the tensions between text and text, between rite and rite, between rite and text, between what the ritual upholds and what the people do. The poetic eye looks beneath and beyond the surfaces of texts and rites, yet is suspicious of any claims to have reached secure foundations, whether in a mythic sense of the holy, in a metaphysics, in a divinely ordered structure, or in access to human interiority. In all of this, what is more and more evoked is the Christ story as the story of a self-giving that is part of this *chaosmos* of the world and of the quest for the divine.

Even within this changing reality, the memorial of Christ remains alive, but how this is to happen is addressed here with certain suppositions in mind. First, the mediation of sacraments in bringing about a divine presence and a human transformation is taken as a given, and the validity of the religious experience of Christian sacrament is affirmed. Second, however, it is likewise affirmed that the Christian tradition of sacramental celebration allows of cultural adaptation and needs to be able to incorporate the realities of contemporary, and temporally bound, human experiences. Third, in face of the human experience of the epoch, sacramental celebration is faced with the Gospel imperative of attention to those who suffer, who are excluded, who are in the 30 percent of the refuse of global communication and organization. Fourth, and in conjunction with this, there is the demand that we make the critique needed, of society, of Church, and of liturgy, and that we seek out the counterknowledge that Christian remembrance offers. Fifth, even while heeding the critique of religions, symbolic orders, institutions, theologies, an appeal can be made to available resources that allow the poetic expression of Christian tradition to emerge and surface with greater vigor. Sixth, since sacraments are the memorial of Christ who in his empathy for those whose lives are semantically empty, himself self-emptied out of love, there may be a resort to the stories and symbols of Christian tradition that forgotten or neglected peoples and minorities can appropriate, and in so doing enrich their lives with the faith and hope of God's great love.

By Way of a Table of Contents

To work out what sacramental interpretation entails in the context outlined, the book is divided into three parts. In the first, the current disarray and disagreement over the interpretation of sacramental tradition is surveyed and explained, and in this light the approach to sacrament as language event is proposed. Chapter 2 may be considered as pivotal to the book. In the second part, since together they make up the complex action of sacramental memorial, the interpretation of ritual action, verbal expression, and visual representation is dealt with, item by item. In the third part, it is asked how we may render an account of this way of considering sacraments, by an interpretation of doctrines, a critique of traditions, a systematic and comprehensive reflection, and a sacramental catechesis.

There is considerable risk in interpreting a field in which such diverse arts as doctrine, theology, history, anthropology, sociology, and art criticism, have a place. There is also considerable risk in covering a liturgy that has so many diverse traditions and trajectories of which to take account. However, since all these fields converge in celebration, the risk has to be taken. Since the field is indeed complex, the work is not intended to be a comprehensive coverage or synthesis. It is offered more by way of a heuristic, a way of taking cognizance of what is involved in interpreting sacramental traditions and in ordering present celebrations.

I have had to be dependent on many sources of information and may readily have omitted some to which attention ought to be given. It is hoped, therefore, that with putting the accent on the heuristic process, the inevitable shortcomings in treatment may be surpassed by drawing attention to the trajectory, which of its nature opens the door to improvement and to continued conversation. Despite specializations and despite pluralism, people can still talk intelligently and feelingly to one another, allowing room for shifting horizons, even when consensus is di/eferred.

Some reviewers referred to an earlier book on the symbolic nature of liturgy as a sacramental theology inspired by Paul Ricoeur.[29] Certainly, much inspiration was taken from his writings, and this indebtedness was clear. However, he may well not have been pleased with what was done, since in the course of the book I retreated into the metaphysics of sacramental causality. At the time, it was my thought that the book would not get much readership in Catholic circles without use of that theorem. This present book could not have been written without having read Gadamer, Ricoeur, Chopp, Marion, Mveng, Tracy,[30] Kearney,[31] Chauvet,[32] and others. However, I would never claim that I have followed their thought through, or that I have been faithful to their insights in working out a sacramental theology. The book hence will not be sprinkled with references to these authors, except where the text requires a direct note or citation. Once and for all, however, the debt to them is here acknowledged, though they are not to be held accountable for the debts to creditors to which the book may give rise.

---

29. David N. Power, *Unsearchable Riches: The Symbolic Nature of Liturgy* (New York: Pueblo, 1984).

30. See especially, David Tracy, *The Analogical Imagination: Christian Theology and the Culture of Pluralism* (New York: Crossroad, 1985).

31. See especially Kearney, *The Poetics of Imagining.*

32. Louis-Marie Chauvet, *Symbol and Sacrament: A Sacramental Reinterpretation of Christian Existence,* trans. P. Madigan and M. Beaumont (Collegeville, Minn.: Liturgical Press, 1995).

Part I

Sacramental Traditions
in Transition

— *Chapter One* —

Tradition and Change

In Christian Churches today, the celebration of sacramental liturgies is under much scrutiny and is subjected to much criticism. As liturgies are revised, the nature of the revision is much contested, with frequent appeals either for preservation of the past or for more far-reaching change, showing quite divergent views about what it is to be faithful to tradition. In such a situation, Churches have to be more aware of the interpretations they give to texts, rites, and other monuments of their liturgical heritage. As one writer, Jean Grondin, has remarked, "making things understood becomes an acute problem only when it no longer works. The necessity for express consideration of interpretation — of the primordial event of language as interpretation (repetition of thought) — is owing to the experience of the unintelligible."[1] Hence the purpose of this opening chapter is first to survey various approaches and attitudes to sacramental renewal, and then to suggest some guidelines for interpreting and appropriating traditions, in the interests of celebration.

Renewal within Tradition

In revising the liturgy of sacrament, Churches wish to give proper value to early Church tradition, to what is peculiar to their distinctive sacramental practices, and to the exigencies of responding to the world and culture in which the Gospel is preached and Christ's mysteries celebrated. How this is to be done is viewed quite differently, and this may be illustrated by contrasting an official Roman Catholic approach with a process among many of the faithful which will be spoken of here as *ritualization*.

Roman Instruction on Inculturation of the Liturgy within the Roman Rite

In the 1994 Instruction on the Inculturation of the Liturgy within the Roman Rite, Roman authorities enunciated the principles of adaptation or accommodation within what the document calls the substantial unity of the

---

1. Jean Grondin, *Introduction to Philosophical Hermeneutics*, trans. Joel Weinsheimer (New Haven and London: Yale University Press, 1994), 23.

21

Roman Rite.[2] The revisions of several sacramental orders of the Roman Rite had already given directives for their adaptation to different cultures, even for that far-reaching adaptation foreseen in *Sacrosanctum Concilium* among non-Western peoples (SC 39–42).[3] The instruction starts from there in an attempt to establish what constitutes the substantial unity of the Roman liturgy. This is in itself an interesting use of terms, seemingly borrowed from the Council of Trent, where it was stated that while the Church has authority to modify and change rites, it has no authority over the substance of the sacraments.[4] The word *substance* was used analogically, in a commonsense way, to refer to whatever Jesus Christ had determined by divine power regarding the sacraments, their rites, and their conferral of grace.

The 1994 Roman Instruction on Inculturation, following the norms for adapting rites given in the Second Vatican Council, seems to take this Tridentine teaching as background for another issue, to wit, the process of change within the Roman Rite in different places, as it encounters various cultures. The instruction is not treating of sacraments as such, but of sacraments and other liturgies as they have developed within the Roman tradition. The reference is not directly to Christ's intention but to what is venerable within the practice and tradition of the Roman Church, which makes it serve as a sacramental model across continents and cultures. In adapting the Tridentine principle to speak not of *substance* but of *substantial unity,* the instruction indicates that there is a certain coherence within the tradition of the Roman Rite that must be respected in adaptations made to its usage in different places and cultures. Thus one has to figure out what is unchangeable, as well as give attention to how the modification of a part may affect the whole. Deciding on what belongs to this substantial unity always requires investigation into tradition and a grasp of its coherence and inner unity.

The discussion of what is substantial to the Roman Rite recalls the adage about the *genius of the Roman Rite,* used by Edmund Bishop when he related the liturgy to the early history of its development in Rome and to the expressions or modalities it borrowed from Roman culture.[5] These cultural characteristics contrasted with northern and Hispanic sensitivities and modes of expression, so that when the Roman books traveled north there was a great difference between their Latinity and sober, though hieratic, ritual and the

---

2. Official Latin text, Congregatio de Cultu Divino et Disciplina Sacramentorum, "De Liturgia romana et inculturatione: Instructio quarta ad exsecutionem Constitutionis Concilii Vaticani Secundi de Sacra Liturgia recte ordinandam (ad Const. art. 37–40)," *Notitiae* 30 (1994): 80–115. Published in English under the title, *Inculturation of the Liturgy within the Roman Rite* (Vatican City: Vatican Press, 1994).

3. Some clear examples are found in the rules adjoining the revision of rites for the sick, for marriage, and for funerals.

4. The phrase *salva eorum substantia* is used in the decree on communion under two kinds, in the context of distinguishing between what the Church can and cannot change. See DS 1728.

5. Edmund Bishop, "The Genius of the Roman Rite," *Liturgica Historica: Papers on the Liturgy and Religious Life of the Western Church* (Oxford: Clarendon Press, 1918; repr. 1962), 1–19.

expressiveness of the Nordic peoples. Bishop's notion of the Roman genius has to do with style, not doctrine, and he clearly thought the Roman style preferable to the Gallican and Hispanic. Indeed, he considered it a matter of rejoicing that with the work on liturgical books done since the Council of Trent, the exercise of the devotional spirit of other peoples had been placed plainly outside the liturgy and not allowed to infect it from within.

The Second Vatican Council wished to see devotions revised and renewed to put them in harmony with the spirit of the liturgy. Clearly, however, it was not thinking of the genius of the Roman Rite in terms such as those of Bishop and clearly was not anxious to canonize the division between the liturgical and the devotional, of which he approved. More significantly, it formulated principles for quite far-reaching adaptations of the liturgy in non-Western cultures. These principles have been echoed in the revisions of different liturgical books, especially in those for the celebration of marriage and the celebration of funerals. How these are to be respected, drawing resources from a variety of cultures while still remaining within the substantial unity of the Roman Rite, is somewhat enigmatic.

Ritualization

It is not only in African and Asian Churches that the need for cultural change in sacramental celebration is perceived. Within the Western world also there are those who believe that ways of accommodating current cultural changes have to be found, and some think that how this is done emerges from celebration itself, rather than being pursued on purely theoretical grounds. As congregations celebrate a sacrament, with authorized books at hand (if not always in hand), a process has come to the fore which can be best understood under the name of *ritualization*. This means attention to known and traditional rites, along with attention to other ritual forms, and a somewhat free way of accommodating to community situations. There are patterns but they are not rigid. The community knows the traditional, but it tries in its own accommodations to negotiate the meaning of this tradition, to weave it into the lives of the congregants, and to invest the rites with their faith perceptions, social concerns, and cultural forms. There is always some play between the written and the oral, the known ritual actions and the enfleshment of these rituals in actual practice.

A measure of ritualization takes place at any time, no matter how consolidated the ritual code may seem to be. Congregations always accommodate this to their own situation in life, culture, and society. It is the extent and diversity of this phenomenon which marks the life of Churches in these decades. Communities are experimenting more with liturgies and more consciously diversifying or adding new elements, drawn from a variety of sources, not exclusively from recognized Christian traditions. The ritualization process is not uniform, nor motivated by the same aspirations. Some resist changes in sacramental ritual, in favor of what they have known, or heard of, from the past, which they find more sacral and more cohesive. Hence, despite the official changes they find ways of ritualization within their own sense of tradition. For example, exposition of the Blessed Sacrament gains new momentum, or devotion to the saints and to Mary can overshadow Sunday liturgy, as with celebrations in honor of the Divine Mercy on the Sunday after Easter. In other cases, and among rather different kinds of communities, primacy is given to the devotions associated with the enigmatically labeled popular religiosity, to feasts in honor of Our Lady of Guadalupe, St. John the Baptist, and local patrons. Others find that the *editio typica* of many a sacramental rite retains too much of the hierarchical, of the boldly masculine image of God, and so even within the execution of the newly revised liturgy incorporate more communal rituals, more inclusive language, and more roles for the nonordained.[6] On some continents, people incorporate rites that they know from cultural religious traditions, such as the veneration of ancestors, forms of communion with the dead, or healing rites.

Much is done by instinct for what is suitable, but it can resist clear articulation of meaning. Catherine Bell has pointed out the difference between the ritual mastery which enables congregations or communities to appropriate the traditions in their own way, and the insight into all that they do and effect in this process. As she says:

> [Ritualization] is a way of acting that sees itself as responding to a place, event, force, problem or tradition. It tends to see itself as the natural or appropriate thing to do in the circumstances. Ritualization *does not see* [emphasis added] how it redefines or generates the circumstances to which it is responding. It does not see how its own actions reorder and reinterpret the circumstances so as to afford the sense of a fit among the main spheres of experience — body, community and cosmos.[7]

This paragraph reminds us of the important relations to which community gives shape in Christian liturgy, as in all ritual. Even the naming of God is done within a certain compass, pointing to the body-self, to the community to which one belongs (or from which one distinguishes oneself), and to the cosmos, earthly and heavenly reality, in which the human community must find its place. In the process of ritual sacramental change, it is helpful to know that these realities are involved all the time, however clearly or less distinctively invoked.[8]

---

6. On a variety of practices in feminist liturgies, see Marjorie Procter-Smith and Janet R. Walton, eds., *Women at Worship: Interpretations of North American Diversity* (Louisville: Westminster/John Knox Press, 1993).

7. Catherine Bell, *Ritual Theory, Ritual Practice* (New York and Oxford: Oxford University Press, 1992), 109.

8. Ritualization is not to be confused with liturgical miming, which is the endeavor to set ideas or ideals to ritual enactment. If people think up a rite, even one using traditional ele-

An Example: The Handling of Texts

This play with ritual and text is more notable where communities specifically set out to explore rites and accommodations. It goes on, however, in varying degrees in almost every congregation. One specific example can illustrate how this involves changing perceptions of what constitutes revelation itself and fidelity to its transmission. This has to do with the handling of texts.

Islam, Judaism, and Christianity are commonly invoked as religions of the book, and of course scriptures are vital to their religious belief and tradition. These are interwoven with rites and customs and respect for holy places, as well as supplemented by other texts, so that the precise role of the sacred book is constantly changing. These specifically religious expressions are in turn interwoven with cultural perceptions that emerge within the way that people live and relate, and with their basic systems of communication. How Christian liturgy treats the printed text in its sacramental celebration is therefore of interest.

In fact, the actual handling of texts is informative about the place given to them in sacramental celebration, as for the place of written texts in any tradition, civil or religious. The heavily illuminated codices of the Bible and the liturgical books of earlier times indicate both reverence for them and a kind of interpretation of the text through the means of adornment. After the Second Vatican Council both liturgical reform and theological reflection placed emphasis on the primacy of the Word of God as proclaimed in and from the scriptures. Reverence was shown for the book of scriptures in the disposition of places of worship and in ritual processions. Nonetheless, a large dissemination of scriptural texts was done through cheap printing or in many another throwaway form. Even in ritual processions one can see the odd proximity of the ritual reverence with which the lectionary is carried and the choice of ill-produced volumes that command little respect. It is like displaying a paperback edition of Dante at a symposium on his work, instead of a reproduction of an early manuscript or edition, or a leather-bound volume of more recent production.

It is in such ritual performance that one finds what counts for those who gather in Christ's name. One needs to look at what is done in order to discern how people think that God is addressing them and where the power of the Spirit is working. Though the Word of God is read from the text of the lectionary, if this is not well presented materially, it loses significance. One has to look for signs of where else people are looking for God's Word and may find that it is in the testimony and wisdom of other persons' lives. In African Churches, foreigners learn that it is a mistake to read directly from a book, whether in proclaiming prayers or in proclaiming the scriptures. People quite readily turn to talk to one another or to singing hymns when they see

---

ments such as fire and water, to express ideals which they have in mind, this is miming, not ritualization.

that the minister is "talking to the book" or getting wisdom from the book, while they are attentive to what comes "from within." In different places, some communities have adopted the practice of receiving testimony from its members on particular occasions. Thus during Eastertide, neophytes speak at Sunday liturgy of their experience. They may be joined in this by their sponsors. On some Sundays, parish council members may speak, or those who oversee planned giving, presenting all this as a faith experience. It can also happen that married couples give testimony on a significant anniversary, and when parents present their children for baptism something more is expected than a simple "book response." In North American Churches, these testimonies are received with great enthusiasm and applause, so that this says much of where the congregation believe that God is speaking and working among them.

This kind of liturgical usage may tell us that it is not so much the text itself that earns respect as the diffusion of the word among the people and their reflection on it. Or it may also say, dependent on other circumstances and practices, that the scripture actually has little moment, and that other things count for more, such as preaching, prayer, or testimonies of life. This may mean that the expression *Word of God* is given quite variant meanings, suggesting different ways in which God is understood to speak to people. In the first place, of course, it is used to designate the book of scriptures in which divine revelation is recorded and taken as a divine address to Israel and to the Church. In the second place, it refers to preaching and all exposition of these scriptures, since this is considered to continue God's address. In the third place, however, *the Word of God* or some similar expression is used to cover a variety of other ways in which believers may consider that they find God communicating something to them. Thus people will say that the rites speak to them, or the example given by others, or a story told, or shared thoughts and feelings. All of this can be considered quite important and even crucial to the communication of God's word and will. People are also affected by seminars on the scriptures, by small group sharing, by personal reading, and by being able to play with or chat about texts on the World Wide Web.

All this being so, it is not to be lightly assumed that the Word of God is transmitted simply through the scriptures, or even through the reading of the scriptures, even when as befits a culture of writing this remains a primary referent. In fact, however, it is the living word within the community that counts in liturgical action, as it connects with the living word of Christian behavior. The visual, the actions enacted, repeated patterns of speech, creative oral utterances, and communication via the Web, all belong to the transmission of what is celebrated by Christians as the Word of God. This then constitutes an essential part of the interpretation of the scriptures and of Christian belief that is given in sacramental action. Hence, to speak of the Word of God active and present in the Church, the Bible is located within an interpretative tradition, and more immediately within a community of proclamation and sacramental celebration.

Such processes of ritualization are better understood when it is noted that established ritual sets boundaries for a community, configures power and its influence, welcomes people into a community, and gives it solidity. But in face of change in the life-world, it then breaks open or breaks down, so that another way of moving, being, acting within the tradition has to be found, without giving up on the role of ritual and on its commonality from one celebration to the other. To engage in ritualization, as here named, is to redraw the boundaries, the exercise of power, the cultural determinants within which memorial is kept and traditions handed on.

Some see a betrayal of ritual in ritualization, because they think that it is in ritual handed on exactly and correctly that the Church's symbolic capital is transmitted, and that the correct exercises of power are expressed in and through it. Others see this process as the precise realization of ritual tradition and as the greatest fidelity to traditional rituals, because it releases the symbolic capital and energy which rite transmits, allowing it to embrace forms that merge more with the lives, social reality, and experience of those who celebrate it, without, however, subjecting this capital and energy to subjectivity or the tyranny of the times.

Sociological Critique

In a sociological critique of liturgical changes, especially in the Roman Catholic and Anglican communions, Kieran Flanagan discusses how the crisis of the modern works out in the field of liturgy.[9] Flanagan's main complaint is that liturgists, and oftentimes priests, have so secularized the liturgy that it is devoid of the sense of the holy and ruined as a means of grace. Like Victor Turner before him, he suggests that there was too conceptual, and somewhat behavioristic, an approach to liturgical reforms. Liturgical scholars and practitioners sometimes made matters worse by injecting change with large measures of ideologically inspired purpose.

Much of this has been noted by people of quite varying points of view, but what is distinctive in Flanagan's work is the apparent supposition that ritual, whether Catholic or Anglican, was functioning well before changes were made. Though he professes the need for conversation between theology, liturgy, and sociology, one has to wonder whence Flanagan derives his sense of what constitutes the Catholic or Anglican repertory of rites and what is to be judged proper in these and other rituals. His problems appear to be with the crisis of the modern, and the issues raised by the trend dubbed post[-]modernism, as this affects liturgy among other religious institutions.

9. Kieran Flanagan, *Sociology and Liturgy: Re-presentations of the Holy* (New York: St. Martin's Press, 1991).

However one agrees or disagrees with his critique, it serves to pinpoint what is problematic in the interpretation of sacramental tradition when liturgy is caught between the modern and various forms of the post[-]modern.

As Flanagan puts it, society, and the Church in particular, have a fund of rites and institutions whose raison d'être is the pursuit of love and the receipt of grace. He contends that since the Vatican Council the Catholic Church has failed in the "management of its symbolic capital." The trends among linguists, theologians, and liturgists are seen as the fruit of a secularized modernity. The modern is ordered, logical, convinced of its insights into reality. What is at fault in our present age, according to Flanagan, is not modernity as such, but secularization, that is, the ordering of human resources toward secular ends, to the detriment of the religious. What he looks for in the field of religion, and of liturgy in particular, is some return to the foundations of modernity, to wit, foundational truths, grand narratives, the ideal of progress, and a managed and reasoned employ of symbolic capital which has its base in these truths, narratives, and hierarchical institutions. He is ill at ease with whatever questions fixed truths and forms, or questions the use of power in symbol systems. He looks askance at those who point to the polysemy of language, or look with suspicion on grand narratives that place everything about human life in an ordered universe. For Flanagan, this is to destroy the possibility of the holy, since it is the holy of sacral forms of expressions that offers a sense of grace and spiritual insight. His appeal is largely to the embodiment of the holy in places, rites, and even what often falls, somewhat ambiguously it is true, under the designation of popular religiosity. This last directs attention to the sense and reactions of the people rather than of the priest or the liturgist for appreciation of the tradition's symbolic capital and its expressions of holiness and divine grace.[10]

The English Dominican Aidan Nichols, in his little book *Looking at the Liturgy,* reviews the criticism of liturgical reform made by Flanagan and those to whom he often refers, Victor Turner and Mary Douglas.[11] It is not difficult to agree with Flanagan and Nichols on some of the defective points in the execution of this reform. Among these are the banality of language that results from a quest for a watered down intelligibility of rites and texts, the difficulty of finding suitable vernacular translations of the scriptures, the adoption of some very poor music for liturgical use, the tendency among some congregations to be so turned in on themselves and their reactions that they obfuscate

---

10. One has to applaud the advocacy of hermeneutics in Flanagan's work, whose tenets are drawn by him from parts of the corpus of Hans-Georg Gadamer and Paul Ricoeur, but it is doubtful that these hermeneutical works taken in their totality support the critique or the resolutions that are advanced. For one thing, it is only to what is now being changed that he applies the hermeneutic of suspicion, leaving the reader to wonder why it is not used of the past which he lauds.

11. Aidan Nichols, *Looking at the Liturgy: A Critical View of its Contemporary Form* (San Francisco: Ignatius Press, 1996).

divine transcendence and mystery, and the fixation with having the presider face the people in celebrating the Mass.

However, when Nichols turns to his "practical conclusion," one sees the basic fallacy of his critique, which is that it is the Roman Rite in its medieval form, or the "Roman rite in its earlier incarnation," which constitutes the historical and spiritual patrimony of the liturgy.[12] There is much romantic fascination with the old Latin liturgy, whereas those with longer memories know how poorly it was often done and how little the average Catholic parish knew of Gregorian chant or of the High Mass, and of how dependent people were on all kinds of devotions rather than on the liturgy to keep in touch with the holy. More fundamentally, however, it is revealing to note what is at the center of this fascination with late medieval and post-Tridentine liturgy, namely, the focus on the consecration in the celebration of the Mass. Nichols quotes the Anglo-Welsh poet David Jones, who takes the consecration of the host in the Western Mass as the context for the universal epic of his poem *Anathemata*.[13] Quite contrary to the idea of a liturgy which has this as a central point, true renewal will make the communion table where all the Christian people receive the gift of the body and blood of Christ once again (*sic*) the center of all sacramental and liturgical action. If one were to ask for one sole indicator of the need for the liturgical renewal affirmed rather than started by the Vatican Council, it lies precisely there. Much in the execution of the renewal has been badly handled, but we have to keep attention focused on the active participation of the Christian people in the sacraments which Christ and the Spirit give the Church. It is around this that the importance of ritual, which Flanagan and Nichols properly note, may be retrieved.

Theological Critique

The problem raised by commentators such as Flanagan, when they see the efforts being made to renew liturgical forms or to relate liturgy to culture, has been given theological expression by, among others, Joseph Cardinal Ratzinger. Ratzinger does not simply note the erosion of the holy in some contemporary liturgies, but he decries what he sees as the befogging of the mystery of the Church and of Jesus Christ. For Flanagan, objections to liturgical renewal are grounded in sociological insight. For Ratzinger, any use of sociological categories seems suspect. Thus in his collection of conferences, *A New Song for the Lord*, he blames much of what he sees wrong in liturgical action since the Vatican Council on the use of sociological categories.[14] He is

---

12. Ibid., 119, 122.
13. Ibid., 111.
14. Joseph Cardinal Ratzinger, *A New Song for the Lord: Faith in Christ and Liturgy Today*, trans. Martha M. Matesich (New York: Crossroad, 1996). His critique is particularly strong in the essay "The Image of the World and of Human Beings in the Liturgy and in Its Expression in Church Music," 111–27. See also Nichols, *Looking at the Liturgy*.

persuaded that far too much attention is given to the human group in liturgical practice, whereas it is the mystery of the Church which ought to prevail, so that the gathering of the faithful may well mean the bringing together of strangers, who in the sacraments acknowledge one another as brothers and sisters in Christ.

Ratzinger may well misrepresent the use of sociological insight made by liturgists and theologians. Sociology is an auxiliary science, which brings insight into the functioning of human communities and societies, and thus can be an aid to theological reflection. Those whom Ratzinger specifically names do not substitute sociology for theology. In the article in an Italian liturgical dictionary which he singles out, there is no mention whatsoever of the text in Matthew that speaks of two or three gathered together in Christ's name (Matt 18:20), though Ratzinger takes this to be the unjustified basis for appeal to sociological categories.[15] The authors are working with a eucharistic ecclesiology and with the principles of inculturation. Ratzinger appears to promote a very abstract notion of Church. It is a mystery, waiting to take flesh in place and celebration. For Ratzinger, this has a very distinctive form, which is Roman and hierarchical. Whenever he mentions Church, in the background there is the ordained priesthood and the authority of the See of Rome. These represent some kind of divine and christological form, which is then to be bestowed on individual congregations, through the liturgy. When those whom he criticizes make some appeal to sociological insights, it is to follow the principle of incarnation of Church and Gospel enunciated by the Vatican Council in *Ad Gentes*. Insights from the human sciences do not substitute for theology, but they give some perception of how the body of Christ takes on flesh and form in human cultures. The transmission of the Word of God, the government of the Church, and ritual practice need to be understood in their innerworldly forms.

The Post[-]Modern and the Holy

Quite opposite to the assessment of liturgical change made by Flanagan, Nichols, or Ratzinger is the exigency for change and the critique of reforms that arises from what might be called post[-]modern criticism. This is a criticism addressed both to medieval and post-Tridentine patterns, and to some of the more recent introductions of the liturgical reform effected after the Second Vatican Council. It is a critique derived from a different sense of the holy and of its expression from that professed by such as Flanagan and Ratzinger.

As mentioned in the introduction to this work, the post[-]modern is often taken as synonymous with the turn from metaphysics in thinking about di-

---

15. He takes issue with an article in the *Nuovo Dizionario di Liturgia* (Rome, 1984), by F. Rainoldi and E. Costa, "Canto e musica."

vine revelation,[16] or with the move away from rooting all understanding of reality in considerations of the human subject. One option in face of this has been to look to process philosophy as a way of accounting for the coherence of Christian theology. The option examined here is the turn to language, which allows us to examine revelation and Christian tradition as a cultural and linguistically expressed reality.

The accent on culture and language, however, gives rise to diverse approaches. On the one hand, there are those who acknowledge diversity among Churches and theologies but underline the cultural coherence of different traditions. Whether Catholic or Protestant, for them the strategy in face of the modern is the retrieval of biblical and premodern religious systems, with their inner coherence and poetic of holiness. On the other hand, there is a quite opposite turn to language in all its forms which points to discontinuity and diversity, not only between different traditions, but even within a single tradition from one epoch to another, and from one place to another. The basis of this is the problem experienced in arriving at a universal, uniform, and standard interpretation of texts, rites, and institutions. In revelation itself, because it is so bound to historical event and circumstance, there is thought to be a built-in fluidity and a diversity which demand the constant effort of interpretation under circumstances that do not coincide with the original.

This is not a purely speculative concern. The need for a fresh theological and ecclesial approach to revelation and to worship is inspired by a sense of modernity's social failure and of the Church's hesitancy, or even inability, to speak to a suffering humanity. What the post[-]modern critique contends is that the response to failure and its attendant suffering cannot be given through any grand scheme of things or through any symbol system that pretends to incorporate human tragedy into its perception of the whole. The divine response, if at all, can come only piece by piece, story by story, enough for each day's wisdom and without grand pretensions. What then is to be retrieved from within tradition that enables Churches to remember the Christ event in more diverse ways, but always so as to hear it speak to human suffering?

This critique of symbolic expressions that have long prevailed is itself destined to a retrieval of the holy. It allows for perceptions of the holy in ways and in areas whose expression has been suppressed in the drift of Church systems. It goes with the hope of an era, in which the world will not rely so fully on the organizational systems and informational hubris of modernity. When the critique is addressed to sacrament, it shows the deficit of the instrumental use of language and rite, and of an excessive ordering. It also shows that

---

16. A clearly presented synthesis of postmodern turns in theology is offered in Terrence W. Tilley, *Postmodern Theologies: The Challenge of Religious Diversity* (Maryknoll, N.Y.: Orbis Books, 1995). See also Frederic B. Burnham, ed., *Postmodern Theology: Christian Faith in a Pluralistic World* (San Francisco: Harper & Row, 1989).

the hieratic has distanced Jesus Christ and the ministry of discipleship from human life, where it remains only as a power that dominates and at times beneficently intervenes. When this critique gives rise to fresh insight, it allows for the intuition of the holy within a greater pluralism of expression. In its very suspicion of the grand narrative, the sacralized institution, or a symbol system of domination, it alerts us to other expressions and locations of grace and holiness.

These occur in that area of the semiotic which Julia Kristeva contrasts with the symbolic, which she identifies with institutionalized and power-controlled mediations of holiness.[17] What Kristeva claims is that there is an underlying fund of feeling and expression that does not find its place within the prevailing Western symbol systems. Within history and within the present time, this finds its own modes of transmission, as it were, on the margins. It is to be found extensively in women's religious experience and expression, but it may also be found among various social minorities. This way of looking at the relation between the contemporary and tradition is equally applicable to the Christian and indeed to the Catholic tradition. There is some parallel to this concern in the effort on the African, Asian, and American continents to retrieve the language of the holy found in ancient religions that predate the advent of Christianity, and to relate them to Christian faith and vice versa.

The poet Seamus Heaney gives helpful insight into what has come in the wake of change, by way of loss and by way of the need to regain something of a lost vision, while at the same time showing perfect sensitivity to the oppressiveness of much in the old religious system. On what has disappeared from Irish Catholic consciousness, he has this to say:

> I would say that the more important Catholic thing is the actual sense of eternal values and infamous vices which our education or formation gives us. There's a sense of profoundness, a sense that the universe can be ashimmer with something, and Catholicism ... was the backdrop to the whole thing. The world I grew up in offered me a sense that I was a citizen of the empyrean — the crystalline elsewhere of the world. But I think that's gone from Catholicism now.[18]

We can appreciate what Heaney sees as loss, and the yearning for something as strong to take the place of the old verities. On the other hand, the same poet has an ear for the subjection imposed by the old ways and so expresses no desire to return to them as such. In his mother's many devotions and prayers, common to the women of his boyhood, he sees indeed the closeness to God and to the world of spirit, but he also finds the sounds of protest, protest voiced in the only language available to her against life's burdens and

---

17. See Julia Kristeva, "From Symbols to Sign," and "Semiotics: A Critical Science and/or a Critique of Science," in *The Kristeva Reader*, ed. Toril Moi (New York: Columbia University Press, 1986), 34–88.

18. Interview with Seamus Heaney, *Irish American*, May–June 1996, 28.

injustices. The prayers and devotions of the women of his boyhood, subjected to a certain way of life as child bearer, mother, housewife, he sees as both "a wilful adherence to the compensations of Catholicism" and "a cry of rage and defiance."[19] Is it then still possible to release the power of the symbols of the holy within Christian tradition, even though they may have been submerged within the rigidity of religious and social systems? A positive answer to this requires a fresh recovery of the things of earth so vital to Christian sacrament, of the word of the Gospel, and of the voices that have so often been silent within society and within the Churches.

Christianity, the Social, Cultures

Disaffection with what is modern and with organizational approaches to liturgical revision have an important impact on the celebration of sacraments. The effect of cultural changes in modes of communication is not to be ignored, since this has much to do with the place of liturgy in a culture. In the past, the cultural, the social, and the religious often converged. The clearest example of this is the way in which baptism, confirmation, and marriage became symbols of human passage, of life transitions, for the newly born, for children or adolescents, and for those entering the state of marriage. Of themselves, none of these three sacraments is related to these moments of life, but in a Christian society their symbolism served to connect rites of life passage with faith. This is of considerable significance because it is at these moments that a culture's own cosmic and kinship symbolism emerges most strikingly. Since, however, the symbols and rites of a culture are dislocated in times of cultural transition, the sacraments are affected to the extent that they have drawn on a cultural heritage. Since the relation to culture, however, can never be passed over, it is helpful to take note of recent writing on different kinds of culture, especially as they are related to styles of communication.

Types of Culture

Generally, writers distinguish two types of culture in relation to the use of texts and of oral tradition.[20] The first is referred to as a culture of writing, for in it written documents hold authority and constitute the core of what is passed on by tradition. The second is spoken of as an oral culture, since it is oral communication and oral transmission which is of primary importance. With the developments in contemporary means of communication, to these

---

19. Ibid., 27.
20. Walter Ong, *Orality and Literacy: The Technologizing of the Word* (London and New York: Methuen, 1982); idem., *Faith and Contexts*, 2 vols. (Atlanta: Scholars Press, 1990, 1995). See also Jack Goody, *The Interface between the Written and the Oral*, Studies in Literacy, Family, Culture and State (New York: Cambridge University Press, 1987); Paul Zumthor, *Oral Poetry: An Introduction*, trans. Kathryn Murphy-Judy (Minneapolis: University of Minnesota Press, 1990).

we now need to add what can be called digital culture. The distinction is not to be too rigorously imposed, but it provides a useful heuristic.

Since in the West we live in a culture of writing, much of how we live is regulated by what is written. In the United States, even the Constitution is written and provides the reference point for all legal and constitutional questions. The written table itself is treated with great reverence, enshrined as something sacred, or reduplicated only in respectable form. Nonetheless, other traditions are created by custom and precedent, filling out practical interpretations of what is given in the code of the constitution. There are also venerable rituals, such as the swearing in of officials, from the president of the commonwealth to local judges or sheriffs, or the daily raising and lowering of the flag. Other customs are more in the nature of folk customs, such as the annual menu for the Thanksgiving Day dinner or the fireworks display that marks the Fourth of July.

In oral cultures, rituals of passage, healing, and reconciliation, as well as oral transmission of myth, saga, or proverb, prevail in setting the way of life and rule for the people. Even when writing and the written word provide certain supplementary points of rule, wisdom, and expectation, the power of the oral is still strongest. In many African countries today, written constitutions and texts set standards, but oral traditions are important to the people as a whole and as a community. In the course of transition from tribal and kin communities to democracies and societies organized around industrial production, it is difficult to provide stories, rituals, and wisdom that guide nations as readily as those that satisfied the needs of tribal welfare. The respective roles of writing and oral expression are in flux. Hence we need to ask how change in the modes of communication changes culture.

Culture, Communication

In the 1930s the Canadian sociologist Harold Innes drew attention to how the telegraph influenced the lives of both native Americans and immigrant peoples, with deep cultural consequences for how they perceived and lived reality. One of the primary consequences of this new way of communicating was that it affected commerce and economies, for all concerned. In the fur trade, the traders coming from abroad could access markets around the world, influencing the laws of supply and demand, and thus of the exchange of furs. Since the native Indians and Inuits were caught up in this exchange, their old ways of hunting animals, of dealing with the carcass, and of trading furs were disturbed and changed. This meant a whole new relation to the environment and to creatures. It also meant a transfer of power and control outside their own indigenous systems. Furthermore, the telegraph, followed by even more advanced means of communication, meant that the traders could recognize a center of control, wealth, and authority on the old continent. As a result, they could keep a cultural identity that was not totally bred in the place where they worked and lived. For native peoples, the effect was to distort their own self-identity, since their source of reference in living was now also outside their own orbit.

This one case is a fascinating example of how central forms of communication are to culture and to identity, and of the deep consequences of changes in these forms.[21] In the different kinds of culture there are different ways in which communication determines the meaning and shape of communal life, its exchange, its perception of environment, its relations to those outside its boundaries, its covenants, its meanings, its traditions, its ways of knowing, its aspirations. The issue here is not whether people read and write, whether they use technology in communication or not. The issue is really what in the mind-set of a people carries most weight and to what must other forms of communication be referred.

In a written culture, in social matters and in matters of values, morals, and religion, the referent is to whatever is written. In oral cultures, on the other hand, whatever may be written and read, it has no weight unless transferred to, or referred to, the oral domain, where the spoken voice, the wisdom of the elders, and the stories of beginnings or of heroic deeds have authority. It would be wrong, however, to think that so-called oral cultures always live within the unfettered immediacy of oral exchange. They too have their forms of distanciation and codification that govern and influence communication. Though not in writing, the tradition exists in rites that are traditional, in forms of expression that have to be respected in telling stories, in addressing people, or in singing poems. There are also the kinship codes that determine the boundaries within which people live, or the expression of relation to ancestors, to nature, and to the supernatural. It is on the basis of such codes and modes of expression that African or Asian writers today develop philosophies and ontologies that they consider built into the way of life of peoples of oral culture and tradition. Sometimes Western authors refer to these codes as "arch-writing," in order to bring out the point that any culture has its modes of distanciation that both allows for tradition and calls for constant reinterpretation, in light of new events and new conditions of life. This, however, constitutes a different kind of distanciation and a mode of interpretation different from the mode of producing written texts.

Digital Culture

Nowadays, both cultures of writing and cultures of orality are being overtaken by digital culture, i.e., a culture where digital forms of communication are the referent and dominate the mind-set of communication.[22] Radio, tele-

---

21. For what follows, with bibliographical references, see James W. Carey, *Communication as Culture: Essays on Media and Society* (New York: Routledge, 1992); John Fiske, *Media Matters: Everyday Culture and Political Change* (Minneapolis: University of Minnesota Press, 1994); David N. Power, "Liturgy as an Act of Communication and Communion: Cultural and Practical Implications in an Age Becoming Digital," *Mission* 3, no. 1 (1996): 43–62.

22. The expression *digital culture* is motivated by the title of the book by Nicholas Negroponte, *Being Digital* (New York: Knopf, 1995).

vision, computer information and composition not only have impact on how people communicate and on communication skills, but they have affected the ways of perceiving reality. They are also changing the locus of reference for judgment, and hence replace the exchange of words and the reference of writing as point of authoritative reference. Many people can read of events in newspapers and still look there for detail and for comment, but they want to see things happening on television. Indeed, the networks themselves have already extended this to their Web sites on the Internet.

These forms of exchange give a sense of immediacy, of being part of something, and indeed even seem more convincing. Ironically, with this creation of immediacy there is found, consciously or unconsciously, an odd distancing from what is represented and from what is learned. The possibility of multiple representations, each with its own twist, becomes obvious and builds the perception that there is some distance between oneself and the event or the information, as well as between the event (or the theory or the piece of art) and how it is represented. Those with some radio and television skills and the vast number of those with computer skills also learn what part they can play themselves in creating reality and in forming opinion. It is because of the vast possibilities of technical communication, both in accessing and in creating, that it is more and more common to think of belonging in a world of virtual reality, that is, of a reality that can be shaped and bred through the active and creative use of the communications code.

Churches and their communities make use of these media, though maybe not always aware of how much they affect the realities represented. The Bible and the works of early Church writers are out on the Internet. The Bible can thus be explored in different languages, or in different versions of the same language, almost simultaneously. What does this do to understanding it and exploring its meaning? The person on the Internet can do all the intertextualizing desired and can also communicate on Web sites with others about the text. The Vatican can put the latest papal discourse on the Internet, with very little control over how it is received or how it is treated when placed there. People with these virtual possibilities are those who form the liturgical congregations of the day.

All of this is important to the sacramental code and its appropriation. Whatever the changes, sacrament is always an event of oral exchange, whatever may lie behind or beneath it. The orality, however, is not the same for all peoples, for the simple reason that the nature of oral exchange in sacrament is affected by the place that orality has within the culture of those who celebrate. The predominance of one or other of the forms of expression discussed here in constituting authority gives rise to a difference in the forms and power of oral exchange. In the case of a culture of writing, the orality that exists can be called, with Walter Ong, secondary orality. Primary orality is exercised when it is the oral exchange, and the face-to-face encounter, that is in and of itself effective, and it is this which is considered of primary importance. Secondary orality means an exchange of words in oral form between persons who have some written (or digital) source in mind and adjudicate by way of reference to it. A classic example of secondary orality is a reading of Plato's dialogues in a college class or a reading of poets and classical novels. A classic example of primary orality is the telling of tales about the ancestors during initiation rites among some African peoples, or the folk stories passed on for many centuries in the west of Ireland without ever being written down. Now cultural anthropologists hasten to get recordings before such story-tellers die out, but this changes the whole power and medium of the story.

The purpose of communication is always to bring people into interaction and to assist in the forming of societies and communities, and for those oral and interface exchange is always needed. The form of the oral differs, however. In any cultural setting, elements of primary and of secondary orality go together, but in different mixes, and this is pertinent to interpretation, to appropriation, and to celebration. To be post[-]modern is to be aware of these fluctuations. With this awareness, some want to resort to older and more stable forms, while others look for the possibilities of the holy within this diversity.

Key Questions

Against the background hitherto described, some key questions for the interpretation and appropriation of sacramental traditions may be noted. These have to do with what is meant by sacrament, what is meant by tradition, and what it means to take guidelines from hermeneutical practice.

What Makes for Sacrament?

This question of what constitutes a sacrament has been asked and answered many a time. It is asked here of practice in order to give a descriptive and practical perspective, one that helps in grasping what has to be interpreted. This is to say that instead of using a theorem and definition of sacrament as guide to practice, sacramental celebration itself must be read and interpreted. Sacramental liturgy is in fact a mixture of appeal to written text, oral expression, and nonverbal, bodily, and visual involvement, within specific cultures. The relation between the oral, the bodily, the visual, and the written is constantly in flux, and quite dissimilar in different cultures, as explained above.

To treat, then, of sacrament, the first thing is to have a broad enough perception of what is done in sacrament, of what forms and means of communication are employed, and of that to which it refers, lest it be reduced to the ritual alone, or its word be reduced to ritual consecration, ritual narrative, or ritual proclamation. Scholastic theology had indeed defined the sacrament in terms of its ritual action, its immediate and remote matter, and its form that resided in specific words. But this reduced the essence of sacraments to certain actions and words of the minister, isolated from the rest of the celebration for the sake of defining essence. This was not the way in early and early medieval theology of sacrament, where the interplay of scriptural texts and their interpretation was taken as vital to the action and meaning of sacramental memorial. Today, however, much more attention is given to insight from ritual studies in the fields of anthropology and sociology and to their pertinence to the functioning and understanding of Christian sacrament. This, however, is not enough but needs to be linked with the interpreting of traditions.

Several cautions about appeals to liturgical history are to be kept in mind. In keeping memorial of Jesus Christ, the role of the word, proclaimed, reflected upon, affirmed for its truth and its ethical consequences has always been the key, though this cannot be divorced from simple bodily actions, which retain some constancy within cultural diversity. While there is a tendency in liturgical history to look for one single pattern of worship, or for what Gregory Dix called the Shape, this should not blind us to the fact that communities wrestled with memories, with an intertextuality which yielded constant reinterpretations of the Christ event commemorated. A contemporary attention to diversity can be retrieved only if we somehow get beyond the notion of sacrament as reenactment, or free ourselves from the notion that images give orderly and almost pictorial representations of event, reality, or person. Likewise, it is unwise to think that we can grasp truth and reality in a clear consciousness that makes what is remembered formally present to the inner self. Sacrament also needs to be unburdened of the notion of a single foundational narrative, given that the foundation event of Christian faith comes to us from the beginning in a variety of narratives, not reducible to an *ur-story*.

Sacraments have rites, indeed in some sense take place wholly within a ritual context, but they are not reducible to rites, and indeed are always in a situation in which the word proclaimed, the memory kept, the divine gift offered are "crossing out" ritual sedimentations, as one crosses out something in a written codex by writing over it. Change is needed in order to express what is handed on by ritual, endeavoring to subsume what was affirmed into another form of exchange. The form of exchange is communicative, oral, and performative, and it is interpersonal, asking for the personal engagement of the participants. It is this which requires breaking the ritual elements, or breaking away from rite, in order to engage prophetically and wisely with the event that is commemorated and continues to speak through its transmission. Hence any study of sacramental tradition has to look at the interaction between bodily ritual, word proclaimed and prayed, the visual surround, and living testimonies of faith, and to appreciate how much this interaction may vary.

What Makes for Tradition?

Since we are talking about staying within a sacramental tradition, it is necessary to consider the meaning of this term. Tradition may be confused with what is fixed and decisive. In doctrine, it may be thought of as the passing on of truths, well conceived and defined. In morals, it may be taken to indicate standardized values, even describing some of them as absolute. In sacrament, it can be heard to point only to what is ritually fixed and unchangeable. In fact, however, tradition is first and foremost the transmission of life in Christ and the Spirit, down through time and across cultures. This has its doctrinal, theological, sacramental, devotional, and sacramental expressions. As far as these are concerned, the action of tradition involves a constant process of interpretation, a process of retrieving the past as we redress the present. Indeed, there is a sense in which the present is always in the very act of passing, since what brings a people into the future is the core concern of tradition.

As long as no new questions emerge, a community may continue to repeat what is found in the past, doctrinally, morally, ritually, devotionally, and institutionally. The scrutiny of the traditions that serve Tradition is, however, recast when the conditions of an age in the life of the Church and of those to whom the Gospel is addressed bring forth new issues and new questions. The conditions may be such that coherency in Church life vanishes and ecclesial life, as it were, becomes a muddle. This is why some "redress" is needed, some way in which the imagination, nourished from Christian sources, "presses back against the pressures of reality," to quote Seamus Heaney.

In writing of the role of the canonical scriptures as a text in the life of a Christian community, Paul Ricoeur takes the process of interpretation as one which discovers "something *revealing* that is not frozen in any ultimate or immutable texts."[23] These texts are related to life, to other texts, to rites, to institutions, to personages, and in the process their meaning and gift emerge anew. What is thus said of canonical scriptures has application in the broad field of the sacramental tradition and the sacramental imagination.

Far from signifying a linear progress of history, even of the history of the Church, fidelity to tradition means allowing for moments of evangelical retrieval within the disruptions of history. It looks back in memory to the Christ event and to the evangelical tradition recorded in the scripture, both to call certain developments into question and to find a point of reference within the flux of coordinated time. It can also record the memory of persons and occurrences, and indeed of doctrinal formulations, which have served as inspirational expressions of Christian faith and of the work of the Spirit. The same is true for sacramental tradition. It is always referred back to evangelical origins, and it brings the light of past expressions to bear on the present. There can be no presumption of progress, however, and each age has to allow

---

23. Paul Ricoeur, *Figuring the Sacred: Religion, Narrative, and Imagination*, trans. David Pellauer, ed. Mark I. Wallace (Minneapolis: Fortress Press, 1995), 72.

its modes of celebration to be called into question by the very desire of being faithful to tradition. Christian tradition, or sacramental tradition, belongs
within the larger human drama, so that its efficaciousness in bringing the
memorial of Christ to bear on human affairs belongs to the appropriation
of tradition. As Pierre Gisel puts it, Christian tradition does not provide a
dwelling-place.[24] On the contrary, in face of human events it provides the
Church with a pluriform memory, which, however, always refers back to one
specific historical event. It looks to narratives, images, institutions, persons,
sacramental celebrations, and diverse monuments, on which it draws in faith
to find a way of being in the present time that is both a memory of the past
and an expectation of the future promised in the Pasch.

In conjunction with the understanding of tradition, it is also asked what
constitutes revelation. In fact, there are several different ways of answering
this query, all of them connected with one another. There is a description
of revelation in terms of "truths revealed," meaning what is given themati-
cally in the scriptures, then explicated by the magisterium as doctrine, and
personally appropriated in faith. In a fuller sense, revelation is Jesus Christ,
the Word made flesh, and for some this gives rise to the task of historical
reconstruction of what is narrated in the scriptures and their spiritual interpretation through communion with Christ. Closely tied with this, revelation
can be said to be the history of God's action in earthly historical events,
which are made known through the scriptures. Finally, revelation is also
sometimes described as God's present action, through the experience of grace
that is now mediated in memory of Christ and by the power of the Spirit.
In this case, the theological quest is to explicate this experience through a
correlation of the analysis and formulation of this experience with a reading
of scripture and its mediation through traditions. What is important is the
presence and action of God in human lives, in virtue of the gift of the active presence of the Spirit and the memorial of Jesus Christ as conveyed by
tradition. In this case, sacramental liturgy belongs within revelation, since it
is the communication of the Word and the Spirit to those who live by the
memorial of Jesus Christ.

What Is It to Be Hermeneutical?

In light of the foregoing considerations, it can be asked what it means to take
a hermeneutical approach to sacramental tradition and its appropriation.[25]
What is emphasized here is the ongoing activity of interpreting and of appropriating what is passed on into the life of the Church. This is not simply a
matter of knowing what was done or written, or why at that time this was
done and written. A hermeneutical approach has its feet in the present. It is

---

24. See Pierre Gisel, *Corps et Esprit: L'excès du croire. Expérience du monde et accès à soi* (Paris:
Desclée de Brouwer, 1990), 79–95.

25. On the use of the term *hermeneutical*, see the introduction, pp. 5ff. above.

to ask what is being passed on in the life of the Church to the present generation of Christians, and how it is being received by them, and to be critically conscious of all that is involved in this process.

Certain characteristics of this approach are important. First and foremost it is the Tradition in the fullness of its varied expressions which is to be interpreted. In other words, for sacramental traditions this means everything that is there is to be harvested, all the actions of a ritual, and all the rituals of different families. This harvesting, however, cannot be a simple picking and choosing, but it has to go with the insights gained into the dynamics of actual sacramental celebration.

It is helpful to note, without overusing them, the distinction between operations made by Paul Ricoeur in an interpretation of written texts to see how they operate in retrieving and redressing sacramental traditions. The distinction is between explaining, understanding and appropriating.[26] Explanation means responsibility to the "text," i.e., to all that we can know of what was celebrated and of how it was celebrated, and within what ecclesial and social context this was done. In this regard, we can recognize that in the canon of sacramental remembrance there belong texts proclaimed, texts spoken, actions performed, elements used, institutions incorporated, and places that gather. They postulate our attention and respect, granted that there is always a limit to the retrieval and explanation of data, in their original form and in the way in which they belonged to a lived practice. Once the texts, in the broad sense of the term, are known, the genre or form of each and every kind of text has to be considered, as well as the interplay of different elements, literary, ritual, and institutional, within a celebration or an order for celebration.

A minute example is provided by the study of the Roman Canon of the Mass, so highly venerated on the one hand and so reviled on the other. Explaining it means attending to the meaning, in context, of the verbs that express offering, as well as attending to how interceding and offering are interrelated, or how the biblical types of sacrifice are invoked. It also means tracing through the *Ordines Romani* to see how it was actually prayed, with what gestures and in what tone of voice, and within what ecclesiastical structures. Another precise example would be to see what concerns about sacrificial action and devotional reform were behind the composition of the Prayer of Humble Access in the communion service of the *Book of Common Prayer*, and how these were resolved in the words of that prayer, together with what perceptions of ministry and sacrament.

Understanding comes with insight into what is projected through the data retrieved, into what is passed on to the present through their appreciation in light of Christ's mystery. This is analogous to a reading of the scriptures.

---

26. Paul Ricoeur, *Interpretation Theory: Discourse and the Surplus of Meaning* (Fort Worth: Texas Christian University Press, 1976), 71–88.

By entering as it were into the flow of the text, its meanings and references are grasped. This does not mean that we will simply repeat what is there, but rather that we gain an insight which helps creativity in the present. This is why such retrieval is called an understanding of virtual reality, that is, something that can be brought to being if the insight is well fostered. It is often indeed an insight into possibilities that the past itself has not realized, even though it virtually maintains them. To go back to the example of the Roman Canon, the explanation of what it meant by *offering* actually enables us some freedom in face of the notion of propitiatory offering that in the period after the Reformation predominated in much Catholic practice. This insight could then be integrated into a new prayer, in a different cultural and congregational setting. A further example of helpful understanding or insight could be taken from what we learn of the meaning of the Eucharist from the prayers of nuns or layfolk that were used, first for communion and then for recitation at the elevation of the host.[27] These are insights that can be incorporated into other parts of the Mass, with special attention to the significance of the visual.

Explanation and insight do not come from a purely intellectual or cerebral pursuit. They involve a high degree of creative imagination, the readiness to play with rites and words that reveals their meaning through the play, and an affective, devotional, and intellectual openness to conversion. It is for this reason that feminist hermeneutics insists on the importance of actual celebration in exploring the fruits of tradition and the possibilities of renewal.

These examples illustrate the fact that understanding goes in tandem with appropriation. The engagement of the community in the life and truth that any tradition proffers is the ultimate intention of sacramental celebration. It is therefore also the ultimate criterion of authenticity and can be judged only by attention to ethical and spiritual fruits.

The Limits of Understanding and Appropriation

The appropriation of what is given through the tradition is, however, done within limits. Two points, already indicated in the introduction, are here recalled. First, in considering established rites and texts there has to be some concern about elements that have crept into sacramental order which are not necessary to fidelity to the Gospel and may in fact even obstruct the free flow of grace. This belongs within what is called the hermeneutics of suspicion. One has to ask, in other words, whether the ritual or the signs may mask some ideology, some domineering power structure, or some conceptual attempt to place God and God's action within controlling limits. One has to ask the same of standard theological and catechetical images and interpre-

---

27. See David N. Power, *The Eucharistic Mystery: Revitalizing the Tradition* (New York: Crossroad, 1992), 187–92.

tations, such as hierarchy or causality. Only by such a critique is the action of grace liberated.

This means a deconstruction of formulations of doctrine or ritual structures that claim to be irreformable. The control of what is done in sacramental celebration has to be placed within its proper limits, the inherent ideological elements of such control have to be unearthed and other possible meanings of the rites and symbols allowed to emerge. This affects the intellectual control exercised by way of a metaphysics of God, the institutional control exercised by an appeal to divine origins, or the cultural control exercised by using cosmological theorems of order and hierarchy. While these may have served an era in guiding the celebration and understanding of sacraments, any suggestion that their claims are absolute only hinders appropriation of sacramental celebration into new cultural, historical, and social situations.

Second, there is always retrieval and reconstruction in the appropriation of Tradition. Earlier meanings may be renewed, or possible meanings not yet noted may come forth from ritual and text or from the interplay of rites and texts in a context in which historical and cultural factors have changed. Examples of this process will occur in the following chapters.

Some Guides to Interpretation

The foregoing has pointed out the fluidity of traditional practice and interpretation and underscored some of the reasons for this diversity, as well as questions facing the Churches today in renewing sacramental celebration. While the community has its texts, both scriptural and liturgical, to which it looks with reverence, their interpretation is done from within a living situation of belief, institutional structure, practice, and cultural horizons. All of this raises questions for the Church today, so it is useful to suggest some guides, or working boundaries and orientations for interpretation, that draw on the past while being appropriate to the present situation.

As noted in the introduction, what is called the post[-]modern arises principally from the loss of confidence in holistic, symbolic, and organizational systems and in rationality. It is modern in that it accepts the departure from cultural forces and models of hegemony and totality. It is modern also in that it attends to the subjective and to the individual. It is post[-]modern in that the turn to the rational and the organizational, with supreme confidence in the power of the human to dominate the world and to create a new kind of unity, is outclassed.

In sacramental thought and practice, there has been some loss of confidence in certain ways of envisaging sacramental representation, so that new queries have to be considered. This means a new awareness of the other whose voices have to be heard, who have been excluded or marginalized. It means intertextuality, instead of the assumptions of unity, whether of the texts, of institutions, or of sacramental actions. Community-wise, it has to allow an ethical moment in the overlapping of concerns where communities gather in conscious attention to diversity, in readiness to listen and to hear. Against modernity, it means a new search for the holy, and a quest for what joins the human with other beings with the world around it in interdependency, instead of acting out of the assumption that we are "stewards of creation." In sacrament, the earth speaks, the cosmos speaks, and humans need to listen. We need to develop a greater sense of living by gift, by what is always coming, adventing, eventing, being offered. There needs to be a heuristic of attentiveness to the symbolic in all its modes, rather than a resort to a set sacramental paradigm.

Too much liturgical revision has been behavioristic and functional, and unfortunately banal. This is not overcome by a return to the premodern, but by moving into a new cultural and religious phase. The poetics of the sacrament calls attention to the interlocking of text and practice, of doctrine or theory and practice, in history and in the present. It attends to intertexuality, even to the tensions between text and text, between rite and rite, between rite and text, between what the ritual upholds and what the people do. It looks beneath and beyond the surfaces of texts and rites, yet is suspicious of any claims to have reached secure foundations, whether in a mythic sense of the holy, in a metaphysics, in an divinely ordered structure, or in access to human interiority.

In writing of the search for an alternative to metaphysical or liberal theology, the Swiss theologian Klauspeter Blaser has distinguished four types of what he calls post[-]modern theology.[28] He dubs them reconstructionist, liberationist, nonfoundationalist and nonapologetic, identifying them particularly with American writers. Both Blaser and, in the same volume, Denis Müller classify process theology as postmodernist, under the heading of reconstructionist.[29] Given the systemic concerns of process writers and their abiding confidence in some form of metaphysics, not much attention is given to that approach in this work.

Other forms of reconstruction are of greater interest, because they give greater attention to language and its various operations. There are theologians who think that the response to the decline of a metaphysics of being and of philosophical foundations is to be found in a theological aesthetics.[30] When this is done, there is often a strong influence of Hans Urs von Balthasar at work. This seems to be due to two factors in his writings. The

---

28. Klauspeter Blaser, "Variété des théologies postmodernes et crise des 'fondationalismes,'" in *La théologie en postmodernité*, ed. Pierre Gisel and Patrick Evrard (Geneva: Labor et Fides, 1996), 189–212.

29. Denis Müller, "La théologie postmoderne constructive et la situation actuelle de l'éthique théologique," in ibid., 213–28.

30. See Pierre Gisel, "Résonances et mise en perspective: La théologie en condition postmoderne," in ibid., 415–17.

first is his proposal of a metaphysics of beauty, which avoids the confusion of created being with divine being but does allow us to see created being as its participation.[31] Created Being is to be understood as the *actus essendi*, which is God's creative act in the world and leaves humans open and transparent to the divine. The second factor is von Balthasar's own theological aesthetics, which in the form of the Incarnate Word, and in the form of the Church, sees an aesthetic wholeness and integrity centered around the revelation of God's *agapé*.[32] While this influence is most marked in Catholic theology, there is the counterpart in Protestant theologies, when cultural forms of interpretation of the Word of God are affirmed to replace the appeal to metaphysics or to an appeal to the human subject.[33] Some relate the retrieval of the aesthetic especially to the scriptures and to narrative, particularly the narrative of Christ's passion and resurrection, inclusive of the Last Supper and the bestowal of the eucharistic memorial on the Church. Others highlight what they see as the aesthetic of the forms of Church order and ecclesial life.

There are, however, two problems in some of this writing that make it difficult to do full justice to the pluralism of scriptural, sacramental, and institutional expression. First, there is an assumption that the foundational narrative of the passion and resurrection is available in a clear, unfragmented form, whereas in fact the story of the event of the Cross from the beginning is transmitted in a variety of narratives that are irreducible to one single narrative form. The second difficulty lies in assumptions about the form of the Church, which is taken to be harmonious in all its parts (traditions, canon of scriptures, institutions, and rites) and well established from the beginning. Any critique of the life of the Church would thus be a critique of how faithful it has been in act to this form. This, however, seems to elude the fact that the Church can be thought of only as the communion of Churches, each having its own peculiar characteristics, even as all seek a unity in faith and in practice that transcends differences. The aesthetic approach also overlooks the possibility of a contamination of ecclesial forms by ideologies.

Following Blaser's classification, we can say that the needed reconstruction has to do justice to critical hermeneutics. This engages in a critique of the metaphysical, epistemological, and institutional factors which have served as

---

31. See Hans Urs von Balthasar, *The Glory of the Lord: A Theological Aesthetics*, vol. 4: *The Realm of Metaphysics in Antiquity* (San Francisco: Ignatius Press, 1989), especially the pages on Thomas Aquinas, 372–412.

32. See especially *The Glory of the Lord: A Theological Aesthetics*, vol. 1: *Seeing the Form* (San Francisco: Ignatius Press, 1982; repr. 1989).

33. In reference to George Lindbeck, Stanley Hauerwas, and John Milbank, Müller calls this a return to a magisterial approach to theology as the response to the criticisms made of theology in the deconstruction of metaphysics. See Müller, "La théologie postmoderne constructive et la situation actuelle de l'éthique théologique," 228. Milbank, it must be noted, while he gives first place to the Christian narrative, does find a place in theology for the language of being. See John Milbank, " 'Postmodern Critical Augustinianism': A Short *Summa* in Forty-Two Responses to Unasked Questions," *Modern Theology* 7 (1991): 225–37.

foundations of theory and practice in the course of Christian history. Its prag-
matic concern lies in the endeavor to retrieve metaphors from the tradition,
especially from the scriptures, which in this age can best serve the reconstrual
of the understanding of revelation and the reconstrual of institutions and ethical norms. The liberationist current is of course very broad and includes the
voices of all those who are seen to have been victims of modernity, and indeed often of Christianity in the way in which it has served the ordering of
Churches and of society. This reconstruction can include a nonapologetic retrieval of the cultural forms which Christianity has adopted, recognizing this
to be an inherent necessity of passing on a tradition. In its endeavor to account for multiformity within the expression of Christian belief, its intent,
however, is to be open to ecumenical and interreligious interests. Reliance
on cultural theories cannot be turned into another, nonmetaphysical, form of
foundationalism.

Proper attention to the plurality found in traditions responds to the concerns of both nonfoundationalists and liberationists. As Blaser states it, the
hope of some of its proponents is that it may make it possible to account
for the concerns of such as feminist theologians, Hispanic theologians, and
African American theologians, since it can blend what comes from tradition
with other symbolic expressions that are more directly addressed to their interests and experience. Reconstruction also opens the door to conversation
between Churches and among theologies on different continents, and indeed
also to dialogue between religions.

Taking account of all this within the compass of a hermeneutical approach
to sacramental tradition and understanding, some points can be made. First
of all, a critique of foundations is necessary. Sacramental practice has been
founded on notions of hierarchy and priesthood on the one hand, or of the
Word of God on the other, that need a critique that opens the door to reconstruction. Second, attention to culture is of great importance, especially in
face of present concerns about inculturation that affect Churches and their
sacramental practice on all continents. In looking at the past, one has to be
able to see what belongs to cultural particularity in sacramental traditions
and is not necessarily linked with the Gospel. One also has to see the extent
to which the Church rejected cultures in its missionary work, so that some
kind of cultural and liturgical redress is now necessary. Third, one has to ask
whether it is desirable to look for any overarching construct within which to
place God language and religious expression. Is there not a pluralism inherent in Christianity from the very beginning, even where there is the common
memory of the one foundational *event*, which is the story of Jesus of Naza-
reth and his crucifixion? Fourth, none of these concerns can be properly met
without the reconstructionists' attention to language and its genres and to
language usage.

If then it is perceived that both foundational narrative and ecclesial form
are fragmented, even in their unique reference to Jesus Christ, the cue to

the investigation of sacramental tradition will be taken from David Tracy. In writing of the need to adopt a hermeneutical approach to Christian tradition in the context of plurality and ambiguity, Tracy has set out certain suppositions, which both offer possibilities of more extensive inquiry and set limits within which to engage in the open-ended process of reflection and interpretation.[34] He takes the actuality of event as key, that is, event as something which happened, and attaches three characteristics to the originating event of Christian faith· (a) event as a happening of language; (b) event as divine self manifestation, or disclosure; (c) event in and of the Word of God, Jesus Christ.

Tracy is here addressing the plurality and ambiguity of interpretation which is current in face of religious texts and of the Christian scriptures in particular. He recognizes that it is impossible to rely on a propositional rendering of their truth. At the same time, he refuses to go with free-floating readings that have no point of reference in the persuasion that texts say something about something to somebody. The historical event of Jesus Christ is a reality, however difficult it may be to historically reconstruct both his words and his deeds.[35] Hence Tracy chooses to take event as the controlling point of reference and to link this with a grasp of the role of language in shaping reality and in handing on what has been revealed. Within such a perspective, one can affirm an event as having occurred without having to determine the details of its factuality and its meaning beyond all doubt or possibilities of further interpretation.

If event is the key, first it is noted that revelation itself is a language event, for it is the proclamation of salvation through Jesus Christ, not simply the fact itself of his life and death. The primordial historical event, however, to which texts refer is the event of Jesus Christ, as both facticity and proclamation, or language. This Tracy takes as an event in which God has given self-disclosure to humankind, a disclosure embraced by believers. It is in the historical person of Jesus that Christians believe God to have disclosed the divine self and poured out divine love. The proclamation and poetics of Christian language is devoid of sense without this affirmation. While the search for the historical Jesus can never be concluded, it is always necessary, for the word about Jesus can be apprehended only in reference to him as the Word of God. This event, however, is made significant and is transmitted through language, and in tradition through written texts. These belong within a believing community and have to be interpreted. Through interpretation, which occurs in many forms,

---

34. David Tracy, "The Word and Written Texts in the Hermeneutics of Christian Revelation," *Archivio di Filosofia* 60 (1992): 265–80.

35. Post[-]modern labeling seems quite divergent on this point. I have heard Dominic Crossan, for example, accused (*sic*) of remaining tributary to modernity and liberalism in his writings about the historical Jesus, while in other circles I find him regarded as post[-]modern, because of the way in which he allows that diverse narratives come from the same event and that it can be accessed only through and within this diversity.

literary, practical, and didactic, and so occurs itself as a language event, the Christ event continues to come to the Church. Tracy's concern in this is to be faithful to the origins of Christian revelation, in the person of Jesus and in the primordial texts, while at the same time allowing for an interpretative tradition, which takes account of the irreducible plurality built into the texts themselves.

To deal specifically with sacramental tradition, I would accept these premises and boundaries, adding others. To the language character of event, I would add the need for attention to the fullness of language, so that it includes the ritual and symbolic. I would find it important to qualify self-manifestation as self-gift. To the primacy of reference to the Word, Jesus Christ, I would add the presence of the Spirit, inner testimony to this Word and inner vitality to the life and sacrament of a Christian community. I would also add that no interpretation and no appropriation of a tradition takes place without engagement with the ethical as a necessary part of the hermeneutical task.

Thus taking the cue from Tracy, some working rules can be stated. They are given here rather schematically, since their meaning ought to become clearer as the work progresses:

1. Sacrament is a memorial of the Christ event, of what is narrated in the Gospels as his Pasch, in which there is a divine self-manifestation and self-gift. The celebration brings this event to the present of the community, to event again within it, embodied in that body which is the living body of Christ. The ultimate referent of interpretation is always the Christ event, even when through different texts and rites the event continues to be re-interpreted. The sacramental action, as an action and event of God's grace, is guaranteed by the presence of the Holy Spirit working in the Church.

2. Sacraments have to be interpreted as liturgical celebrations, and this includes word, blessing, and ritual action. This approach is a heuristic rather than a model. That is, it attends to operations, to word, blessing, and rite as actions and seeks insight from their interaction into what it is to keep memorial of Christ's Pasch and to enter communion with him through such celebration.

3. It is the proclamation of the word and the memory of the gift expressed in prayer which leads the community to the font, or the sacramental table, or the blessed oil. On the other hand, presence at the table, at the font, around the oil, shapes the being of the community and its relation to its environment, earthly, human, and social. Hence, the interpretation of word and rite belong together, and they need to be understood in their interaction.

4. Interpretations of the sacraments have to face the diverse character of the scriptural texts proclaimed in their celebration and of the rites celebrated. They cannot reduce the texts to a single grand narrative or overarching symbolism, nor the rites to a clearly demarked essence of matter and form. Interpretation respects the pluriformity of faith in Christ already evident in the

New Testament, as well as respecting the Hebrew and sapiential scriptures as stories of salvation in their own right, not to be reduced to typologies of Christ and Church. It respects the relation between rites and peoples, between rites and cultures, and attends to the diversity to which this may give rise.

5. All interpretation is contextual and intertextual. When new liturgical rites are composed, or when people ritualize, usually many texts and rituals are retained from the past, but now placed in new situations and put into a different sort of intertextual play, which gives rise to new meanings.

6. All interpretation is perspectival, that is, it is done within the preunderstandings of the interpreter or the interpreting community, though it is ready to let these preunderstandings be challenged. To say that it is perspectival does not mean that it is purely subjective. Representations have their own power within them, to which people are invited to open themselves. However, they do come with their preunderstandings, and these are bound up with the conditions of their own being. There is thus an encounter between the world to which the participant belongs culturally and historically, and the world of being presented in the language of the tradition. Interpretation, in Gadamer's phrase, is to work within the fusion of horizons, out of the desire for being and for truth that is given voice or expression both in the work and in the participant.

7. All interpretation is anticipatory, open to whatever possible meanings and actions the interpretation of the word and the rite make possible and open to whatever "comes from the future," anticipated in the passing present of the memory of the past.

8. The aim of the interpretation is not to find ideas about sacraments, but even within the confusion of ideas it is to try to be open to "what is going on" through these words, what attention to language tells us about the kind of participation in being and life that sacraments offer, and within what language and ritual limits, whatever the possible distortions, this remains "on offer."

9. The rites and texts are ever brought into a speech situation, a situation in which there is communion/communication, which is not reducible to passivity, but supposes appropriating activity of all members of the community. In this the interplay between rite and word is vital, for the word in its multiformity and polysemy goes beyond the ritualistic and the propositional.

10. The speech situation is one into which are drawn persons who are shaped by cultures and live in given societies. The connection between the liturgical ordering and the cultural and social ordering of life to which those in the sacramental community subscribe, or to which they are subject, has to be taken into account in tradition's appropriation. The justice of God's kingdom is expressed in sacramental symbols, but not in the abstract. It is an encounter with the other that is culturally, economically, and historically grounded. The sharing of wine, bread, and water, as well as the healing power

of oil, have far-reaching implications, affecting both those who share, and what is shared, through these symbols and rites. The ethical is inherent in sacramental expression, and in its appropriation. How the ethical commitments of a community are affected by sacramental exchange is vital to the interpretation of the tradition and to its appropriation.

Conclusion

In this chapter, the purpose has been to set current understanding of sacraments within a current situation of change, and even of disagreement on what is proper. This makes it clearer why we can usefully adopt a hermeneutical approach to sacramental traditions and the explanation of sacramental celebration. First, the desire to revise the Roman Rite within its own substantial unity was contrasted with the phenomenon of ritualization. Then, some sociological and theological critique that affirms the loss of the holy in sacramental renewal was taken into account. This was followed by giving attention to an alternate, post[-]modern critique of sacramental practice and language. Subsequently, the connection between liturgy and cultural changes in communication was noted. On the basis provided by this analysis of present currents, key questions about sacrament, tradition, and interpretation were spelled out. Finally, some guidelines for interpretation were suggested that meet present needs and that can help to develop sacramental understandings attuned to the present.

— Chapter Two —

Sacrament:
Language Event

The issues about the celebration of sacramental liturgy noted in the previous chapter are issues about language. Some contend that the former language of the holy should be preserved; others that it needs to be changed. In the meantime, changes in the modes of communication change language usage, and in some parts of the world the effort is to retrieve a language of the holy that belongs to cultures hitherto neglected by the Church's liturgy. Touching on these debates, what was noted was that all celebration in its use of words, symbols, and rites involves the interpretation of the tradition handed on. It therefore seems appropriate to present a theology of sacrament that brings language to the fore. This enables us to grasp what is taking place, as well as how we are dealing with liturgical traditions.

What is proposed is that a sacrament may be viewed as a language event. This offers a theology that is oriented to practice, and at the same time meets the post[-]modern perspectives already mentioned. To develop this approach, first some sacramental theories of the past are reviewed, to harvest their insights and to note their limitations. Second, the place of language in human life is explored. Third, on this foundation a heuristic of sacraments as God's Word Eventing in Spirit is proposed, relating it to the problematic of human time and of changing cultures.

Sacramental Theories: A Review

Within the last seventy years, sacramental theologians and liturgists have paid considerable attention to the sign function of sacrament, countering the stress on causality by looking to the perceptible signification of sacramental celebration. The Vatican Council itself highlighted this aspect of liturgy by calling for the people's active and conscious participation and asking that revisions of the rites would make signs available and open to all. There have also been the widely known endeavors to relate signification and causality by attending to contemporary understandings of the symbolic. Even while moving from these theories into other areas of interpretation, even while being

51

critical of them, their gain is not being discarded. It is never possible to think beyond a theory, without thinking through the theory.

The theory of instrumental causality assured that sacraments would be seen clearly as works of Christ, *ex opero operato Christi,* as the adage went originally. It also presented sacraments in ecclesial and historical perspective. The historical perspective was expressed in terms of the relation between past, present and future, in an act which is one of memorial, of commemorating a particular event, which is the passion of Christ. This historical presentation was clearly eschatological, because the intent attributed to keeping memorial was to attain to the life of glory in God, where all will be one.

Thomas Aquinas

The ecclesial perspective also emerged, despite what is said in criticisms to the contrary.[1] To begin with, as Thomas Aquinas explained it, baptism is an initiation into the priesthood of Christ and the public worship of the Church, and it is for this reason that it sanctifies. Further to that, there was the strong scholastic insistence that sacraments were to be ministered in the faith of the Church and ecclesially meant nothing if ministered otherwise. The central role of the Eucharist in the sacramental system was also well brought out within the model of sacramental causality, since all sacraments were said to include a *votum,* or desire, for the Eucharist and to be intrinsically ordered toward it.

Whatever its suggestions of productivity, justly criticized as too narrow a focus, the theory of instrumental causality established the link in faith and action between God, Christ, Church, minister, and recipient. Inasmuch as it built up the notion of causality by relating it to the function of sign, it underscored the fact that sacraments are signs of faith and are to be celebrated as such. This also permitted an appeal to Christ in his passion as exemplary cause of Christian life and the form communicated through the sacramental action to those who receive the sacraments and are configured to him.

To recognize the limits placed by Thomas himself on the theory of efficient causality, it has to be related to the genus of sign within which he first puts sacrament. The sacramental sign in its signification is threefold. While it speaks of something in the present, of what is done in the moment, it does so by signifying what is past, that is, the passion of Christ. It is only in virtue of this that any present reality is signified and effected. This puts limits on the extent to which the mystery of grace is "presented." Furthermore, the sign also points to the future, expressing the expectation of what is to come in glory, in the fullness of communion with God in Christ. This too limits presence. Hence the advertence to the fullness of sign and signification

---

1. On what follows, see David N. Power, *The Eucharistic Mystery: Revitalizing the Tradition* (New York: Crossroad, 1992), 216–36.

severely limits any accusations made that Thomas gives excessive attention to theologies of presence.

On the other hand, it is the appeal to sacramental causality, as it is also the appeal to substantial presence in his eucharistic theology, which shows the limits of signification. Whatever may be conveyed through sign, and so grasped by the human mind, there is a divine activity and a divine presence, and an activity and presence of the risen Christ, which is not captured in the sign.

Aquinas also related the entire sacramental economy to the Eucharist, and specifically to the communion in the body and blood of Christ whereby he joins the faithful to himself in the communion of the Church and thus brings them into his communion with the Father. For him, this central act of worship is one in which Christ acts directly, without the mediation of a minister, creating a spiritual communion in which the Church is "as though one person" with himself. This aspect of the sacramental economy also points to the limits of the theory of sacramental causality, as well as to the limits of the power of rites to signify Christ's relation to his members.

Bonaventure

One should not, in any case, think that the scholastic theory of causality was uniform despite a certain consistency of vocabulary, established because of the authority given to the *Sentences* of Peter Lombard. The particular position of Bonaventure is instructive on that score. Two problems usually arise in discussing Bonaventure's theology of sacrament. These have to do with how he conceived sacramental grace and with his explanation of sacramental causality.

Bonaventure writes of sacraments as remedies, as healing grace, rather than as sanctifying grace.[2] Yet in the *Breviloquium* of the Eucharist he says that because Christ himself, the Principle of sanctification and redemption, is present, it infuses the flame of love into the heart.[3] This is consistent with his notion of redemption as restorative. Christ, the Word of God, is the Principle of both creation and redemption. He is an incarnate principle, that is, he took on flesh, because humankind needed to be restored to the grace in which it had been created and from which it had fallen by sin. Remedy, therefore, is to restore grace and love in the human heart.

While, in keeping with the tenets of scholastic theology, Bonaventure calls sacraments causes, he says that this is only *senso extenso*.[4] The sacraments are more vessels of grace than instruments. It is by a divine pact or covenant that when the sign of grace is expressed in sacrament, God grants grace. There is no causal activity intrinsic to the sacrament as such. This sacramen-

---

2. See Bonaventure, *In Sententias* IV, dist. 1; *Breviloquium*, Part VI.
3. *Breviloquium*, VI, 9.
4. *In Sententias* IV, dist. 1, part 1, art. 1, qq. 2, 3.

tal principle is the Franciscan principle, which was somewhat exaggerated by Duns Scotus, who seemed to attach a certain arbitrariness to it, because of his doctrine of divine voluntarism. In Bonaventure, however, it is meant to emphasize the divine gift given in sacrament, rather than any innerworldly activity. It is also in keeping with the precedence that Bonaventure gives to love over knowledge, whether in writing of God or of the human person. What is signified in sacrament is this divine love, and what is given in sacrament is love, the sacraments culminating in the Eucharist wherein Jesus Christ is present, love itself. One can also note, as does Bernard Cooke, that Bonaventure is molded by the Franciscan sense of the ever pervasive presence of God in creation and in created things.[5] The divine love penetrates all things and draws human beings through the love shown forth in them into communion with God.

From a contemporary point of view, benefit is to be drawn from the accent that Bonaventure gives to the divine presence in the sacraments and to the precedence of love in thinking about the economy of creation and of redemption. Furthermore, his general view of the created and redemptive order affirms their unity and integrity, or wholeness. It is in that sense that he reads the scriptures, explained according to the teaching of the four senses.[6] That is also the way in which he sees the relation of sacraments to one another, within the vision of Christ, the Principle.[7] There is an integrity, a completeness, to divine order, and it is manifested in the order and unity of the universe and of history.

Reformers

The relationship between word, sacrament, and faith was a key issue for the Reformers of the sixteenth century. Indeed, it could be said that the understanding of language precisely as event has roots in the sacramental theology of the Reformation. Martin Luther was devoted to the scriptures and their proper interpretation, but he put this in the context of preaching and proclamation. Word is not just knowledge, but it is communication and address, asking for a response. Luther, while of course he wished the congregation to hear and understand, kept alive the biblical and prophetic sense of the Word of God as a salvific address. He brought this into his reforms of the Mass or Last Supper, in which he wished the words of the Supper narrative to be truly a proclamation, carrying with it all the vigor of a divine promise.

In the sacramental theology of John Calvin there was also a reminder to the Western Church to take due account of the action of the Spirit, without which there is no communion in Christ and no life-giving presence. In this he was indeed much accountable to a Western writer, St. Augustine, according

---

5. Bernard Cooke, *The Distancing of God: The Ambiguity of Symbol in History and Theology* (Minneapolis: Fortress Press, 1990), 161–64.

6. *Breviloquium*, Introduction.

7. Ibid., Book VI.

to whom actions could be correctly celebrated and the effective Word of God enacted in the prescribed forms without a communication of grace, where communion in the Spirit is absent.

Problems lay in the passage from theory to practice. Some Reformation liturgies seemed to be so concerned about the intelligibility of the Word that its nature as an event of salvation was obscured. It may also be true that the Reformation in its reaction against the magic quality invested in sacramental practice lacked a good appreciation of the role and symbolic function of sacramental signs and rites.

For an appreciation of the dual action of Word and Spirit in sacrament, we can look to the theology of the Eastern Churches. There sacraments are envisioned as the celebration of the Church which is the *koinonia,* or communion, of the body of Christ. It is in the communion in the Spirit that the Word is heard in faith, as it is in the communion in the Spirit that God is blessed in the name of Christ and the gifts transformed. It is thus also in the communion in the Spirit that the gift of Christ's body and blood is received, the Church entering through this communion into the divine mystery of the eternal communion of Father, Son, and Spirit.

Contemporary Theologies

In contemporary Protestant theology, Peter Brunner has made a significant contribution to the relation between word, sacrament, and prayer in worship.[8] The presence of God in Word and Sacrament confronts the congregation on the one hand. On the other, there can be no proper proclamation of the Word or reception of sacraments without an invocation by the Church of Word and Spirit. As Brunner says, "That God approaches us through Word and in Meal with his incarnation-presence is not a mechanical, but a pneumatic event."[9] It is the action of the Spirit in the response to the Word that is the ground for a good appreciation of the eschatological character of sacramental worship, for it is the pouring out of the Spirit which is the eschatological reality given to the Church, in anticipation of the fullness of the kingdom of God.

In his interpretation of Melanchthon on the relation between sacrament and sacrifice in the Eucharist, Brunner underlines the need for a worship that integrates both aspects. While the Lord's Supper is primarily sacrament, the offer of God's promises made in Christ, the Church is moved by Word and Spirit to make its sacrifice of praise and thanksgiving, of its service to the poor, and of its own self, in and through Christ. The two are integral parts of worship, not two distinct types of service.[10] It is in his appreciation of the role of liturgical arts in worship that Brunner does justice to the nature of

---

8. Peter Brunner, *Worship in the Name of Jesus,* trans. M. H. Bertram (St. Louis: Concordia Publishing House, 1968).
9. Ibid., 201.
10. Ibid., 123–24.

sacrament as symbolic.[11] He contends that God can be discernible only in the symbolic, which points away from itself and toward the mystery which is represented. The analogy at this point is with the role of icons in the worship of the Byzantine Church. Such an accent on the symbolic could of course be applied to what is most central, the sacramental action in the bodily elements of bread, wine, oil, and water.

The development of the Thomistic theory along the lines of symbolic causality by Karl Rahner and Edward Schillebeeckx enriched it in a contemporary vein. Drawing on insights from contemporary philosophers and from anthropological studies, these writers enlarged the understanding of sign so that it could be better appreciated as an act of self-communication, both divine and human, and an encounter in grace. Based on that insight, they and others were able to express how grace works through the symbolic action, and not merely as it were alongside it, or in conjunction with it. Following Rahner's specific contribution in his vision of creation as an action of divine grace, it was possible to relate the vision and grace of sacrament to the workings of grace in the whole of human existence. With a Heideggerian perception of humanity's oneness in being with all reality and of the self-realization of the human in this givenness of relationships, sacrament's encounter with God and Christ took on the proportions of the wholeness of human existence and its transcendental desire.

There have been gains from this turn to the subject for sacramental theology, whatever the questions now put to what it has inspired. For Karl Rahner, all knowledge and all love are linked with the sensible and linked inexorably with our being in the world, and the sensible, historical, conditions of this being, or *Dasein*.[12] The communion with the world of creation is already a communion with a loving and saving God, because in the action of creation itself there is a divine self-communication, whereby there is a divine presence in all things. For the human to know and to love, there is a necessary presence of the sensible world to the human, and even the other person is sensibly present as a condition of being present in love. This expresses in a renewed way the Thomistic insight of the need for matter in sacrament and shows how God comes to us and invites to personal communion through a sensible presence. This sensible presence is both the presence of the whole world of creation through objects such as bread, wine, oil, and water, and the presence of God who is present in these things through the creative act of self-communication. Further to this, it can be noted that the persons in the community are sensibly present to each other in what is done, together, to and with these things.

Within time and space, the human person is awakened through this sen-

11. Ibid., 281.
12. The key essays are in Karl Rahner, *Theological Investigations* IV, trans. Kevin Smyth (Baltimore: Helicon Press, and London: Darton, Longman & Todd, 1966).

sible communion to the infinity of forms and to the horizon of being. From the preapprehension of the infinity of forms, there emerges a sense of the infinite which cannot be contained in forms. From the preapprehension of being, there comes the conscious awareness of absolute being as the ultimate horizon of all knowledge and love, and a desire for communion with this being that is not yet available, because of the limitation of forms and the limitation of being in time and place.

Revelation is both an action within God and a historical act, or an act within history, reaching from particular history and event to embrace all history. It is the act of God which restores the divine presence in creation and the presence in love to humans, subverted by sin. It is both event and Word, events of saving action and Word that speaks of the divine salvific love that is expressed in these actions. It reaches its acme in Jesus Christ, who is the Word of God Incarnate, the ultimate presence of God in love in and to the world, of whom the Word of the Gospel and of the Church speaks. Word and thing merge in sacrament, in which are remembered the event of the Pasch and the restored presence of God to the world through this event.

Furthermore, Rahner probes the notion of symbol as self-presence and self-communication. It is an expression not just of immediate knowledge but of the horizon of knowledge, not just of being but of the desire for being, not just of immediate love but of love without bounds. The divine symbol, who is Jesus Christ, present in sacrament to a community in place and time, is total self-presence and total communication. There is no coming to knowledge and self-presence in God. For humans, self-presence and presence to the other is rendered possible through symbol. The symbol is given as sign of God's presence, but it is also given as means whereby the human person and the human community can become self-present, both as being loved by God and being in love with God. It is grounded in human ways of knowing, loving, and personal growth, but it speaks to it within its ultimate horizon, giving the possibility to attain this horizon in a divinely given fulfillment.

This way of seeing sacrament has given us much that cannot be discarded, even within a post[-]modern critique. It grounds the sacramental in humanity's being in the world, in the facticity of humanity's being in the world of creation, and in the concrete conditions of historical being. It shows how celebration of sacrament is both a divine presence through the memorial of Christ and a divine openness and promise of what is to come. It likewise shows the relation in sacrament of the event remembered, the action of and in things, and the role of the word. It speaks of sacrament not as a product, but of a being-together-in-communion of Church and of Church with God.

However, while the virtues of the models of instrumental causality and of symbolic causality are affirmed, it seems pertinent to the current problematic already presented to step back from them. They can too easily be related with the notion that signification is something conceptually clear, both to priests and to people. Causality is also associated, partly because of some of the standard examples, with models of production, which are ill-suited to the gift of grace and to interpersonal exchange. Furthermore, the renewal of the paradigm of causality as symbolic causality by Rahner and Schillebeeckx relies very heavily on the turn to the subject. In this turn, it assumes a self-knowledge and self-presence on the part of the subject, individual or collective, which the post[-]modern critique calls into question. The risk is that of replacing a metaphysical foundation with the foundation of self-consciousness, spelling out the power of sacrament in these terms. Even the appropriation of insights from anthropological and cultural studies can be very readily assimilated into such a perception of self and self-presence.

The questions that a current critique put to this sacramental vision have to do with the horizon of being and with the degree of self-presence assumed. While Rahner acknowledges the role of the sensible and of the word in human self-presence, he seems to assume that ultimately knowledge and love come from the presence to self that is attained. With this, there goes a view of representation which would assume the presence of God, of Christ, of the event remembered, present to consciousness. Certainly, Rahner takes account of the limits of knowledge, self-presence, and representation. Sacraments can and must needs develop, as does the grace of Christ, but they have an assured starting point in human consciousness, certainly in the consciousness of the Church, even when personal self-presence falters. The critique of this position associated with post-modern concerns, pries open the notion of self-presence and representation. The very variety of traditions, the changes in form throughout the ages, the polycentrism of Christian communities, express a limit to these possibilities. If Christians remain always "hearers of the Word," it is because of the limits of word, the polyvalence of words, and the subjective limits of interpretation and self-presence. The Christ event being necessarily present in the manner of historically conditioned symbol (word and sign) is not present in itself, but in a variety of historically conditioned symbolizations. It is thus absent, even in its being present.

More deeply, the critique asks whether the knowledge of God, and especially the knowledge of God in Christ, can be thought through in terms of the horizon of being. Rahner of course posits God as absolute being, known now not in the form of such being but by analogy and in the apprehension of ultimate desire. However, it remains that God is thought out in terms of being and the Christian revelation of love and gift are also thought through in these terms. First, this is to subject the horizon of human desire to the structures of being in the world, however much these may seem to be overcome and superseded. Second, it is to condense the gift of God and the love of God within the structures of being.

Consequently, some theologies now want to express the gift of God and to think of God in ways not limited to the horizon of being. There is an excess to God which cannot be apprehended at all in these terms, just as there is an excess to human desire which cannot be apprehended within the horizon of the preapprehension of being. This is not to say that the excess of God and the excess of human desire converge. Far from it. It is simply to appeal to this excess of desire to make us aware of what it is to limit what is beyond limit. Hence, sacramentally, in the event of Christ remembered there is the intuition of the excessive which can never be bound within our ways of thinking. Rather than developing a theory of self-expression through symbolic language that relies on consciousness of the self, the turn to language and hermeneutics takes the detour to knowledge of self through language and symbolic expression, allowing for no direct and immediate access to consciousness. If this is indeed the case, then the knowledge gained through the process of interpretation of signs is subject to the deconstructive reading of these signs, but it allows for their multiple and pluricentric appropriation.

A way to get beyond the problems raised about the theories reviewed here is to address the nature of sacramental action and memorial as language event. In proposing this approach, the intention is to take it as a heuristic rather than as a paradigm. A paradigm serves as some kind of model within which to situate different elements. Thus instrumental causality or symbolic causality are paradigms, for it is then asked how different elements in the celebration belong within this perspective. A heuristic on the other hand means attending to a set of operations. If one attends to what happens or goes on in a celebration, then insights into its meaning are gained from this. A heuristic is also more open-ended than a paradigm and more likely to serve within different ecclesial and cultural settings. To attend to language event is to attend to how language operates and to look for insights into sacrament from this, insights which are as much practical as theoretical.

Language

A turn to language in sacramental theology means looking to the established traditions and codes of celebration, as well as to performance, in order to develop an understanding of what happens in and through celebration. This makes it possible to underline both what is common and what is pluralistic in sacramental memorial, in principle and in fact. While traditions and meanings are handed on, some specific determination of meaning takes place in practice within each particular celebration. A language event does not go purely according to predetermined meanings, unless it is extremely manipulative. Even indeed when manipulation is attempted, the meanings engendered escape control. There is something very wise to the saying that any priest who thinks that the people think what he thinks when he baptizes a child had better think again. What happens, what exchange of grace occurs, is specific to each particular sacramental event, granted that it happens within a certain universe of meanings, rituals, and encounters.

As explored here, language is not restricted to the verbal, but refers to all human media of encounter and exchange, bodily and ritual, as well as verbal.

While the importance and role of the written is to be taken into account, the notion of language event means the living exchange in a dialogical situation. The use of language is governed by intent. Intent is not here understood as a clearly formulated intention. It is rather a human drive, a search for the sense of being and for meanings by which to live. It is the drive to look into reality and humanity's place within the complex of things. In using language, therefore, there is the intent to express meaning, the intent to explore the meaning of things and of life, and the intent to communicate and to share meaning, so as to share life.

The Study of Language

First something can be said about the field of the study of language. The terminology itself is fluid. According to some, sem(e)iotics explains codes and their inner interaction and intersignification, as this would be set down, for example, in a grammar or explained in a dictionary. Semantics has to do with usage. It is thus attentive to the particularity of every use of a code, the particularity of meaning and reference, the particularity of what are brought together in the language spoken in this situation, the innovations which occur in usage, and the type of encounter engendered. Umberto Eco prefers to use the term *semiosic* for the study of a code and *semiotic* for the study of its usage and employ by person or persons.[13] Here we can stay with the terms *semiotics* (omitting the second e) and *semantics* to distinguish between the study of a code as transmitted and reflection upon its actual usage.

There has been considerable interest in taking ordinary, everyday speech as a foundation for all studies of language. This is the language that emerges from humanity's initial being in the world, the initial encounter with things and the need to find a place among them. The language of the daily cycle, of the seasons, of the things that pertain to ordinary living, the sayings and maxims of pithy wisdom, proverbs and folk-tales, emerge from ordinary speech, expressing how human persons find their basic relations to creation and to one another. There is also an ethical edge to daily language, since it betokens our relations to others, to things, and to life itself. On this ordinary language, then, much else is based in the elaboration of language genres, and understanding a culture means attending to this basic fund of exchange.

The language of oral exchange becomes more elaborate in formal settings, but it always retains something of the ordinary in the desire for some immediate communication. For this reason, there is an instinctive unself-conscious quality to speech, though its uses can be brought to conscious reflection and

---

13. See Umberto Eco, *Semiotics and the Philosophy of Language* (Bloomington: Indiana University Press, 1986). For an overview of how this is used in the study of liturgical rites, see Gerard Lukken, "Liturgy and Language: An Approach from Semiotics," *Questions Liturgiques* 73 (1992): 36–52.

it itself can become more self-conscious. It takes up what precedes all differ-entiation between subject and object and between classes of persons, since it expresses the being at one with things that precedes such differentiation. It expresses not merely the human, but allows things to show forth in their own being, as well as displaying how they are brought into the human situation.

The nature of language as an act of communication has been probed by use of Austin's discourse on how to do things with words, where both the performative and the illocutionary qualities are laid bare.[14] Within this ap-proach some lay stress on the fiduciary use of language, on the understanding that participants abide by the meanings intended by the language code and tradition.[15] This has been helpful up to a point, but if stretched too far high-lighting the performative can turn out to be another type of instrumentalist thinking and use. Before asking what those who use language specifically in-tend, one has to attend to what the language in its code, its usage, and its literary output has to pass on. A good use of performative theory in fact looks to the language code itself, not into the minds of actants.

These perspectives have been complemented by looking at how language in the act of communication may be dysfunctional, or even imbedded with ideology.[16] When not all are familiar with the language code, those who are better versed enjoy an disproportionate use of power, or indeed may be in a position to manipulate other members of the society. It is also possible that over time the code has been invested with certain ideological inter-ests that give some dominance over others. This is a concern that is raised, for example, about racially and ethnically prejudiced terms, or about the use of gender usage that is noninclusive. In these cases, both the code and its uses have to be scrutinized, and a language has to be developed that fos-ters the emancipatory interest of those who are subjected by its common or privileged usage.

As foundation to these specific interests in the study of language systems and language usage, there has to be a fuller exploration of the relation be-tween life and language. On this score, something will be said about language and thinking, language and reality, language event, language and ethics, with a final word on the poetic, or poetics.

Language and Thought

To begin with, it can be noted that language is the sole medium in which to express thought. Beyond that, one has to say that it is the medium in which

---

14. J. L. Austin, *How to Do Things with Words*, 2d ed. (Cambridge, Mass.: Harvard University Press, 1975).

15. See Jean Ladrière, "The Performativity of Liturgical Language," *Concilium* 2/9 (1973): 50–62.

16. This was the concern of Jürgen Habermas in his reaction to Gadamer's hermeneutics. As an example, see the essay "The Hermeneutic Claim to Universality," in *Contemporary Hermeneu-tics: Hermeneutics as Method, Philosophy and Critique*, ed. Josef Bleicher (London: Routledge & Kegan Paul, 1980), 181–211.

to come to thought. Ideas do not exist first to be given expression, but they originate and take form themselves through the use of language, listening to language, and playing with language. Debates about universal ideas have gone on for a long time. It is a mistaken approach to see them as ideas that can be given expression in words, for it is only through words that they can take any shape or form. In that sense, the universal is more an ideal than a reality, for even what we contend to be universal is tinged with the particularity of what is said in any given set of circumstances. There is a desire for universal understanding within the human spirit, but it comes to realization only through expression and reflection upon it and is always in tension with the particular. This is equally true for what belongs in a community and in a culture, where the expression of language is the medium for coming to a fund of agreed orientations and meanings, or to debate about what these may properly be.

The relation of speech or writing to thought and to what is thought is problematic. There was the ancient and medieval supposition that language is the expression of thought that precedes its expression. Now, we have to see that the thinking goes along with the speaking or writing; it is as it were a "joint venture." Likewise, it was supposed that empirical contact with things gave sense perception, from which arose understanding and thought about things, and then language to express this. But now we see that things themselves come to expression in speech, by "giving" themselves, and it is in language that they are experienced as "near," and brought to thought. As Grondin writes, "to hermeneutically understand language is precisely to pierce through the facade of uttered language in order to bring attention to the things which our words attempt to share, but without fully succeeding."[17] It is not precedence of one over the other that needs to be asserted, but the simultaneity and the interaction of feeling, of things that impress upon us, of thought, and of language, that needs to be appreciated.

There is a certain "prelinguistic" understanding to our ex-isting: we dwell with things and with people, we know how to go about activities, the uses to make of things, etc. But even this is largely shaped by language, by the traditions handed on, by what is said of things and people, by the wisdom transmitted in various forms of expression. The understanding of things needs to be opened up beyond this "prelinguistic." A person may know what a jug is prelinguistically, use it instinctively for the right purpose, and yet miss its full significance in belonging to the world in which the person lives. This is opened up by the poet, as in the poem by Georg Trakl about the table laid with bread and wine,[18] or as with the decorative form of an Etruscan jug.

Thus in interpretation and understanding, one is preceded by the things

---

17. Jean Grondin, *The Sources of Hermeneutics* (Albany, N.Y.: SUNY Press, 1995), 143.

18. "A Winter's Evening," in *Song of the West: Selected Poems of Georg Trakl*, translated with an introduction by Robert Firmage (San Francisco: North Point Press, 1988), 6–7.

that are "given" to one, in the situation of facticity, as also by the linguistic, artistic and metaphysical traditions that speak of them. To understand is to be able to live in the midst of things and in the repetition of the past in such a way as to be authentic, free in choosing potentiality and action, by conscious activity and not simply by compulsion from without. In a language-exchange, what is heard "brings tidings" about being and about what is beyond being. What is heard is a message, a challenge to what is the given of one's world and understanding, the possibility from (maybe another) tradition (or time) to live through the possibilities that it offers.

Language and Reality

However much speculative discourse endeavors to distinguish and separate the language user and that of which it is used, there is still an inevitable involvement that conjoins speaker, the spoken, and the spoken about, or similarly the writer, the written, and the written about. Using language is a way of being. The use of language shows how understanding and existence, perspective on life and living, go hand in hand. It reveals how people are, how what they are and what they think or feel belong together. The language traditions in which people belong show how life addresses them, how they address it, and how its possibilities, comedies, and tragedies are projected into some kind of living venture. This is why conversation or dialogue is often seen as paradigmatic of language usage, because it clearly engages us with others and with life itself. However, the engagement is present in all types of language, including the written, and not only in verbal discourse but also in bodily expression of feeling and in ritual.

Language also richly engages the imagination, not as fantasy but as insight into and projection of life in the world.[19] In this, it keeps a connection with the practical and with the sought for. It is in the practical order that people find the way of mediating between knowing and feeling, and it is in the practical order that a link is found between people's lives as they are, immersed in those things that constitute the stuff of daily existence, and the possibility of seeing beyond these limits and striving in action and suffering to go beyond them. When imaginative language is rooted in this ordinary, it also expresses the *telos* of what is beyond it, of what can be realized from moving within the practical and yet not being confined to the present practice. In other words, the imaginative expression of language, be it ever so daily or ever so poetic, construes the practical and lived world as one fraught with possibilities. While engaging people in the limited world of their apparent possibilities, it projects for them a world of greater possibility into which they can move, without having to deny the world in which they are from

---

19. Seamus Heaney spoke/writes of a double adequacy of poetry, namely, the adequacy which allows it to address the harsh realities of life as lived, and the adequacy to what is larger and more true than what factually is. See *Crediting Poetry: The Nobel Lecture* (New York: Farrar, Straus & Giroux, 1995).

day to day and from which they take their character, their social reality, and their cultural horizons. In this sense, the reality of language cannot be grasped without recognizing the coordinates of listening, writing, ritualizing, speaking, suffering, and acting.

All reality is given to us through language that is embedded in being and culture, even the civility of how we eat. However much some writers may use the expression "prelinguistic experience," that should not be understood to mean that something occurs in human life before language encounters us, or as though experience is not always in some way articulated. It is used rather to avoid giving language and language system some kind of ontologized being in itself, or to make sure that the entire human person is taken into consideration in considering the role of language. Different kinds of language shape human existence: the ordinary language of day-to-day intercourse, the scientific language used in those fields where the ambiguous would be disastrous, the martial or the emotionally laden language that rouses a public to an overriding sense of unity, and the poet's and the artist's language for deep-down things. Though it has grown over time and continues to grow through its employ, language is always there before the people, always passing something on to them through the code and through the authority of a tradition. Even those who fight the tradition acknowledge it and its power, reality being shaped by its existence within language. It has been spoken by generations prior to us, and they have injected their horizons, their aspirations, and their perceptions into the code. In the end, it is the things that make for human being that speak to us through language, inviting into a conversation that probes the good and the true.

It is quite true that language should not be taken as an abstract and ontologized reality in itself, because it is spoken by somebody about something. It is also true that language does what its nature intends, when it is brought from code or tradition or page into the dialogical, into a situation in which persons are communicating with one another. Yet even in such situations it holds what is unspoken, what is the unsaid of discourse, it is an address from without the boundaries of the immediate human community, so that hermeneutics can be called the quest for the unspoken of human discourse.[20] It is thus true that language comes to us "from the gods," or in Christian vocabulary, that it is the Word of God, as conveyed by the Church. Even then it has to be taken as a Word that infiltrates into the human, that conceals even while revealing, that bespeaks and offers more than is said, that requires an inner and spiritual conversation, as it were beneath or even within the words. This is not purely and simply because humans cannot fully grasp what is said, but because the thing that is said is also in the saying unsaid. It offers itself as gift, but through the foreshortened means of language, whose power is

---

20. See Grondin, *Sources of Hermeneutics*, ix–xiii.

matched by its powerlessness. The deity, no less than humanity, cannot find the words adequate to the gift offered, and yet it keeps on offering the gift.

Sometimes it is therefore said that language precedes the persons by whom it is spoken or written. In the first place, this points to language traditions that have been built up and constitute the orientations of a people into which one is born or with which one associates oneself. More deeply, it means that language is rooted in humanity's being in the world, its being together with other things, working out its destiny with them and in relation to them. The things that constitute human beings' environment come to speech in what humans say, since these impress themselves upon human consciousness. Beginning with ordinary everyday language the manner of our being with things, being one with them by the very nature of the universe, comes to speech.

Language Event

To see the relation between language and the events of which it is spoken, a good approach is to talk about language event. As has been noted, in this present age people are struck by a sense of how history is disrupted, or they are perplexed by a series of events over a period of time that do not seem coherently connected. The march of human progress which the Enlightenment, and the vast range of invention that left its stamp on human life ushered in, has been disrupted by a host of disasters, ecological and human. Thinking instinctively in terms of cause and effect, we are inclined to see history, on a large scale or on a smaller, even family, scale as a series of events that can be explained in this way. However, disruptive forces make it impossible to sustain this perspective. It is more difficult to see the relation that exists between events.

In recounting beginnings races oscillate between stories of mythic origins and stories of origins borne by events that happened and are retained within human memory. When it is myth that prevails, it is not necessary to trace events back to the moment of beginning. Myth expresses rather a connection between all that happens among a people and some dynamic creative force that is always at play, but not within a chain of events explicable as a sequence of cause and effect. Creation myths or heroic epics function in this way. On the other hand peoples who look to some historical event as a beginning, or as a new beginning, like to be able to trace the power, the inspiration, the movement, of present events back to this one. That is how the French may look to the Revolution and to the Declaration of Liberty, Equality, and Fraternity. That is how the people of the United States may look to the War of Independence and to the writing of the Constitution. That is how the Irish look to the Rebellion of 1916 and its declaration of an independent Republic.

Or rather, that is how these peoples looked to these historical events. Today, with revisionist history in favor, the connections are less obvious. It is otherwise that they find a beginning and a hope in these episodes. They are not active in the present simply because they set off an explosion and movement of vital forces.

If we ask how it may be that such events continue to be alive among peoples, despite their disrupted and often tragic history, we appreciate this through an understanding of the link between event and language. Events are brought forward not through the set of operations which they set in motion, but rather through the language that shapes its usage in reference to them. Not only then may we talk of an event brought forward by language, but we can talk of a language event. It is through the events of the use of language among peoples and communities that historical origins or new departures or mythical beginnings are themselves present as events. As humans find their dwelling place in language, so do the events that shape their destiny.

Looked at in this way, the relation of event to time becomes clearer, clearer because it allows for ambiguity and for disruption. What communities want to know first and foremost is the impact of remembered events on the present, even on the day to day. The ordinary time in which they live is affected by the recall of events through the right kind of language, that is, when it is language that relates to this ordinary being in time. The sense of a place in historic time is also spoken and transmitted through a certain type of language. This is not language that tries to establish cause and effect, nor the kind of language used to write histories that account for as many facts as possible. It is rather language that expresses the vital forces and inspirations, the values and the hopes, that are taken to be embodied in the events remembered.

There are furthermore kinds of symbolic and mythic language that relate human persons and human communities to a time that is larger than the ordinary, that the ordinary measuring of time tries to approximate in some way, but never wholly succeeds. This is cosmic time, the time of the earth's revolution, the time of the planets, the time of an ever increasing space around us, without perceptible limits. Symbol and myth allow us to express the connection to this time in an imaginative, and so creative, way. There is also a memory of events that belong outside any image of time, or we might say time immemorial, or time unimaginable, using the term *time* itself metaphorically. Mythic language also meets this need, as when it bears the stories of creation or final destiny and apocalypse.

There is always some other who addresses people from within the remembrance of past events and their recounting. The others who lived these events, or the others who exact their remembrance, are voices that address those who keep memory. Their testimony cannot be reduced to what is said, for there is more to the saying than to the said. As Emmanuel Levinas reminds us, the saying of language, whether spoken or written, is always larger than the said.[21] It is an *other* who speaks, remaining other, and not reducible

---

21. Emmanuel Levinas, *Otherwise Than Being Or Beyond Essence,* trans. Alphonso Lingis (The Hague, Boston, and London: Martinus Nijhoff Publishers, 1981), 34–38.

either to what that one has said or what others have said about the events in which the testimony was given. When something is set down or spoken, something is left unsaid but the memory of the saying keeps itself open to further expression. That is why hermeneutics is sometimes called the art of discovering the unsaid of discourse, in the recognition of the effort to say which is behind the said and continually transcends it in the quest to communicate and to express meaning.

To dig further into this heuristic of language event, we must see the link between written text and oral performance. Language as oral encounter is what constitutes the proximate bringing of the past into the present. It is there that the language event gives body to the community as community, placing people into a living relation with one another, with their origins, and with their shared sense of destiny. Ritual action serves to establish the space and the interaction within which spoken language occurs. Oral and ritual performance moreover express the lived connection with the past and with forebears, and with the future that the past promises. Peoples who have a strong sense of living ancestors more readily find that this is also a way in which they speak and are now present. Communing with others who are present with us, we commune with the other whose word (saying and said) is transmitted from the past and brings us beyond the present, and indeed beyond the mode of being in time.

The connection of oral performance and exchange with the past involves a link with a written text.[22] It is in the nature of a written text to be in time and space removed from the original event or the original speech situation. Its role is not to make it possible to reread the past exactly, nor to allow the possibility of penetrating the mind of the author or of those who engage in the occurrences narrated, sung about, or eulogized. Some endeavors along these lines are surely possible, but this is not the primary role of handing on a tradition through written texts or oral compositions. What writing does is to put an event into writing in such a way as to express a meaning that is not tied only to those who lived or witnessed the event. It distills inspirations and values and promises and prognostications from the event. Established through these traces as the property or treasury of a people, it is possible for the event to be taken into their living communion at any time. Written down, an event is then open to constant interpretation and appropriation.

This oral and ritual performance that looks to the heritage of what is handed down is itself a creative act. It is one that inserts what is written into the living present. The written as it were becomes generative by inspiring interpretation and a new expression. Not only its content but its forms of expression can be taken up into the lived encounter of peoples. Epic and lyric

---

22. In cultures of oral tradition, a comparable function is carried out by oral literature and established rites that have to be "handed on" with fidelity.

poetry, narrative of events, hymns and blessings whose texts are transmitted give rise to new creations of like and even expanded genres.

The interpretation of orality within oral cultures, connected with field studies and studies of the development of literature by writers such as Jack Goody, Ruth Finnegan, and Paul Zumthor, is of aid to liturgists in probing the reality of the oral even within other types of culture.[23] The following points can be taken into account whenever in oral and communal celebration a sacramental tradition is being appropriated. First, the oral is linked with bodily performance. The sound goes out through the body. Bodily postures and rhythms, both those of speakers/singers and those of hearers, affect interpretation and assimilation. The voice displays itself particularly in the face and in the hands. The tones of voice are clearly important, but the sound can also be enhanced by instrumental accompaniment. Some kinds of sound, such as that of the drum, are particularly resilient in aiding speech and listening and in relating the community with the sounds and rhythms of earth.

In this bodily performance, insignia and tools of office play a part in stressing the importance of the moment of celebration and of certain words spoken as words arising from the authority invested in the speaker. Thus the axe-head of the staff of an African chief suggests the decisive and cutting effect of his word. Masks make it possible to bring ancestors and spirits into the ritual action, joined to stories told or words spoken. Some of this is found even in Christian liturgy. A bishop speaks staff or crozier in hand to show the power of his word. The vestments worn by a celebrant take what he says into the realm of the sacred. In the Roman Rite, the pallium worn across the shoulders at a liturgy gives extra weight to the words of an archbishop.

Secondly, the oral is centered on the present, breathing a sense of communality among the gathered, while also relating them to all the sounds and rhythms evoked through speech and performance. Sometimes it is said that the oral centers so much on the gathered community that it fails to effect the sense of a communion beyond the gathering. This may be true up to a point, but one cannot forget how sound and voice can invoke the past ancestors and all that inhabits earth and sky. One also has to take note of the body vibration and created responsiveness that carries over from one gathering to the next, and the sense of one community calling out to another across space, or meeting with the sound of another in air and space. In the Valley of a Thousand Hills in Natal, on a Saturday evening the fires of different gatherings signal to each other, and the sounds arising from each converge and cross one another in the night skies.

Thirdly, the oral screens tradition in making it pertinent to the immediate present. By mnemonic devices, standard recitations, rhetorical cadences, and

---

23. Jack Goody, *The Interface between the Written and the Oral*, Studies in Literacy, Family, Culture and State (New York: Cambridge University Press, 1987); Ruth Finnegan, *Oral Literature in Africa* (London: Clarendon Press, 1970); Paul Zumthor, *Oral Poetry: An Introduction*, trans. Kathryn Murphy-Judy (Minneapolis: University of Minnesota Press, 1990).

verbal repetitions, it serves to give the sense of a tradition alive now within the congregation, as well as the sense of something to be passed on to the next generation. Fourthly, and in conjunction with this, the oral allows a community to bring together into one place and meeting various stories and remembrances, even crossing from one community to another, dependent on the extent of hospitality.

This oral reality is tempered and modified by intersection with writing within a people whose orality is more in the line of secondary orality. What attention to writing brings out is the fluidity of what is remembered, the need to wrestle with interpretation and with the possibility of recasting and retelling the story as it is appropriated in different circumstances. Written narrative is more free to break the plot, to rewrite with different sequences, interjections, and metaphors, without disturbing the sense of passing on a foundational story. This is apparently more readily appreciated when secondary orality prevails over primary. Accepting the distanced and even dead nature of the story as sealed in writing does not harm its transmission, but does awaken people to the realization that its future lies in its interpretation, whatever forms even of retelling this may allow.

The functioning of secondary orality in the creation of community and tradition requires a different kind of setting from what occurs among peoples of dominantly primary orality. Secondary orality is more self-conscious, more reflexive of its moves and of the exchange between persons. The individual person is less readily absorbed into the congregation, but has to be brought in with a higher accent on what is called the interpersonal, the sense of person encountering person, rather than simply being one of a community. Furthermore, those who come to ritual from their own personal reading of the scriptures, or from exchange in small groups, or from exchange on the Internet, will not become as readily absorbed into the recitation in community. They have to be ritually invited to do so in ways that respect the personal endeavor to interpret. Prayer too is less easily repetitive, needing to bring in new needs, new formulations, new aspirations on practically every occasion, even while still drawing from a known repertory. This need for a more conscious interchange between those gathered is enhanced within digital culture, where persons are more accustomed to active exchange and to the possibilities of virtual representation.

Paul Ricoeur has helpfully distinguished three moments, or three levels, in the remembrance of events, or in what he calls *mimesis*.[24] He shows how remembered events must first be related to the world in which people live and to which they already give shape and meaning through their cultural heritage. This is expressed in rites, tales, institutions, proverbs, and other symbolic modes that belong within their heritage. For a remembered event to

---

24. Paul Ricoeur, "Mimesis and Representation," in *A Ricoeur Reader: Reflection and Imagination,* ed. Mario J. Valdés (Toronto: University of Toronto Press, 1991), 137–55.

be effectively remembered, it has to adopt something of the expressions and perceptions of this heritage. The second moment is the narration of the story of what is to be recollected. It is told as a plot, as a meaningful configuration of episodes and sayings, that can be projected into another situation, or as it were written into this situation. The third moment is thus the relating of this second form of *mimesis* to the first, or to the cultural world of the people. When the key event that is narrated comes from another culture, it has to be creatively transposed to find a home there. This is done in some measure by literature and writing itself, but it is more effectively established as a people's own living heritage when it finds its way into ritual performance.

It is possible to add another link between the present and the past event by employing the notion of testimony. We can say that in original events persons testified to something vital and important and to something that was to be carried forward. The written account is the expression of this testimony, but it is also the testimony of those who remembered what they had perceived and in which they believed. In this sense, the interaction of written text and oral performance is an engagement with the original testimony of the actors in an event and with the testimony of those who wished to keep this alive by their own testimony in narrating it. The duty to nurture this twofold testimony is transmitted to living communities, who are to testify in how they live from this memory and are to find fresh ways of transmitting it in language, written, spoken and ritualized.

Language and Ethics

In many of his writings, Paul Ricoeur has repeatedly referred to Aristotle's connection between *poetics* and *praxis*, sometimes himself contrasting *mythos* and *mimesis*.[25] The point of this is to say that the way of describing human action is itself to establish an ethical horizon. The poetic, in the large sense of the term, illuminates the meaning and horizon of the good in acts described in narrative or lauded in lyric and drama, or confessed in contrition, as it also infers judgment on other actions that are false to this horizon. Thus language discloses an ideal way of acting, even as it refers to the concretely historical or describes a fiction. To affirm the truth of such language, to consent to what it discloses, is to embrace in principle a way of acting. It is to engage ethical perceptions, as one will also return to language from ethical engagement in order to shed light upon it. In this process, the interchange between action and language, undertaken in two directions, influences the interpretation and the tradition of community texts.

This is not to claim that ethical questions are resolved in language alone, or even in discussion about values and horizons. Deliberation on the concrete

---

25. For a relatively recent summation of Ricoeur's position, see the essay "Pastoral Praxeology, Hermeneutics, and Identity," in Paul Ricoeur, *Figuring the Sacred: Religion, Narrative, and Imagination*, trans. David Pellauer, ed. Mark I. Wallace (Minneapolis: Fortress Press, 1995), 303–14.

must follow, but it is done within the perspectives set by the language code and use professed by a community. The thought of Jean-Marc Ferry is helpful on this score, as it also relates well to the contemporary sense of fragmented identity.[26] Ferry first points out that the received language itself needs critical consideration. Violence, discrimination, and oppression can be affirmed in and through received language traditions. Therefore a people has to stand back from its traditions to deliberate their full significance and import. He also points out that if the voices of victims, especially of the past, are to be heard, a reconstructive hermeneutic needs to be done. That is to say, in the case of particular, not generic, suffering, there has to be a critical and deliberative reconstruction of the reasons and motivations of acts of violence. Third, he notes that it is difficult to find one common narrative in which all the stories of injustice and oppression, and the resolution of their issue, can be accommodated. Therefore, any people or community has to be ready to receive and heed the stories of the "other" and has to deliberate on the stories that intersect and cross one another, seeking to resolve the particular as much as the general.

These insights of Ferry meet what has been said already about the fragmented sense of identity that is common in our day. It also gives some more insight into what has been said about the pluriform character of the Christian poetic and tradition. Within sacramental liturgies, the community is engaged in listening to a plurality of stories. What may prompt the fresh hearing and reading of the scriptures may in effect be the readiness to heed the stories of victims, or even more simply the stories of other cultures and groups. All stories, however diverse, are heard within the horizon of desired reconciliation and communion. Aware of diversity, but within the shared desire for communion, each community has to work out its sense of identity, as it also has to reflect upon its ethical choices in the light of this pluriformity, in the light of the efforts at reconstruction and in the willingness to be open to the voice of the other.

The Poetic

In many cultures, either oral poetry or writing serve as the medium through which insight into reality is further expressed, shaped into plot and reflective values, and then pondered. Thus in ordinary language, people mark time by sunrise, high noon, sunset, and twilight. Poetry then, such as that found in the Hebrew psalms, ponders this marking of time for deeper meanings, which in the case of the psalms are religious.

The poem presents an ideal model for semantic study, since of its nature it is exploratory and innovative, even while working with a language

---

26. His thought is summarized in the short work: Jean-Marc Ferry, *L'Éthique reconstructive* (Paris: Éd. du Cerf, 1996). Ferry acknowledges the affinity of his thought with that of Jürgen Habermas.

code that it supposes known by its readers/hearers. It is clear that in the poem this, and only this, expression satisfies. It cannot be as such transferred into another expression of reality. When Seamus Heaney asks of Kevin, in whose outstretched hand the blackbird has nested, "has the shut-eyed blank of underearth crept up through him,"[27] the dictionary provides no warrant for creeping underearth, but the intuition simply cannot be transmitted into other terms.

In Western traditions the poem, however, gets writ and passes on, in its many readings, as writ. Actual recital also has its innovations, much more particular to the moment, and usually not captured for posterity. This is verified in other forms of tradition as well. For example, liturgical orders at times catch an innovation in its occurrence, but the fact of writing it down already takes it out of the sinews of exchange. When on entering the sanctuary, the bishop of Rome first thought to dismiss his assistants with the kiss of peace, a master of ceremonies wrote it down and it then became custom (*Ordo Romanus* I).

The term *poetic* can be used in a broader sense than what is customarily meant by *poem*. It is used to express a quality of expression, as *poetics* means the effort to uncover it.[28] This is that quality of language, verified to greater or lesser degree, which in its imaginative use includes reference to what is beyond immediate perception and everyday functional discourse. While the spoken word or the enacted rite seem to address the present, they are always open to the future. Poetic language strains for what may come to light through innovative and imaginative expression. It seeks to give form to what is to be brought to act, or for what may come to the speaker when the right expression meets the right moment and desire. In this sense, the poetic within a written or oral tradition displays the innovative and creative uses of language rather than the purely directive. It is always open to that fresh reading and hearing within which its power is newly revealed. Besides what is transmitted through texts and rites, there can also be a poetic turn of verbal or nonverbal character of a more passing quality in each celebration, by which the immediately present is lit up, but then passes from view. The way the sun shines through a window at a particular moment of a celebration, the way in which the newly lit candle flickers, the turn of phrase used in a homily or a prayer, the way in which a parent answers the question of what is sought

---

27. "St. Kevin and the Blackbird," in Seamus Heaney, *The Spirit Level* (New York: Farrar, Straus & Giroux, 1996), 24–25.

28. Paul Ricoeur describes poetic language this way: "(a) Poetic language is language that breaks with everyday language, and that is constituted in the crucible of semantic innovation. (b) Poetic language, far from celebrating language for itself, opens up a new world, which is the issue of the text, the world of the poem.... The world of the text is what incites the reader, or the listener, to understand himself or herself in face of the text and to develop, in imagination and sympathy, the *self* capable of inhabiting this world." This essay "Naming God," is included in the collection *Figuring the Sacred* (Minneapolis: Fortress Press, 1995). The quotation is from page 232.

through baptism, belong to the poetic of actual liturgical celebration. They are all moments based in a code of ritual, but carrying its meaning forward within interplay and exchange.

The poetic must integrate the tragic and the comic of life, within a vision of the future. The centrality of metaphor to the poetic indicates how this is done. The place of metaphor in the play of language is to open up new possibilities of meaning and of being, in our being in the world and in our being in time toward death, to be linked to the comic and the tragic. The comic is to reveal the disproportions of life, that which is illusory to our self-conceits and pretensions, but showing them in their folly. The tragic is to enter into the play without being able to clearly envisage the end, but accepting the struggle as one's destiny.

The tragic of human life includes also the suffering imposed, the suffering to which people are submitted without willingly entering into it, but forced in by duress. Auschwitz has taken on a strong symbolic resonance in our time, because of this. When writers discuss such suffering, they may refer more readily to pathos than to tragedy, because it is something from which there is no escape, whether it be willed or not. The question for the language which is a construct of human time and being is the same: is there redemption from this suffering, even unto death, or from the suffering which lasts in the mind and soul long after it is over physically? Can victims, those who are victims pure and simple, be brought to a share in life? After All. For those who survive, there may be some kind of catharsis in face of evil, through faith/fate and through remembering the ethical demands of the other that the memory of victims imposes. But for the victims of evil, those who have disappeared in face of evil? There is no logical or rational answer to this, but does the remembrance of solidarity call them to life? Only poetic language, the language of *poesis*, can speak to and of this.

Toward Silence

Language is the expression of intent. Without it, the mind and heart cannot be in touch with the inspiration and the horizon of human being and desire. At the same time, its intent is to bring to humans the gift and the invitation into a communion that transcends the limits of the particular. Hence, of its nature language has a horizon beyond the perceptions which it itself voices. It is in language that the voice of the world in which humans live and the intent of the heart come together, not in the placid satisfaction with things as they are but in an intent and within a horizon that is beyond the said. It is in this sense that we can take what philosophy says of an inner word. This inner word is not to be confused with images or concepts that are then brought to speech. It might better be spoken of as quest, as the desire to know and love, but whose outlet and expression is spoken and written language. Language is the effort to let this desire attain its intent, it is the way of bringing humans into communion with that which is sought. It is the limits of language in achieving this which requires that it rest in silence. Humans need the times of silence for two reasons. First, they need to gather in what language says and to reflect upon it. Second, they need the silence to be in touch with the intent of language which is beyond language itself, and thus in touch with the intent of the heart which opens up horizons beyond the expressions of whatever language has brought to expression and to being. It might almost be said that language brings us into silence. On this earth, however, and within mortal existence, the horizons of heart and language are not reached, so that this silence itself must again take up speech in the continuing quest for mystery.

Sacrament: God's Word Events through Spirit

Before giving a more ordered presentation of this explanation, we can note how the above considerations on language pertain to Christian sacrament.

Sacramental Language

Christian sacrament is so fascinating because in its tradition, and potentially in any given assembly, it embraces many forms of language. It includes clear prescriptions about sitting, walking, and the kinds of things to be used and without which there is no rite. It can be examined as a ritual with anthropological and sociological insight. It is put under the microscope of the examination of a semiotic code. It has been analyzed as performative language. It has been dogmatically interpreted with an effort at precise definition of how it functions as an instrument of grace. It is explored within its aesthetic wholeness, fitting the pieces together into harmony and symphony. On the other hand, it is received in all the enigma of its disjunctive pieces and its ambiguous phrases. It is taken up for its power to give speech and expression, beyond what has been said, but which lies before one in its imaginative potential. All of these approaches reveal aspects of sacramental language and say something true about sacrament, but any one approach begins to be false when it is given privileged place as the privileged discourse about the reality that is revealed, given, and concealed, in liturgy.

In the realm of the holy, the poetic must win out, though the organizational, the socially binding, and even the conceptually correct are needed and for this reason may make a bold bid for priority. This is as true of bodily language as of verbal. The bodily expression of rite can often seem to have most to do with community organization or with rites of passage, but at its core it brings to heart the deep down sense of things with which humans have communion, such as the things of earth, the seasons of the year, and the pouring out of life. Sacramental language is a polyphony of sounds that speak to the core of our belonging to and being rooted in the world, while totally related to the transcendent mystery of the Pasch. It lauds the glory of this mystery, indeed calls us to bathe in its glory, letting its incandescent light shine through. The different roles played by different forms of speech and different forms of bodily action belong within the poetic and will need exploration later. It is in the interplay of forms or genres, and in the exchange between persons, and between the present and the past, that the poetic emerges.

In sacramental language, the tragic and the comic are appropriated into the horizon of faith and worship. This is done with faith and hope, but not with sight. What Paul says of wisdom as folly is the comic of life, that which is the illusion of philosophy and religion to clarify or to set in order. In this light, ritual cannot take itself too seriously when it has to do with roles and offices and mediations. What Philippians says of the *kenosis* of Christ, or Peter of the descent into hell, draws us into the tragic of the death of Jesus. Preaching the blessings of the reign of God, he has to meet death. He does so, entering into death, which is expressed as a metaphoric combat, combat not as an act of human power but as an act of entering into destiny, confronting that which seems to overpower, but which the metaphor suggests is in fact reversed by "exaltation."

These are not words of consolation, though they may be words of defiance. There is so little logic to them that they cannot console, there is no pretense in them to a grand theory of providence, or of a path to good through the reversal of evil. They are simply words that bespeak an unwillingness to lose faith in God, even when they are words spoken from faith in God that has been broken, and yet remains. They are words without logic, at times almost devoid of plot, but they find place in a world of *pathos*, where God often hides amid suffering instead of being made manifest in power.

As has been said, the power of events in effect depends on being put into language that seeks to reveal their potentiality and be thus transposed into new contexts. It is the proclamation of the Cross that gives it its power in human history, and it is the expression or word and rite that gives the risen Christ the power to transform lives and communities. God is not simply using a power over souls of which the word speaks, but the speaking is doing the efficacious acting.

It is this heuristic of language event that serves insight into the nature of sacrament. It seems an apt heuristic with which to engage the note of the discontinuous and the disruptive that marks our sensitivity to broken time. It allows us to see God's action in the past and in the present, without having to relate them by an unbroken sequence of events and without having to look for some causative force outside language usage itself. A ritual or sacramental event relates to an event within time past through the capacities and power of language to carry it forward and to allow it to enter afresh into lives, however they may have been disrupted and broken. By that same token, the heuristic of language event brings sacramental expression into the realm of the practical. Redescribing reality through remembrance of the Cross, sacrament points to the Christian praxis which goes with such remembrance. On this account, the heuristic of language event could also be called a heuristic of *poesis* and *praxis*. It is concerned with the forms and power of language and at the same time with the paradigms of Christlike action that are evoked through this language.

As a language event, the Christian sacrament is the event of God's Word in the Spirit. Jesus was manifested at his baptism and on the Cross as the Word coming forth from God, and those who believed gave testimony to this in their preaching, in their lives, and in their writings. The written Word passes on the sayings and teachings of Jesus and the narratives of his passion and death. In the narratives of the resurrection in the Spirt, there is added the hope of the Second Coming, the assurance of the presence of Christ in his body the Church, and the gift of the Spirit to animate this body, enabling it to keep memory and interpret the truth, in word and in deed. It is in what is proclaimed as the Paschal event that the redemptive operation of Word and Spirit has its center, and it is this which is at the heart of sacramental remembrance in the Church.

To interpret this sacramental event of Word and Spirit, we need to examine the sacramental action in its entirety and as a unity. It is composed of ritual action, word proclaimed, and blessing prayer. The three together constitute the language event, and insight into meaning and into what is done derives from seeing them in their intertextuality.

Since they incorporate many of the insights mentioned into the use of language, the blessing prayers of Christian sacraments provide an apt heuristic key to the understanding of sacraments as language events. Hence we will take a special look at these, in order to forward this heuristic. From there, we can move to considering the nature of the action as that of Word and Spirit, understood here through the analogy of inner and outer word. Since sacraments are described as the memorial of the Pasch of Christ, we can next ask how this mystery is expressed and how the genre of language event can be used to express its commemoration. Fourth, we move to an understanding of sacrament as gift of God. Fifth, since the sacraments are actions of the Church, using the heuristic of language event, it is possible to see how the Church bodies forth and takes shape through sacraments, in a way that involves evangelical and ethical commitment. Sixth, we turn to how the naming of God occurs within sacramental actions. Finally, we can move from these considerations to what it means to describe sacraments as memorials, or in traditional terms as *anamnesis* and *mimesis*.

Blessing Prayer as Hermeneutical Key

The Word of God is addressed to a particular community through its own traditions. It is a Word heard in the power of the Spirit and a Word which in this same Spirit moves the community to the blessing of God which it prays over the elements and in conjunction with the ritual action. It is indeed the blessing prayers of sacramental rites which reveal how the Word proclaimed, the inner action of the Spirit, and the rites that surround the use of the sacramental elements come together in a single act of communion. In formal terms, we could talk of the blessing prayer as the active, Spirit-led, interpretation and appropriation of the Word proclaimed and shown forth in the ritual action, into the life of a believing community. The eucharistic prayer is the most obvious example to consider. The blessings for other sacraments have a similar format, and what they do is to bring people through different passages to the communion of the eucharistic table.

The mystery of divine love is expressed with fullness in sacramental blessings. In them, there is a threefold invocation of God, related to the threefold aspect of this mystery as it is made known in revelation. First, there is the invocation of God as creator, in the remembrance of the gift and love of God shown in the blessings of the earth. Second, there is the invocation of the God of the covenant, who takes an initiative in addressing humankind by a Word of love, law, and salvation, intervening in human life and history in a gratuitous and unexpected manner, to call humans into a new relationship with the divine self. Third, there is the invocation of God as the Father of the Lord Jesus Christ, made known and present to the world in the self-emptying of the Cross of Jesus and in his being raised from the dead, in the power of the Spirit, overcoming the powers of evil. These invocations are not simply complementary to one another, in the sense that they build on one another. There is rather an intertextuality, a play between the invocations, which is kept alive in sacramental blessing. The key to the exchange that takes place in these types of invocation is always found in the remembrance of the Cross of Jesus Christ. It is in receiving the gift poured out in this self-emptying, in the communion with that love, that the relationship to God who creates and who makes covenant is truly appropriated. The relationship to God as creator becomes one of "having everything and possessing nothing." The relationship to the God who is covenant maker is that of unfailing trust, moving through and beyond fidelity to precepts to a relationship of love, in the wonder at the life which is poured out as pure gift. When some writers today stress the symbolic exchange which takes place in sacramental worship, what they are bringing to the fore is that life achieves its climax when it is lived in the purity of relationship rather than in the sharing of things given, though of course these are not eliminated from the picture.

Though it may be more common to consider the confession of sin as a distinct type of prayer, it is to be noted that this too is in some manner incorporated into prayers of blessing. As memorial, these prayers recall the history of salvation, and hence of sin. They also include the Church's acknowledgment of how it is party to the sin, standing always in need of forgiveness and redemption. While blessing prayers recall the act of creation and of humankind in the image and likeness of God, they connect both divine covenant and sin with it. The story of the first sin does not have the same place in history as stories that are remembered. It exercises the role of the myth or symbol which expresses the human condition within history. In creating humankind, God took it into a special relationship of friendship, freedom, and obedience, but this creation covenant is broken by sin. The covenant with the patriarchs and with Israel is a necessary backdrop to the reading of the myth of creation, divine friendship, ordinance, and disobedience, just as it in turn illuminates God's relation with Israel, and then the redemptive relationship given in Christ. The mythical recall of the story/stories of creation and sin expresses humanity's relationship with the whole of creation, the relation to which God calls them in love, and the divine love which is spoken in the promise, and thus in the realization, of atonement. The confession of sin included within blessing thus relates to the invocation of God as creator, as a covenant God, and as the God of Jesus Christ, and the invocation itself is conditioned by the confession of sin.

For sacramental blessings to be given a concrete and historical place within human time, from the start one has to attend to the things over which blessing is made and the actions which it accompanies. It is over the core realities which connect human persons with creation that God is blessed. They are those things which stand at the heart of human life and of its communion with earth and all creatures. They represent the scene of God's forgiving and life-giving love. As represented by bread, wine, oil, and water, humanity's participation in the life of the earth is faced with plenty and with want, with joy and with sorrow, and there can be no commitment of human persons to each other and to God without a commitment to the things of earth.

The passage from sin, or through a life-discernment which is a conversion to Christ, is signified by the passage through water and by an anointing with oil. These elements are not used as abstract symbols, but the fact that they belong to the rites of initiation and illumination expresses the birthing, the conversion, and the abundance of life which are found in God, but only through a communion with the cosmic and the earthly. The use of oil in the sacrament of the sick is in its own way a commentary on illness and on passing through it, either to healing or to a fresh perspective on life. It is the use of hands which comes to the fore in the blessing of the passage through ordination and penance that leads to a renewed place at the communion table of the covenant people. In marriage, both a joining of hands and a giving of gifts express the union in which a couple thenceforth takes part in the life of the eucharistic Church. Their communion in love has to embrace all the material and spiritual realities of life, and this is expressed both in the ritual gestures and in the blessing prayers found in various liturgical traditions, whether they are pronounced in the home or pronounced in the church building.

When the faithful gather, they hear the Word proclaimed, the Word written for their sake and interpreted in the living reality of a communion in faith, hope, and love. In the power of that Word, they turn to God in prayer, blessing the divine name over the elements of their earthly existence.

The language of address or blessing prayer is that of praise, thanksgiving, intercession, and doxology, which is a polyphony of sounds and meanings.

The doxological character of the Church's blessing prayers is important to note. While this is voiced particularly in the concluding words of each prayer, it can also be said to run through the prayer as a whole. In fact, while the main content is that of thanksgiving for the works of creation and redemption and of intercession for the Church and the world, the giving of glory is not confined to the concluding doxology. In Eastern prayers, it is introduced through the first and introductory part of the prayer, wherein the Church joins the heavenly liturgy, where from all eternity the angels worship the Father, the image of the Father which is the Word and the Spirit of truth who is made manifest through the Word, and who is the life-giving power that in the time of the economy sanctifies the world. In this exordium of praise, both the eternal mystery of God and the works of redemption through the mission of the Word and the Spirit converge but are not mingled.

In recalling God's action through the two missions of Word and Spirit, the Trinitarian structure of the blessing is creedal in structure, made to reflect more basically creedal statements such as that found in the Symbol of the Apostles or in the baptismal evocation of the faith of the catechumen. It ought not to be lost to view, however, that the creedal format relates to narrative of events and depends on the narrative remembrance of the works of the Trinity. In this narrative the action of the Spirit is recalled along with the action of the Word in the works of creation and redemption. In short, the meaning of the thanksgiving and its Trinitarian structure cannot be opened up unless it is read and prayed against the background of the narrative of events in which the divine action testifies to God's gracious gifts.

Blessing prayers commemorate the twofold mission of Word and Spirit. These missions are concomitant, that Word and Spirit are at work in all the actions of God in the world, from the very beginning. There is no temporal sequence to these missions, but any Trinitarian theology has to account for their simultaneity and complementarity. This avoids the Western ecclesiastical and theological tendency to posit the mission of the Spirit after the fulfillment of Christ's Pasch, or to make it dependent on Christ, or even on the primacy of the Word, as though in some fashion the Word was sent first.

One may also note that the intercession included in blessings, as prayer in the Spirit and in the name of Christ is a language of communion. In the mutuality of this intercession for one another the members of the Church express how they are bound as members of Christ's body, living in expectation of the kingdom of God. As a community of believers, they are joined in union not only as an assembly but with all who profess the name of Christ, and with all who passing from this world are still one with the living in an ecclesial and divine communion. The communion may also be stretched by the intercessions to take in the peoples of other faiths and the suffering of past and present time, all too often absent from the pool and the table. The invocation of the Spirit, or epiclesis, is couched both as a request for the transformation of the elements and as a petition for communion of the faithful in the mystery celebrated. Both go together, for the communion is brought about through communion in the elements as they are blessed by the proclamation of the Word, in the power of the Spirit, within the gathering in faith through Word and Spirit.

That God is revealed and active in the Church's own prayer, spoken as a response to God's creative and saving Word, is expressed by reference to the memorial command which grounds the sacramental event. The eucharistic prayer has incorporated the Supper narrative, with its memorial command. The blessing of water at baptism is given a grounding in reference to several scriptural texts.[29] First, there is of course the mention of the risen Christ's mandate to baptize. Second, there is frequent recollection of Jesus' own baptism as the motivation for Christian baptism. Third, there is occasional reference to the changing of water into wine at Cana of Galilee, this being taken as evidence of the power that Christ can exercise over human life by his power over the water itself.

In brief, then, in relation to the triune God, the language of blessing has several characteristics. It relates God's action through Word and Spirit to creation, to covenant, and to redemption from sin and death. It is symbolic, relating participation in the life of Father, Son and Spirit to the communion of table and service in the Church. It is prophetic, because the eucharistic sacrament is given to us by God through the triune action of grace, and through it God addresses us as God's own people, and forms us as such. It is creedal, because it embodies a tradition that has its origins in the epiphany of the Paschal and Pentecostal event, and it is out of this tradition that the Church has the power to live as God's people, always in expectation of the kingdom. It is narrative, because revelation and divine life are given to us through the events in which God gives testimony to unoriginate love, and these events need to be remembered and told in order to offer their power and testimony to our lives. It is eucharistic, because we are called by God's address into relationship with the mystery of eternal Trinity, and speak within the sacramental communion of the body of Christ, empowered by the Word that is given to us by this same Christ, and moved by the Spirit to communion with him and with the saints. It is grounded in God's own Word and mandate, delivered through Christ. Finally, it is doxological in the wonder expressed before the mystery of God's triune and eternal holiness, open to the silence in which God is present beyond words.

---

29. See the examples of the prayers for the Gelasian and Armenian rites given in the next chapter.

The Inner and Outer Word of Sacrament

For insight into this gift of the love of the Three in the economy, as it is given to the Church in the language event of sacrament, we can draw some orientation from three elements in the work of Basil the Great. First, he uses the image of Word and Breath to illustrate the coming forth from the Father of Son and Spirit. Next, in his treatise he says that the Spirit illumines the mind so that it can see the icon of the Father in the Word made flesh.[30] Third, his anaphora states that the Son manifests or reveals the Spirit.[31] It is the simultaneity, mutuality, and complementarity of the two missions which stands out, Word and Spirit interacting in the entire economy, and now in the life of the Church, as expressed in its Eucharist. If a sending forth of the Spirit can be rightly related to Christ's resurrection and ascension, it is not because this is the first sending of the Spirit, but because the Spirit is after Pentecost particularly manifest in the rebirth of this new people which is the sacramental body of Christ, his visible presence in the world and in human history.

Drawing on these assertions, to clarify the mutuality of the two, several comparisons help. First indeed is the analogy itself of Word and Breath, external and internal manifestations of life. Second is the analogy of the relation between visible action and inner insight. Third is the image and reality of the body, which both has its visible and sacramental, even institutional, form and is moved by an inner freedom which allows movement and diversity in shaping this form.

It is in the nature of God's self-emptying love to take visible form, within the circumscriptions of historic event and cultural form, and by pouring forth into our hearts an indwelling of this same love. But the Word is the Word of the Cross, which means both the self-emptying unto death and, in the words of Stanislas Breton, the crossing out of whatever human and visible forms it adopts, since they limit the presence of the one who is beyond limits.[32] Paradoxically, the once and for all historic event of the Cross of Christ can be given sacrament and spoken among many peoples, only in the many forms of local Churches that both negate each other's claims to be the total form of the body and interact with each other in a dynamic of cross-cultural living. It is in the Spirit that the Word continues to be present and active in the Church.

Another way to express this is through the contrast between outer and inner testimony, noting their interaction. The Spirit, indwelling love and discernment, allows us to appropriate the outer testimony of the Word and Cross of Jesus Christ, testimony to the name of God as Love. At the same time, in

---

30. Basil, *On the Holy Spirit* 18.47.

31. For the text, see A. Hänggi, *Prex Eucharistica*, Spicilegium Friburgense 12 (Fribourg: Fribourg University Press, 1968), 240–43.

32. Stanislas Breton, *Le Verbe et la croix* (Paris: Desclée, 1981), 101–30.

this very appropriation the Spirit moves us to love of the other, to a practical and discerning love which holds on to nothing for oneself and yields all for the sake of the other. By force of the indwelling Spirit, those who love in Christ hold no form or representation of the event remembered or of the community formed above the call of love. They hold on to nothing, in the urge to embrace through action, and give vitality and a place within God's love to others. The self-emptying, or *kenosis,* of Christ on the Cross calls forth the self-emptying of those who are his disciples, a self-emptying which acknowledges the limits of all representation and is ready to cross out whatever representations hinder the gift of love and its testimony in the breadth and universality of God's giving.

The historical and visible testimony of the Cross is complemented by the inner testimony of the Spirit. Through this double testimony, Churches are given the inspiration and the freedom to continue to appropriate this Word of love in the many embodied forms that offer its appropriation to many races, through many generations, and in many tongues. They are given the freedom to embody Christ again, even when language has been dislodged from its complacency, even where suffering has taken on the qualities of the absurd, so that the Word and Cross must event again, through the language event that is rooted in this people's story and remembrance.

The Paschal Event

It is the event of the Pasch of Christ which is at the heart of sacrament, since by definition the sacrament is its memorial. What is stressed here is that it is in the very medium of language that the event enters into human lives and history. It is through the very means of language, and within both the power and the constrictions of language, that the Word and the Spirit are present in the Paschal memorial. Once this is perceived, we can see that the sacramental remembrance of the Pasch may take on varied religious and cultural expressions over the course of time.

Down through history, Christian communities have expressed the plot of the Paschal story in different ways. Even as they heed the original story in faith, they retell it in the symbolic language of their own cultures. Both the language of the Gospel and the plot of the story are reappropriated. In this, liturgical action has played a considerable role. Thus the Pasch of Christ has been recast and remembered in a variety of narrative and ritual plots, with the result that sacramental memorial and *mimesis* takes on comparable but divergent forms. It is possible to distinguish between three prevailing ways in which this has been done.[33]

A tradition associated with Syria and Antioch proclaimed and celebrated

---

33. The liturgical has always been accompanied by the devotional, such as the veneration of the Cross or passion dramas. Sometimes these are partially incorporated into liturgy, but whether or not this is so, they are part of the Church's tradition to be harvested.

the death of Christ through the imagery of his descent into hell.[34] This spoke of the suffering which he endured and of his deep, mortal association with human death and suffering. The plot, however, presented this descent as the way in which the child and servant of God, Jesus Christ, conquered sin and mortality. Well-known examples of this way of remembering the passion, with its moral implications for the Christian believer, are found in the Paschal Homily of Melito of Sardis[35] and in the eucharistic prayer of the *Apostolic Tradition,* which has provided the foundation for the revision of this prayer in Churches today.

Another tradition, which is associated with Origen and the School of Alexandria, took the image of passage as the primary metaphor for plotting the Pasch of Christ and the Christian's participation in it, through sacrament and the spiritual life. Moral and mystical conversion supplied the paradigms for telling the Christ story, which is thus presented as a passage from the world through death into life with the Father. When this plot presents the incarnation as the descent of the Son, or of the Word, into the world of human death and sin, the passage then becomes a return to the Father, with the Son taking humanity with him into this glory.

The medieval West, for its part, interpreted the death of Christ as a vicarious and redemptive sacrifice for sin, through the interplay of the metaphors of merit, redemption, sacrifice, and satisfaction. It is this highly priestly plotting of the story of Christ's death and passion which provided the form in which the Roman liturgy celebrated the Paschal memorial.

These three examples show how interpretive language, with its use of metaphor and image, diversely appropriates the original narrative, placing these narrative and ritual interpretations at the heart of sacramental *mimesis.* The question today is whether, in a different time, in the midst of different human and historical experiences, and in different cultural settings, Christian communities may take a hold of different images and metaphors in the ways in which they hear and appropriate the passion story which they commemorate.

Fresh attention to the diversity between the four Gospel accounts of the passion, and fresh attention to the core symbols and rituals of bodily and cosmic reality, may enlarge the possibilities of diverse appropriations. The time of the kingdom of God is always an enigma, but as lived by those who keep memorial it is lived day to day, with a wisdom that keeps faith in God in the midst of lesser things and in the presence and advent of suffering. The symbols are the symbols of life in common and of life lived in communion with the things of earth, according to the cycle of the seasons, but the memory

---

34. Sometimes this is referred to as a perception of the Pasch as *passio,* because it underlines the truth that Christ won victory through suffering.

35. For the text, see Melito of Sardis, *On Pascha and Fragments,* texts and translations by Stuart George Hall (Oxford: Clarendon Press, 1979).

grafted onto them is one that generates the salvific hope of a salvation that comes into this time from an advent, a gift, that comes from God.

In the discussion above of language event, the connection between narrative and written remembrance on the one hand and oral performance on the other was noted. This is also operative in the sacramental memorial of the Pasch. The immediacy of the presence of God's love and gift is given expression in rite and oral speech, according to traditional patterns and also in inculturated forms. When account is taken of the transmission of revelation through the written word in the oral discourse of sacramental celebration a community is more conscious of the fact that it is not passively receiving, but in fact interpreting and as it were transposing this word. It is in the nature of a written text to be in time and space removed from the original event or the original speech situation. This is all the more apparent when, as in the Gospels, the event is narrated with different nuance by different writers or the sayings are transmitted in varying versions. It is not possible to totally reconstitute the event or regain the sayings as first spoken, nor to enter anew into the mind of the author of the text. What is written is given credence because of the testimony of the lives of those who passed on the Word, claiming to speak in the Spirit. It is linked with the testimony of those who have continued, and now continue, to appropriate the Word and transmit it into lived and living reality. Interpretation is always a condition of this transmission, an action which time and time again the believing community measures anew by fresh readings of the original word, and checks against the testimony of living witness.

It is over the earthly elements, over persons, and over their actions that the prayer is invoked. Thus the Paschal event is recalled and represented in the things and actions of the community and in their living communion. This is not a figurative representation, but an imaginative one, which relies on the play of the image that is spoken before it is seen. The bread and the wine of the Eucharist may be looked at "as though" they were the body and blood, and the oil as though it were the presence of the Spirit who gladdens with anointing. However, the immediate significance of the elements and the action is first to make present the table shared with the other or the water and the oil through which communion is initiated with others. This is what is immediately present, and the presence of Christ and of his salvific actions is mediated through this. In other words, Christ and the share in his mystery is mediated through bread and wine *shared,* and shared with the other with whom we come to table. The bread and wine are filled with the presence of earth and human hands and with the presence of table companions with whom there is a shared hospitality. What is being done at the table is to constitute here and now a communion between "others," in a shared table, and with this is associated the memory stored in writing, the story, the fragment, of the event of the Supper and the passion, to indicate that these are given to us truly in sign, but under the conditions of their distanciation. This is the mode of Christ's bodily presence and the medium of sharing in his Pasch.

The presence of the others at table brings their stories and their sufferings into the assembly. Furthermore, the presence of some calls attention to the absence of others. It so happens that it is often the poor, the socially marginalized, the victims of history and social organization, who are absent. Their absence at a banquet to which all have been invited is a kind of discomforting presence, which distances the remembered Pasch even further, and most especially its eschatological promise. As Melito of Sardis in his Paschal homily saw Christ suffering in the sufferings of Abel, Joseph, David, or Jeremiah, the Christian community has to see him suffering in the sufferings of the people of the Christian millennia and in the suffering of the present time. The *passio* of the Paschal event has to be more starkly recalled, for it is in this that communion must be born if there is to be communion in the *eschaton*.

In short, through the sacramental blessing prayers we see all that pertains to the sacramental action and how this is a memorial of the Paschal event. These blessings are prayers of the community of disciples, addressed to God as Creator, Covenant-Maker, and Father of Jesus Christ who shares in his lordship through communion in the Holy Spirit. They are prayed in the power of the Word and of the Spirit, God's gifts to his people. Through the inner testimony of the Spirit, the Word in the community expresses itself anew in the action of the believing community and testifies thus anew to God's love. The blessings recall the original testimony of the Paschal event so that it events in this community in ways appropriate to its own story and existence. The blessings are invoked over the things of earth, over persons and over their lives, and breathe the Word and Spirit into them. The many blessings of the economy radiate from and gather to the communion table of the Eucharist, where the Church is born and confirmed as the one body of Christ in the Spirit, the living testimony of God's gracious goodness to the world.

Sacrament as Gift

The twofold mission of Word and Spirit comes from the Father, as his gift. The sacramental elements of bread, wine, oil, and water are already an expression of gifts received. Humans receive them from the earth, and through them they receive life and communion together. To express his own self-giving, Christ took what by creation and earth's bounty are already gifts given. Through this medium, he gave sacramental form to his own self-giving. The gift/giving of God through Word and Spirit is continually manifested in the sacramental self-giving of Christ through the memorial of his death and in the gift of the Spirit which works from within to allow the Church to take this memorial into the actuality of Christian community. The gift was given in the sending of the Word and the Spirit. It was given through the self-emptying of Christ in his mission and on the Cross. It is given through the sacrament left to the Church on the eve of the passion and as a memorial of this passionate self-gift. The Eucharist is an economy of gift, where the gift is from God, of and through Christ and the Spirit, and the communion table is the central rite, not the consecration nor any gift made by the Church to God.

The giving through the twofold mission of Word and Spirit reveals the gift that comes from God as the gift of love, total and self-emptying love. While love is certainly associated with the Spirit, the gift of God within the heart, it is just as much associated with Christ, who gave his life and gives his sacramental self in love. Indeed, he is rightly said to be the icon and the expression of the love of the Father. In other words, understanding of the economy of grace and of the Trinitarian gift can be derived from the naming of God as love, a naming that occurs in and through the twofold mission. What is given in the Word and in the Spirit are the forms in which the love fills the world, and in particular the Church, which is the communion of God in charity.

The interplay between praise, thanksgiving, and doxology both shows the difficulties inherent in the appropriation of gift and keeps open the horizon of gift. The problem in underscoring *thanksgiving* is that it seems to provoke the need to make some offering in return. Those who receive, whether the gifts of creation or the gift of grace, turn very readily to giving something back in offering. How is it possible to be in reception of gift without entering into this economy of returning gift? There is discussion among liturgical historians, which will be looked at again later, as to whether Christian blessing is properly praise or properly thanksgiving. While the weight of opinion now seems to favor the specificity of thanksgiving, there is much to be said in favor of giving priority to praise, and with this giving more attention to the doxological conclusion that leads to silence. Praise is given in virtue of wonder. It allows the sheer wonder of the gift/presence of Word and Spirit to stand forth, as they are contemplated in the events of grace in the actions of all the *dramatis personae* of salvific action. Thanksgiving comes as it were in second place, by way of acknowledging the origin of these events and their grace in God and in God's love. That in turn gives place to doxology, which is the silent return to a contemplation of the divine mystery which is most truly present, but beyond comprehension, and indeed inevitably somewhat subverted by the words and signs that show forth its presence.

The Church Eventing

The dynamic of the action of Word and Spirit in making memorial is profitable in understanding the reality of the local Church as primary manifestation or sacrament in its Eucharist and sacraments of initiation. The inner movement and wisdom of the Spirit, along with the tradition, word, and ritual and institution of the body of Christ, which comes from the apostles, allows for pluriform expression. This great sacrament of God's love is always the completeness of the divine gift, and yet always historically and culturally realized within the concreteness of human experience. It always has an ethical implication, since it raises the issue of how Christians live, and what relations to God, neighbor and world believers appropriate, and how suffering is shared and lived through.

While the sacramental event is that of the language addressed to a particular community in Christ's name and that of the language spoken by the community in Christ's name, it is always the same Word which finds speech in many forms. The language event of Christian sacrament is the event of the Word of God, through the creative testimony of the Spirit, taking root again, in rich diversity, in time and place. It forms anew and it builds up a body which in its celebration and action testifies to the gift of God at work in the world and inviting into the divine communion of Father, Word, and Spirit.

Sacraments do not stand on their own. They are interwoven with institutions, lives, histories, personages. The exploration of a liturgical tradition involves connecting the liturgical actions, known through the evidence of traditions, with these realities. When a priest speaks and acts, it is asked what institutional support is behind him and how he relates to others within the institutional structures. When a people celebrates a Mass of Thanksgiving, one inquires about the events for which they give thanks and how being thankful for those particular events reflects the horizon and the values thus embodied in the liturgy. We also want to know whom a liturgy commemorates, and how and why. We can be even curious to find what is known of the recorded personalities of persons like Gregory the Great, Basil of Caesarea, Charlemagne and his chancellor Alcuin, Martin Luther, Thomas Cranmer, the Tridentine reformers, and the Wesley brothers, who left their stamp on liturgy.

Of particular importance both to interpreting and to appropriating sacramental tradition is insight into the physiognomy of cultures. How does a culture relate to the cosmos and to its earthly environment? How does it perceive and name things? What persons are revered within it? What forms of language discourse have greatest impact?

While we know that sacramental liturgy combines a variety of linguistic prayer forms, we cannot be sure in a purely a priori way of how they interchange. In practice, thanking, interceding, praising, confessing, singing, lamenting, are diversely appreciated in different cultural traditions. There is room in studying liturgical celebration for a deeper insight into how these forms modified each other in the past. The dispute about the relation between praise and thanksgiving in Christian prayer has been mentioned. While this is a historical question, it may be that it has no one solution, for the interplay between the two may well be different in different traditions. Furthermore, while there are the existing historical forms of liturgical language, this does not mean that they realize the full potentiality of speech in giving expression to the Christian mystery. As the Gospel encounters new cultures, the question has to remain open about other particular cultural forms that may yet be received into the liturgy. Even the simple and basic sacramental elements, bread, wine, oil, and water, are differently obtained, differently perceived, differently respected, and differently shared, in different peoples. In all these areas, there is always room for the two-way action, enunciated by John Paul II, of letting the Gospel take root in a culture and of letting the culture find a home within the Gospel, thus enriching the Gospel tradition itself.[36] It is thus that local Churches come into existence, and every other activity of such Churches finds a center in the sacramental economy.

This body is a community of disciples, and so engaged ethically on the way of discipleship. A community that in worship lauds the actions of Christ in hymns of praise, and narrates them as the actions of God's Word among us, takes up the following of Christ according to the measure of this Word. At the same time, the ethical engagement itself is brought back to worship and influences the way in which worship is celebrated, in both its words and its ritual actions. The interplay between worship and ethics is inescapable, but it is built into the character of language as such, since *poetics* expresses the ideal of *praxis*. The role of prevailing metaphors or paradigms put to play in celebration and in its interpretation is crucial in setting the ethical horizon for a Christian community. The metaphors that have served the memorial of the Pasch in different Churches have already been recalled. Clearly, these paradigms affect the manner of Christian relationship to the world, to activity, and to suffering, as well as the relationship to God. They all, however, call for a praxis that is born of the poetics of celebration. The Church in a culture is embodied on the one hand in its sacraments and in its institutions, but it is also embodied in its ethical engagement with the world that is shaped by this sacramental memorial.

Naming God

Within the sacramental assembly of the Church, it is through the different literary genres of both scripture and prayer, and through the actions of the body in its immediacy to earth and to humans, that God is named. God is not named outside this sacramentality, but is named there as Creator, as maker of covenant, and finally as Father, Son, and Spirit. These last distinctive names, however, are not to be confused with the essential nature of the Godhead, as though they expressed the ineffable divine being. They are relational names, names of God in relation to creation and salvation, and showing forth the divine mystery, as it supersedes and transcends within itself the realities of divine gift within the world. This is how they are recited in the Creed and invoked in blessings. They signify the relationality within the divine action and presence to the world and within the mystery of divine life. The three

---

36. See John Paul II, "Litterae Encyclicae de perenni vi mandati missionalis," no. 52, AAS 83 (1990): 300.

thus named are really distinct, not to be collapsed into each other, each name relationally signifying the Godhead present and not just some one aspect of God's mode of being or subsisting. To speak that way would be to subject God to ontotheology, configuring the divine as being within the structures of being, though transcendentally. Since the naming takes place in such diverse circumstances and with such historical and cultural discontinuity, and with address to such manifold and untellable suffering, it has to be done anew each time, and it has to find resonance in each situation.

The naming of God occurred within the economy of redemption, as Jesus was acclaimed as Savior. It cannot be taken outside this economy in some abstract or conceptual manner. The name of God as *Father* was a naming of the Father of the Lord Jesus Christ. It is a postresurrection naming and occurred in the overcoming of the scandal of the Cross, affirmed as the true relation of the crucified Jesus to the God of the Law and the Prophets. God was thus named *Father* in conjunction with the naming of Jesus as *Lord*, and it is in this that he is *Son*. This naming, which was done in proclamation of the good news, was integrated back into the narrative of the baptism of Jesus and of his conception and birth. It is thus revealed in and through the descent of the Spirit, who empowers Jesus for his messianic mission and who is in turn named as the Spirit of the Father of the Lord Jesus Christ, or simply as the Spirit of Christ. In conjunction with this threefold naming within the economy of redemption, the teaching and works of Jesus are likewise embraced in memory and narrative as the teachings and works of the Word and the Wisdom of God, of him who is the *icon* of the Father who invests him with his own name. Christians are baptized in this name/naming. They are children of God in the Lord Jesus and in the Spirit. This is what is affirmed in the baptismal formula and in the doxology of Christian prayer.

Doxology expresses the truth that these are not proper names of Godly being, though they place us in face of God, whom we cannot see, image or name "properly." They express God present to us, and when taken up by us place us in face of God, but they fall short of God. They are icons of God invisible, ineffable, and unnameable. They lead us to contemplation, if they are invoked in a truly personal and committed way.

What has been pointed out in some recent theology is that these three namings relate to Love, to Divine Love, poured out. Love reveals what God is when present to the world through this threefold naming. It is mediated as a gift that has its origins in God through this naming, which takes place in sacrament. It is concretized in the advent, experience, phenomena, stories, prayers, of the assembly, and in the presence of/to the other of earth and human brought there by/in the sacramental signs. It comes to us, as gift, through these media, under the conditions of these media.

Because the names of Father, Son, and Spirit are not proper names of the Godhead in its essence but of relations, names, that is, of Love adventing, some claim that they can in sacramental formula and creed be changed.

What is signified archivally by these names is taken by anamnesis and appropriation into the advent/event of another situation. In this, there is some redress of story, some retrieval in culture and struggle of the signs by which love's presence is given. To take two examples, Christ is now called by some Sophia, and once in Syrian Churches the Spirit was called mother dove. Within the redress of story and original naming, brought now to flesh and to expression, there may also be some redress of names without transgression of the Trinitarian revelation of this Love.

If the divine names are modified in keeping with other sensitivities, the relation to the economy of redemption and revelation has to be kept. Some inner critique of whatever formula were to be adopted would also be needed. Just as in their original revelatory use, the names Father, Son and Spirit cancelled out what was culturally meant by such names to fill them, in the process, with new meaning and desire, so all redress of names at any moment has to meet the exigencies of this process. To substitute *parent* for *Father*, for example, is pure banality, simply replacing image with image for what cannot be imaged. Perhaps "Love that is without begetting, Love that is begotten, and Love pouring forth in bonding," is a move in the direction of redress, but probably too "nameless" and lacking in a clear relation to the Cross and the lordship of Jesus, to the name given to him by the God whom he proclaimed. Ancient of Days, Wisdom, and Love might serve as a naming to fit the relational presence of the unnameable, provided wisdom is related not only to the wisdom inherent in creation but also to the wisdom inherent in the Cross. Mighty God, Word of God, and Breath of God, could suggest the relation to the presencing through outer and inner testimony. In naming God, the Church cannot be deaf to the fact that the question of the names is raised most terribly by those who have known suffering and oppression under those who have appealed to them most strongly. The resonance of the names in a world of suffering, where the kingdom of God's justice is not yet established but is yet expected, is the testing point.

On a whole, one should not tamper too readily with the divine names found in the tradition, but by setting the familiar names in different contexts which transgress whatever images the names suggest, they may remain "pure" names, without content of substance but bespeaking an ineffable presence of the gift of Love. This is not of course to assume that we know what divine Love is, except in its revealing and under the forms of its revealing. The advance in naming is to realize that the naming of the three has to do with love given that is self-giving, and that the threefold naming is related to this. Much more might well be said on this and on the connection between Love and Justice in naming God, but this is not the place for that.[37]

---

37. The matter of names is further discussed in chapter 8, in connection with feminist critique of sacramental history.

Anamnesis / Mimesis

While in systematic sacramental theology the choice is often to begin with some discussion of the meaning of memorial, or *anamnesis*, here the choice has been to conclude with this consideration. This is first because a good appreciation of memorial requires insight into the nature of sacrament as language event. Second, coupling the words *anamnesis* and *mimesis*[38] provides a way of unifying all previous reflections.

The language event of sacrament engages us at the level of the daily, the bread and the wine, the oil and the water, within the time that is the time of living day to day. It puts the daily into the longer time frame that is called history. It opens it out to cosmic time, and to what comes into time by divine advent, but at the point where creatures have their being in the time told by these earthly elements. In keeping memorial through proclamation, prayer and rite, the sacrament brings the Paschal event, the event of God into the world through the Pasch of Christ into daily and historical time, though it is not of this time, but comes from "beyond time." Entering time by the grace of God, as sign of the presence of the Word and of the Spirit, the sacramental presencing of this event interrupts, even disrupts, the flow of daily and historical time.

The word *anamnesis* brings the act of remembering to the fore, an act which as said before is the working of the Word and the Spirit in the action of the Church when it keeps memorial of the Pasch, in the midst of human life as this is represented in the rites. It is as an act of remembering, within the play of the language event of celebration, that the relation of the Paschal event to this human life is forged. The event is represented in the distanciated form in which it is given shape in the memory of the Church, expressed in its written tomes, its rites, its institutions, and its monuments. It is by reason of this kind of distancing that it takes shape anew in the sacramental action of each and every Christian community or Church. Since the celebration is a complex interplay of text, prayer, and ritual, through this language the event remembered is configured to the human reality of the people, and their reality is configured to what is represented to and for it. The distinction made by Paul Ricoeur between the three stages of *mimesis*, where he adopts the Aristotelian term to express story and plot, gives insight into the working of this sacramental memorial. In noting this distinction earlier, it was seen that the story of the Pasch is not simply proclaimed from the scripture, but it is proclaimed or retold in a way that brings the original into conversation with the speech of the community and its people. The *anamnesis*, or act of remembering, assumes the language of the culture lived by this people into its recall of the Pasch in a variety of ways. These include their own particular

---

38. The word is not used now as it is used by Ricoeur in his distinction of the triple mimesis of story, but in a sense taken from Christian usage, as will be explained below. On the use of these two terms, compare R. D. McCall, "Anamnesis or Mimesis? Unity and Drama in the Paschal Triduum," *Ecclesia Orans* 13 (1996): 315–22.

choice of scriptural texts, the homily and comment upon the texts, the language of prayer in which some key metaphors in which to sum up the story stand out, the music and body rhythm with which the remembrance is conjoined, the particular way of determining the use of the core elements and actions with bread, wine, oil, and water, the ritual manner in which bonding in marriage or entering ministry is expressed. All of these words and rites at one and the same time bespeak the life of the people and the remembered event of the Pasch. It is through this door of language that the memorial done in Word and Spirit enters the life of the community and configures this to the Pasch, changing peoples' horizons, giving them the gift of the hope of the reign of God in which the renewed possibilities of acting and suffering in Christ's name can be taken up.

This remembering relates the Pasch to the time of the community, or lets it enter this time and simultaneously bring it into another kind of time. The time of the community, expressed most vehemently in its bodily rituals, is daily time, historical time, and cosmic time. Each of these, and the intersection of these, is in itself an enigma. Human effort often concentrates on bringing the three together into some linear conception of historical time, where a sequence of happenings is affirmed and explained and a future can be reasonably projected. The memorial of the Pasch disrupts any such effort. When we see that it is through a language event that it is represented, we are aware that the sacramental action does not express any clear linear sequence of historical events, or even institutional continuity, with the historical time of Jesus. It is always as an event remembered that the Pasch is represented, made possible only by the play of language and subject to its conditions. In that sense, it has its impact only when constantly brought back into time, and not as the simple result of some dynamic forces inserted into the sequence of ecclesial or human actions. Word and Spirit are indeed present in human history, but within the modalities of language event. Hence within the ordinary or historical time of a human community, the Pasch occurs sacramentally as a kind of irruption, indeed disruption, always adventing "anew." It is in this way that it opens to the future, an eruption as it were setting off new hopes and possibilities when its interruption of the course of events is allowed. This is the sense in which to understand the eschatological quality of Paschal remembrance. Humans experience the difficulties of harmonizing daily time, historical time, and cosmic time. Indeed, in relation to each of them the experience is that of broken time, of time disrupted and discordant. Yet it is under these very conditions, in the midst of life and time thus broken, that the gift of God's healing, reconciling, and hope-filled love is imparted.

These considerations sparked by the term *anamnesis* indicate how sacramental remembrance introduces the Paschal event into time by way of extending it, so that relation to the day, relation to history, and relation to cosmos, are all made new when the vigor of the Pasch disrupts and enlarges the actualities and the possibilities of human action. It is the coming into time of the salvific event from the past that is brought to the fore. Both the event and the memorial are God's gift, the action of Word and Spirit, and they hold the promise of future gift. Or, in other words, they express the truth that God keeps on gifting. By way of deliberate contrast with *anamnesis*, the word *mimesis* expresses how the Church relates to the divine from which the gift comes and which is present in the gift.

The cue to the use made here of this word is taken from the mystagogical catechesis attributed to Cyril of Jerusalem.[39] In contrast with the truth, or *aletheia*, of the actual events of the crucifixion, burial, and resurrection of Jesus Christ, Cyril calls the sacramental participation in this mystery a *mimesis*, and to this relates the other terms *eikon* and *omoioma*. The first of the three is generally translated as "imitation," the second as "image," and the third as "likeness." They are used concurrently by Cyril, not to express the kind of imitation which goes with acting out something or with figurative representation, but to speak of a participation in the reality remembered and ritually represented in a form which in appearance is quite different from it. The three terms are then put in context by another word, *koinonia*, which means a communion and a participation in the mystery. The words can be used to speak of all the rites and actions of the service of Christian initiation, but in a particular way they are applicable to the key moments of baptismal immersion, anointing with oil, and eucharistic communion, and then spill over into the kind of rebirth and new life which mark the participants as they continue their earthly journey.

The impact of these terms is to suggest that what is wrought by *anamnesis* in bringing the Pasch into rite and thereby into human life is a participation in the here and now in the divine mystery of love revealed in this salvific event. In that regard, it could be said that the sacramental moment is a moment "out of time," since it is a moment of communion in the mystery of the Triune God. This is of great significance in an understanding of human existence. As it will be spelled out further in writing of rituality, the rites of bread, wine, oil, and water and those of human transition reveal human existence at its most vulnerable, enigmatic, and fecund. These rituals point to the very heart of human life, to its key energies, and to the search for an insertion of this life into a greater horizon that extends the limits of its given perceptions. To relate the rebirth in the Spirit, messianic anointing, marriage exchange, the healing given in the Cross, the communion in the body and blood of Christ, to these precise moments is to relate them ecstatically to a communion in God's own mystery and love. This moment of human existence, and potentially any moment of human existence, while it is lived out in the kind of time relation expressed in remembrance/*anamnesis*,

---

39. This is found particularly in his comments on baptism. For an English translation, see Edward Yarnold, *The Awe-Inspiring Rites of Initiation*, 2d ed. (Collegeville, Minn.: Liturgical Press, 1994), 77–80.

is also a moment of communion in the divine, because it is a communion in the Pasch. While *anamnesis* represents a participation extended over time, under the conditionings of remembering, the mimetic action of ritual orients human existence "beyond time" and "beyond being," certainly as something not yet consummated, yet as something truly already shared. Like metaphor, rite gathers and scatters. It gathers all that is proclaimed into one key moment and expression, but in doing so it gives this mysterious exchange the power to disseminate itself throughout the whole of human living, acting, and suffering. Narrative, blessing, catechesis, testimony, bring it back into the flow of living, but without overshadowing the truth that each moment, each action done in truth, each suffering taken up in hope, each living communion established, is a share in the divine and eternal mystery of God's love.

It is of the role of the poetic language in which the death is remembered to keep this ritual "nonclosure" open for the whole course of ecclesial life. Remembering Christ eschatologically does not mean that we expect him to return "as he was" and as he appeared in the resurrection, but to return as Judge of all that has been done in his name, to intrude upon it, judging it on the ground of an ethical remembrance of a "nonclosure." It is also the remembrance of the gift offered through the ways of the flesh and through symbols, as it was offered at the baptism of Jesus in the Jordan and at the Supper, repeated then at Emmaus in the light of the Law and the Prophets. While the giving is always realized through time and under the conditions of temporality, the gift enters from above, from the God who transcends time and being, yet projects the image of the divine self-giving in the *icon* who is Christ and in the *icon* of the sacraments, in which this gift continues to be present, present, however, not in its completeness but in the traces of its earthly passing.

Once again we can appeal to the anaphora of Basil of Caesarea to give an example of how this conjunction of historical remembrance and here-and-now communion is expressed.[40] Basil's anaphora brings those who pray through the events of salvation to lead them to the Supper narrative and eucharistic action, with the recall of the memorial command. All is related back to the heavenly liturgy and to the dissolution of God's creative intent through sin. The Law and the Prophets are recalled as the preparation for Christ. Christ's own mystery is first put into the imagery of self-emptying, or *kenosis*. After this, the text of the anaphora commemorates the incarnation, the teaching of Christ about the Father, the mystery of communion with him as a royal and priestly people through baptism and thus the oblique recall of his own baptism in the Jordan. The text moves on to the Cross, the descent into hell through the pains of death, the rising on the third day, the ascent into heaven, the session at the right hand of God, and the expected coming in judgment. At that point the text turns to the Supper action as the ac-

---

40. *Prex Eucharistica*, 260–63.

tion by which we are given the command and ritual of the memorial of this mystery. The invocation of the Spirit over the elements and the congregation gathered around them then inserts the remembrance, and the moment of communion in the body and blood anticipated, into the communion of the Church and through extended intercessions into the complex reality of human living, as Church and as citizens of the world.

The distinction here developed between narrative remembrance of the mystery and communion in it fits well with the Eastern distinction between the cataphatic and the apophatic, between divine revelation and the mystery revealed. The cataphatic, or positive theology, expounds and safeguards the ways of revelation. The apophatic is the way of negation of creaturely and temporal restraints inherent in the way of revelation in order to enter into contemplation of the mystery. Along these lines, we can see that sacraments are *anamnesis* inasmuch as they recall and commemorate the deeds of Christ's flesh through which the divine entered the world, but that they are *mimesis* or *mysterion* inasmuch as they bring us into the mystery of divine giving and of divine life, which is inexpressible and beyond being and time.

Conclusion

Presenting Christian sacrament as a language event enables us to attend to how the sacrament is the event of God's Word and Spirit that relates the Church to the Paschal event of Jesus Christ. Various considerations on the understanding of the term *language* were developed, showing how this serves as a heuristic of sacrament as a language event, simultaneously *poesis* and an exercise in *praxis*. In this way, it proved possible to take all its elements into consideration and to relate it to the Paschal event through which the twofold mission from the Father of Word and Spirit took shape in the convocation of the Church. The reality of sacraments as *anamnesis* brings this mystery into time, even in its brokenness, and yet as *mimesis* it assures an ever present participation in divine mystery and in divine communion. Pithily, one might say that the event of Christ's Pasch, which is the event of God's gift of Word and Spirit, events again in the event of Church becoming through sacrament, and in virtue of this the sacrament brings the Church into a communion with the eternal mystery of the Triune God. Taking a hermeneutical cue from blessing prayers, the chapter concluded with a dialectic between *anamnesis* and *mimesis*. This highlighted the fact that while the Church lives in the confidence of presently sharing in divine mystery and divine life, it does so in the context of broken time. Within the very experience of living in diverse kinds of time, which cannot be harmonized and which are fragile in claims to continuity, the sacramental Church constantly looks to the future for the gift of divine love and self-emptying which may come into human lives in ways not planned or foreseen, finding a place in the flux of human existence in virtue of this memory and this hope.

Part II

The Complexity
of Sacrament
and Its Interpretation

— Chapter Three —

Community, Sacrament, Interpretation

Before considering the diverse elements found in sacramental celebration, some examples can serve to show how complex and interwoven sacramental liturgies have always been, and how on some past occasions sacramental texts have been interpreted. This serves as a concrete induction into the exploration of sacramental rites, one that helpfully precedes the more theoretical and general reflections of the following chapters.

For this purpose, in the first part of the chapter two canons of baptism are explored. In the second part, a look is taken at two diverse interpretations of the same text. In a third section, the case is taken of a preacher who wove scripture, rite, and Christian life together in his interpretation of the sacrament of ordination. The choices could be considered random, but any specific case is a good way of alerting ourselves to what is involved in rite and what is involved in interpretation. The exercise of reading involved makes later considerations less abstract.

Baptismal Liturgies in Two Different Traditions

These examples demonstrate the interplay between scriptural selection, euchology, ritual action, and visual perception.[1] This historical survey will continue to serve as a point of reference in later chapters.

The liturgical texts chosen from the past have the practical advantage of being readily accessible in published translations, as well as in editions of the manuscript evidence.[2] The one is the canon of baptism in the Armenian Ritual, as edited by F. Conybeare,[3] and the other the order of baptism at the Paschal vigil according to the Gelasian sacramentary, as edited by

---

1. Though there is no way of connecting the rites considered with a specific building, information will be taken from some baptistries of an early age to suggest connections between rite and place.

2. For our purposes here, there is no need to take up the questions of critical redaction and historical reconstruction which are sometimes discussed.

3. *Ritual Armenorum*, ed. F. C. Conybeare and A. J. Maclean (Oxford: Clarendon Press, 1905), 89–101.

L. Mohlberg.[4] Both orders are conveniently available in English translation in *Documents of the Baptismal Liturgy,* published by E. C. Whitaker.[5] Both services reflect practice in a period when children and adults were baptized according to the same rite, which originated for use with adults.

The Armenian Rite is known from a thirteenth-century manuscript, and since the candidates were small children there is no eucharistic celebration. Instead, when the newly baptized are brought into the congregation they are placed on the altar and a host touched to the child's tongue. Adult neophytes in earlier times would have joined the community in the eucharistic action and communion.[6] It seem that this rite reflects the custom of baptizing candidates on the Feast of the Epiphany, which was done because on this day the Church commemorated the baptism of the Lord in the Jordan. While in very early times, immersion took place in a river of flowing water, later the service was located in baptistries which were part of the church complex.

The Gelasian rites also suppose child candidates, but they too reflect earlier practice with adults. The sacramentary has adopted the practice from earlier times of scrutinies and other ceremonies for the elect during Lent. It also places the renunciation of Satan and the profession of faith on the morning of Holy Saturday. Parents, sponsors and children apparently attended the vigil of readings, at the end of which they went in procession to the font. It was in the baptistry that the water was blessed and rites of initiation performed. The candidates were then brought back to the congregation for the Eucharist. There are several changes in this ritual, due to the candidature of children rather than adults. The fourth-century Jerusalem liturgy, as we know it from an Armenian codex, is the background to the Gelasian Paschal vigil and initiation rites, since it had considerable influence on developments of both the Paschal vigil and the baptismal liturgy. From this we know that the Gelasian has changed the practice of doing the baptism during the vigil of readings. Baptism had in earlier times been done in the baptistry, while the congregation celebrated the vigil in the church. The neophytes were introduced into the congregation at the end of the Old Testament vigil of readings to take their part in the liturgy of the resurrection. In their presence, the resurrection of Christ was proclaimed through New Testament readings and the Eucharist was celebrated. At this, they partook of the body and blood of Christ for the first time.

For each baptismal liturgy, we will distinguish the ritual actions, the proclamation of the scriptures, and the euchology, or prayer texts.

---

4. *Liber Sacramentorum Romanae aeclesiae ordinis anni circuli,* ed. Leo Cunibert Mohlberg (Rome: Herder, 1960), 70–76.

5. See *Documents of the Baptismal Liturgy,* ed. E. C. Whitaker, 8th impression (London: SPCK, 1960, 1993), 61–68, 166–96.

6. For a detailed study of Armenian initiation, see G. Winkler, *Das armenische Initiationsrituale,* OCA 217 (Rome: Pontifical Oriental Institute, 1981).

Armenian Rite

Ritual Actions

First noted are the actions that are integral to the Armenian canon. The service begins with the reception of the elect at the door, and the liturgy of the word celebrated at that point is followed by the procession into the church. In blessing the font, the minister pours blessed oil crosswise into the font. The candidates are stripped and washed with a triple immersion, and then anointed with oil. They are then brought to the church, welcomed by the congregation, made to kiss the altar, and given communion.

While the baptism is done with water and oil, these actions have a cumulative significance that in some sense precedes and then completes the signification of the scriptures, prayers, and formulas proclaimed and spoken. The procession to the font sharpens the sense of a journey of faith and of entry into a new community. The pouring of oil into the water in the Armenian Rite is a vivid expression of the dual action of Word and Spirit. The reception by the congregation and the eucharistic action are the climax of the rite.

Scriptures

The liturgy begins at the door of the church, with an office prayed by the clergy "over" the candidates. Three psalms are prayed, followed by litanies and prayers, the renunciation of Satan, and the profession of faith. As the text stands in Conybeare's edition, this profession is made both according to the ancient baptismal formula of question and response and by the recitation of the Nicene Creed.

The psalms used are Psalm 14[15], "Unto thee, O Lord, have I lifted up my soul," Psalm 25[26], "Judge me, O Lord," and Psalm 50[51], "Have mercy on me, O Lord, according to thy great mercy." On entering the church, Psalm 118[119], "Confess ye unto the Lord, for he is good," is prayed with the catechumens to celebrate their entry, both into the building and into the congregation. The typological and accommodated use of these and other psalms is evident. The forgiveness of sins is accentuated in these texts, but they also celebrate God's loving care and the entry into the community of the Church, wherein the candidates receive the sacraments of water, oil, and the table banquet of the body and blood of Christ.

The preparation of the font and baptismal immersion is then preceded by an office. The readings for this are Ezekiel 36:25–28, Galatians 3:24–28, and John 3:1–8. The psalms are Psalm 28[29], "The voice of the Lord is upon the waters," and Psalm 23[24], "The Lord shall be my shepherd and I shall not want." There follows a litany, the blessing of oil which is poured into the font, and the blessing of the water thus prepared. Each prayer has its scriptural references, which will later be considered. When the candidate has been plunged three times in the waters with the baptismal formula, Psalm 34[35], "Many are the afflictions of the righteous," is sung. It is preceded by the formula "You have been baptized into Christ." A reading of Matthew 3:12–16 follows, which is the story of Jesus' baptism in the Jordan. After this, the neophytes recite the Lord's Prayer. They are then anointed and communicated with the holy mysteries, and the service ends with the singing of Psalm 31[32], "Blessed is he whose sins are forgiven."

In the choice of readings, this service combines different genres. There is first the prophetic text from Ezekiel which promises the cleansing of sins. This is followed by the moral exhortation of the letter to the Galatians which proclaims the dignity of all baptized in Christ and the overcoming in him of basic divisions and distinctions. Chosen from the Gospels, there are two foundational, or founding, stories. One is the account of Jesus' own baptism, and the other is the promise of rebirth through water and the Spirit, given by Jesus in his conversation with Nicodemus.

While intertwining different genres in the selection of texts, the readings also harmonize different images for the meaning of baptism. These are the cleansing of sins, the forming into one body of all, whatever their distinctions, and rebirth in the Spirit. The reading of the account of Jesus' baptism in the Jordan, when the Spirit descended upon him and his sonship was manifested through the voice of the Father, offers this as the basic paradigm for Christian baptism.

Euchology and Scripture

The euchology of the service completes the significance of the ritual actions and of the scriptural selections. As mentioned, during the blessing prayer of the font, oil is infused into the baptismal water. This is to express the role and action of the Spirit. The newly baptized share in the anointing of Christ by the Spirit, as members of his holy people. The entry into the font expresses washing and rebirth. The accompanying rubric interprets the triple immersion as oneness with Christ in the three days of his burial, but this is not otherwise mentioned in the texts, though it was a frequent theme of mystagogical catechesis. In fact, the baptismal service makes no explicit mention of Christ's death and resurrection. What it accentuates is forgiveness of sins and rebirth in Christ as members of his body, through the grace of the Spirit. In this, it is significant that the paradigmatic text is the baptism of Jesus in the Jordan. The image of regeneration, however, in its own way expresses death, as does the plunging into the water. One cannot be reborn without losing a previous form of life, and candidates are plunged into the formless chaos of water in order to emerge as from the womb/tomb newly formed. The paradigm of Jesus' baptism fits into this horizon. It was when Jesus had joined humanity in the baptism for the forgiveness of sins that he was anointed as God's Son and driven by the life of the Spirit to dwell peaceably among beasts, wrestle with Satan, and be ministered to by angels. These three things signify a new way of being on earth for God's Son, and in him for all God's children. Some death is implied in entering the water in the expectation of the coming of a new era in which the old is to be refined by fire, as proclaimed by John.

The prayers take account of these texts and add imagery from other sources. The prayer of exorcism and preparation at the beginning of the service invokes the name of Jesus as Lord, proclaimed in the hymn in Philippians 2:10f., and relates this to his power over the evil spirits that assail the candidates. It also brings in the baptismal text of 1 Peter 3:21, where the typology of salvation in the ark is brought to a conclusion by presenting baptism as a cleansing of consciences. In the preparation of the font of water, a number of scriptural texts are incorporated. In the blessing of the oil which is to be poured into the water, the grace is asked for entry into the holy race and chosen people mentioned in 1 Peter 2:9. Along with this, images of adoption and inheritance are taken from Galatians 4. In the blessing of the water, the creative power of the Spirit in bringing life out of the waters is recalled from the story of creation in Genesis 1. While the baptismal command of the risen Christ in Matthew 28:19 is given due place to guarantee God's action, the baptism of Jesus and rebirth through water and the Spirit have primary importance as baptismal figures. When the prayer invokes the descent of the Spirit into the water, it is asked that the water may be cleansed as were the waters of the Jordan at the baptism of Christ, and that it be given the power of regenerating those who descend into it.

Asking what meaning of baptism emerges from this use of scriptures, one has to see it within the ritual unity of exorcism, profession of faith, water blessing and immersion, anointing with oil, and eucharistic communion. Within that ritual flow, the newly baptized are configured to the baptism of Jesus, when he is declared the Christ and the beloved Son, and where he is empowered by the descent of the Holy Spirit. Through this configuration, they receive rebirth in the same Spirit as God's children, are anointed with the anointing of Christ, receive forgiveness of their sins and are freed from the power of the evil one, and become members of God's holy and chosen people. By this action they are brought into the unity in Christ in which there is neither Jew nor gentile, slave nor free, male nor female, that is, into a unity which no difference or distinction can disrupt.

Gelasian Liturgy

Ritual Actions

In the Gelasian sacramentary, there is a procession to the font for the baptismal rites at the end of the vigil of Old Testament readings, but, as remarked, in earlier times these rites took place during the vigil. In blessing the water, the minister is to sign it with his hand. The candidates are to be dipped thrice in the water. They are then to be signed with chrism, not by the bishop but by a presbyter, and then they are to receive the laying on of hands from the bishop. The signing of the water in the Gelasian service is a visual reminder of the saving Cross of Christ. In both cases, the triple immersion pinpoints the profession of faith in Father, Son, and Spirit, while also expressing the entry into the chaos of water from which birth in this faith emerges. In the Gelasian, assigning the chrismation to a presbyter and the laying on of hands to the bishop expresses a difference in the role of these two actions. The liturgy resumes with the singing of the Gloria, which begins the liturgy of the resurrection in which the neophytes join.

Scripture

The setting for the rite of baptism in the Gelasian sacramentary is the Paschal vigil, so that the texts which serve the commemoration of Christ's Pasch also serve to express the meaning of baptism. This is brought out particularly in the petitionary prayers which follow each of the readings and which introduce christological, ecclesial, and baptismal typologies into the reading of scriptural texts.

This set of readings for the vigil is not the same as that associated with the Church of Rome in the Gregorian sacramentary and other sources.[7] It is in fact closer to the readings located in the Church of Jerusalem by what is called the old Armenian lectionary. In this latter lectionary the continuity with the Sinai covenant and with Jewish vigil worship is to the fore, and it is in this setting that the sacrament of baptism is celebrated. The stories of creation, of the binding of Isaac, and of the Paschal Lamb in particular make this connection, as they also present types for the redemptive work of Christ. The prophetic readings then express the passage toward the new covenant in Christ. After the readings, the neophytes entered the church with the bishop for the eucharistic service, which began with the proclamation of the resurrection in 1 Corinthians 15:1–11 and Matthew 28:1–20. It is this ritual and lectionary sequence which expresses the meaning of baptism.

The Roman vigil of Gregorian heritage, as it has been reconstituted by Herman Schmidt, veered away from the expression of continuity with things Jewish in its sequence of readings. While it had the readings about creation and the sacrifice of Isaac, it omitted Exodus 12. There is also a reading of Moses' final exhortation to the people in Deuteronomy 30 and his appointment of Josuah (Jesus) as the new leader who will bring them into the promised land, when they again cross the waters of the Red Sea. The prophetic readings are different from those of the Church of Jerusalem and have more to do with redemption from sin and with the Church as God's vineyard. The baptismal typology is that of passage and of salvation in and through the Church, and the relation to Christ is that to the one who leads them to salvation.

---

7. For a summary of studies on the readings for the vigil in different locations, see Thomas J. Talley, *The Origins of the Liturgical Year* (New York: Pueblo, 1986), 47–54. For a study of evolution in the Roman rite, see Herman A. P. Schmidt, *Hebdomada Sancta*, vol. 2, *Fontes Historici: Commentarius Historicus* (Rome, Freiburg im Breisgau, and Barcelona: Herder, 1959).

The Gelasian vigil retains more of the readings and focus of the Armenian lectionary, though its sequence is not identical with that of Jerusalem. The texts proclaimed include a number of narratives. These are Genesis 1, the creation story; Genesis 5, the story of salvation from the flood in the ark; Genesis 22, the story of the "sacrifice of Isaac"; Exodus 14, the crossing of the Red Sea; Exodus 12 on the Paschal Lamb, and Deuteronomy 31, which is the last testament of Moses to the people of Israel. The accompanying prophetic texts are Isaiah 54, on making of the gentile peoples God's heritage; Isaiah 4–5 which is the song of the vineyard, and Ezekiel 37 on the valley of the dry bones which come to life when God breathes on them. To these are added the blessing prayer of Moses which concludes his testament and Daniel 3, which is the hymn to creation of the three children in the fiery furnace. Psalm 41[42] is then added for the procession to the font.

The most basic narratives have a focused christological meaning. These are the story of the sacrifice of Isaac and of the Paschal Lamb. On the one hand, these readings make the link between the Old Testament and the New, or the former covenant and that established in Jesus Christ. They also serve to bring the salvific sacrifice of Christ to the fore and the saving power of his blood. In this sense, they interpret the passion narratives that were read during the week, and maybe even sometimes on that night. They also show whence the baptismal water receives its power to cleanse, to give life and to free from sin and evil.

The Genesis story of creation belonged in the old Armenian lectionary. It carried over from the meaning given to the Paschal night by the Jewish people, who related the expectation of the Messiah to the story of creation. Exodus 12 also connected Christian vigil with Jewish vigil. For the Jews, it was and is both a story of liberation from slavery and the establishment of cult, in commemoration of the Exodus event. At the Christian vigil it offered a prototype of Christ as the true Paschal Lamb and foreshadowed the new cult inaugurated in memory of him. In this context, baptism had a clearly covenantal and cultic meaning.

Some of the other readings, found here but not in the liturgy of the Jerusalem Church, changed the perspective on the relation between Jewish covenant and new covenant and also reflected another attitude to baptism. The story of the creation is followed by the story of the destruction of the world by flood and of the ark in which a few are saved. This put more focus on sin, as well as on salvation in the ark which is the Church of Christ. It seems that the passage of Exodus 14 was read in the Church of Rome, which omitted Exodus 12. The omission played down the continuity with Jewish cult and also showed a preference for the symbolism of baptismal passage through the water attached to the Christian reading of Exodus 14. The Gelasian vigil has both readings.

The prophetic readings from Isaiah are about the redemption of Israel, which typifies the Church in which the baptized are saved. Isaiah 54 proclaims the salvation given in Christ to all peoples. The song of the vineyard is a song of God's loving care for sinners, but also something of a warning about what happens to the unfaithful. In context, the text from Ezekiel is about the life given in baptism to those dead in sin. The prayer which follows it relates it to the promise for the future received in the Paschal sacrament. Through the canticles, these stories and prophecies are brought into the living context of grateful praise and the acclamation of God's glory, as revealed in creation and in the works done for the people.[8]

Within this setting, some of the narratives refer most particularly to the power of the baptismal water. The narratives of creation and the flood serve to typify the life-giving and cleansing powers of this water. The crossing of the Red Sea by the Israelites typifies the passage through baptism from slavery into freedom and the destruction of the devil and evil forces that have enslaved the candidates.

Euchology and Scripture

The blessing of the font and the baptismal immersion used to be joined with the profession of faith. The baptism is still followed in the Gelasian by the anointing with chrism and the episcopal laying on of hands for the sevenfold gift of the Spirit. It is completed in the eucharistic liturgy. The resurrection narratives were proclaimed in the liturgy that followed baptism, and possibly also Romans 6 or 1 Corinthians 15:1–11, which was used in the Church of Jerusalem according to the Armenian lectionary. These readings locate baptism as a baptism into the death and resurrection of Christ.

The blessing of the baptismal font for its part relates the imagery of rebirth through water and the Spirit to the baptism of Jesus in the Jordan, rather than to his sacrifice or to the mystery of his death and resurrection. The prayer may well have its origin in another setting than that of the Roman Paschal vigil. By some it is thought to have associations with Peter Chrysologus, who lived in the fifth century and was bishop of Ravenna, a city whose baptismal fonts testify to the typology of Christ's own baptism. In any case, the effect of the ritual unity of diverse texts is that in the Gelasian the figures of the prayer are related to the Paschal mystery by the context of vigil, readings, and eucharistic prayers.

The primary historical references in the blessing of the font are to the creation story, the story of the flood, the changing of the water into wine at Cana, the walking of Jesus on the waters, Jesus' baptism in the Jordan, the flow of blood and water from his side on the Cross, and the baptismal command. Their placement within the euchology is of interest in giving a more precise meaning to their citation. The blessing has an introductory collect,

---

8. It is Herman Schmidt's opinion that the Roman vigil at one time may also have included a reading from Baruch 3. If so, this would have been an inclusion of wisdom literature, for though Baruch is listed among the prophets, this chapter is a song of wisdom. See Schmidt, *Hebdomada Sancta*, 832.

which invokes the images of a new people (1 Pet. 2) and of adoption (Gal. 4 and Rom. 8). The blessing prayer includes an invocation of God's power, an exorcism, an epiclesis, and a petition for the effects of the blessing in the lives of those to be baptized. The image of the Spirit hovering over the waters of creation is introduced both into the exorcism and into the invocation of God's power. The story of the flood serves in the exorcism to typify God's dual action in destroying wickedness and in giving regeneration.

In the invocation of God's power, the baptismal command of Matthew 28:19 gives authenticity to the action by appeal to a divine imperative, which is the sole guarantee of salvific sacramental action. The baptism of Jesus is again invoked as type. The Cana narrative records both Jesus' manifestation as the Messiah and his power over water, while also introducing festive and nuptial imagery. The story of the walking on the water is a story of Christ's power over the elements and a story of salvation, since he saved Peter from sinking through fear and lack of faith. The flow of blood and water from Christ's side on the Cross typifies the origin of the sacraments of baptism and Eucharist in his death. In the final petition, when the descent of the Spirit into the waters is asked, the effects of baptism are registered through the scriptural imagery of regeneration, washing away of sins, and the restoration of humankind's original form. The prayer concludes with a doxology, which acclaims Christ's power as judge, by which he separates the good from the wicked at the end of time, further illustrating the introduction of the baptized into his kingdom.

The preface for the Mass of the Paschal vigil in the Gelasian sacramentary celebrates the regeneration into new life of the neophytes. This regeneration comes in virtue of the death and resurrection of Christ, hailed as the dawning of the light of a new day that dispels the night, as the breaking of the bonds of hell (death and the underworld), and the raising of the victorious banner of the resurrection. Sacrificial imagery is introduced by quoting the Pauline phrase "Christ our true Passover was sacrificed for us" (1 Cor. 5:7), and the Johannine acclamation of "the Lamb who has taken away the sins of the world" (John 1:29).

These two rites, Armenian and Roman, show how scriptural texts are interwoven together and how they are interwoven with prayer to interpret the meaning of baptism. The imagery of incorporation into the death, burial, and resurrection of Christ, so prominent in catechesis, is absent in both these baptismal canons, but it was introduced in other ways in the Roman liturgy.

Postscript: Current Rites

We can complete this examination of old liturgies by seeing how some current rites in revised books compare with them.[9]

---

9. For a comparison between current rites of the Roman Catholic, Episcopal, and Lutheran Churches in the United States, see Philip F. Pfatteicher, *Commentary on the Lutheran Book of Worship* (Minneapolis: Augsburg Fortress, 1990), 28–58.

In the current Roman Catholic lectionary for the Paschal vigil, at which adults are baptized, the readings given are: the creation story (Genesis), the sacrifice of Isaac (Genesis 22), the story of the crossing of the Red Sea (Exodus 14), followed by the canticle of Moses, two readings from Isaiah (54 and 55), a reading on wisdom from Baruch 3–4, a reading from Ezekiel 36 on the cleansing with water and the new covenant written on peoples' hearts, Romans 6 on baptism, and of course the proclamation of the resurrection. This retains some of the readings in the Gelasian, but introduces new ones. The most noticeable omission is that of Exodus 12 on the Paschal Lamb. The most notable introduction is the Pauline reading on baptism in the death of Christ, which leads to a share in his resurrection. The concern to relate the scriptural readings of the vigil to the death and resurrection of Christ is evident. This is also apparent in the blessing of the font, which unlike the Gelasian prayer introduces an explicit reference to sharing in the death, burial, and resurrection of Christ. Otherwise, it retains many of the old types, such as creation, the flood, the crossing of the Red Sea, and the baptism in the Jordan, as well as recalling the baptismal mandate of Matthew 28.

For baptism, the American *Lutheran Book of Worship* retains three Old Testament readings.[10] These are: the parting address of Moses to the people in Deuteronomy 30, Jeremiah 31 on the new covenant, and Ezekiel 36. These three readings omit the baptismal types but stress the covenantal character of baptism. The service book then offers a large selection of New Testament readings. Some have to do directly with baptism, such as Romans 6:3–5, Titus 3:4–8, and John 3:1–8. Others have to do with the forgiveness of sins through Christ, the new Adam (Romans 5) or life in the Spirit (Romans 8). Still others have to do with the nature of the Church (1 Pet. 2:4–10; Eph. 4:1–6; 1 Cor. 12). The choice to base baptismal teaching mainly in the New Testament is obvious, and even the Old Testament texts are not typological but underscore the reality of the covenantal people, gathered on God's merciful initiative. On the other hand, the thanksgiving over the water keeps some of the types, in particular creation, the flood, and the crossing of the Red Sea. It sustains the New Testament references to Christ's baptism in the Jordan, his baptismal mandate, the cleansing of sins, and participation in his death and resurrection.

The Presbyterian *Book of Common Worship* foresees the holding of the service of baptism during the Paschal vigil.[11] The Old Testament readings which it selects for the vigil are Genesis 1:1–2:4 (creation story), selections from Genesis 7, 8, and 9 (story of the flood), Genesis 22 (story of Abraham's sacrifice of Isaac), Exodus 14 (Israel's deliverance at the Red Sea), Isaiah 55:1–11

---

10. *Lutheran Book of Worship*, prepared by the churches participating in the Inter-Lutheran Commission on Worship (Minneapolis: Augsburg Press, 1978), 308–12.

11. *Book of Common Worship*, prepared from the Presbyterian Church (USA) and the Cumberland Presbyterian Church (Louisville: Westminster/John Knox Press, 1993), 294–314, 403–18.

(offer of salvation to all), selections from Proverbs 8 and 9 (the wisdom of God), Ezekiel 16:24–28 (a new heart and a new spirit), Ezekiel 37:1–14 (valley of the dry bones), and Zephaniah 3:14–20 (the gathering of God's people). These are completed by the Easter readings from the New Testament, and it is after them that the service of baptism occurs. In the actual baptismal service, pride of place is given to the dominical command in Matthew 28:18–20. The thanksgiving over the water incorporates the imagery of the work of the Spirit at creation, the story of the flood, the story of the crossing of the Red Sea, the baptism of Jesus in the Jordan, and the "baptism of his own death and resurrection."

From the above, we see all that is interconnected in the baptismal act: the interweaving of a selection of scriptural passages, the prayers said, and the rites performed. All of these together constitute the language event of sacrament. The action of grace runs through the whole. The meaning of this sacramental action, with its possibilities for a new life, emerges from this totality.

Place and the Visual

There is no evidence of an early baptistry for the Armenian Church with which we could compare the canon of the Armenian Rite published by Conybeare. Even the tenth-century Church of the Holy Cross at Aght'amar has left no evidence of a baptistry.[12] For the Roman Church, of course, there is the reconstruction of the baptistry of St. John Lateran, adjoining the basilica. From this we learn more about the shape and decoration of the font than about sculptures or paintings which gave life to the building. The font was octagonal, with the heads of deer at each corner, from which the water flowed into it. We also have the text that was inscribed on the wall, celebrating the mystery of baptism. This place, however, was not that which served for the celebration of the baptismal action recorded in the Gelasian sacramentary, which did not serve the papal liturgy at the Lateran.

Given the lack of more information on space for the Armenian and Gelasian canons, another example may serve us better as a starting point to show how actions and scriptural interpretation would have been affected by the shape and decor of the place of celebration. Though the Church of Naples would not have celebrated the Roman liturgy, it is of interest to note the remains in that city of a baptistry that existed prior even to the Lateran baptistry in Rome. This is the baptistry of San Giovanni *in Fontes*.[13] The baptistry was annexed to the basilica, to the right hand side of the sanctuary, with a door through which the neophytes entered for the eucharistic celebration. Its shape was octagonal, and in the dome above the font there was a

---

12. J. G. Davies, *Medieval Art and Architecture: The Church of the Holy Cross, Aght'amar* (London: Pindar Press, 1991).

13. See Jean-Louis Maier, *Le Baptistère de Naples et ses mosaïques* (Fribourg: Éditions Universitaires, 1964).

mosaic representing the monogram of Christ, the Cross with the Greek letter Rho (✗) atop it. It is placed against the background of a blue sky, illuminated by stars. A hand is placing a wreath above the Cross, a laurel of victory. On either side beneath the transept bar, there are the letters Alpha and Omega.

The Cross was surrounded, at a lower level of the ceiling, by mosaics representing biblical scenes, some of which are extant but some missing. Those extant represent the marriage feast at Cana, the encounter of Jesus at the well with the Samaritan woman, the holy women at the tomb, the miraculous draught of fish, and Christ giving the Law, with Peter and Paul accompanying him on either side. It is surmised that among the missing mosaics there was a depiction of the baptism of Jesus by John at the Jordan. Outside of this circle, there were the four winged figures of Ezekiel, representing the four evangelists.

The biblical scenes represent narratives that are associated with baptism in liturgical texts. These recur in baptistries in different locations in early Christian centuries, with greater or less prominence given to one or to the other.[14] At Dura Europos, the primary depiction, within the niche over the basin, is that of Jesus, the good shepherd, pasturing the sheep. At the baptismal pool in the cemetery of St. Pontianus in Rome, pride of place is given to the baptism of Jesus by John. This is also true of the two well-known baptistries in Ravenna.

The impact of the visual form of the baptistry on the celebration of baptism is threefold, as can be exemplified by reference to San Giovanni and other places. First is its location outside the main place of assembly, but adjacent to it. This meant that the rites of immersion and chrismation were included among the rites of liminality. The final configuration to Christ of the candidates for Church membership was completed here, and the integration into the community as full members was symbolized by the entry procession and the sharing in the eucharistic sacrifice and table. This leads us to remark that nowadays, when the adult ritual of initiation is celebrated in full view of the assembly, the meaning of these rites of immersion and consignation is changed, and the relation of the candidates to the community is differently expressed.

Second in what is visually noteworthy is the shape of the building and font.[15] At San Giovanni it was octagonal, in the center of the building and below floor level. In fact fonts could be below floor level, or built into the wall. Their shape was diverse, allowing for a circular form, hexagonal and octagonal forms, a square, a quadrilobe, a rectangle, and possibly the form of a cross (if excavations at Emmaus are reliable). The size and depth of the fonts

---

14. See Robert Milburn, *Early Christian Art and Architecture* (Berkeley: University of California Press, 1988), 203–13.

15. For a useful overview of fonts, though not of the buildings and the art, see S. Anita Stauffer, *On Baptismal Fonts: Ancient and Modern*, Alcuin/GROW Liturgical Study 29–30 (Bramcote, Nottingham: Grove Books Limited, 1994). The survey does not include San Giovanni in Naples.

differ, with different possibilities for either immersion or pouring of water over the head of the candidate. The font at Dura Europos, for example, is built into a niche in the wall and could not allow for a person to stand in it. Some think that it may have been possible to sit therein, or alternately to bend the head over it. Even with pools that allowed standing, the manner of immersion is not clear. Candidates stood in the water, which apparently was not very deep. Possibly the minister then poured water over their heads as they stood there. Possibly their heads were placed beneath the inflow of water, as would have been possible at St. John Lateran, where the water flowed in from the corners. Possibly at the crucial moment candidates were lowered into the water by the attendant minister, that is, deacon or deaconess. As can be seen, the symbolic shape of the font and the action it allowed were not universally identical. There was room, as it were, for symbolic play in relating the water rite to the mystery of Christ and to biblical symbolism, and this shows itself both in the visual aspects of the place and in the way the rite was performed.

The third noteworthy thing about the visual aspect of baptistries was their decoration. This served to represent the mystery of initiation in diverse ways, relating it to the mystery of Christ. Thus the biblical narratives painted in San Giovanni *in Fontes* relate the act of baptism to the Gospel story. The icons of the evangelists accentuate both the importance of the Word and the eschatological expectation signified in the prophecy of Ezekiel, which supplied the figures. In places where the baptism of Jesus was given primacy, the location fitted well with the paradigm evoked in the texts which we have seen in the Armenian and Roman canons. In other buildings where the ministers and candidates looked upward to the Chirogram, they were drawn into the victory of Christ's Cross and into his glory. At Dura Europos, the candidate was bathed under the watchful eye of the good shepherd leading his sheep to pasture.

This overview of baptismal services in two different canons, together with the information given about the shape and decor of baptistries, introduce us to the way in which action, scripture, prayer, and place are interwoven. Together they express the meaning of sacrament.

Interpreting Sacramental Liturgies

With this overview of liturgical interweaving, we may now ask if some insights may be had from past interpretations of sacramental rites and texts. Baptismal catechesis and the contrast between two interpretations of the Roman Canon can serve as good examples, keeping in mind the problems that these raise for us today.

Baptismal Catechesis

In the mystagogical catechesis of the fourth and fifth centuries, the typological interpretation of both scripture and rite was prevalent, and the two were closely related. What was told of in the scriptures was enacted through the sacramental rites. Indeed liturgy was a privileged place within which to interpret the scriptures, precisely because in it the scriptures were proclaimed as the scriptures of the believing community and their meaning was clarified by being related to the ritual celebration of the mystery of Christ. The scriptures themselves were closely woven together, since they were all read, both Old and New Testament, in relation to Christ. This manner of interweaving the texts of the sacred book is clear from the examples of the two rites just presented. The catechesis and the scriptural selection show the same approach to the Word of God and the mystery of the two testaments.

That this is the background to the choice of scriptures for sacramental celebration is a problem today, when scriptural exegesis gives more attention to literal meanings, to historical reconstruction, and to literary forms. It is not possible to be as sure of the intention in the original event of the Pasch as were early and medieval commentators, nor to read the crossing of the Red Sea purely and simply as a type of salvation through the waters of baptism. These stories are about a people, a people that lived then and a people that lives now by the memorial of this event for what it is in itself, not for what it says of Christ and Christians. However much the events and passages of both testaments may be linked as stories of salvation, they cannot be reduced to a single overarching reading.

Present-day readers and hearers of the scriptures, who have some background in exegesis, may well be struck by a sense of discontinuity when faced with the current lectionary selections. There is historical discontinuity between Judaism and Christianity and between their respective readings of the Hebrew and sapiential scriptures. There is also discontinuity between early Christian and current readings of both testaments, and more deeply a discontinuity in the sense of the history of salvation. Hearing the reading about the Paschal Lamb and about Christ's death in the same celebration, it is not possible to resort to the easy typology of early Christian interpreters. There is in effect a historical discontinuity between them, introduced by the division between the Jewish people and the Church. The Paschal Lamb is *not* in and of itself a type of Jesus Christ, whatever may be done by way of drawing on the imagery of this story to convey the salvific intent of Christ's death and shedding of his blood.

Even if the texts are related to the mystery of Christ and its celebration, there is need for a fresh reading. When the story of the passage through the Red Sea and of the drowning of Pharaoh's army is heard as a baptismal allegory and the congregation responds with merriment, acclaiming in song the hurling of horse and rider into the sea, the effect is highly disturbing to anyone not given to this sort of typological interpretation. How can it be that God's lordship over Israel demanded such awful slaughter? Is there no thought in hearing this story for the Egyptian soldiers? That God sets a people free belongs to the revelation of the divine name, but what does it mean that the freedom of one people has to be bought in God's name only through the destruction of some earthly power? What helplessness is there in seeing that the proclamation of the one true God brings such bloodshed with it? How does the memory of such events, so intrinsic to the transmission of our faith, both disturb and challenge us in a century of the slaughter meted out to one another by neighboring nations?

A different reading of this text, in fact, suggests that the freedom which God promises and grants and which a people claims in God's name is opposed by temporal forces and often results therefore in violent clash, where the claim to freedom and the claim to dominate are at odds. Unhappily, the invocation of God's name in this world inevitably occurs within such contexts, and even the believer is caught in the temptation to dominate in turn, with the difficult option of seeking the way of peace and reconciliation. This may well indeed fit into a hearing of the Word that prepares for baptism, but not in the easy manner of a spiritualized allegorical interpretation. Hence the community is compelled to ask what this really says of God, if it be within the compass of naming the divine and within the compass of divine self-gift that such episodes occur and are even set down "for our edification." The stories recounted may be such that they disturb as much as they console and have to be heard and received as stories that claim faith in the redeeming God within the harsh realities of power structuring, of claim and counterclaim, that human societies breed.

The New Testament texts also have to be read with more attention to their content and form. The passion narratives, for example, cannot be reduced to one synchronized story or some kind of comprehensive grand narrative. Each of the narratives offers its own unique way into the passion of Jesus Christ. The same is true of the resurrection narratives. Each of the four accounts of the Last Supper also has its own irreducible characteristics, and this diversity or polysemy is increased when due thought is given to the testamentary tradition of the washing of the feet in the Johannine Gospel. The way of discipleship is also opened up in diverse ways through the parables and sayings of Jesus. Symbolic reductionism is not workable in sacramental celebrations which include scriptural readings, and hearers have to be open to the "conflict" of texts as they make their journey into the mystery of Christ.

Sacramental Prayer: Two Interpretations of the Roman Canon

What becomes clear in these two interpretations of the same prayer for the eucharistic liturgy is how far prejudgments have played a part. The two examples are the commentary of Odo of Cambrai on the Roman Canon, and Martin Luther's attack on this same prayer.

Odo of Cambrai

Odo of Cambrai was abbot of Cambrai and later archbishop of Tournai in the eleventh century.[16] In his commentary on the Canon, he has reduced the essential exposition of the Mass to its presentation, and even that he takes, as commonly understood at the time, to begin after the Sanctus with the Te igitur. The commentary extended thus from the offering made in the opening portion or prayer to the consummation of the sacrifice with the kiss of peace. The gloss on the text of the Te igitur shows clearly what he had in mind:

> *Therefore we ask you, most merciful Father,* that you may accept the sacrifice from us. And because you admit our voices to be joined in suppliant confession, *we suppliantly ask you, most merciful Father, through Jesus Christ your Son,* to accept this real sacrifice, so that the substantial sacrifice may follow the praises of our voices.[17]

Odo here refers to the singing of the Sanctus, seeing in it the sacrifice of praise foretold in Malachi 1:11, in order to contrast it with the real sacrifice offered through the Canon. This sacrifice is that of the body and blood of Christ, of those very gifts (*dona*) which the Father gives the Church to offer. Consequently commenting on the words of the Supper narrative, beginning at *Qui pridie*, it is the change of the bread and wine into the body and blood of Christ by the action of blessing and the words of Christ which Odo stresses. It is because of the faith in the change that takes place in the elements that the Church can offer sacrifice, whether as a congregation of clergy and people, or as a solitary monk celebrating in a communion of faith and prayer with the whole Church. Expounding on the words over the chalice, Odo concludes:

> And because this faith is one throughout the whole Church, he is one who is then and now offered; therefore the chalice also is accepted, and it is one by divine words, just as it is said that there is one altar in all Churches, because on that altar, according to one faith, one sacrifice of the body of the Lord is daily offered.[18]

Odo expounds on the entire Canon, both before and after the words of the narrative, in light of the twofold insight given in his explanation of the words and blessing of Christ: the bread and wine are changed substantially into the body and blood of Christ, and they are given to the Church by God both

---

16. Odonis Cameracensis *Expositio in Canonem Missae,* PL 160: 1053–70.

17. *Te igitur, clementissime Pater,* rogamus, ut a nobis sacrificium accipias. Et quia nostras voces supplici confessione admittis, *Te igitur, clementissime Pater, per Jesus Christum Filium tuum supplices rogamus,* et reale sacrificium acceptari, ut laudes vocum substantiale sequatur sacrificium (PL 160: 1055).

18. Et quia haec fides una est in tota ecclesia, et ille unus est tunc et modo offertur; ideo et calix accipitur, etiam ad divina verba est unus, sicut et omnium ecclesiarum altare dicitur unum, quia in eo secundum unam fidem, unum Dominici corporis offertur quotidie sacrificium (PL 160: 1062).

to be offered and to be consumed. Since he gives little attention to externals or to actions (apart from the stress on the word *benedixit,* which for him meant the action with the hand which the priest used in the Mass order of the time), the accent of his commentary is first on the truth of dogma, that is, substantial change and sacrifice, and then on the inner spiritual attitude of service with which the offering is to be made. This reflects intense devotion to God, deep faith in Christ and in his memorial, and a communion of faith with all the Church, which unites those not physically present to each other as much as it unites the members of an assembled congregation. Right through the commentary, it is a mixture of dogma and devotion which guides Odo.

Martin Luther

In turning from Odo to Martin Luther's tract *On the Abomination of the Secret Mass,* which is also a commentary on the Roman Canon, one finds all Odo's positions reversed.[19] For Luther there can be no sacrificial offering, whether of the Church's gifts and prayers or of the body and blood of Christ. Luther was of course acquainted with the commentary of Biel on the Canon,[20] with the stipendiary system of the era, and with the manner of celebration affected by priests, which was often much related to monetary gain and to promises made to the faithful of the benefits of the Mass. Hence his commentary on the Canon is a diatribe against sacrifice and offering and amounts to condemnation of the entire prayer. Of the prayer Unde et memores, where indeed Odo found an offering to God of the gifts given to the Church by God through the consecration, Martin says:

> The priest offers up once again the Lord Christ, who offered himself only once, just as he died only once and cannot die again or be offered up again. For through his one death and sacrifice he has taken away and swallowed up all sins. Yet they go ahead and every day offer him up more than a hundred thousand times throughout the world.[21]

Luther and Odo evidently find the same meaning in this prayer, but judge it differently, given their diverse ways of reading the Supper account of the New Testament. For Odo, it is this gift and offering which Christ left to his Church, and hence the Church rightly offers with faith and devotion, and in memory of Christ's death. For Martin, the words of Jesus are, however, a testament, as he had already expounded them in *A Treatise on the Mass, That Is, the New Testament.*[22] It is the inheritance and promise of the forgiveness

---

19. Martin Luther, "The Abomination of the Secret Canon," *Luther's Works* (Philadelphia: Fortress Press, 1959), 35:311–28.

20. Gabriel Biel, *Literalis et mystica missae expositio,* ed. H. A. Oberman and W. J. Courtenay, 5 vols. (Wiesbaden, 1963–76).

21. Ibid., 320.

22. *Luther's Works,* 35:75–112.

of sins that is given in the words over the bread, "Take and eat, this is my body, which is given for you." He chides the Canon for leaving out the words "given for you," thus obscuring the sense of the donation or gift in order to uphold the meaning of substantial change and sacrifice. Of the words over the cup, he remarks that the priests do not obey them, since they deny the chalice to the laity, favoring all the time offering. The institution narrative must be proclaimed as the Lord's testament and inheritance, the assurance of the forgiveness of sins through his sacrifice on the Cross. The communion in the body and blood, truly present, is but the seal and sacrament of this testament. The words of forgiveness predominate; the sacrament is necessarily related to these words. There can be no sacrifice of the Mass in the true and proper sense.

After Luther's attack, the Catholic apologists included the defense of the Canon in their defense of the true and propitiatory nature of the eucharistic sacrifice.[23] They of course found terms of offering in the prayer in abundance and were quite undiscriminating in the meaning which they gave to them. This carried over into the debates of the Council of Trent and into its eventual defense of the Canon in its decree on the Sacrifice of the Mass. The curious thing about these apologetic writings is that writers found it necessary to give an apostolic origin to the Roman Canon, with considerable contortions, since for them it constituted a potent argument from tradition for the propitiatory nature of the sacrifice of the Mass. But it is clearly their adherence to a belief that determines the interpretation rather than an attention to words giving the meaning to belief.

Conclusion

From the two commentaries we learn how interpretation of a liturgical text is determined by what each commentator believes to be done in the liturgical mystery. Even in doing a detailed reading or analysis of a text, Odo and Martin Luther were guided by dominant beliefs or systems to which the text is to be related. The meaning of the whole prevails over literary exegesis. Today, when the Roman Canon is considered in its genesis and according to its literary structure, neither the blessed Martin nor the monk-bishop would be taken to be correct in his interpretation.[24] The same is true for their readings of the Supper narrative in the scriptural text or in the liturgical tradition. For all that, we know that each author placed the reading of the text into the context of celebration, and it was also the celebration which guided their understanding of the Supper narrative cited within the prayer. They also related the parts of the rite to the whole, each item in the place, each

---

23. See David N. Power, "The Priestly Prayer: The Tridentine Theologians and the Roman Canon," *Fountain of Life*, ed. Gerard Austin (Washington, D.C.: Pastoral Press, 1991), 131–64.

24. On the Roman Canon, see Enrico Mazza, *The Origins of the Eucharistic Prayer*, trans. Ronald E. Lane (Collegeville, Minn.: Liturgical Press, 1995), 240–86.

word, each ritual action, taking on a meaning within their vision of what the Eucharist is.

Looking at these commentaries raises the question of current prejudgments and understandings that are brought to sacramental celebration. First, if we attend to what is found in the traditions examined we have to ask with what faith and belief may we ourselves celebrate. We cannot choose one approach as correct and dismiss the other as wrong, but neither can we reconcile their diverging points of view. Second, we need to ask what beliefs or systems dominate in congregations that hear and pray the same or similar texts. The liturgical texts and rites as such do not yield the operative meanings. Performance, inclusive of ritualization, and the community's meaningful reference points need to be grasped. If the traditional doctrinal or theological approaches, found in different confessions and Churches, do not seem to satisfy, in what way can a contemporary congregation affirm and nourish its faith in its celebration of the Pasch of Christ and the Church's participation in it? We will also recognize that the reading of the scriptural texts which relate to the sacraments are influenced by the celebration and by beliefs about them.

Leo the Great as Mystagogue

Many commentaries on the rites and texts of initiation are known to us, so we could go back to figures such as Origen, Ambrose, or Cyril of Jerusalem for examples of sacramental interpretation. However, we choose rather to look at Leo the Great's interpretation of sacramental ordination, placing it in the context of his general approach to sacramental liturgy.

The sermons of Leo the Great for the anniversary of his ordination as bishop of Rome exemplify an interpretation of liturgy which integrates the proclamation and reading of the scriptural text into the meaning of the sacrament.[25] The texts to which his sermons refer belong either to ordination rites or to the marking of an episcopal anniversary in Rome. These are Matthew 16:13–19, on Peter's commission as the primary text; 1 Peter 2:4–10, on the priesthood of the Church; Hebrew 7, on the priesthood of Christ, which he collates with John 17:11; Psalm 110 [111], interpreted as God's consecration of the Son as priest; Psalm 114 [115], as a thanksgiving prayer for the mission and the grace received by the ordained.

In these sermons, as in others, Leo looks upon the liturgy as *sacramentum et exemplum* of the mystery of Christ, now actively participated by the Christian people.[26] The *sacramentum* is the mystery expressed in the liturgical symbols, with reference to the events told and remembered in the scriptures, to the fulfillment of this mystery in the glorification of Christ in which the

---

25. Leo the Great, *Tractatus in Natale eiusdem*, 1-V, CC 138, 1–25.
26. On this, see M. de Soos, *Le mystère liturgique d'après saint Léon le Grand* (Münster: Aschendorff, 1958).

saints are joined with him, and to what now takes place in the Church through the liturgy. It is not only sacrament or symbol, but it is also *exemplum* because it acts as a form imprinted on the Christian life and is the root of Christian action that configures the people to Christ himself. The mystery of Christ is thus present not simply in the liturgy, but in the lives of those who live by this configuration. It is the power and intercession of the risen Lord, the eternal priest, which brings about this configuration through the liturgical action.

When Leo explains how this sacramental action works, leaving its imprint on Christian life, he points to the entire liturgical action, in all its moments, with a key role played by scripture. The people of Rome gather for the anniversary of their bishop as the priesthood of the elect of Christ (1 Peter 2:4–10). They gather at the tomb of Peter, which is the living sign of Peter's presence in this Church of which he was the first bishop. They gather around their bishop, to celebrate their own priesthood and the special mission given to him in virtue of the mandate and authority which Christ gave to Peter. The power of the sacramental action, for Leo, comes first from the proclamation of the Gospel and the sermon which serves and protracts the action of God's word in the Gospel. This power thus announced is then exercised in the rites performed and in the prayer of the assembly and of the ordained minister. Finally, it continues to act in its power as *exemplum* in and through the lives of all those gathered.

Leo's exposition of Matthew 16:13–19 illustrates how the scriptural word comprehends and forms the mystery celebrated, and then lived, in various ways. According to him, the firmness of Peter's faith, here at Philippi confirmed by Christ, is the foundation on which the Church is built. It is communicated to the other apostles by Peter, who with him share the mission to pass it on to the faithful. It is thus on this faith, expressed by bishops and by people, that the Church continues to be founded. In the liturgy, by the very word of Christ proclaimed in the Gospel, this faith is confirmed in the bishop ordained, as well as in the faithful who look to him as teacher and leader. In their different ranks, as Leo sees it, all share in the priesthood of Jesus Christ, and thus in his glory and in the power of his heavenly intercession. In the Church of Rome, this has a particular force and significance which comes from the presence of the tomb of Peter and from his patronage of this Church. Peter shares in the agency of Christ in the ordination of Rome's bishop, because through the glorification of his own martyrdom he now shares in Christ's own glory and intercedes for the Church along with him. The Church of Rome, according to Leo, has a special role among the Churches since it was founded on the two great apostles, Peter and Paul. The proclamation of the Gospel and its sacrament therefore has a special resonance in the liturgy of this Church. The mission of Peter is confided in a special way to this Church and especially to its chief pastor and extends through this proclamation and sacrament to the other Churches and their bishops. The prayers of the liturgy, for ordination and for its anniversary, in their communion with the priesthood of Christ carry the mission and the mandate of the Gospel into the priestly intercession of the Church, so that the *exemplum* is formed in the minds and hearts of all, according to their place in the Church.

In elaborating on the scriptural proclamation and its effect in the sacramental celebration, Leo takes the entire celebration into account and links the proclamation and interpretation of the Gospel to the rest of the liturgy, as an integral whole. While he is careful in his reading of the text and in collating it with other scriptural texts, his sermons also show the influence and integration of certain ecclesial and cultural perspectives. The notion of patronage attributed to Peter has its antecedents in Roman civil practices, as well as in the veneration of those dead who are considered to continue to befriend their descendants. While he is very careful to show how the mystery of Christ, and especially the mystery proclaimed in this Gospel, is verified in the lives of all, Leo adopts terms for authority from Roman law to explain the ordering of the Church and the role of its bishop.

In all of this, the sermons of Leo are a good example of how scripture has been interpreted in the past as an active part of sacramental liturgy, not simply as an antecedent to it. They are also a good example of how participation in the mystery of Christ has to do not only with worship but more fully with a life lived as a share in this truth and example.

Conclusion

The examples of rite and interpretation given in this chapter show how complex sacramental celebration is in itself, what was involved in interpreting sacramental texts at given moments of history, and how belief, scripture, and sacramental action were seen in relation to one another. In this way, they are a good introduction to a more formal discussion of the ritual action, the verbal polyphony, the visual components of celebration, and the ongoing interpretation of sacrament, that occupies the following chapters.

— Chapter Four —

Ritual Action:
The Sacramental Body

Participation in the language event of Christian sacrament is grounded in bodily ritual. The memorial of the Pasch is kept through ritual actions that are celebrated with the common earthly elements of bread, wine, oil, and water. It is around these that communities are gathered together and around them that the word is heard and the sending of the Spirit invoked. What is done with these things expresses the reality of being community and of its being in the world. What is proclaimed by the word is given symbolic focus in the blessing and in the use and transformation of ritual elements in ritual actions.

One of the criticisms of Enlightenment philosophy, with its effect on human disciplines and on the use of language, is that it fostered a disjunction between mind and body. There has also been some criticism of the liturgical renewal of the last few decades which accuses it of being behavioristic, relating bodily action to mental knowledge, rather than allowing the body its own perceptions and activity. It is the work of sacramental theology to redress this impasse and to give due place to the corporeal in the expression of faith and in enacting ecclesial communion.[1] This means allowing for a renewed interest in ritual as a bodily action, which is to be related to the words used, but not to be seen as simply enacting what words signify.

In looking at the canons of baptism in the Gelasian sacramentary and in the Armenian Rite, we have already noted the ritual components of each and how they are interwoven with word. This attention to specific rites serves as a good background to this chapter on ritual, which is divided into four major sections. First, something is said about developing bodily ritual in a period of change in sacramental liturgies. Second, a relation between community ritual and corporate memory is examined. Third, there is the topic of the place of bodily ritual in developing community and social belonging. In the fourth section, the discussion is about the relation between ritual and being in time, and what this says to keeping memorial of Christ.

---

1. For an overview of this concern in sacramental theology, see Aldo Natale Terrin, ed., *Liturgia e incarnazione* (Padua: Edizioni Messagero Padova, Abbazia di Santa Giustina, 1997).

Bodily Ritual and Sacramental Renewal

It is commonplace knowledge that the bodily, both in materials used and in action, is essential to sacrament. The sacramental order is built around bodily actions done in bread, wine, oil, and water, actions performed in giving and receiving the body/self in marriage, and the giving or receiving the laying on of hands in other sacraments. The bodily rite belongs to sacrament as sign, and for theories of causality of course also as cause, and no age has ever neglected this factor, but it has been approached in different ways. Interpreting bodily rites, however, raises particular problems in a period of ritual change and cultural transition, so this needs to be noted, having in mind the issues raised in the first chapter.

To put the question in focus, some historical questions are first revised. Then something is said about contemporary issues and controversies over bodily posture.

Scholastic Theology

Some questions of interest arise already from considering differences of opinion in scholastic theology on why the use of material signs is intrinsic to the sacraments instituted by Christ. Bonaventure, for example, following the line of thought pursued by Hugo of St. Victor, focused on the medicinal and remedial character of sacraments as corporeal and visible signs.[2] Their role lies in healing the breach between body and soul and in controlling the passions that sought satisfaction counter to the domination of spirit. As Hugo had explained it, the institution of sacraments was a remedy against the ignorance born of too much attention to the body, and its celebration was a discipline to learn anew the ways of right and proportionate action in matters of body and mind.[3] It was also a humiliation for one who thought to attain all knowledge by the mastering of all things material. Thomas Aquinas, on the other hand, while he found place for these explanations of sacramental medicine and discipline, gave a more radical place to sacrament in the divine economy. The root reason for having corporeal sacraments, according to him, lies in human nature itself as created by God, for it is only through the body and the imagination that humans have any access to knowledge or to the life of the spirit.[4]

From this divergence in explaining the purpose of the bodily act in sacrament, questions arise about the signification of bodily action in itself. What does it add to the meaning of the words, precisely as a corporeal sign? At times, Thomas seemed to take the bodily action as simple illustration of a spiritual meaning, as, for example, when he pointed to washing in water as

---

2. See Bonaventure, *Breviloquium* VI,1.

3. Hugo of St. Victor, *De Sacramentis Fidei* II, 3: PL 176: 319–22. He also related this to the history of redemption as restoration.

4. Thomas Aquinas, *Summa Theologiae* III, q. 61, art. 1.

sign of a spiritual cleansing.[5] Over all, his insight into the role of sense and imagination in intellectual understanding posited the foundation for later theology. It is of the very nature of human existence to relate to even the highest realities through the body, and this order of things is integrated into the economy of grace.

Sacramental Character Revisited

In the traditional doctrine of the sacramental character there is insight into the fact that through the interaction of body and word communion in faith is ingrained as communion in a social body. The character was said to express a person's relations to the Church and to arise from the celebration of the sacraments of baptism, confirmation, and order. These marked forever the recipient's place among the people of God, with ritual and social implications for all the members. Augustine and Thomas Aquinas both explained this belonging through a relation to the Church's worship.[6]

St. Augustine, in upholding the permanency of the sacrament of baptism, compared its lasting effect to the brand or character on the forehead of a soldier. Once baptized, one always belongs to the visible institution of the Church and will be recognized as a member. However, if one does not partake in a communion of charity in the faith, worship, and actions of the Church, this marking out is at a loss for meaning. St. Thomas's approach to the issue of the character was to say that baptism introduces one into the corporate worship of the Church and its exercise of Christ's priesthood. Introduced by this sacrament to a place in the Church which is visibly apparent, the recipient is also armed with the knowledge of its signs and with the faith that allows participation. The distinctions of the character of confirmation and of that of order have to do with the different places given in the one body to its different members. It is in relation to the Church as a visible and corporate institution, which engages at its heart in worship, that this traditional insight has been more recently explored with the help of anthropological insights into rite and body.

Ecumenical Perspectives

During the sixteenth century and beyond, Protestant liturgies and Catholic liturgies divided over the respective roles of word and sign. There was a theoretical basis to this in the controversies engaged in the twenties of that century between Martin Luther and the Catholic apologists.[7] Luther's reaction against the dominance of act and body over the hearing of the word was involved in his attack on the theory of *ex opere operato* efficacy as he

---

5. Ibid., q. 66, art. 1.

6. Explained in clear and concise fashion in Edward Schillebeeckx, *Christ the Sacrament of Encounter with God* (Kansas City: Sheed Andrews & McMeel, 1963), 153–73.

7. For these controversies, see David V. N. Bagchi, *Luther's Earliest Opponents: Catholic Controversialists 1518–1525* (Minneapolis: Fortress, 1991), especially 118–46.

saw it implemented. In itself, this medieval scholastic theorem, upheld by the apologists, was designed to underscore the work of Christ in the sacrament rather than that of the minister or of the believer. This in itself sits well with Luther's concerns. However, for him the way in which this theory affected practice seemed to downgrade the role of word and faith and to attach an efficacy to the rite itself, even regardless of faith in Christ. It was for him an issue of the primacy of God's Word, spoken in Christ, and of the truth of justification through faith in Christ's Cross, something which he thought displaced by the focus on ritual.

In recent decades, there has been some meeting of the ways. Catholic theologians recovered an understanding of the power of the Word, often rooting this in biblical study available to scholars across denominational boundaries. This influenced practice in the promotion of scriptural proclamation within sacramental liturgy, as it influenced a catechesis which unites a scriptural catechesis with a mystagogy of sacramental rite. For their part, Anglican and Protestant scholars have attended to the power of sign and symbol in sacramental celebration. With this ecumenical convergence in theory and a growing convergence in the practices of celebration, there is a new desire to appreciate the power of symbol and rite more fully. This is helped by an appeal on all sides to philosophical, cultural, and anthropological sciences. Such modern interest is of course now quickly overtaken by post[-]modern quandaries, so that the ambiguity and polysemy of both word and rite, as well as of their intersection, come to the fore.

Current Issues

The 1994 Roman Instruction on Inculturation devoted a section to gestures and other bodily factors in liturgy, noting these as an important area of adaptation.[8] Similar materials and gestures do not mean the same thing for every people. Thus the document adverted to the fields of sound, music, instrument, and material things, as culturally differentiated and hence "adaptable." On the other hand, it repeated that no adaptation can touch the essence of a sacrament, including what authentic tradition has determined to be materially essential to it.

The signification and cultural adaptability of the bodily element in sacrament is not addressed without controversy. One example illustrates the point. In North America at present there are acrimonious disputes over whether the congregation ought to kneel or stand during the eucharistic prayer, with the episcopacy inclined to advocate kneeling. This is said to express greater reverence for the presence of Christ in the sacrament. Consequently, ancient voices, such as those of Justin Martyr and Basil of Caesarea, which spoke for standing in communion with the risen Christ, are not considered and apparently counted irrelevant.

---

8. As cited previously, p. 21 above.

Arguing in scholastic fashion, one could say that this is inconsequential, or at least does not touch on the essence of the sacrament. However, it has everything to do with its signification and with participation in it, and in this sense is indeed, in more colloquial terms, an essential matter. This is not to say that one has to choose between one position or the other as the necessarily correct one, but what is conveyed needs careful consideration. In this particular case, the divergence in posture at the Eucharist is not even simply a choice between standing and kneeling. In some countries sitting on the ground would be the most reverential attitude to adopt for so important a prayer.

Christian sacramental rites have a center in the sharing of a loaf and a cup, an immersion in water, uses of oil for anointing and soothing, and the touch of hands. At the same time, there is more to sacramental signification than the minimal assignment of matter and form, whereby some few words and a slight bodily action are isolated from the rest of the service. As more attention needs to be given theologically to the entire use of word in sacramental liturgy, so also more attention has to be given to the complex bodily action.

A further factor is the need to express gender differentiation adequately in the symbolism of the body, personal and corporate. On the one hand, the particularity of women's experience tends to be submerged within a sea of masculine structure and symbol system. On the other hand, often when it is symbolized, or at least spoken of in connection with sacraments, a way of understanding the feminine is adopted that is gender biased. Feminist theology and women's celebrations are therefore factors to be taken into conversation in sacramental theology.

Ritual and Corporate Memory

Current liturgical studies draw on the anthropology and sociology of ritual. A great deal has been learned of the role of the body in rite and tradition from African customs and African scholars. Greater place for body movement is also found in the northern hemisphere through learning from African American, Native American, and Hispanic ritual performance. Women speak of and express embodiment in ways that demand attention.[9]

Rites are a primary way of passing on a tradition, its ordering of the world, and its wisdom, and for initiating the young into a community. They are ways of achieving harmony with the order and rhythms of the universe and of keeping in touch with the spirits of the dead. In ritual practices, the use of certain substances, of bodily rhythms, of music, and of masks are all noted and can provide analogies for inquiry into Christian liturgy.

---

9. See Susan A. Ross, "God's Embodiment and Women," in *Freeing Theology: The Essentials of Theology in Feminist Perspective,* ed. Catherine Mowry LaCugna (San Francisco: HarperSanFrancisco, 1993), 185–209.

What are the legitimate and enlightening aspects of the insights thus gained for interpreting Christian traditions? To treat the issue in a helpful way, so that the focus is truly on the place of the body in rite, several steps will be taken. First, it will be shown how ritual belongs to the constitution of the Church in its relation to tradition. Second, some consideration will be given to the relation between memory and body. Third, the notion of distanciation, which has been operative in looking at the role of writing, will be applied to sacramental practice.

The Church Writes Itself

The French philosopher Stanislas Breton, in order to find a metaphor to enlighten what it means to see the Church as a people and a community, has used the wonderful expression "the Church writes itself."[10] The phrase means that as a corporate and visible reality and in obedience to its tradition, the Church determines its form and historical being in every place and age, especially through its institutions, its customs, its sacramental life, its devotions, and its life-witness. Breton relates this to the fact that the Church has been given the Gospel in written form, so that the primary source of its tradition is something written. As such, this continues across centuries and across cultures at the heart of the Church, but it always stands in need of being fleshed out in practice. Drawing from its written heritage, the Church continues to develop its sacramental life, its institutions, its customs, its living testimonies, and its ongoing stories. It continually takes bodily shape through these factors, which are bound to tradition but also of their nature open to some change, within the passage of time and within the passage from one people to another.

The metaphor of "writing itself" expresses this being within tradition. As writing gives form to a blank page, so the Church gives form to itself as a people, drawing on the heritage passed on to it, and working from the traces of God's actions that are written on the pages of the scriptures. The writing now, however, is not simply on the page of a codex, but it is a writing in the flesh and life of those who at different epochs and in different cultures make up the Church.

In considering the force of this metaphor, one may distinguish three kinds of body that coalesce within the community of the Church.[11] The first is the body/self of each and all the members. The second is the social body that supports community. The third is the reality of the Church as the body of Christ, presence and sign of God's saving action in the world and one with the Trinity in its eternal communion. The first and second are related to the third and form themselves within the life of this reality of Christ's body. At

---

10. Stanislas Breton, *Écriture et révélation* (Paris: Éd. du Cerf, 1979), 131–52.

11. This is developed by Louis-Marie Chauvet, *Symbole et sacrement: Une relecture sacramentelle de l'existence chrétienne* (Paris: Éd. du Cerf, 1987), 206–32.

the same time, it is only within the first and second that the body of Christ takes shape.

Bodily Memory

This leads into a consideration of the body as the bearer of memory, something that can be said either of the individual body or of the social body. The bodily impact of ritual can be compared to the marks on a body which are embedded into the flesh and continue to enlarge and take shape as the body grows. An excellent example of this are the scars of initiation rites left on the face or torso or back, or even the limbs, of initiates among some African and Asian peoples. These are marks of identity, significant both to the bearer and to the rest of the people. As such, they are marks which are legendary, that is, that can be read as signifying and bearing the history and beliefs of the culture.

This example illustrates, beyond the fact of such markings, the force of bodily ritual, even that which does not leave a physical mark. While we might most readily think of memories as stored in the mind, they arise in the body and have an abiding place in the physiognomy of the person. In adulthood, one remembers in physical and emotive reactions some of the events, practices, and rites of childhood. If a child learns from sad experience to fear dogs, even as an adult this person reacts in the body to the presence of dogs, due to the physically imbedded memory. If one was accustomed in an English childhood to eat with fork in the left hand, accustoming oneself to the American right-hand use or the Asian use of fingers remains even after years of usage in some tension with the more instinctive habit.

The anthropological comparison invites reflection on the bodily impact of Christian rites. The Church's sacraments leave no visible traces on the bodies of agents or recipients. They do have psychosomatic effect, so that in this way members carry about in their bodies the marks of Christ and of his Spirit and the memory of Christian belief. Some rites performed only once leave a lasting bodily, psychosomatic memory, because of the force and power of the ritual complex. Most adults who have no memory of baptism because they were baptized in infancy have lasting memories of first communion. Given how they were instructed at the time, maybe some never get used to letting the consecrated bread touch their teeth. More importantly, the memory is of how they were related to family and to Church through this rite. Those baptized as adults will always be inclined to tell stories of the catechumenate and of that particular Paschal Night when they received the sacraments. The plunging into the water, the touch of hands, the scent of oil remain vivid in such memories and their recounting.

Other rites are purposely repetitive and work their way into persons as actions almost instinctively performed. When a community assembles for Eucharist, the people stand, kneel, process, and the like, without having to consider what to do next, because their bodies have the rites inscribed on them. We know more about the force and the implications of this from the recent liturgical history of negotiating change. The changes in rites meant bodily and emotive unlearning and relearning, to which some indeed have never accommodated themselves.

Bodily Performance

Sacramental actions embrace different modes of communication and authoritative reference. The purpose of communication is always to bring people into interaction and to assist in the forming of societies and communities, and for this oral and interface exchange is needed. The form of the oral, however, differs. In any cultural setting, elements of primary and of secondary orality go together, but in different mixes, and this is pertinent both to interpretation and to appropriation. There are situations of strong oral exchange in any culture, but to understand how they fit into the overall pattern of cultural communication is important to the ways of dealing with sacramental tradition.

Liturgy brings people together in a way in which they share the spoken and the ritual action. Humans cannot honor God only in their hearts, but must do so with their lips. God is not deemed to act sacramentally, except through the body and through the lips. In normal circumstances the use of oral forms has a social and communal impact, whether in passing on tradition, creating tradition, or binding a gathering around what is proclaimed. This retains a particular importance within a people of digital culture, for what the liturgy continues to do is to gather them around the elements of bread, wine, oil, and water, so that the possible depersonalization of the digital is gainsaid within the face-to-face of encounter and the search for the spirit that binds and unites.

There was a time when in Catholic sacramental liturgy the only voice heard in church was the male voice. Nowadays, women are heard reading, singing, and praying aloud, but never from the presider's chair, nor over the sacramental elements. This is officially considered foreordained by Christ and justified by the use of bride/bridegroom symbolism that is attached to a body experience that belongs in a society wedded to a particular, historically determined way of ordering public relations between man and woman. Bringing woman's embodiment and the female voice into sacramental ritual has considerable significance for the integrity of Christian ritual.

Music and Ritual Memory

Music is an essential part of bodily performance and corporate memory. With regards to this, ethnomusicology has shown how it belongs within an entire cultural system of signs, perceptions, and values, or in other words how musical texts and usage have to be interpreted within the cultural system to which they give sound.[12] One of the things that emerges from such studies is that music is a movement of the body, first a sound within the body and next one that is one with bodily posture and action. In its own way, this principle has always been inherent in liturgical composition in that different kinds of chant and musical expression belonged to different moments of the liturgical action.

Vocal and instrumental music accompany and assist, or on the contrary weaken, the effectiveness of either primary or secondary orality by bringing the body into tune with the expression of the words, and the words into tune with the expression of the body. Sounds that catch the harmony of the human with the rhythms of the universe go with primary orality, since they express the oneness of human being with the being of things. Sound can also bring to body expression the feeling of disjunction that in many respects marks the person's relation to things, thus deepening the sense of discordant concordance with which humans contend and which they try to resolve. Other types of vocal and instrumental sound are more distanced from primary feelings, and more reflective, so that they go with that reflection on what has been proclaimed, which is of the nature of secondary orality.

Among scholars of liturgical music and chant, there are different approaches to its relation to sacramental worship. One can be called functionalist, in that it interprets and assesses pieces directly in relation to the ritual action. In this way, music is thought to accompany rites and the meaning derives from the text or from the ritual action, not primarily from the music itself. There is likewise the opposite approach, which is to take music as self-referential, listening to it to see what relation to body it has and in a particular way what kind of living relation to being in time it suggests. A third approach can be called referentialist. Its practitioners emphasize the internal relation of song and music to culture. They locate musical composition and rendition to the symbolic world of a culture, looking for its meaning as it fits into the gamut of symbolic references found therein. For liturgy, of course, this would have to be another very important area for the encounter between the Gospel and a culture, between the Christian sacramental system and cultures.

Music today, in a time of cultural transition, serves to enhance a sense of dissonance with the socially and culturally acceptable or with the meaning and events of the times. Taking one example, Richard Fragomeni has written of some contemporary music of mass death as a dissonant composition that jars the collective memory. In some Jewish and Christian compositions, it emerges as sound form that "takes older forms and texts and strains to discover the power of the memory it seeks to communicate by twisting a

---

12. A helpful article summarizing positions on the relation of Church music to culture is that by Mark P. Bangert, "Dynamics of Liturgy and World Musics: A Methodology for Evaluation," in *Worship and Culture in Dialogue: Reports of International Consultations, Cartigny, Switzerland, 1993, Hong Kong, 1994,* ed. S. Anita Stauffer (Geneva: Lutheran World Federation, 1994), 183–203.

new sound and a new form of communication."[13] When a liturgical community needs to explore the Word anew, to probe it and recast it in face of its own experienced reality, this kind of musical sound may serve to deepen the corporate and body-centered involvement in this search.

Timing and Ritual Participation

The memory and the sense of time expressed in bodily ritual involves in performance a proper sense of ritual timing. The rhythms of body movement and the rhythms of sound are meant to enhance the high moments of ritual, not to create a kind of ritual impertinence by drawing attention away from them. Something is wrong when movement and sound so take up the congregation at other moments of liturgical action that the table sharing, the immersion in water, the anointing with oil, the exchange of consent and of gift in marriage, are diminished in practical importance. Movement and sound have their place in creating a sense of community and communion, but above all they should enhance attention and openness to the word and participation in the key sacramental moment of any celebration. Active participation is not guaranteed by keeping active, but it is in essence the attuning of the body to what is key. In assuring this, there is a rhythm of timekeeping. Calendar time and daily time are not lived as though all moments had the same value. The body is shaped by actions and repose to adjust us to lived time and to differentiation between hours of the day and days of the year. A comparable strategy enters into any good sacramental action. There are sounds and movements appropriate to particular parts of worship, and movement and sound have to be well coordinated to achieve this. It is disconcerting to take part in a liturgy where the gathering and the leaving receive the greatest "sound effects," and nothing whatever is done to initiate a congregation into good body posture when attending to a prayer of blessing, witnessing a baptismal immersion, or accessing the table of the Lord's body and blood.

Rite and Distanciation

The memory that is inscribed is in the first place a memory of the body and of bodily actions, but rooted though it is in the body it is more than that. It is a memory of meanings, a memory of stories, and a memory of a ritual complex of persons interacting. Bodily performance writes these memories into the self of participant and of community. It also "rewrites" through the process of ritualization mentioned before, in whatever measure it is employed. Even those who remain quite faithful to the directives of liturgical books use body language and vocal sounds that in every celebration are both an appropriation and a reappropriation of tradition.

The kind of total involvement that rites engage is a way of being caught up both with the community and in what is being marked by the celebration.

---

13. Richard N. Fragomeni, "The Dissonant Sounds of Hope," *Concilium* 1993/3: 104.

The immediate impression is that of being in touch with those present and with what is represented. There is, however, a distanciation at work in ritual enactment.

The tendency for religious people may be to attach themselves to what is immediately perceptible. The history of devotion to the presence of Christ in the sacrament of the Eucharist tells its own tale of how memories and persuasions are attached to things that can be seen and touched (or deliberately not touched). While Christ is present in and through the sign of bread and wine, some devotion tends to associate an immediate and direct physical presence with the sacrament. It is provoked to this by the bodily perceptions and imagination. In an analogous way, all sacramental action gives the sense impression of "being there." As the Jewish Paschal Seder puts it in telling the story of the escape from Egypt and associating it with the foodstuffs and the wine on the table, "you yourselves" passed over the Red Sea, not simply, that is, "your ancestors." The useful side of this sense of immediacy is of course that it brings participants into lively interaction within the community and with what has gone before. It serves that sense of tradition which sees people of all generations caught up in the same reality. It also enlivens the faith in the presence and action of Christ and of the Spirit.

Nonetheless, the process of distanciation noted in the reality of writing is at work also in rite. To note this is particularly relevant in a time of change and of sharp controversy over change and difference, when quite divergent appeals are made to tradition. The fact is that an exact reconstruction of the origins of sacramental rites is impossible, and this is even further true of the reconstitution of the events remembered. Today, we know them only from the written and archeological evidence, as well as from within the rites themselves that have been passed on. Even as they are celebrated, they undergo change over the course of time. As therefore the written scriptures are as it were rewritten when taken up by a culture, so too the rituals of early Christian origins continue to be redrawn and reshaped, affected both by cultural energies and by the change of social reality across time.

The presence of Christ in the sacraments is linked to the memory of an event always being reconstrued. It is the presence of the risen Christ to his body, the Church, through signs that bear the imprint of both distance and absence. It is the constant reconstruing of ancient rites, as they are accommodated to cultures and to times, that is at the base of inculturation, and indeed its warrant. Without a sense of the process of distanciation, however, this will inevitably be blocked. Other bodily signs are substituted when some are lost, just as showing and looking took the place of eating and drinking in eucharistic history. When this occurs, the reasons have to be considered, and the relation of rituals to their evangelical origins has to be taken into account. In this way, some judgment of appropriateness can be made. It is not a matter of finding out exactly what the rite was in the beginning but of relating what is done now to the way of discipleship and to the meaning that was

attached to rites, which for all that we lack knowledge about particularities
is passed on to us in ritual practice.

Ritual, Socialization, Community

In the Church, as in any corporate reality, we distinguish between what constitutes community at the level of participation in reality, and what pertains
to its social construction. While this is not confined to sacramental worship,
it is above all in that domain that the two come together. To reflect upon
this, this section of the chapter is divided into five parts. First, the analogy
of rites of passage is probed. Second, on this basis we look at the relation
between social body, physical body, and the body of Christ in sacramental action. Third, there is the question of rites of social differentiation within this
one body. Fourth, we look for a link between living at the margins of the
Church and sacramental rites. Finally, it is asked how sacramental worship
affects the relation of Christians to the secular social body.

Ritual and Passage

One of the primary areas from which analogy is drawn in explaining sacrament from the field of cultural and social anthropology is that of rites of
passage.[14] The paradigm for the role of ritual as passage comes from cultural
rituals which carry persons through transitions in life, which in affecting them
affect the entire community. Such are the rites of passage from childhood to
adulthood, from single state to married, rites for becoming a mother and rites
for moving from life through death to the after-life. The status of the person
changes in such transitions, but it must nonetheless take place within the
circle of the community's symbols and horizons. The person takes on a new
position in the community, as adult, as one of a married couple with duties
of childrearing and childbearing, or as ancestor. The symbols and rites enacted negotiate these transitions within the horizon of the cultural cosmos
of a people.

In considering the analogy supplied by rites of passage, appeal is often
made to the perceptions of one author in particular. Following in the foot-
steps of Arnold van Gennep, Victor Turner has had a strong impact on ritual
studies through his theories of passage and liminality and his insight into
the relation between social order and *communitas*. Though primarily a cultural anthropologist, with field studies in Africa, he has indeed made some
applications of all of this to Catholic rites and practices.[15]

---

14. On rites of passage, see Arnold van Gennep, *The Rites of Passage,* trans. M. Vizedom
and G. Caffee (Chicago: University of Chicago Press, 1975). Louis-Marie Chauvet discusses the
relation to sacraments in *Symbole et sacrement,* 368–73.

15. Among his works, one that has had strong impact is Victor W. Turner, *The Ritual Process:
Structure and Anti-structure* (London: Routledge & Kegan Paul, 1969).

As Turner explains, every member of a social body belongs to it in two ways. What is most immediately apparent is the social role that the person has, by reason of status and way of life. This is something that changes as one moves from childhood to adulthood, from being single to being married, from being without child to being mother, and from being one of a living community to being an ancestor. Transition is also involved as a person accesses to positions of leadership. Beneath or behind these transitions, however, is what they serve, namely, what Turner calls *communitas*, where the most fundamental way of belonging to the social body lies. This is that life which is common to all and in which all share, and which is expressed in its stories, its memories, and its values. Rite has to keep a balance between the social structures of reality and the promotion of *communitas*.

This is particularly delicate and important in rites of passage. As one passes from childhood to adulthood, for example, through initiation rites two things happen. First, those to be initiated have to be introduced into those symbols and rites which express the basic life of the society or community. This is the way in which they come to know their own people and all that constitutes the life world of that people. Second, however, these young people have to learn to assume roles of adult responsibility, to learn to respect order, and to earn the respect of others themselves. For this purpose, they are put into a state of liminality for a period of time, which sets them outside the community, even in a physically distinct place. There they undergo trials, learn myths and stories, and perform rites that serve their transition. Finally, through another kind of rite, they are aggregated anew into the community in their new social role. What is done physically to and with the body in this process is very important. To be placed outside, to undergo feats of endurance, to receive the markings of the initiate, are an intrinsic and necessary part of the learning process. It is also through the marks received that they are given the stamp that will mark them out as members and adults of their own people.

Elements of such passage are present in every sacramental action, inasmuch as they all have to do with conversion. Turner himself in his comments on Catholic ritual pointed to an element of passage in every sacramental action by writing of its ritual flow. In this flow, the element of communion in Christ stands to the fore, but it has to be such that it also engages the elements of order in the community.

However, the analogy of passage applies most readily to the conversion fostered in the adult rites of Christian initiation, inclusive of catechumenal rites and of the sacraments of water immersion, consignation, and Eucharist. The starting point is to embark on a journey of faith that changes one's world, and the end point is to sit with the disciples of Christ at the communion table of his body and blood. Along the way, one can mark in this journey the starting point of separation from one order, the transitional period of liminality when one's universe is being reshaped by Christian faith, and the point of aggregation when one finds a gifted and responsible belonging in the community. The initial reception and inscription as catechumen, the exorcisms and laying on of hands, mark the break with the old and the gradual configuration to the new. The fact of being dismissed Sunday after Sunday from the congregation puts candidates in a status of liminality. Water immersion is a rite of rebirthing and consignation that of a new configuration, which bring one closer to the aggregation to community. This is perfected at the communion table, with its act of communal memorial thanksgiving and table-sharing of the gift of Christ.

The pertinence of passage to social status is clearest in the sacraments of marriage and of ordination. There is some difference, however, in that the sacrament of marriage may not necessarily be coterminous with entering marriage. Though present legislation requires this, it was not always so. Taking up a new social position as married partners may possibly not be done in such a way that it is a testimony of Christian faith. Were the sacramental celebration of marriage to come later, this would mark a transition in the marriage itself.

In both marriage and order, bodily rites need to be taken into proper account to express their meaning. It is significant, for example, that for the celebration and blessing of marriage in the West the couple are in the sanctuary and that they give their pledge to one another in Christ standing before the assembled community. Even if as an engaged couple they have frequented the Eucharist together, from the time of marriage their presence there is seen differently by other members. In ordination, much of the expression of the role of priest is embodied in such things as prostration, vesting with special garments, and the accession to a place standing at the altar for the Mass. A challenge to ritual performance is to truly allow the laying on of hands stand out as the most distinctive moment, when the action is joined with the invocation in words of the gift of the Spirit.

Apart from these more obvious cases of transition, other sacraments also receive new light when looked at in this way. The sacrament of anointing, for example, is enlightened in two ways by this paradigm. First, it has to do with a change that is a new way of considering sickness in Christ, such as is spelled out in the introduction to the revised order of anointing. The ritual act of anointing both promises healing and configures the sick as sick to the Paschal mystery of Christ. In the second place, in the comforting of a sick or elderly person by its ritual actions of support in faith, a community ritually highlights the special status of these persons in the community, not only comforting them but affirming the unique testimony which they give as members of Christ to the rest of the community.

Using the insight of passage in relation to Eucharist is delicate and not without difference of opinion. Every eucharistic action in its ritual flow carries elements of conversion and journey, but the question is where these belong. Victor Turner associated them with the ritual flow of sacrifice, finding therein, along with other social anthropologists, the elements of dividing off and reconciling. He posited the resolution of division and the act of reintegration in the consecration and the elevation of the host, for he thought that at this moment all participants are at one in the their fundamental communion in Christ in his sacrifice, unmarked by the distinctions of social ordering.[16]

This explanation is unhappily untrue to the eucharistic rite as celebrated throughout the first millennium. Then, the climax and moment of integration was the participation together at the communion table. Ritual itself in its history has not respected this eucharistic *communitas*, inserting many ritual niceties which mark off the communion of the clergy from that of the faithful. Even in the revised Roman Rite such communion is in part negated. The priest still takes communion at a different spot, communicating at the altar/table, whereas the faithful receive communion away from the table. He will always take communion in consecrated bread and wine, whereas quite often the people still receive in only one kind. There is need for some ritual change that marks the undifferentiated oneness in holiness and grace of the eucharistic table.

In the eucharistic rite there is a ritual flow associated with communion, though this needs to be more clearly enunciated in bodily ritual, as well as in word. From the rites which express the approach to the table as sinners, through the liminal status of stepping back from one's life world to hear the word of God, the members move to the table of the body and blood where reintegration into Christ and his Church is effected. The Roman Rite places a penitential rite at the beginning of Mass, but allows for the possibility of placing it after the liturgy of the word. This inserts penance both as a response to the word and as a preparation for the eucharistic offering. In this case, the preparation of the bread and wine takes on the appearance of a marginal moment, when in penance people take cognizance of having nothing and yet having all, and of placing their lives before God to be healed and made one in Christ.

In Anglican ritual, from the time of Cranmer, the separation from the holy by sin is marked within the prayer leading to communion, and it is in the "creeping to the table" that people take cognizance of their liminal status, to be taken up into Christ by the word and gifts of his forgiveness. In all such ritual, the key expression is that in being called by Christ we are stripped of status and self-reliance and find a common humanity in this quasi-reduction to nothingness, only to be reintegrated into his body by the ritual and gift of communion.

Social Body, Physical Body, Body of Christ

Anthropologists and sociologists favor the title of Eucharist as sacrifice because they think that this deals with division.[17] On a social level, offering

---

16. Victor Turner, "Ritual, Tribal and Catholic," *Worship* 50 (1976): 504–26.

17. For example, John Bossey, "The Mass as a Social Institution 1200–1700," *Past and Present* 100 (1985): 29–61, and Turner, "Ritual, Tribal and Catholic."

sacrifice can unite all strata of society in one ritual, without destroying distinctions to the ordering of society. Thus instead of putting the focus on the common table where all eat the same food and drink the same cup, they point to those bodily rites in the course of the Mass which both maintain division and express unity. Among these rites, they privilege the exchange of the kiss of peace as it is passed through the congregation, beginning at the altar and with the clergy. The image of sacrifice is also thought to address those divisions which are caused by sin, or those faults in the body-self which keep from peaceful participation as one social body or one spiritual body. By bearing our sins, even now, Christ expiates fault and heals divisions. In this perspective, the image of the scapegoat is thought to nicely complement that of sacrifice, or even fuse with it.

Given the strong association that has grown up between sacrifice and making propitiation, the imagery of passage might in fact better express the constant coming to be as communion which occurs in the Eucharist.[18] The image of the body of Christ is an image of communion, of being one in mind, heart, and action through a communion in the divine communion of persons. It is a union achieved through reconciliation in the power of God's mercy, making one out of those who were separate and divided. Augustine exploited the metaphor of the one loaf in order to illustrate the process through which neophytes have to go in order to enter this communion. They are ground and milled through exorcism and fasting, they are moistened by the water of baptism, and then baked with the fire of the Holy Spirit, and thus they are made the bread which is the body of Christ.[19]

The sacrifice of Christ is once and for all, and not to be repeated, and more basically in itself it transgressed the procedures of sacrifice, so that sacrifices need no longer be offered. It was not a propitiation offered to God, but a self-giving act representing God's merciful expiation. The offer of love and mercy, when given in the flesh, was refused, so that the death ensued. The death itself, the intimate communion between Father and Son in the Spirit, wiped out the attempt to propitiate, so that the offer of forgiveness and mercy is now given in the sacrament. It is as innocent death, death unwilled even by the Father except as an act of self-giving that runs counter to religious and secular violence, and thus reveals divine justice, that Jesus' death is redemptive. It is in receiving the gift of this self-giving that communion is made possible, not by incessant propitiating. Both Augustine and Aquinas had pointed to this Christian peculiarity in writing of the death of Christ and of the Eucharist, in the use which they made of the image of sac-

---

18. The suggestion is derived from the discussion of Christ's redemptive death in A. Vergote, "La mort rédemptrice du Christ à la lumière de l'anthropologie," *Mort pour nos péchés: Recherche pluridisciplinaire sur la signification rédemptrice du Christ* (Brussels: Facultés Universitaires Saint-Louis, 1976), 45–83.

19. Sermon Wolfenbüttel 7, in *Eucharist*, ed. Daniel Sheehan, Message of the Fathers 7 (Wilmington, Del.: Michael Glazier, 1986), 99–102

rifice. The description of Christ's sacrifice and ecclesial communion in this sacrifice, which both used, Aquinas following Augustine, was in fact a negation of propitiatory sacrifice.[20] For them, the meaning of Christian sacrifice is fulfilled by acts of mercy which lead to a perfect communion or holy fellowship, a *perfecta societas*, in the true meaning of the Latin word *societas*. Hence, as Aquinas points out, the order of divine justice is not an order of retribution, but an order of mercy and forgiveness. In shedding his blood on the Cross, according to Thomas, Christ acted with excess, out of an excessive love.[21] It is this which the fellowship of the Church must mirror, and it is this which is signified in the Eucharist

The bodily ritual of the Lord's Supper and Holy Communion must, however, respond to what is still felt in the flesh, namely, sin and division. Social divisions, racial divisions, gender divisions, ethnic divisions, are brought to the table of the Lord's body and blood. They are not to be hidden or camouflaged. The very invitation to the table, the passing over to the table, at which there is no discrimination or division calls for penance and the request for mercy. The *Didache* cited Matthew 5 in conjunction with the preparation for the Eucharist to make this point.[22] Anyone conscious of division must first seek reconciliation before coming to the "sacrifice," which is the Lord's table. Rites of penance, which are reminders of baptismal gifts and covenant, and the kiss of peace may signify the willing address of sins of division. In the bringing of bread and wine, together with what else is shared with the poor or with one another, we submit ourselves and our being together, being together even with the earth that gives to us, in praise and thanksgiving for God's gracious blessing.

Openness to the other, the human other and the earthly other, is a condition for eucharistic communion, but this too is a gift given to us through the blood of Christ. The rites of celebration can either ignore such need for social healing, or they can choose to bring it to the fore. When the bishop of the small Syrian community, whose ritual activities are recorded in the *Didascalia*, gave his seat in the assembly to the poor man, he had found a way of ritualizing the Christian love celebrated in the feast. The association of going on pilgrimage with penance is another way in which the call to a oneness, "already and not yet," is brought forward in the body. Unhappily tourism may have attenuated the experience of being pilgrim with a motley of other motivations, but of old pilgrims encountered persons of all kinds along the road

---

20. See Augustine, *The City of God* X.6 and Thomas Aquinas, *Summa Theologiae* III, q. 48, art. 2.

21. When Aquinas writes of satisfaction in this context, it is to say that it is the love which sets aright an order of sin and opens the way to the flow of divine mercy. Without such generosity of love, there could be no retribution, that is, no recapitulation, to use another term which in an earlier question he used to speak of our relation with Christ, with whom we are "quasi una persona." See *Summa Theologiae* III, q. 8, art. 2, c.

22. *Didache* 14. See the text in Lucien Deiss, *Springtime of the Liturgy* (Collegeville, Minn.: Liturgical Press, 1979), 77.

to their shrines, where they were to eat and drink together in the hostels and receive the sacrament of penance and the sacrament of Christ's body and blood. It is this kind of transgressing of wonted social boundaries which serves to display the order of justice which is celebrated at the Eucharist table, with its implications for the order to be promoted in society.

Words give contours to the actions, with the result of accentuating some rather than others. It is quite curious that the eucharistic action in and of itself as a bodily act is one of commensality, and yet in celebration it is the action of offering which was for so long privileged, even to the elimination of table sharing. This could only be because of the ideological images imposed on the action by words. Now it is time to return to the import of the action itself when it is restored as commensality.

The various examples given above are intended to exemplify insights into sacrament that come from analogies with rites of passage, especially as this means conversion and affects how members belong to the community of Church. Some connection has also been made between sacrament, passage and social division, pointing finally to the eucharistic table as the arrival place of passage, the place that countenances no division, but anticipates eschatological reconciliation. But differences prevail, and are even served by some types of ritual action, so the matter of societal differentiation within ritual needs further reflection.

Ritual and Soci(et)al Differentiation

The foregoing considerations have raised the question of societal differentiation within the body of the Church, as this is marked by sacramental rites, whereby as a social body the Church "writes itself." As an interpersonal and social body, the Church differentiates itself through ritual, creating the ordering that befriends sacrament and serves the ritual action of the memorial of Christ's mystery. The ordering takes place in a variety of ways, some of them scarcely noticed and yet effective, but always to be put to the test of their value in serving communion.

As a concrete example, the revisions of the rites for the sick may show how rite expresses differentiation and can in subtle ways change it. When the revised *editio typica* called for the ministry of the baptized in ministering to the sick, it asked for ritual changes in liturgies of prayer, in communion to the sick, and in the rite of the sacrament itself. This virtually changed the ordering among members in Christian communities, since it spelled out new ways of relating that had been unknown for a long time. For several centuries the entire rites of communion to the sick and of extreme unction were between the priest and the sick themselves. The ritual performance suggested that the priest alone could bring spiritual comfort and grace and that he alone was responsible for the sacramental action. Today, with provisions for bringing communion to the sick that engage the laity, with the provision that others receive communion along with the sick person and with the presence and participation of others at the anointing, the meaning of the rite is much more clearly related to the community and to a differentiation of roles not confined to the sacrament of order. Communal celebrations of anointing, either in the parish church or in a hospital, also affect the whole sense of order within the Church and the meaning of its sacraments.

Whether a ministry of service should endow the minister with special status is an open question, but that it has done so for centuries cannot be contested. Pope John Paul II in writing of the exclusion of women from ordination was not unaware of this dilemma of status in the Church. In *Christifideles laici* he put forward the view that confining candidature to males had to do only with symbolic action, and not with dignity and grace, in which in Christ all are equal.[23] The point is clear, but the problem is that there seems to be a split involved in thinking about the relation between the symbolic and the real. To be excluded from the role of presidency and, according to the explanation given, from that of representing Christ, does affect status and participation in sacramental reality. It says something about womanhood's relation to Christ that has much to do with a social and symbolic ordering that affects the life of grace and dignity, unless dignity is given a rather abstract definition.[24]

Rather than pursue the question of women and sacrament at this point, let it be noted that many of the issues associated with Church order today concern ordination, candidacy for ordination, and the power and presidency of the ordained in relation to the roles of all the baptized. On this score it is not only the rite of ordination that needs revision, but there are ordination practices that have to be subjected to reconsideration.

Recent popes have made a practice of themselves ordaining bishops for dioceses around the world in Rome. The bishops are then received in their own cathedrals, in a kind of paraliturgical ordination ceremony, where they enter mandated and empowered by the bishop of Rome. This has an entirely different bearing on relations in the Church to what is signified by ordination within the diocese, in the presence of the faithful and the clergy. The relation to the diocese in the first instance implicates the empowerment by the pope and makes him a kind of superbishop to the diocese. The relation to the diocese in the second instance is one of being born as it were to ministry and nurtured and empowered in it, within the Church to which the bishop is called to minister. It is then much more clearly as bishop of his Church that he enters communion with the Church of Rome and with its bishop.

There is an analogous difference when a candidate for priesthood, for example, in a religious order, is ordained in his home parish, only later to be assigned and sent to another Church. This kind of "absolute" ordination gives

---

23. John Paul II, *Christifideles laici* 51.
24. The precise issue of ritual and woman's body experience is taken up in more detail in chapter 8.

the impression that the priest possesses a power, valid in itself without specific relation to the people with whom one is Christian and for whom one is minister.[25] It is totally different from being received and accepted among the people as a Christian, and then ordained among them and for them to ministry.

There are also strong ecumenical repercussions to the readiness to share, or the refusal to share, publicly in sacramental ritual. If ministers of two distinct Churches share together in the blessing of a marriage between members of their communities, something is said about the basic communion in baptism. If the couple, though belonging to different confessions, take Eucharist together on that occasion, this speaks not only to their relationship but to a relationship between the Churches that goes beyond the mutual recognition of baptisms.

The question of eucharistic sharing between Churches, and of recognition of order, is sometimes wrongly seen as a matter of acknowledging, or refusing to acknowledge, the eucharistic reality of another Church. In fact, one can affirm that another Church has the true sacrament of Christ's body and blood and yet refuse eucharistic sharing as a matter of policy, and indeed of faith. In this case, the ritual decision points to differences in perception of other articles of faith or in the perception of what the Church of Christ ought to be.

Rites on the Margin of the Church

Bodily ritual in the first instance orders life in the community and expresses the universe of being and a people's or community's part in the whole rhythm of creation and passage of time. The cases looked at in the preceding paragraphs illustrate this. However, ritual performance can also express a sense of marginalization and dislocation among its members.

This marginalization occurs in two ways. First, within a community of people some members experience a marginality in relation to the exchange of life and power within the body and its rites. This shows in the way in which they take part in rites or perhaps begin to develop rites of their own to express a troubled belonging. In the second place, it has to be asked of practitioners of religion or members of a Church how their practice affects them in their relation to the culture of their daily lives and surroundings. Do Christians ever feel marginalized in society because of their creed, and how does this surface in ritual?

The question of feeling marginal to the Church in its ritual has only recently begun to be explored. Ritual expressions, however, that express this marginality within ritual or outside the mainstream are quite ancient. Much of this went unnoticed because it belonged in the area often called devotion or popular religiosity. We saw in an early chapter how the poet Seamus

---

25. Canonically, of course, the candidate has a title because he is a member of a religious community, but what is here meant is that the rite has little apparent relation to ministry and assignment.

Heaney saw in his mother's devotions both a way of coming to terms with her place in life and a woman's protest against occupying the place in society where her Catholic faith and culture placed her. Studies of habits of fast and eucharistic communion among medieval women are now often understood as indications of a sense of marginality. In the writings of Jacques De Vitry on Marie d'Oignies, for example, we see how women denied frequent access to communion could in fact obtain it through their excessive fasting.[26] In the *Herald* of Gertrude of Helfta, there are many stories of a woman's personal ritual that gave her an intimacy with Christ, who even gave her a role as his messenger and as a teacher of others, though Church order at the time did not allow women any public office.[27] When only the priest could communicate regularly or when a local Church interdict denied communion to her convent over a period of time, the ritual of preparing a bed for the crucifix on some holy days was a ritual of the communion thus denied. Today, more reflexively conscious of their marginal status, many women explore their belonging to Christ, to community, and to creation through the process of ritualization already discussed in chapter 1.

Marginality may also come about as a result of unwanted change to rites that are deeply ingrained in personal and community behavior. There can be some attempts to retrieve older forms, but if this is done, the retrieved rite is not identical in meaning with its original use, but expresses the protest of those who feel left at the margins.

Rituals for Christian Marginality

A difficult matter is the extent to which Christians are marginal to their surrounding culture, and what their rites do to give them either a feeling of well-being within it or a feeling of some dissociation. In other words, it has to be asked how participation in Christian sacramental ritual relates members of the Church to the broad culture and social reality. Today, most countries follow the principle of the separation of Church and State, but Christians maintain a broad interest in keeping alive Christian principles as norms of behavior. However, it may well be that in relation to much that is accepted in mainstream culture, the rituals of adult initiation, of infant baptism, and of weekly Eucharist will inevitably convey a sense of marginality for their participants. The beliefs there expressed about the human person, about the universe, and about social and moral values, are less and less mainstream orientations in Western societies. Do we feel this in the body when we come to the communion table, or is this so anesthetized that it fails to register its extraordinary affirmations?

The British social anthropologist Mary Douglas, in her book *Natural Symbols*, gave attention to the connection between ritual and marginalization

---

26. Jacques De Vitry, *Acta Sanctorum Junii* (Paris and Rome, 1867), 547–72.

27. See Gertrude d'Helfta, *Le Héraut*, or *Herald*, bk. 2, in *Oeuvres spirituelles*, vol. 2, Sources chrétiennes 139 (Paris: Éd. du Cerf, 1968).

among minorities in England.[28] Her first study on this matter has to do with Irish Catholic immigrants in large English cities, who continued the ritual of abstaining from meat on Fridays and found in it a public mark of their own specific identification. The custom helped its practitioners to mark themselves off, in culture and in faith, from those among whom they lived. It also helped them to identify together as a community and to maintain a sense of social and cultural stability in a foreign country. Douglas lamented the change in laws of fast and abstinence that came in the sixties, not only because of the part they played for this immigrant group, but more generally for what it meant in giving Catholics a sense of bearing some specific difference, even when seen in public places.

However, it also needs to be noted that the more the Irish integrated into English society and found that they could compete in all spheres of life, the less they needed such rituals as cultural markers. This is not to say that fast and abstinence do not have a signification that still holds in religious observance, but the imprint of its meaning is tied to cultural factors. Relinquishing its role as spelling out Catholic identity, the Church has not succeeded very well in expressing its religious, ascetic, and communal significance. Possibly this is to be retrieved not by holding to its particularity as Catholic, but by realizing that it is a practice which offers common ground to persons of diverse religious persuasion. Beyond the particular question of abstinence, however, there is the question of whether Christians simply merge with their surrounding culture, or whether there should not be rightly something in their ritual to express some degree of marginality to it. To this, we can return below.

The other study in Douglas's book is even stronger in showing how ritual expresses a sense of marginality and an attempt to keep in touch with spiritual forces proper to one's own culture. This study has to do with ritually evoked trance, and Douglas shows its importance to West Jamaicans in England.[29] Certain kinds of rite, such as smoking specific substances, use of incense, and ritual dance, can induce a state of trance. Within this state, where the participant feels in touch with ancestral spirits, persons speak in tongues, give messages to the congregation, and dance according to certain rhythms of sound and body. As Douglas sees it, the state of trance and the esteem in which it is held are joined to the feeling of being in a foreign place, among foreigners. Leaving the body, or distancing from its sense of specific location, characteristically induced through body movements, puts the person and those who observe the trance in touch with religious and spiritual powers which are alien to the culture and society of the host nation.

To the examples and insights offered by Douglas, it can be noted what

---

28. Mary Douglas, *Natural Symbols: Explorations in Cosmology* (New York: Pantheon Books, 1970), on "The Bog Irish," 37–53, and "The Two Bodies," 65–81.
29. Ibid., 79–81.

ancestral rites mean for peoples caught in the process of cultural change, and specifically in our time of wholesale functional, social, and cultural modernization. Among African youth in some cities on that continent, there was a tendency to abandon ancestral rites, and in particular the rites of initiation. This spread too into villages, with the intake of Western norms and methods of education, and with the changing aspirations of young people and of parents for their children. Now there is a trend among those educated in the new ways to recover such rites, including the rites of initiation. Within the cultural flow of the times, they help participants to keep a sense of heritage and identity, to which the religious is key, and to maintain religious, kinship, and social wisdom and values. There is in this a challenge to suitable ritual development. If these rites are kept intact, without relation to new situations, they become folkloric, or they are in time experienced as failing in purpose. If the economic and community conditions of peoples have in fact changed, the ritual has to integrate this awareness and detach itself from suppositions of time, place, and transition which are no longer verified.

From these examples, we see different ways in which bodily action relates participants to cultural traditions. In the one case, it passes on a tradition and a spiritual force that remains dominant among a people. In the second case, its significance lies in what it does for people who are cut off by place and the transition of time from long-standing cultural roots, but still want to keep some connection with them. In the third case, the rites are taken up in the midst of change in the exploration of ancestral traditions and of the power that they may still carry.

How much do we expect religion and culture to coincide or interact today? In a volume of *Concilium* entitled *Liturgy and Human Passage,* Aidan Kavanagh asked the apposite question of the degree to which Christians could be content with the rites of passage of the surrounding society and culture to mark the seasons of life, thus avoiding their confusion with Christian initiation.[30] The question can be more broadly asked, in light of the rooting of the Gospel in non-Western cultures. In some African Churches, for example, it is now more readily agreed than before that young men and women would properly participate in traditional initiation rites, affecting their integration into their own culture. Traditional burial rites can also be respected, without excluding the memorial of the dead in eucharistic celebration and Christian prayers in the course of such ritual. Even in Western countries, the habit of deferring baptism, first communion, and marriage has grown. This is quite a complex pastoral issue, allowing of no easy solution, but it does provide the opportunity to keep Christian sacraments as sacraments of conversion distinct from passage. Christian teaching and ritual celebration can always complement the more cultural or secular rites of passage, but it does not

---

30. Aidan Kavanagh, "Life-Cycle Events, Civic Ritual and the Christian," *Concilium* 112 (1979): 14–24.

have to replace them. It is only when these rites are alien to Christian beliefs that their participation is to be dissuaded. The health of Christian sacrament, as such, is best served by grasping its somewhat antiritual or antitypical character, and its celebration of discipleship and communion with Christ in the mystery of his self-gift in the Spirit.

Such issues are not accidental to how sacramental traditions are kept and develop. They question how people take in traditions, how they relate to society and its values, how they live their place in a culture, from within their faith as Christians and their affirmation of it. Identifying with Christ and his Church, can the ritual of their sacramental worship give them a perspective on what it is to be citizens of a culture and a country? The forms of bodily ritual, and not simply the words, have much to do in expressing this. That is because body movement has a strong impact in relating people to place, time, and traditions.

Ritual and Being in Time

Rituals are deemed a theurgy, an action of transcendental or divine power. They are actions that order life and order community, that resolve conflict, that reconcile members, that guide through transitions, and that bring healing. They are said to engage with mystery, or in Turner's phrase they introduce into *communitas*, while still respecting and maintaining structures and their socializing power. In all of this, the energy and power of the rite is attributed in a particular way to bodily action.

But what does Christian ritual say to humanity's and the Christian mystery's relation to time?[31] Bodily rites, in their very intensity of rhythm, bring to the surface the sense of being in time and space, together with the tensions inherent in this condition of being human. Rites associated with birth, marriage, adolescence, and death express the enigma and vulnerability of existence. In times of transition, from childhood to adulthood, from single status to marriage, persons are caught in a present that has an ambiguous relation to past and future. Rites associated with seasons underline the debility of human control over the very necessities of life and dependence on much greater forces which humans cannot even understand. They look for harmony with these forces, but cannot guarantee it without appealing to higher powers for their clemency and bounty. Rites for the assumption of office look to that level of communion in life where there is no differentiation, and in that very act reveal how fragile communion is. Rites of healing touch the forces of evil to which humans constantly feel subject and from which they need release.

When these enigmas, these mysterious encounters with time and with cosmos, are made to surface, myth or saga eases the transition and projects a

---

31. For comparison, see the discussion in chapter 3 on the relation between *anamnesis* and *mimesis*, and the relation of sacrament to daily, cosmic, and historical time, and to what is beyond time.

universe of order in which human beings have a place. They promise healing and pretend to a coherent whole. If the myth or saga comes into question, when the body language associated with them continues to be used it creates feelings of dislocated being. Myth and saga are social and cultural responses to this enigma. They offer a wholeness within cosmic order. They project an imagined time outside the time of both humans and cosmos, an imagined but ultimately unidentifiable time within which both find a place. Passing over into it means renouncing all desire to remain permanently in human or cosmic time. In that sense, even within paradigms of wholeness there is a disjunction between given existence and desired existence.

Sacramental ritual often assumed many of the qualities of mythical projection, offering the vision of a well-ordered universe where all falls under divine providence and plan. Now, however, with the dissolution of such certainties, the unique character of the Gospel's response to ritual desire comes newly to surface. It radically demythologizes the quest for lasting life and the quest for cosmic order by asking for identification with Jesus Christ in his self-giving and self-emptying.

Accepting the disjunction between being vulnerable and the desire for life without death, all the enigmas of *chaosmos* are handed over to a divine wisdom that is loving but quite often incomprehensible. It is a wisdom located not in the vision of a cosmic order, but at the table of a repeated and constant table-sharing among the weak of the earth. That is where initiation, the passage through conversion and the struggle with the elements of life and death in the chaos of water, leads disciples.

Ritual Transformed

There is a ritual distinctiveness in Christian sacrament that puts the focus on domestic rites, not on festive or cosmic ones, however much of these is appropriated or respected. It is this which gives the particular sense of being in time that is proper to the memorial of Christ. When cultural transition is at stake, one has to ask with what kind of symbolic identity, ritual being, and cultural wisdom would one start to teach about God's kingdom. The ritual transfer from sacrifice, rites of passage, cosmic rites, indeed from the whole language of cosmic identity, to the loaf and the cup, to the tub of water, to the jar of oil, shared in daily living, parallels the transposition of the Christ story into a people's parabolic language. A people has its identity and its relations to things of life and of earth and to the transitions of time in these rites in ways that ground any spoken word.

One does not obviously dismiss the festive rites of life and season in inculturating worship. The enigmas of life, the search for oneness with all being, with the cosmic, with the spiritual, with ancestors and spirits, that get expressed in these rites have to be brought to the hearing of the Gospel and given new forms in the sacramental rites of the Church. Through the avenue of a people's own more parabolic ritual, however, these questions are introduced with metaphoric transfer of language and expression into the rites of table, washing, anointing, and touching that are the core of Christian sacrament and its memorial.

This is an extraordinary transition. Other religions of course have their common meals, regular as well as festive and cultic. The Gospel makes the daily meal, the regular sharing of a community, the centerpiece of its communion with and in the divine, as proclaimed in the Christ event, in the self-emptying of the Cross which is a pouring out of the Spirit. All of the aspirations to communion with cosmos, to communion with spirits and deities, that religious ritual brings to expression, are finally located at this table. They are invested in this act of sharing the one loaf and the one cup, with the food and drink of daily toil, daily sustenance, and daily want. This is what is symbolic or metaphoric about Christian sacrament: it makes religious aspiration, all that is customarily located in sacrifices, in temples, at altars, in seasonal assemblies, in rites of passage, converge at the common table of weekly gatherings. There is ample room for the recovery of a greater esteem for the body, in the regard for bread and wine, and in the esteem of the hands that sow, harvest, knead, bake, and crush, and in the pleasures of bodily sharing, as well as in the distress of bodily want. There is place too for the recovery of new forms of social ordering and relating, when the focus of ritual is truly on the preparation of the table and on sharing at it, where what is remembered is the self-gift of Christ and what is shared is the body broken and given, the blood poured out in a covenant of grace. Christians belong most truly to time at the common table. It is there that they discover their relation to cosmic time, to the time immemorial of the world's beginnings, and to the "time beyond time" in which they enter the mystery of God.

This is a practical wisdom learned through ritual that bears on love between neighbors and love between foreigners and on the care of those who need care. It is a wisdom of trust in a divine providence and presence that touches daily lives. It is all that Jesus taught about the presence of kingdom of God "today." It opens table participants to open to the outflow of the Spirit that touches all flesh and teaches us to say, "Abba, Father," in the quest for daily bread, enough for the day and no more. It is from within this wisdom, gained from parable[32] and from this prosaic ritual of shared daily communion, that a community hears and confesses the proclamation of the Cross, with its own renunciation of mythic, religious, and philosophical wisdom, as well as its promise of life.

The entry into unending life is offered to those who like the grain of wheat are ready to die, ready, that is, to give up the concern with self and one's body to the mystery of God's love and the life that is in God. This has been the aspect of the Gospel that has most defied the human imagination, so that history is replete with all the efforts, artistic and vulgar, to depict life after

---

32. On this, see the following chapter.

death or eternal life, and the abode of the dead or the abode of God. The urge for holistic symbolism is constantly in tension with the unique symbolism of the self-emptying of the Cross and the death of the grain of wheat, which so pleased Paul when he wrote of the resurrection from the dead.

This entails entering a new horizon. It means taking the enigma of death and of life, of past and future, into the Cross of Christ, at the table. The rite in which death and life are faced "in their battle" is the daily rite of table-sharing, the rite of putting bread and wine on the table, to be shared as one loaf and one cup. It is from day to day that the Christian faces death and is renewed in the promise of life. It is in what is required to live day by day with others and for others that death is faced, and the constant passing from past to future, with no very tangible hold on the present. Only parabolic wisdom serves in this encounter. There is no great myth or saga to encompass all of reality in an imaged wholeness. The Gospel heard at this table is made up of *petits récits*, of unsynchronized stories of passion and death, offering different paths of entry into the one Christ, who bears the face of all suffering and is without comeliness.

The struggle of Christian sacrament, and struggle it has been, is to maintain this simplicity of washing in water, soothing with oil, and sitting at table. In other words, other religious or cultural interests intervene constantly to turn evangelical beginnings into more splendid rituals. Even today, even four centuries after the Reformation, even after the Catholic liturgical renewal of the twentieth century, it seems impossible to recover the table rite and the eating together in service of the one loaf and drinking of the one cup. More orderly and hierarchic interests constantly intervene, or the common imagination finds this unsatisfying.

The domesticity of Christian ritual and the teaching of parable go together in constituting the setting within which the proclamation of the Cross and the transformation of the elements into divine gift take place. Just as it is the bread, wine, oil, and water of human life that are brought forward to be blessed, so it is the life expressed in parable that is brought forward to be transformed. The truth of the Cross and the power of God's Word and Spirit have effect in what is represented by the parables and by "what is at hand" in bread, wine, oil, and water. As the gift of the grace and the active presence of Christ take body in these elements, so too they take form in the body of the people, which is the Church of Christ.

Other Rituals

It is normal and to be expected that Church communities develop a galaxy of other rituals, such as those for celebration in times of human passage and in times of seasonal passage. These, however, should not crowd out sacraments in their core simplicity, nor become confused with them. There is something very important in the Protestant insistence that there are only two sacraments, baptism and the Lord's Supper. Catholic doctrine and theology in their own way account for this with the distinction between the major and minor sacraments, thereby acknowledging the centrality and unique character of these two.

Within the culture of Christendom, baptism, confirmation, and marriage became rites of passage, extreme unction and Christian burial completing the ritual of the four seasons of life and death. Many liturgies in old liturgical books also served to mark the stages of the four seasons of the year. Quite rightly, some contemporary liturgists write of the importance that rites of passage may have in retrieving a respect for nature and for human harmony within the Church. Their relation to sacrament, however, requires considerable theological and pastoral prudence.

The Reformers wished to undo the absolutism of Christendom and the sacralization of the whole of life, recognizing both the reality of personal faith and the independence of secular matters from ecclesiastical control. Hence their liturgies, to greater or less degree, undid the holistic cultural approach of Catholic symbolism. It has been suggested that the whole Reformation liturgy failed to replace this with the rites and symbols that could touch people in the issues they faced in the course of their lives, so that people often had resort to rites outside sacrament that were not truly Christian. This coincided with the tattering of the cultural synchronism of Christendom.

While there is merit to this criticism, it also has to be remembered that Catholic practitioners often had their own array of quite magical practices that entered in where liturgy and clergy failed to touch on issues of life and death, or sickness and healing, as well as problems of weather, harvest, and the like. The many blessings of the late Middle Ages, many retained in the Roman Ritual of 1614, were at any rate an attempt to bring the power of sign and symbol into the whole gamut of life experience.

Conclusion

In this chapter, the use of bodily ritual in Christian tradition has been considered, in the light of how it joins with words in the language event of sacrament. Its role in keeping memory as well as its affinities with the anthropology of ritual were taken into account. On the one hand, it was asked what analogies may be drawn from the anthropology of ritual to help understand the process of Christian sacrament. On the other hand, it was shown how Christian sacrament relates the Christian community to the questions of being that surface in bodily ritual. The most significant conclusion is that in Christian sacrament rite joins word at the point of parabolic wisdom. Sacrament signifies and celebrates the presence of the divine and the presence of Word and Spirit in the daily wisdom of practical living and the common table. It is this which it takes up and places within the compass of what comes in the Cross and resurrection of Christ, and what is promised to us in that memory. It tells us that we have access to this mystery from within the ordinary of human existence, that we do not have to enter some mythic time to be saved. This ordinary of life and the extraordinary of divine presence are expressed chiefly in the sharing of bread and cup that Jesus left his disciples as a memorial and testament. Their convergence is taught in the wisdom and the parables of the kingdom which are the teachings of Jesus, the Christ. To have access to such a table is indeed a passage, a conversion, an entry into a new horizon, a new way of being, in time and in place, living for others and in harmony with the things of earth, but always looking to what it is that God brings and will bring, beyond what humans imagine or ritualize.

— *Chapter Five* —

Verbal Polyphony

People enter into sacrament first through their bodies. Though words determine the significance of rite, they can be interpreted only within the ritual context. It is the ritual which determines the setting and the communion within which the word is heard and prayed. While individual words or sentences have long been presented as the form of sacramental actions, determining the significance of rites, they have been isolated from a larger context. Some attention may be given to other images and metaphors used in prayer, but what merits more attention is the interplay of the different verbal genres that work together, and work with ritual, in the celebration of this language event. The foundation for this exploration has already been given in chapter 2, where the sacraments were presented as language events of Word and Spirit.

In looking at the Gelasian sacramentary and at the Armenian rites of baptism, we already noted the use of different kinds of scriptural readings and the interweaving of scriptural readings into prayers. This occasioned some thought on intertextuality, that is to say, on the interaction in one liturgy of different genres of scriptural proclamation and of scripture with prayer. It is now appropriate to carry these considerations further. To do this, we can first examine the effect on sacramental memorial of interweaving different genres of scriptural texts. After that, we can give similar attention to the diversity of genres used for prayers. In both instances, it is the category of literary genre which is the focus of attention, and not simply content. This is because genre is vital to the creation of meaning and the engagement of a congregation in the sacramental action. Furthermore, when the use of genres changes in the course of handing on tradition, this affects sacraments quite deeply.

A preliminary note to this study of texts has to do with the appeal to literary genres. In the wake of the work on metaphor of Paul Ricoeur, it is frequently noted that metaphors are not simply rhetorical ornaments of speech but bearers of meaning. A metaphor, by relating two unlikely terms, opens the way to the construction of new meaning. In this, it also reveals something about reality and about truth, involving the reader or the hearer in this quest. To speak, for example, of fire in the belly is to say something about the viscerality of human commitment and about the relation of the whole person to the quest for truth and for the good. It was Ricoeur who pointed out that a metaphor is not simply an image used, but that it lies in the predication of one thing of another. In similar fashion, he drew attention to the nature of parables as extended metaphors, being stories that draw out unlikely comparisons and so reveal something of the nature of the reign of God. Thus in the parable which likens the reign of God to the failure of a builder to provide enough stone for the building of a tower, the Gospel attends to the zeal and providence which is required in the pursuit of the goods of this reign. The insight is indeed inspired by the very fact that such goods are unlike what is put into the project of erecting buildings.

Pursuant on this notion of metaphor, there follows a larger attention to diverse genres of texts in generating meaning, or different modes of discourse.[1] Genres such as narrative, wisdom writing, and legal code draw the reader into a horizon of meaning and truth, and this remains true in their public readings. What that meaning and truth is appears not only in a single type of writing or speech but in the intertextuality of genres, that is to say, in the interplay of different kinds of text. Literary forms of discourse, whether in writing or in speech, are more originary forms of meaning than abstract propositions. Propositions are indeed abstract-ed from those types of discourse in which meaning is first expressed and have to be checked and refreshed by reference back to them. The composition and intertextuality of types of discourse do not simply generate subjective meaning. They refer to reality and to the quest for truth and good, but open up this reality and truth to insight and to their appropriation into a meaningful life.

With this prelude in mind, the interpretation of both lectionary texts and prayer texts will draw largely on insight into the diverse genres or types of discourse used.

The Lectionary Use of Scriptural Genres

Lectionary

Some words on the composition and nature of a sacramental lectionary are here placed before the consideration of genres. The two canons of baptism previously examined illustrate the way in which sacramental lectionaries in different traditions constitute a canon within a canon. The scriptural canon is universally recognized in the communion of Churches, but each Church makes its own selection from within this canon for its liturgical canon of readings. Thus this liturgical selection becomes integral to the way in which a particular tradition interprets the scriptures and passes them on, relating them to the Christian mystery commemorated in sacraments. Given the kind

---

1. For one pertinent examination of modes of discourse, or genres, see Paul Ricoeur, "Philosophy and Religious Language," *Figuring the Sacred: Religion, Narrative, and Imagination*, trans. David Pellauer, ed. Mark I. Wallace (Minneapolis: Fortress Press, 1995), 35–47. This type of investigation recurs in many of the essays in this volume.

of typological reading that has prevailed in selections of the liturgical canon, a critique of this canon can arise not only from scientific exegesis, but from within the assembly itself because of the way in which it relates to experience and to the knowledge of the scriptures.

Examples readily come to mind. At the Paschal vigil, in preparation for the sacraments of initiation, there are readings from the Book of Genesis about the sacrifice of Isaac and from the Book of Exodus about the destruction of the armies of Pharaoh at the crossing of the Red Sea. These are given a typological and baptismal reading. There are two reasons why this sounds improper to some congregations. First, there may be more sensitivity to the place of these scriptures within Judaism itself, and so some dissatisfaction with a Christian reductionism. A second reason is that both readings associate the action of God with very bellicose actions and attitudes and can conjure up images that do not have an adequate relationship to the historical events recorded.

A second example can be taken from the reading at a marriage liturgy of Ephesians 5, which relates marriage to the mystery of the union between Christ and his Church. This itself is a most fruitful comparison and conjunction, but the metaphor in the scriptural text is followed by a recitation of what were then prevailing household codes, and the author seems to sanction them in the name of Christ. Many a bridal couple and assembly therefore find this reading inappropriate, since in relation to their own experience the relation between husband and wife within the mystery of Christ and the Church needs a different kind of explanation.

Genres

While historical criticism is always applicable to the formation and transformation of a lectionary canon, we cannot afford to miss the fact that whatever selection of texts is made a certain number of literary genres inevitably recur in scriptural readings. The interaction of such genres has significance in itself, and maintaining it provides some norms for interpreting the proclamation of the word. In the texts used for baptism studied earlier, we could see the role of the different kinds of readings chosen. It is not only the imagery that draws hearers into the mystery of Christ, but according to their literary form the texts invite different kinds of response. What stands out within liturgical canons is the presence of narrative, prophecy, hymn (psalm and canticle), and wisdom literature.

Two things therefore have to be considered in seeing the role of the scriptural usage within sacramental worship: (*a*) what these different scriptural forms contribute to sacramental remembrance and appropriation of the mystery;[2] (*b*) what it means to interweave these types of reading with each other,

---

2. For an overview of scriptural forms, see the work of Walter Brueggemann, *The Creative Word: Canon as a Model for Biblical Education* (Philadelphia: Fortress Press, 1982).

either by setting them side by side or by taking them into prayers that are used. The significance of different kinds of text will thus be considered one by one, and in their relation to each other. Since it is a problematic issue, a special word also has to be said about the use of Old Testament stories in sacramental worship.

Narrative

The role of narrative is basic to keeping the memorial of past events. Four kinds of narrative are distinguishable: institution narrative, foundational story, foundational myth, and parable. Incorporated into sacramental worship, all these narratives are passed on from generation to generation and constantly repeated, with their promise of new beginning for each community that gathers to hear them. They call for a hearing that is fresh, with an openness of spirit that is not cluttered by presuppositions nor impeded by firmly entrenched systems of life or of thought. They carry the testimony of the One whose action is narrated and who is named within the narrative and are borne by the testimony of believers and messengers who pass on the story. They are repeated as stories of power and promise, but not within a repetition of events traceable in linear time. Rather they are always heard as an irruption into life, as an interruption of the tempo of life and the sequence of happenings that go on within the ordinary efforts of managing time. While they are stories for all who believe, they are always an address to this particular assembly, gathered within this rite and in this place. Hence in being there repeated, they are also there interpreted, for this people and in relation to their experiences, sorrows, and hopes.

Institution Narratives

Behind an institution narrative, there is always the larger story of beginnings and foundation. The Paschal Seder provides a good example of how the two kinds of story belong together. This order includes the story of the Paschal Lamb, with the command to keep this memorial rite. Behind this, there is the second type of foundational narrative, that which tells the events which brought the people into being. This includes the freeing from the slavery of Egypt, with the call of Moses, the plagues, the crossing of the Red Sea, the destruction of Pharaoh's army, the wandering in the desert, and the entry into the promised land. Both kinds of story have to be remembered, passed on, and repeated with ritual performance.

What the Church has been wont to call upon as an institution narrative can actually come in different forms. In the New Testament, the most obvious instance of a story of ritual foundation is that of the Last Supper, with the memorial command given by Jesus to the disciples. On the other hand, the baptism of Jesus in the Jordan, coupled with the story of the sending of the apostles with the mandate to teach and baptize, took on a similar foundational role for the sacrament of baptism. The other five sacraments of Catholic practice do not have clear institution stories, but liturgical traditions have in some sense provided one or another to fill this role. Thus the Byzantine liturgy of marriage recounts the story of the marriage feast at Cana, while the Western rites call on Jesus' prescription in Matthew 19 about fidelity to the original monogamous plan of creation. For the anointing of the sick, the sending of the disciples by Jesus with the command to preach, cast out demons, and anoint the sick (Mark 8) is sometimes used. The precept given in James 5 to pray over the sick supplements the story by way of providing an apostolic command. While penitential traditions[3] invoke Matthew 18:18 or John 22:21, sometimes Luke 18:9–14 on the humble confession of the publican, recommended by Jesus as an example to his followers, is drawn into this role.[4]

This appeal to what are called "institution narratives" is not without ambiguity. Both the story of the baptism of Jesus in the Jordan and the story of the Last Supper are told differently in the New Testament sources. This becomes more complicated when it is recognized that later tradition, homiletic and liturgical, diversifies the interpretation even further. The diversity in the Supper traditions is well known, but the stories used as mandate for baptism are also differently told. According to the text of Mark, by asking baptism of John Jesus associated himself with the sinners to whom John promised judgment and the Day of the Lord. Coming up out of the waters, out of this expression of solidarity, Jesus was given a revelation of God's love through the name bestowed on him and through the descent of God's Spirit, promised in the prophets for the Day of the Lord. This initiated him into a different perspective on God's kingdom, and so he went out among beasts, where he was tempted by Satan and ministered to by angels. It prepared him to preach the advent of God's reign and a Gospel of repentance. In the light of the Jordan revelation, however, this repentance is something new, as illustrated in the stories which follow about the call of disciples and the controversies over the interpretation of the Law.

In Luke's Gospel, it is the epiphany of Jesus as the beloved child of God on whom the Spirit descends which is put to the fore. Luke brings this out more strongly by associating this event with the genealogy which links Jesus with the beginnings of creation and with the story of salvation. The baptism is also prelude to a lengthy account of the testing in the desert, not found in Mark, which is the occasion for more elaboration on the nature of the kingdom of God which Jesus is to preach.

---

3. See David N. Power, "Contrition with Tears: Motivation for Repentance," *Church and Theology: Essays in Memory of Carl J. Peter,* ed. Peter C. Phan (Washington, D.C.: Catholic University of America Press, 1995), 216–22.

4. Behind these institutional narratives are the passion narratives, along with the various hermeneutical keys provided in the New Testament to the reading of this story: for Paul the Cross, for Philippians self-emptying, for Mark the Son of Man, for John the Word Made Flesh as servant of God/disciples. In each case, it is the language of rupture which is employed to give the meaning and reference of the story.

Homiletic and liturgical traditions associate this story of Jesus' baptism and mission with others, especially with that of Jesus' death or descent into Sheol.[5] When this connection is made, it appears that God's righteousness is fulfilled in Jesus when he descends into the Jordan. That is to say, it is time for God's righteousness, prepared in the Old Testament, to manifest itself. Liturgical texts also develop the theme that Jesus has purified the waters, so that demons have been expelled and believers can find cleansing from sin and rebirth. The event is given cosmic significance by associating the freeing of all creation with the baptism. This is graphically represented in the iconographical tradition which personifies the river Jordan and makes it an awed spectator of the scene. Finally, the theme of epiphany is given great prominence, and on this basis the gift of the Spirit in Christian baptism is made to stand out very clearly. With this reading of the baptismal narrative, it is clear that taking it as an institutional narrative for the sacrament of baptism has many implications.

The advantage of having variant traditions and interpretations of the one event is that it allows different communities to appropriate these founding traditions to their own situation and reading. The Word gives itself delightfully in its own polysemy, allowing the promise of God's kingdom to come about in different ways, as communities in their own experience of life find the meaning of their sacraments in these narratives. Jesus' solidarity with sinful humanity, his vision of God's kingdom, his wrestling with Satan, the purification of the waters for the cleansing from sin, the gift of the Spirit, or the symbolism of cosmic struggle and renewal, can each in turn be taken as the ground and warrant of baptismal practice. The personal promise given to candidates, the challenge to be reborn in Christ and to follow him, and the promise of the reversal of a wonted order of things must always occur, but they will occur differently, with variant interweavings of the stories and interpretations of tradition.

Founding / Foundational Story

Beyond or beneath the stories of institution, there is the story of the beginnings of what is celebrated in sacrament. An excellent example of how a foundational narrative is in its own way the foundation for cult is Deuteronomy 26.[6] This text is seen as the very basis for the story of the Exodus from Egypt and the story of the patriarchal covenants and call. It is a brief account of the original wandering of the one called by God and of the bounty which God bestows on him and his descendants. The setting for the story is cultic. When the people bring the baskets of their first fruits for the offering of sacrifice, they are to put them aside and first recall the story of their origins

---

5. See Kilian McDonnell, *The Baptism of Jesus in the Jordan* (Collegeville, Minn.: Liturgical Press, 1996).

6. For this insight, appeal is constantly made to G. von Rad, *Old Testament Theology*, vol. 1, *The Theology of Traditions*, trans. D. M. G. Stalker (New York: Harper & Row, 1965).

and give God thanks. Then they may give their offering to the priest. In a similar way, within the ritual of the Paschal Seder, the ritual mandate to eat the Paschal Lamb as an act of remembrance is set within the commemoration of the larger story of the liberation from Egypt.

The founding narrative is a word proclaimed from the past, but always addressed to the present. In liturgy, it is passed on not simply as a written text, but as the living remembrance of a living community. It comes wrapped in the testimony of all those witnesses to Christ who have translated this story into their own lives. It is thus a story about a time that was, but likewise about a recurrent coming into time that is irruption, interruption, and eruption. In that sense, the narrative is an eschatological proclamation, speaking of an event that by its continued force points to an origin of life outside the experienced flow of time. It allows something new to come into time as it is lived. The events it narrates are not reducible to delineation along a projection of linear time. Hence, on each occasion it has to be heard anew, received, and reinterpreted, in relation to this now present, in the gathering of disciples around the table of communion, where the gift proclaimed in the narrative is embodied. It is completed, in some sense made actual, by its juncture with the parabolic word that is about living by the wisdom of this story. Though the rites are cosmic and belong within a tradition, in virtue of the founding narrative each gathering is like a particular event, in response to a particular call, that interrupts the facticity of time. It is an interruption of the "course of events," and is to be heard with this sensitivity to the event and action proclaimed, and now irruptive.

The foundational story that grounds the Christian sacramental dispensation is of course the passion narrative, completed by the resurrection accounts. The examples of baptismal canons which have been given above, especially that from the Gelasian tradition, show how Christian commemoration interprets the passion and resurrection narratives by linking them with other types of story. At the Paschal vigil, where the elect were baptized, anointed, and introduced to the communion table, two other types of story were proclaimed. One type is that of foundational myth, provided here by the creation story and the story of the flood. The second type is the historical story, which serves to interpret the Christ event. At the vigil, this includes the story of Isaac, the story of the Paschal Lamb, and the story of the crossing of the Red Sea.[7]

The key thing about a foundational narrative is of course that it is a story in which the hearers identify their origins, with which they can in turn identify and which forges the identity to be passed on from generation to generation. Since it is a story of action and suffering, with plot and purpose, it supplies a model for action, bringing out the possibilities of action and ac-

---

7. In looking at blessing prayers, we have already noted how the passion has been viewed variously as combat with evil, as passage, and as sacrifice.

tive suffering in Christian life, indeed the basic way of following Jesus. He himself had pointed this out whenever he talked of the need of the Son of Man to suffer and the need to take up the cross to follow him. While this means openness to suffering, the verb used, however, is one of action, taking up the cross. The eschatological orientation of the story is supplied by the resurrection stories, in which the second coming is promised, the gift of the Spirit assured, and the completion of the kingdom of God anticipated.

As earlier recalled, in the course of Christian history the baptismal narrative, the Supper narrative, and the passion narrative have been given several different forms. These are not reducible by any kind of synopsis to one harmonious account. Starting with the variations in the New Testament accounts themselves, the story is constantly retold in different ways as it meets and converges with historical events and peoples' lives in different places, times, and cultures. The story is challenged at times of crisis, so that a retelling is particularly urgent. This retelling can be more formal, as in the Life of Jesus which inspired Ignatius of Loyola, or looked at through the prism of the life of an exemplary disciple such as Francis of Assisi. It can also work its ways into the devotions of the people, as with the *laude* and the passion plays of the twelfth century onward, or in the way of the Cross, or in the Gospel of Solentiname of the communities led by Ernesto Cardenal. These are tellings which help people identify with the story, and identify in it salvific power for their own lives. What was said before about the effect of working from a written tradition within a living context emerges quite clearly in this recounting of foundation stories.

Narrative / Foundational Myth

Foundational myths, such as that of creation or that of the flood, could for a long time be given a quasi-historical reading that reinforced a prevailing sense of order and cosmos, under the providence of a divine creative and salvific ordering. In face of scientific exploration of the universe and in face of a cultural sensitivity to what James Joyce called *chaosmos,* the stories are demythologized. Unfortunately, that at times means also cast aside, whereas in fact demythologization provides an opportunity to give them a poetic reading and grasp their purpose better, as well as their role as background to the narration of the Christ event. The stories of creation and of the flood were both responses to the calamity of evil and of sin, taking into account the way in which some mythologies presented a cosmos governed by dual principles of good and of evil. They do not pretend to tell historical fact, nor do they pretend to resolve the enigma of evil, but they place those who suffer before the affirmation of a good and provident God, even if in a way they only enlarge the dilemma of believing in providence. By enlarging it, they open up the question of how a good and loving God, who calls people into covenant, enters into the story of good and evil, without this disappearing from the world.

The Italian philosopher Gianni Vattimo draws attention to the opportunities opened by demythization for drawing more powerful spiritual force from the myths passed on by tradition.[8] Reading them for what they intended invites a new approach to truth and a quest for the way of living in *chaosmos* that is not illusory but is responsible and creative. What this means is that one must face the issues raised, even while going beyond the mythological resolution of those ages which gave them quasi-historical status. With this way of listening to the Christian myths, we are put in touch with Jesus' own way of undoing religious traditions that substituted the illusions of order for God's call to justice and the righteousness of the love of neighbor, even to the point of sacrificing oneself. This gift of self is more important in Jesus' teaching than all the ordinances of the Law that attempt to reflect a divinely ordered cosmology. In other words, mythical stories when read at baptism in an era of demythization may lead to the hearing of the passion narrative (or the baptism in the Jordan) in a fresh way.

Narrative / Parable

The role of reading from the parables, and indeed from the sayings of Jesus, in keeping memorial of the salvific event of his passion cannot afford to be missed.[9] The Church, beginning with the Gospels themselves, has allegorized some of the parables told by Jesus, but through exegesis some conjectures can be made about their original form. Some of them are simple stories intended for moral exhortation and instruction, asking from hearers or readers an ethical response to the proclamation of the kingdom of God. The parable of the sower, for example, is like that. Others, however, act more provocatively, calling accepted horizons and values into question in face of this proclamation. Such are the parables of the Samaritan's care for the man injured by robbers, that of the payment of the workers called to the vineyard throughout the course of the day, and that of the unjust steward.

The parables which reflect a reversal of standard moral wisdom are applied by the evangelists to the proclamation of the person of Jesus himself as Christ and Son of God. As it is more or less stated by several writers, in the passion the parabler became the parable. The evangelists themselves make this connection, when in their gathering of the Teacher's parables they relate them to his persecution, suffering, and death. Parables presented as stories about Jesus' suffering are also stories of the kind of extravagant wisdom or justice gathered from a knowledge of God and the divine covenant that

---

8. On this, see Richard Kearney, *The Poetics of Imagining: From Husserl to Lyotard* (London: HarperCollins*Academic*, 1991), 182–85. For a discussion of postmodernity by the same author, see Gianni Vattimo, *The End of Modernity*, trans. Jon R. Snyder (Baltimore: Johns Hopkins University Press, 1988).

9. For a good presentation of contemporary insights into parable and an ample bibliography, see John R. Donahue, *The Gospel in Parable: Metaphor, Narrative, and Theology in the Synoptic Gospels* (Philadelphia: Fortress Press, 1988).

leads to suffering. From this perspective, the wisdom of the Cross, as reflected upon by St. Paul in the first letter to the Corinthians, is the wisdom of the parables translated into the way followed by Jesus himself in contending with the wisdoms of this world, whether religious or rational. His stories and his death serve as a critique of those wisdoms that make order prevail, even over human suffering and the needs for justice.

In an essay found in the collection *Figuring the Sacred*, Paul Ricoeur summarizes how those who read the parables are engaged with Jesus himself, brought by them to a recognition and a confession of faith. The recognition, he says,

> this knowledge concerning the narrator of the parables, progresses across the parables by Jesus and about Jesus,...engendering a sorting out of various groups: the crowd, adversaries, friends, and disciples who are thereby placed in variable relations of proximity to the person of Jesus. This sorting is aimed at constituting the community of those close to him who hear and understand.[10]

Ricoeur then points out that the success of the teaching, its acceptance, as well as its rejection, led to a decline in the power of Jesus and to his inability to hold sway in his action for the suffering, against the force of those rejecting his wisdom:

> This advance of the word [through the parables] is paralleled by a decline of the body, if we consider that the success of Jesus the miracle worker on the bodies of those he heals at the beginning of his ministry leads to the defeat of Jesus' body in death.[11]

One might say that if we follow through from the parables to the betrayal, suffering, supper, and death of Jesus, we see Jesus himself progressing in wisdom. From preaching acceptance of God's kingdom, feeding the crowds, and healing the sick, thus exercising God's own power in the midst of the sinful and the sick, he moves to the moment where his only response to sin and to suffering is to accept betrayal. He hands himself over to death and its testimony to the love of the Father and the power of the Spirit. This of course is embodied in the sacrament of the Supper, the body which he leaves broken and crucified, to his followers, as a memorial, in never-ending testimony, and as daily parable of divine wisdom for his followers. It is into this sacrament that believers are initiated by their passage through the teaching and through the death and burial of the Lord whom they confess.

An important contribution of parable to sacrament is that it is the kind of story, and teaching through story, which reaches people in their daily lives and challenges the ethical perspectives which they bring to these. What happens in the parables is "that Jesus places the point of contact between God

---

10. Ricoeur, *Figuring the Sacred*, 162.
11. Ibid.

and human beings in the everyday world of human experience."[12] In other words, it is through the wisdom learned from parables that in living day to day the kingdom of God is encountered. Listening to the parables of Jesus invites interchange with similar kinds of story-telling in a people's own culture. What store of tales does a people have to provide cues to neighborly behavior, or to ways of treating the things of earth, or to attitudes to work and recompense? This is their wisdom and the life in which the Gospel of Jesus Christ takes root. What kind of challenge is presented to a people's traditional story-telling by the parables of the Gospel? The answer to this question may well be given, in proximity as it were to pool and table, by the reversals introduced into the people's own traditional stories as a result of hearing the Gospel stories. Indeed, unless the parables provoke this kind of culture-centered response they remain without parabolic effect. From within the challenge to the way of life presented in popular parable and Gospel parable, a people is readied to respond in faith to the story of the passion of Christ, with its promise of resurrection.

Narrative / Old Testament Stories

The reading of the stories of the covenant with the Israelites is quite problematic, since it is unacceptable to keep on reading them as stories about Christ and about Christians. They are indeed stories of salvation, but they are also tragic stories, full of the enigma of naming God. Perhaps it is as such that they could continue to be appropriated in a Christian community. Each of those chosen for the Paschal vigil raises harried questions about how God is named, as Jewish commentators themselves recognize. In receiving the gift of an heir and with him a whole inheritance of a people for generations to come, what could prevail on Abraham to do this son to death and believe that this was obedience to God? And how is God named, if it was indeed his desire to be known as one who could ask such disposal and renunciation of so precious a gift? Or was Abraham mistaken, led astray by religious expectations, as some commentators have contended? Attending to this story is a way of letting a community be asked about the nature of God's giving and what it is to live of the gifts given. In receiving gifts from God, do we learn to be reckless with the gifts? Is it that no gift is to be stored, treasured, held tight, but that receiving gift is itself for giving? In other words, is there some parable here of the bounty of God's giving in a kind of divine profligacy which carries through into the gift-given people, making them equally profligate in giving, and giving away?

The story of the freeing of the Israelites and of the crossing of the Red Sea is a tragic story, albeit it ends in a song of triumph in which God is hailed as victor over the chosen people's enemies. What naming of God goes on when its glory requires the slaughter of other peoples? What a believing people is

---

12. Ibid., 14.

faced with here is the fact that so often acclaiming God, and indeed in Christian history the God of Jesus Christ, means enmity with others. Not only does it mean that believers may be confronted by enemies who see their faith and their existence as threat, but they themselves set out to defeat and destroy others in virtue of what they proclaim. Can taking life be something that we do in God's name? Do we sing or do we lament when religious conflict brings about the destruction of any life, whosoever's it be.

Perhaps when a community hears the story of the destruction of Pharaoh's armies at the Paschal vigil, it ought to fall into a profound and tragic silence, not burst out in songs of joy. When the story is taken as a type of baptism, it is a double offense. First it offends the place which it has in the Jewish faith, as the story of their beginnings. Second, it offends against the tragedy of the story itself, which tells that faith, true faith indeed, brings conflict in its wake, a conflict resulting in human death. It calls on those of faith to enter the agony of living by faith and the agony of what looking for the glory of God's name may all too often entail. What does it mean to enter into the passion of Christ out of such trials?

Prophecy

In the canons of baptism for the Armenian and Roman Churches, the prophets are read in conjunction with the mystery of Christ and Christian baptism in order to show that there they have been fulfilled. Thus the cleansing waters of Ezekiel 36 are taken to illustrate the cleansing of baptism, and the story of the dry bones in Ezekiel 37 is applied to the new life given in the sacrament. Listening to them today, however, with a better sense of the role of prophecy in the Hebrew scriptures, a different response may be asked which fits in a different manner with the mystery of the sacraments.

Prophecy in the first place highlights God's initiative in dealing with the people of Israel, as well as his loving care and a constant maternal and spousal readiness to renew the covenant. In the second place prophecy translates the story of events into a personal address of love and of loving relationships. In the third place, the prophets call Israel to question its obedience to the Law, making an order of divine justice prevail over institutions, legal, kingly, or priestly. Without prophecy, the proclamation of God's works could not become a word event, because the element of address and covenantal interaction would be missing. The words "Thus says the Lord" need to occur in one form or another within the proclamation of the Gospel and within the celebration of sacrament.

In giving more place in its baptismal liturgy to texts from the prophets than to typological stories, the present Lutheran service for use in the United States exemplifies another way in which they serve this sacrament, and could serve others.[13] What is underscored in the selections made is the reality of

---

13. See above, p. 108.

covenant between God and Israel. Indeed, some Lutheran scholars, particularly John Reumann, have suggested that covenant is a good background to understanding how and why liturgical memorial is kept.[14] All that belongs within a covenantal relationship, on God's part and on Israel's, is transposed to the relationship between God and the Church. In this case, covenant acts more as a metaphor than as a type and is more readily transposed into a different historical setting.

In the third place, prophecy takes up the story of Israel's liberation in face of calamity, interpreting it anew, and even retelling it in face of disaster. Thus Ezekiel 36, which contains the verses on cleansing waters, is addressed to Israel at a time when she has been "made an inheritance to the rest of the nations," who "have taken my land to themselves for an inheritance." The prophet blames the people for not having remained faithful to the Law while under foreign domination, accusing them in God's person of having profaned his name. This goes back to their ways when they were still independent and their laws and institutions failed in keeping them faithful. Indeed, those holding authority are often held culpable, and it is clear that institutions are no guarantee in themselves of fidelity or of security. In spite of this, the prophet assures his hearers of cleansing from sin and of restoration as a people. The prophecy over the dry bones in Ezekiel 37 continues this theme, but then goes on to speak of a future when the power of the covenant shall arise more from being written in the hearts and in the flesh of the people rather than from its laws and institutions. The prophecy calls for a response of confidence most certainly, but it also by its nature asks for lament, which is more than simple repentance over failures.

This kind of prophecy sounds today in the ears of a Church aware of the failures of humanity, with all its skills, to maintain justice and peace. The Church itself is implicated in this, in its own behavior and in some of its traditions, such as its formal way of stigmatizing Jews and subjecting them at times to forced catechesis. This places failure not only in the sinfulness of the members, but points to institutions and to a leadership overburdened with legalistic concerns and with the conservation of order and standing. The sacraments themselves, as ordered by the Church, have in some respects failed as the medium of God's voice and of the grace that builds a fellowship in charity, which is also a testimony to God's grace. Heard at a sacramental celebration, the prophecies invite a remembrance of the counterstories which recall how in its very preaching of God and in its very ordering the Church has subverted the message of the Gospel. From this there may spring a lamentation, which calls for an entering into the Christ story and the Christ event within a new horizon of conversion.

---

14. John Reumann, *The Supper of the Lord: The New Testament, Ecumenical Dialogues, and Faith and Order on Eucharist* (Philadelphia: Fortress Press, 1985), 34–41.

Wisdom

Wisdom literature offers a practical avenue for integrating the reality and the wonder of creation into sacramental memorial. It has to do with the order of creation and with living in harmony with the things of the earth and with the rhythms of the day and the seasons. It locates the providence and care of God in watching over the earth and human life on the earth. It glorifies God's loving and providential care in human life through the image of Wisdom, or Sophia, whose delight it is to be with the children of the earth. It also gives the portrait of the just person who testifies to God's primacy and providence in the midst of human ambition and deceit, ready even to suffer in respect for this providence and promised immortality. God's justice and peace are truly rooted in the works of creation and given to those who in all things recognize God's hand and live a life with others that shows appreciation for God's ways and a love for God's justice.

While wisdom literature itself does not record the act of creation and gives little attention to history, it is read in liturgy against the background of the Genesis story of creation and of God's work for keeping the order of creation and an order of justice, through the divine covenantal dealings with Israel. The order of human harmony with creation advanced in wisdom is grounded in the act of divine love in creating the world and placing human beings in it, as told in the Genesis myth. The role of Israel in salvation is also best appreciated in seeing that the aim of God's covenant with her is to restore the kingdom and order of God's justice to the world, a restoration in which Israel was given a prophetic role among the nations, in her defeats as well as in her triumphs.

In a threefold way, the story of redemption given in Christ draws on wisdom imagery. First, Christ himself is portrayed as God's Wisdom. He takes on the traits of that feminine figure who delights in the world and invites to the love of God shown in the world, when its order is well respected and draws forth wonder. Secondly, he is given the portraiture of the just one who suffers, suffers even death, in testimony to God's life-giving care and the act of living in harmony with the justice built into the act of creation. Thirdly, it is wisdom literature which serves as the basis for the cosmic significance which some New Testament books give to Christ, in his death and in his being raised up as Lord. In these ways, a reflection on wisdom books shows that the act of redemption can be remembered, and its significance grasped, only in conjunction with due wonder at creation and with due obedience to the order of things established through God's wise and loving act in bringing the world into being and in being present in it with wise and loving care.

Wisdom literature fits well with parables, for it is about living the day-to-day life and living human relations to the universe, in the acknowledgment of the presence and the power of God. It asks the hearer to face the realities of life and to face the anxieties of misfortune, loss, sickness, death, in looking not to human wisdom but to the wisdom of God. The sacrament is indeed memorial of a historical event and has to do with the shape of living in time, in looking to the future promised in that event. Christians, however, like all people, live day by day according to a rhythm of day and night and season, and according to the times and places of human life and existence. This life is often troubled, and much happens in human relations with earth and cosmos that defies explanation. What wisdom literature asks is that this be lived in trust in a beneficent God. When it is related to the historic event of Christ, it tells us to look there for the sign and testimony of this love, not to well-ordered plans that smack too much of human ingenuity. Wisdom texts come for the most part from the Hebrew scriptures, but wisdom is found in the Gospels in the sayings and parables of Jesus, and in some of the teachings of the Apostle. It carries over into the psalms, some of which celebrate historical events, while others are prayers of the just who in the midst of life and death trust in the goodness of the God revealed in deeds and in the universe.

Hagiographies

It was a practice for several centuries to include readings from the Acts of the Martyrs in the sacramental liturgy, as it is still today in the liturgy of the hours.[15] In all probability, the hagiographies of holy persons replaced the Acts of Martyrs after the era of persecution. From one point of view this simply expresses the fact that the story of Christ is taken up in the witness given to him in martyrdom or in a holy life, and this belongs to the appropriation of the Christian mystery that takes place in sacramental liturgy. From another point of view one notices certain ideals in these acts that read strangely to contemporary ears. The Acts of the Martyrs focused on the shedding of blood, the complete configuration to Christ on the Cross in anticipation of the configuration to the risen life. This was a complete witness, one given in the flesh and not only in spirit, even to the giving over of the flesh to torment, and in the flesh of the complete self. The idiosyncrasy of this giving of self may, however, appear in clearer light as it is replaced by the importance given to virginity. This too is a giving in the flesh, but in its surrender and in a surrender of erotic desire. In times past it was thought that married persons who live as two in one flesh could never equal the life of virginity, something made clear in the prayer for the blessing of virgins in the Verona sacramentary. Many of these perspectives are not pertinent any more, but the need to look to living testimonies to the mystery of Christ remains.

The hagiographies of holy persons were written according to the pattern of what was known as the *exemplum*. This meant not only that they were pre-

---

15. B. de Gaiffre, "La lecture des Actes des Martyrs dans la prière liturgique en occident," *Analecta Bollandiana* 72 (1954): 134–66.

sented as models to follow, but that in them the living mystery of Christ was seen to shine forth. The life of Martin of Tours is a good case to consider.[16] He was presented as the ideal Christian inasmuch as he was monk, evange- lizer, monastic founder, and bishop. His story is told with borrowings from the Gospels, especially in stories of healings and the gathering of disciples. If he did not conform to Christ in the shedding of blood, he did live out the *exem- plum* of Christ, was indeed himself *exemplum*, in his public deeds and ministry. It can be readily seen how closely this relates to typology, and it is interesting that this remains the model for hagiography even in the life of Francis of As- sisi. In this latter case, the binding to Christ in the flesh, through asceticism and mystical ecstasy, is expressed in the reception of the stigmata.

From a contemporary perspective, one sees the need of a reading of non- scriptural material and a gathering from the witness of Christian life to complement the scriptural narratives. The liturgical reform frowns on adding anything to the scriptures in the celebration of sacrament, whatever it fos- ters for the divine office. However, in itself this is not a sacred principle. What should be read is another matter. If there were some liberty of choice, that made by local Churches would show how they see the appropriation of Christ's mystery within the historical and cultural situation of their own time and place.

The remembrance of the dead has to be wider than the stories of the saints. It is not enough to mention them, but their memories have to be cultivated, inasmuch as they cannot be truly remembered unless their stories are told. In the wake of the Holocaust and of wholesale violence on various continents, we have in our age come to see that the remembrance of victims is vital to the memory of the passion of Christ. Their stories also need to be incorporated into sacramental liturgy, especially around the eucharistic table, where the dead are named as the passion of Christ is recalled.

Psalms and Canticles

In the liturgy of baptism, psalms and canticles are placed in the mouth of the baptized or of the Church which welcomes them into its womb. In their variety and poetic quality, they serve as an address to the God who first addresses us. They also amply evoke the many different prayer forms that belong to this relationship. They continue to serve, both in themselves and as inspiration for hymnodic composition in different cultures. Rather than develop this point further, it is more expedient to move on to the prayers of the Church's own composition.

---

16. Sulpicius Severus, *Vita Sancti Martini Episcopi et Confessoris*, CSEL 1, 109–37. For a critical edition, see *Vie de Saint Martin,* ed. and trans. Jacques Fontaine, SC 133–35 (Paris: Éd. du Cerf, 1967).

Prayer Genres

Liturgical prayers are never simply the prayers of individual believers. Even when they give voice to an individual person, they belong within the community that is gathered. They express this community's sense of self and the manner of its relation with those who speak in its behalf and on its behalf. Above all, they express the community's multiple relation to God and to what it remembers as the stories of God in its past. In chapter 3, sacramental blessings have already been presented as the action of God's gift of the Word and the Spirit in the Church. This serves as background and foundation to the discussion of prayers in this chapter, and reference can be made to that discussion, of which the following is a further elaboration.

In euchological traditions, different prayer genres have emerged in sacramental celebration.[17] Roughly, they include praise, thanksgiving, intercession, exorcism, blessings, and at times even curses, invoked upon persons and things, repentance, offering, and lamentation. Diverse forms can actually be woven into one single prayer, so the most practical way to take up the question of genres is to take examples.

To begin, we can briefly recall what a structural approach has brought to light in many recent studies of eucharistic prayers. From the beginning, prayers such as that found in chapter 10 of the *Didache,* that called after *Addai and Mari,* or the one found in the *Apostolic Tradition* combined praise, thanksgiving, and intercession. The mixture of forms was done with some diversity in the formulas used, so that Cesare Giraudo was able to distinguish between traditions that highlighted thanksgiving and those built for the most part in the form of intercessions, to which the offering of gifts can be readily attached.[18] In the examination of these prayers, there is an ongoing discussion about the difference between prayers of praise, and prayers of thanksgiving. The former type gives voice to admiration at God's name and eternal, ineffable mystery. The latter is an articulation of gratitude that emerges from the recall of God's salvific deeds or actions. Alongside intercession, praise, and thanksgiving, there is the doxology that may conclude all and any of these forms. There are theological consequences to this attention to prayer forms, affecting the placement of the Supper narrative either within the thanksgiving or within the intercession, and hence also the placement of the *epiclesis* for the Spirit in relation to the Supper narrative and the words of Jesus.

Some examples from eucharistic traditions have been considered in chapter 3. Here an analysis of the blessing over the water in the baptismal

---

17. For attention to genres in liturgical theology, see Don Saliers, *Worship as Theology: Foretaste of Glory Divine* (Nashville: Abingdon Press, 1994), 85–136.

18. Cesare Giraudo, *La struttura letteraria della preghiera eucaristica* (Rome: Biblical Institute Press, 1981).

canons of the Gelasian and Armenian rites will be helpful.[19] Both blessings incorporate various types of invocation into the unit of blessing the font.

The Gelasian prayer is preceded, as is the fashion for blessing prayers in Roman liturgy, by a short collect which asks for the presence of God in the sacramental action. The blessing itself is structured as follows:

- Intercession, with elaborate invocation, asking for the action of the Spirit in and through the water

- Exorcism, addressed to the waters, for the driving out of evil spirits in the power of the living God and in the power of Christ, and ending with the recall of the risen Lord's command to baptize

- *Epiclesis* for the descent of the Spirit into the water, for the sanctification of the font, and for the cleansing and regeneration of those who go into it

- Doxology, which is eschatological in character, looking forward to the final judgment

It is generally surmised that the exorcism of the water is an addition to the prayer at a later time, reflecting a growing preoccupation with the work of evil spirits. The exorcism in the Gelasian sacramentary voices a growing concern that the world was infested with evil spirits, and responds to a preoccupation born of the struggle with earthly and cosmic elements particular to Frankish and Gaulish peoples. The prayer holds together as a unit, with or without this section. The intercession, the exorcism, and the *epiclesis* all provide the occasion to recall the deeds of God in creation and the paradigms of baptism in the life of Christ. Since the address to God at the beginning starts with the recall of creation, and the doxology looks ahead to the judgment at the end of time, the entire sweep of salvation history is integrated into the prayer, locating baptism in this unfolding.

The Armenian blessing of the font has this structure:

- Proclamation/Praise of God's works, in creation, in sending forth the apostles to preach and to baptize, in promising regeneration through water and the Spirit

- *Epiclesis* for the descent of the Spirit into the water, as prefigured in the baptism of Christ, and for the cleansing from sin, the regeneration, the adoption as children, and the inheritance of the kingdom for those to be baptized

- Doxology, which foresees the communion of the baptized in God's praise for all eternity

---

19. See above, chapter 4.

This prayer also takes in the whole sweep of God's action from creation into eternity. Unlike the Gelasian it has no exorcism, though there is mention of the cleansing of waters at Christ's baptism.

The *epiclesis* for the Spirit is central to both prayers, along with the remembrance of Christ's own baptism and his baptismal command. This fits the traditional structure of sacramental blessing, which is rooted both in memorial of Christ's mystery and in the recall of the divine command which guarantees the action of the Spirit in the sacrament being celebrated.

It is in the opening section of the blessing that the difference in liturgical traditions surfaces most clearly. The Latin tradition was always inclined to accentuate intercession, even finding this the proper moment at which to recall God's past salvific actions. The Eastern and Syrian traditions were more accustomed to laud God's works, before moving to the petition for the action of the Spirit and all that this brings with it.

The Trinitarian structure of the blessing prayer is not to be missed. Creation and salvation come from the Father. The divine action reaches its apex in Christ, with the Spirit at work both in creation and in the mysteries of Christ. From this divine action in Christ and the Spirit, there follows the work of grace in the Church. It leads to the eternal glory, in which the blessed share forever in the praise of the divine Trinity.

In brief, the qualities of sacramental prayer are illustrated by both these texts. It is Trinitarian, for in itself it is a proclamation and manifestation of the divine mystery of the sending from the Father of the Word and the Spirit. It is commemorative, rooted both in remembrance of God's actions and in the command to keep the sacrament. It is ecclesial, for it is done in the Church and by the Church. It is epicletic, for the power at work in the Church is in fact the power of the Holy Spirit. It is eschatological, for it culminates in a doxology which draws those who here and now celebrate into the eternity of divine glory and praise. It is doxological, for it goes beyond being thankful for what has been done for the world and for the Church into a contemplation of the divine mystery, a sharing in God's own glory.

Doxology

A further word can be said about doxology in its relation to memorial prayer. We need to note the distinction and complementarity of thanksgiving and doxology. This is particularly remarked in Eastern Churches. Basil of Caesarea in his treatise *On the Holy Spirit* distinguishes between two doxological formulas. As he puts it, we address the Father in thanksgiving when we say "*through* the Son and *in* the Spirit," but on the other hand we also address God in giving glory "to the Father *with* the Son and *with* the Spirit."[20] Thanksgiving expresses the economy of grace and redemption, whereas glorification wor-

---

20. St. Basil the Great, *On the Holy Spirit*, chapters 5–8, trans. David Anderson (Crestwood, N.Y.: St. Vladimir's Seminary Press, 1980), 22–42.

ships the eternal, ineffable, and unnameable Trinity, to which Christians may ascend in contemplation. In his treatise, Basil speaks only of the doxological formulas that close prayer. The anaphora attributed to Basil begins with praise of the ineffable mystery, as well as containing a concluding doxology.[21]

Germanus of Constantinople can also serve as an example of this distinction. This bishop of Constantinople at the time of the iconodulic controversies makes a notable distinction at the point of his treatise *On the Divine Liturgy*, where he speaks of the eucharistic prayer and its relation to the table of Christ's body and blood.[22] There he records the action of the Spirit in the prayer of the bishop, sealing, perfecting, and testifying to what Christ gives through his words, namely, his body and blood, for the sanctification of those at table. The divine action is completed in the sacramental gift which Christ gives and to which the Spirit testifies. The prayer itself is called an act of contemplation on the part of the bishop, and the faithful who approach this mystery contemplate it in its sacramental signs and partake of its holiness, doing both in the power of the Spirit. In the sacrament, the mystery of the Godhead is participated through the sacramental economy of grace, but it is also contemplated in itself, in its own inner holiness of the communion between Father, Son, and Spirit.

Both Basil and Germanus, therefore, distinguish in the eucharistic liturgy between the thanksgiving for the works of God in the Word and in the Spirit, and the glorification of the divine Trinity. They also distinguish between the remembrance of the economy of grace and the contemplation of the holy name of God which is revealed through this economy, while ever remaining ineffable and incomprehensible.

In Eastern theology, this liturgical distinction between thanksgiving and doxology corresponds to the theological distinction between *oikonomia* and *teologia*, a distinction still kept, for example, by such writers as Vladimir Lossky.[23] In recent Western theological works, Jürgen Moltmann takes some account of this distinction by writing of both the eucharistic concept of the Trinity and its doxological naming.[24] As he puts it, the eucharistic liturgy reveals the differentiation of divine persons in their work, while doxology returns the community to the sense of the eternal and unoriginated unity and *perichoresis* in the Godhead. In short, what we find in this appeal to the *lex orandi* of eucharistic celebration and commentary is a twofold Trinitarian reference. The one is to Christian participation in divine life through

21. In *Prex Eucharistica*, ed. A. Hänggi and I. Pahl, Spicilegium Friburgense 12 (Fribourg: Éditions Universitaires, 1968), 230–43.

22. St. Germanus of Constantinople, *On the Divine Liturgy*, the Greek text with translation, introduction, and commentary by Paul Meyendorff (Crestwood, N.Y.: St. Vladimir's Seminary Press, 1984), no. 41, pp. 95–99.

23. Vladimir Lossky, *Essai sur la théologie mystique de l'Église d'Orient* (Aubier: Éditions Montaigne, 1944), 5–20.

24. Jürgen Moltmann, *The Spirit of Life: A Universal Affirmation*, trans. Margaret Kohl (Minneapolis: Fortress Press, 1992), 298–306.

God's gracious action. The other is to the contemplation of the mystery of the Trinity in its own eternal *perichoresis*.

Exorcism and Offering

Beyond these most basic forms of prayer, others have also developed within sacramental traditions. Such is exorcism, which has already been mentioned. Exorcism is quite an ancient tradition in liturgy, but its meaning and practice underwent a notable development.

Exorcisms first symbolized the belief that things blessed are for the good of those who receive or use them, for "health of mind and body." The action of God, Christ, and the Spirit is sacramentally mediated through blessed things, and these serve as protection as well as for growth in holiness. Even the early prayers of the Eucharist pinpoint the nature of sacramental food as remedy against sin and against mortality, or everlasting death. Oil, olives, and cheese were blessed, likewise for both growth and protection. The immediate meaning was, however, that it is human beings who are assailed by evil spirits, so that it is they who are freed from them, through the medium of God's blessing of creatures. In this way, the exorcism actually developed a particular aspect of sacrament, which has to do with remedy, spiritual and physical.

Though it has no *epiclesis* because of the tendencies of the author to focus on the Word, a good illustration of the meaning of early exorcisms is the following prayer, found in the *Euchology of Serapion of Thmuis*. It is intended for the blessing of oil and water which those present will take away with them at the end of the Sunday synaxis:

> In the name of your only-begotten Son, Jesus Christ, we bless these creatures. We invoke the name of him who suffered, who was crucified, who rose from the dead and sits at the right hand of the Eternal, on this water and oil. Give these creatures the power to heal, let them drive out every fever, every demon and every sickness. Let them become for those who use them a healing and reviving remedy, in the name of your only-begotten Son, Jesus Christ.[25]

Later, and in particular in the medieval West, the idea grew that things themselves are infested by demons and that they have to be exorcized to be used, and especially to be used in sacraments.[26] Many texts of blessing are given in the compendium of A. Franz, and they often include exorcisms, which reflect the notion that the world is subject to demonic power and has to be released from it by God's intervention.[27] We might be inclined to

---

25. English translation, L. Deiss, *Springtime of the Liturgy: Liturgical Texts of the First Four Centuries* (Collegeville, Minn.: Liturgical Press, 1967), 198.

26. See David Power, "On Blessing Things," *Concilium* 178, *Blessing and Power* (Edinburgh: T. & T. Clark, 1985), 24–39.

27. A. Franz, *Die kirchlichen Benediktionen im Mittelalter,* 2 vols. (Freiburg-im-Breisgau: Herder, 1909; repr. Graz: Akademische Druck, 1960).

dismiss this as superstition, but we need to recall how it conjures up the lives of those who sought these blessings. The poor of the earth, subject to many natural and human catastrophes, encounter life as a constant contention with evil forces, which they personify in their prayer. While such exorcism may be out of vogue in the West, it has some affinities with the ways in which people on other continents see nature and the forces, both good and evil, at work within it and seek harmony with world and cosmos through invocation of higher powers. In some form or another, sacraments have to take account of the evil forces which affect life, and they adopt those forms of prayer which fit into cultural perceptions and bring God's action close to where and how people live.

Offering is also a kind of prayer which took on increasing prominence in sacramental traditions. This is discussed mainly in treating of the Eucharist, though it is not only bread and wine, but such things as olives, water, oil, and fruits, which are offered in early euchological collections. Here it is sufficient to note that offering is another form of relating to things of the earth and of relating them and their use to communion with God in sacrament and holiness. Irenaeus saw the offering of bread and wine as gratitude for the things of earth, similar to the offering of first fruits in the practices of levitical sacrifice. According to prayer traditions God is honored in the use of things of the earth, and God works for humans in and through them. Offering is not a depriving of self of these things, but a way of enjoying communion with God through their daily and through their sacramental usage.

When in later times, offering was looked upon either as foregoing something to honor God or a way of making propitiation, this was part of a spirituality which doubted the things of earth and our use of them. To offer things up was to suffer some loss or pain, it was to renounce them and remove oneself from their enjoyment in returning them to God. This is a contamination of sacramental tradition, not a healthy development of it. The positive side of such a development may lie in its ability to disturb consciences over a self-centered use of earthly goods and a tendency to accumulate them for less than godly purposes.

Martin Luther and the other sixteenth-century Reformers reacted against this kind of offering. They saw it as taking away from the sufficiency of Christ's death on the Cross and as a reliance on human works. Nonetheless, they retained much of the language of offering. Thus they spoke of the sacrifice or offering of thanksgiving, of offering gifts for the poor, and of the self-offering which Christians make when they throw themselves on Christ. None of this, according to them, justifies, since justification is pure gratuity, but it is done through the sanctification given by the Spirit in baptism.

The usages of offering and sacrifice ought not to be dismissed as out of date, for they can undergo further development. They still have significant place in the prayer traditions of some cultures. For example, in the composition of eucharistic prayers for use in Africa, one can note a strong accent on offering and sacrifice and the connection of this with blood. This fits into a tradition of sacrificing animals, of using their blood to signify covenant communion and therewith reconciliation, not only with the living but also with ancestors, as well as to signify protection against malignant spirits. As a prayer form which incorporates the memory of Christ, offering sacrifice or gift readily assimilates the imagery of the blood of the Cross which reconciles and makes covenant communion between God and humanity.

In his book *Worship as Body Language*, Elochukwu Uzukwu cites a prayer composed for use in Kenya. This prayer glosses the word of Jesus over the cup in the Supper narrative in this way:

> All of you, take this, drink this.
> It is my Blood, the Blood of the pact of brotherhood,
> Which begins today and lasts forever.
> It will be poured out for you and for all,
> So that sins may be forgiven.

Further down, the prayer offers the cup with these words:

> Owner of all things,
> We offer you this Cup in memory of your Son.
> We beg you for life,
> For healthy people with no disease.
> May they bear healthy children.
> And also women who suffer because they are barren,
> Open the way by which they may see children.
> Give the good life to our parents and kin who are with you.[28]

This one example illustrates how prayer genres may still develop, heeding both a liturgical tradition and other cultural traditions. In considering prayer genres, we have to remember that sacramental liturgies did not weave their own forms out of virgin cloth, but took inspiration from already existing prayer traditions. The influence of Jewish synagogue, table, and temple prayer has been much discussed in relation to the composition of eucharistic prayers. Account can also be taken of the influence of the Roman prayer form of the *prex* in the genesis of the Roman Canon. There is also a mine of information about how the Roman liturgy was adapted to use by Gauls and Franks in the composition of prayers, with a much greater accent on exorcisms, blessings of persons and objects, and petitions for the dead. Though often now criticized, this is a good example of how early traditions meet up with different cultures and adapt accordingly in the way in which prayer is formulated. Against its historical background, we can see how this kind of

---

28. Elochukwu E. Uzukwu, *Worship as Body Language: Introduction to Christian Worship: An African Orientation* (Collegeville, Minn.: Liturgical Press, 1997), 312–13. For a sample of other prayers composed in African Churches, see F. Kabasele Lumbala, *Celebrating Jesus Christ in Africa: Liturgy and Inculturation* (Maryknoll, N.Y.: Orbis Books, 1998), 35–41.

language may converge with the traditions of non-Western cultures and there develop along other lines.

Declarative Formula

Another development in liturgical formulas of the Latin tradition was the adoption of declarative words, then given more importance than prayers of blessing. For example, the formula "I baptize you" came to be considered essential to the sacrament, where the declaration accompanying immersion took over from the power of blessing and the profession of faith to constitute what was seen as the essence or substance of sacraments. The same thing happened with penance, where the formula "I absolve you" was given primacy over the petition "May almighty God have mercy on you, etc." Anointing and consignation were also supplied with such priestly declarations.

The prayer of early centuries does not use the declarative form, but locates the power of the action of the Spirit in the blessings which accompany ritual actions. Recent liturgical reform follows a compromise, both giving more prominence to prayer and keeping the declarative form. The reason given for the choice of the declarative form was that it makes clear the power and effect of the act of the priest who exercises the power of Christ. This itself is a theological issue, since it separates the presence and power of Christ in the priest from that of his presence and power, through the work of the Spirit, in the body. The issue is one of the theology of ministry, which is amply discussed in many publications, but of course it is more formally one of the theological understanding of Christ's relation to his body, the Church. Further discussion of this is not opportune here.[29]

Sacramental Imagination

The word comes to us as the Word of God, with the gift of the Spirit to enable us to hear and appropriate it into the worship and testimony of our own lives. The word and its inner testimony challenge common ways of seeing things and constructing society. Prayer does not represent the accomplishments of human understanding, but arises from the power of Word and Spirit. Good prayers are subversive of human self-consciousness and self-reliance. They guide and perfect human understanding and human action, but by reversing many of its suppositions. The different forms of word that have been considered help us to see how this divine gift works, and what kind of holy imagination it evokes in construing the world in which to live, as disciples of Jesus Christ, in the sharing of his Paschal mystery.

---

29. For some discussion of this issue, see David N. Power, "Representing Christ in Community and Sacrament," *Being a Priest Today*, ed. Donald J. Goergen (Collegeville, Minn.: Liturgical Press, 1992), 97–123.

Thus a proper appropriation of the various linguistic genres of scripture and liturgical prayer serves to restore the nature of sacrament itself as a divine language event, that is, as an event in which the twofold mission of Word and Spirit takes form anew among peoples called to the Gospel of Christ. Restoring its event character means being duly conscious of what it means for the sacramental imagination to encounter the cultural imagination of today. This is one thing in Western countries, another on other continents. The legacy of sacramental traditions has to be opened to encounters with the other, in view of how peoples live their history in time and place.

When secular and ecclesial traditions are experienced as weak, even though they carry much weight, communities are opened to the variety and nonsynchronic quality of scriptures, liturgical canons, and prayer forms. These perceptions help create a fertile ground for the advent of God's word. Within the confusion of the times, the creative imagination continues to relate the remembrance of Christ and the experience of God to the basic earthly elements of bread, wine, oil, and water, as well as to experiences of community, of body, of cosmos, and of time. The verbal forms are hitched to these ritual elements, examined in the previous chapter.

To open the sacramental imagination, whether to other cultures or to the post[-]modern, communities have to learn by experience to forego that kind of representational imagery which tries to bring the past or the divine into immediate presence, by the power of institution, the power of ritual imitation, or the power of conceptual thought and locution. Some strong traditions, such as those of sacrifice or of priesthood, have to be thought anew, with more attention to their occurrence in Christian tradition as critical metaphors rather than as ritual institutions.

At the same time, it is not on modernity's power to construe the world and its order that we can rely. God's word as it comes to us challenges reliance on human ingenuity and on the power of self-knowledge and self-containment. Instead, through the original stories, in their own shocking originality and diversity, the events of Jesus Christ's appearance, mission, teaching, and passion, are remembered and recounted as stories of "prophetic confusion," offering a critical stance on faith in God and on the tendency of religious practice to identify itself with the holy, and vice versa. They are also recalled as stories which question standard ethics, in the name of a more radical commitment to discipleship and to God's kingdom. Their character as testimony to the advent of God in the testimony of Word made flesh and of the gift of the inner Spirit call for openness to mystery, to the otherness of life and of persons, and to a creativity that goes with the call to all peoples.

The foundational narratives of Jesus' messianic appearance in the waters of the Jordan, of his passion and death, and of his Supper prayer and gift to his followers, invite Christians to attend to other stories of divine manifestation, of suffering and of gift. They intersect with these stories, especially with those of victims and of prophets. They invite into the celebration the testimonies of those who hunger for the kingdom of God and its justice. These stories, like those of Jesus himself, at times spring up from lamentation over betrayal, over loss, and indeed over the confusion of a seemingly divine absence. Myths about origins, whether the traditional Judeo-Christian ones or those of other peoples, are heard with ironic distanciation as expressions of the struggle to find meaning and coherence, where in fact confusion, doubt, and disharmony prevail in the lives of persons, communities, and whole peoples.

It is prophecy which serves to raise the question of fidelity, both God's and the Church's, while at the same time keeping the eschatological promise alive. Through an appropriation of parable and a fresh listening to both myth and story, we can see the active role of the imagination in interpretation. The imagination does not simply store images or conjure up a scene, recording as it were what has been told. It takes the story into converse with lives lived, with affect, with a search for truth, and guides in the construct of a response to the story. In this way, it probes whatever possibilities of suffering and action the narrative offers its readers/hearers when they allow themselves to be creative in the unfolding of the story in new circumstances, open to its questionings, its issues, and its horizons. Linking this with what was said about sacrament as a language event, it is the gift of the Spirit in the hearts of believers that makes it possible for them to remember, to be caught by the truth, to work with the images, plot, and issues of the narrative of the event of the Word, and to think ahead in hope, with commitment.

This can actually work out in practice in quite simple but enthralling a fashion. Some small faith communities among poor people in different parts of the world, for example, in communities in the *favelas* of Brazilian towns and cities and in the inner-city flats of Dublin, approach the matter this way.[30] First, the people are asked to tell their own story, as they see their lives to have been shaped by their circumstances and their surrounds, as well as by their religious inheritance, telling it in face of their present struggles. Then they are asked to tell the story of Christ's teaching and passion, which they do in the common ways of story-telling, maybe even miming or acting out parts of the story. After that, they are invited to tell their own stories again, and this can be done with plottings and insights noticeably different from the first telling. Finally, they engage in conversation about what all this means in terms of living their lives as Christ's disciples, affirming how they feel the Spirit's presence and Christ's love, assenting to what must be accepted, pointing to actions that are possible when they take stock of their own potential, and what it all means in terms of naming and of helping the neighbor. From this, they move to a sharing of bread together, or to a eucharistic sharing of bread and wine, body and blood of Christ, if a priest is

---

30. I am aware of this from contacts with a confrère, Ciaran Earley, O.M.I., who has ministered both in Brazil and in Dublin.

part of the gathering. In virtue of the memorial in word, the presence of Christ in the table ritual is palpable, showing itself not only in the elements but in the hands and faces of those who gather in this way around him to receive his sustaining and nourishing gift.

We need also see how integral prayer is to sacramental commemoration. It is within prayer that the sacramental imagination exercises creativity, construing what has been heard in the scriptures to meet new situations. The people move to the sacramental act, be it table or water or oil, through allowing God's word to enter their lives in the various ways mentioned. But between word and sacramental action, giving form to the action, is the prayer. The different kinds of prayer offer different modes of moving from word to action, different ways of entering the action in which the community is one with Christ, and in Christ. The meaning of the movement and of the action is modified by the prevailing type of prayer. The type of prayer itself is determined by how the word is heard. Moving to water or bread or oil through thanksgiving is not the same thing as moving to it through praise or through intercession. People in the circumstances of their lives and in their recasting of Paschal memories within this context may be moved to any one of these forms, or indeed perhaps also to lament. The kind of prayer betokens the congregation's sensitivity to the hearing of the word and the sensitivity to the presence of Word and Spirit configuring their lives. It betokens the relations to community, to the surrounding world, to one another, and to God which the word engenders and which now form themselves in prayer.

New forms of prayer emerge in Churches today, accordingly as they see the Gospel take root among them in relation to their culture and in relation to the conditions of their lives as cultures change and paradigms break down. As we have see, among some African peoples the eucharistic prayer will embrace memories and attitudes of sacrifice and its reconciling power. In other African sacramental prayers, as in the anointing of the sick, the memory of Christ's healing ministry and of the healing power of his blood is to the fore, and so with this a strong cry of intercession and an exorcism of evil. In some Asian prayers, sacramental prayers are richly contemplative, catching the people in wonder at the all-pervading presence in the universe of Word and Spirit. Some Western Churches, with their harsh memories of centuries of the Christian persecution of minorities and the religious wars between Christians, are moved to lament for deeds done and for what occurs now as a divine absence in their cultures.

In the past, it was said in scholastic writing that the words gave form to the matter. With a much richer appreciation of sacramental prayer and its relation to the hearing of the word, this idiom assumes much larger and more provocative meaning. What is it to enter the baptismal water in awed wonder at the presence of God in the elements of the universe and at the invitation into the *perichoresis* of the world, in which one vibrates with the divine *perichoresis*? What is it to pray over the oil and over the sick in the memory of Jesus' healing touch and in the memory of his blood that reconciles, reconciles even to death itself? What is it to share Christ's body and blood in the lament to which biblical narratives, in conjunction with harassed memories of human deeds, invite? Simple actions like these take on such variant meanings in the power of the prayer proclaimed, but they are variants on the communion that all have in the one God-given Word and Spirit.

Conclusion: Sacramental Memorial

The present chapter has reflected upon the verbal, found both in proclamation and in prayer, thus following up on what has been said about bodily ritual action. First it was shown how sacramental rites deal with the scriptures. The diversity of scriptural texts was then examined for what this says to the meaning of sacrament as a language event and for some of the problems raised by traditional practices. This was followed by a reflection on the kinds of prayer found in sacramental euchology. Finally, some thoughts were offered on the challenges that are to be taken up by the sacramental imagination.

What has thus been said about the verbal elements of sacrament gives insight into the meaning and practice of keeping memorial of the Christ event. To keep memorial is to relate the present, which is characteristically in flux, to the past and to the future. The past does not repeat itself, but it has left its traces and its testimony, and thus transmits its power to change history and lives by a pattern of action which emerges from it. This power, and presence in power, comes through the uses of language and always works toward the future. Narrative construes the plot of the event, the pattern of Christ's being and of the being of his disciples, which is the life of self-giving, for God and for the world. The parables reveal the wisdom and the justice inherent in this pattern of being. The mythical relates it to the dilemmas of human existence, as it is confronted by its own ephemerity and by the chaos and evil in the world, relating Christ's memorial to the enigma of being in time when confronted by mortality and by the challenges to the possibility of being in the future. The prophetic and hymnic texts of God's word place the memorial in the context of communion in being and in hope, of address, promise and response.

Moved and inspired by this advent of the Word and by the accompanying gift of the Spirit, the Church is awakened to keeping memory. It carries over the power of the event, proclaimed and passed on through such variant genres, into its own formative prayer. The event remembered is thus in this prayer, and in the action that forms but one with it, alive in the future-oriented present of each and every Church community and gathering. In its different forms, the prayer spells out the present of diverse ways of relating in community, through Christ and the Spirit, to God. Doxology submits all, in wonder, to the eternal mystery of God, from whom Word and Spirit come, and into whom those who keep memorial are drawn. The ethical is always a factor in keeping memorial. The event remembered is present not only in the sacraments, but in the Christian people, in the life of discipleship, in the action and suffering for justice's sake, to which the remembered event moves participants.

These considerations on the word are related to what was said in chapter 2 about the hermeneutical key provided by blessing prayers and about the characteristics of sacramental action as *anamnesis* and as *mimesis*. Narrative, prophecy, thanksgiving, and intercession relate most readily to expectant remembrance, or *anamnesis*. Parable, wisdom, praise, and doxology reflect most fully the *mimesis* of the communion of Christ with the Father in the Spirit on the one hand, and the communion with his disciples and suffering humanity on the other, as it was expressed in the communion of the Last Supper and in the cry on the Cross. The Church prays in remembrance of the Pasch of Jesus Christ, in whose story it finds its identity as his body and in the hope of which it looks forward to the always unexpected advent of God's reign in times to come. The community is grounded in the universe through creation stories, it is addressed by the prophetic word of God, and it invokes the name of Christ given to him in narrative in order to address the Father, who is known in proclamation as the Father of the Lord Jesus Christ. It is as a Church, gathered in the communion of bread and wine and all that this signifies, as pointed out in chapter 4, that the community prays. Through words of parable and wisdom, Christians find their way of being such a communion, in the knowledge of the ever-present grace and reign of God. In this communion, created in the Spirit, it is both one with the earth and suffering humanity and one in and with the divine communion of eternal, ineffable, and self-giving love.

— *Chapter Six* —

Seeing Is Believing:
The Force of the Visual

Writing of the need for fresh directions in Christian art and its use in worship, John Dillenberger comments that

> the sidetracking of art within major sections of Protestantism, the use of plaster saints in Catholicism as reminders rather than as objects that express the power of art, and the pronounced neglect of the visual arts on the part of most scholars of religion ... have obliterated too much of what belongs to the world's humanity.[1]

The visual is in fact integral to sacramental worship and does much to determine the form, shape, and meaning of sacraments. The action is seen as well as done. It is also marked by its setting, by the place wherein worship is celebrated and with which the sacramental action is one. Just as the rites of tradition need interpretation, so do the places where sacraments were and are celebrated. Ghislain Lafont states this very succinctly when he writes of the relation between word, symbolic action, and space:

> One cannot isolate the linguistic symbols of which [eucharistic language] is made up from the entire complex of plastic symbols to which they are intimately linked. The bond between the articulate sounds of the mouth and the movements of the body is not left aside but rather affirmed: there are prayer gestures which correspond to prayer formulas: they embody them, and in turn, render them more authentic. The exigency of a decor (in the sense that Gadamer speaks of the decorative element in art) is likewise born, as it were naturally, of the type and rhythm of the words which are exchanged in the Eucharist. The language of the latter emerges within a spatial framework and a division of the framework without which the words would not be able to reach the fullness of their meaning: the light, the vestments, the props are

---

1. John Dillenberger, *The Visual Arts and Christianity in America* (New York: Crossroad, 1989), 201.

178

not external to the significance of the language: they create its milieu, whether of superabundance, or of what one could call super-austerity.[2]

To account then for the role of the visual in sacramental worship, we can address five considerations in this chapter. First, something will be said in general about the place of the visual in the act of worship. Second, we will consider the effect of the design of the place in which sacraments are celebrated. Third, we will look at the role and power of interior art. Fourth, we will distinguish between different kinds of artistic representation. Finally, we will reflect on the appropriation of the visual by participants in our contemporary setting, marked in some cases by post[-]modern perceptions and in others by the effort to present inculturated art forms within the liturgical place and the liturgical act.

The Place of the Visual in Sacramental Action

Considering the visual as an element that is integral, and not merely subsidiary, to sacramental form, we can recall what was said earlier about baptistries and the relation of space and figurative art to the service of Christian initiation. One of the earliest reminders of the power that the visual had to draw congregations into the act of worship and to unveil its meaning is found in mystagogical catechesis. Ambrose of Milan started his instructions to the neophytes during Easter Week by drawing their attention to the things which they saw, such as the water, the oil, and the bread and wine. From these perceptions he moved to biblical stories that he related to the things and actions seen, and in this way moved on to explanations of what is done in the sacraments. Theodore of Mopsuestia is also well known for his attention to things and actions seen, sometimes indeed interpreting them allegorically to make reference to the mystery commemorated, as when he likened the deacons laying the cloth on the altar to the women preparing the body of Christ to lay it in the tomb.

The writings of the Pseudo-Dionysius pave the way for the accent on the visual in the worship and catechesis of the Byzantine liturgy. Having explained the proclamation and praise of the mystery of Christ that takes place in the eucharistic prayer, the Pseudo-Dionysius comments on the rite of communion, starting at the point where the hierarch (that is, bishop) unveils the gifts:

This is what the hierarch unveils in the sacred rites, when he uncovers the veiled gifts, when he makes a multiplicity of what had originally been one, when the distributed sacrament and those receiving it are made perfectly one, when a perfect communion of all the participants

---

2. Ghislain Lafont, *God, Time, and Being,* trans. Leonard Maluf (Petersham, Mass.: St. Bede's Publications, 1992), 140.

is achieved. By resorting to the perceptible, to imagery, he makes clear that which gives life to our minds. He offers Jesus Christ to our view. He shows how out of love for humanity Christ emerged from the hiddenness of his divinity to take on human shape, to be utterly incarnate among us while yet remaining unmixed. . . . He shows how, inspired by love for us, his kindly activities called the human race to enter participation with himself and tò have a share in his own goodness . . . [to] truly enter into communion with God and with the divine things.[3]

In this comment, we see how the word, the act of taking communion, and what is seen converge in drawing the communicants into participation. With this accent on the visual, the Byzantine liturgy seems to have developed in such a way that the participation of the faithful was more by way of sight than by way of word and action, though song and the proclamation of the word were never lost. In describing the high point of liturgical development in the Church of Hagia Sophia in Constantinople, Richard Krautheimer portrays the interaction of emperor and patriarch "under the great dome of the H. Sophia":

Both the ecclesiastical and secular hierarchies were permeated by the light of the Divinity which emanated from the center of heaven and spread to the angels, patriarch, clergy, and Emperor. Thus in the H. Sophia the spatial shapes, the light, and the colours all emanate from the center dome. The ordinary people in the aisles and galleries remained hidden in the shadows and behind curtains. Only from afar were they able to see the light, the colours, and the glory that streamed from the center, the seat of Godhead.[4]

However, the primary role of images in Byzantine liturgy was, and is, as it were to make the word visible, especially the Word who is Jesus Christ made flesh. The principal icons that belong in liturgy are those of his salvific events, namely, the incarnation, birth of the virgin Mother, the transfiguration, the acts of his ministry, and particularly all those that belong to the Paschal sequence, that is, the crucifixion, the burial, the descent into hell, the resurrection. Images of angels and saints also belong within the liturgy of the Church by way of expressing its participation in the heavenly worship of the Trinity.[5] Thus these latter coincide with what is said in the words of the Byzantine anaphoras of Basil and John Chrysostom. All defenders of icons,

---

3. *Pseudo-Dionysius: The Complete Works,* trans. Colm Luibheid (New York: Paulist, 1987), 222.

4. Richard Krautheimer, *Early Christian and Byzantine Architecture* (Baltimore: Penguin Books, 1965; repr. 1967), 160.

5. The intention behind the use of icons is explained in the words of John of Jerusalem in the early eighth century, quoted by Hans-Joachim Schulz, *The Byzantine Liturgy* (New York: Pueblo, 1986), 52–54. This writer explained that the paintings present what the sacred scriptures teach, that is, the economy of salvation. He then lists all that is represented, from the incarnation to the ascension, and includes mention of the saints and angels.

such as John Damascene[6] and Theodore of Studion,[7] place the icon within the order of images by which the divine is manifested, and also relate them to the words of the scriptures. It is in reference to the Word Incarnate that the meaning and purpose of icons is understood, as well as their place alongside the words of the scriptures. In the Word Incarnate there is the image and resemblance of the Father. Human beings, the things of the world, images that recall or that foretell salvific events, and icons of Christ, Mary, the saints, and the angels all in differing degrees disclose the divine. They present the divine to those who venerate them, and they draw them into the mystery of what is manifested. Since this mystery cannot be manifested in its own essence, images, like words, allow those on whom they look to ascend beyond the seen to what is unseen. In this, icons do indeed parallel and can be integrated into sacramental worship.

In the Latin West, there was also an accentuation of the visual aspects of ritual, allied with the elements of space. In the early medieval *ordines* of the Mass, when the priest falls silent, attention is drawn to his entry into the Canon.[8] In other words, the very silence is used to draw more attention to what is seen and to find imaged in this the entry into the holy of holies where the sacrifice is celebrated. Ocular vision and imagination are brought to work in concert. Relics were to be beheld and touched. While the sacrament of the Lord's body was not to be touched, it was to be looked at with worship and in the hope of its healing power.

Thus participation by sight eclipsed participation by action and by hearing. The most drastic evidence of this is the way in which visual communion in the Eucharist took the place of going to the table and receiving Christ's body and blood.[9] This remained a devotion to the remembrance of Christ's passion, but this could not be done without resort to words, though the words were privatized rather than given public form. For example, in the twelfth-century *Lay Folks Mass Book*, the devout are given this prayer to say at the elevation of the host:

Praised be thou, king, and blessed be thou, king,
of all thy gifts good and thanked be thou, king.
Iesu, all my joying, that for me spilt thy blood and died upon the rood,
Thou givest me grace to sing the song of thy praising.[10]

---

6. St. John of Damascus, *On the Divine Images: Three Apologies against Those Who Attack the Divine Images*, trans. David Anderson (Crestwood, N.Y.: St. Vladimir's Seminary Press, 1980).

7. Theodore the Studite, *On the Holy Images*, trans. Catharine Roth (Crestwood, N.Y.: St. Vladimir's Seminary Press, 1981).

8. See Michel Andrieu, *Les Ordines Romani du Haut Moyen Age* (Louvain. Spicilegium Sacrum Lovaniense, 1960–61), 2:334, and 3:182.

9. See Edouard Dumoutet, *Le désir de voir l'hostie et les origines de la dévotion au saint-sacrement* (Paris: Beauchesne, 1926).

10. *The Lay Folks Mass Book, or The Manner of Hearing Mass with Rubrics and Devotions for the People*, with appendix, notes, and glossary by Thomas Frederick Simmons (London: N. Trübner & Co., 1879), 40.

As is clear, not only Eastern but Western Churches were adorned with image and narrative painting. The theory put forward of this use by Latin authors put an emphasis on their didactic purpose.[11] The authority most often quoted is Gregory the Great, in a letter to the bishop of Marseilles, Serenus. Images, he wrote, "are to be employed in churches, so that those who are illiterate might at least read by seeing on the walls what they cannot read in books."[12] This is echoed centuries later by both Thomas Aquinas and Bonaventure, the latter, however, more closely following the views of Augustine that images supply somehow for ignorance and the waywardness of human emotions.[13] On the other hand, however, there was the idea that all visible things may lead to the knowledge of the invisible and to God, as signs lead to the signified.

Above and beyond the use of images and the visually perceptible in sacramental action, and beyond the didactic use professed by the writers mentioned, there was in both East and West a veneration of images that gave them an inherent power that instilled reverence and made them the object of cult. These images were consecrated, incensed, illumined by lights, and variously revered and implored. Popular piety may not have made many distinctions, but authorities explained that they were not to be considered to have power in and of themselves, but only as images of Christ, Mary, or some holy person. If they exercised some power of mediation, this was because of their consecration by the Church. Consecration indeed of images supplied both a ground for devotion and an explanation for Church authorities and theologians. Historians of the image, like Belting[14] and Freedberg,[15] comment much on this, but it is a cult that separates images and their veneration from sacramental action.

Naturally, one cannot account for the place of the image in worship without considering the reactions of the Reformers to their use. It was primarily the cult of images in themselves that raised problems for them. At the time of the Reformation, the battle over images was taken up in the context of the appeal to the primacy of God's Word. In *The Institutes of the Christian Religion*, Calvin opposed having images of God, and in this appealed to the authority of the Old Testament and to Augustine.[16] Pedagogically, he could not believe that images would not hold attention, and hence take both from

---

11. An overview of positions may be found in David Freedberg, *The Power of Images: Studies in the History and Theory of Response* (Chicago and London: University of Chicago Press, 1989), 161–91.

12. *Epistola IX. Ad Serenum Episcopum Massiliensem.* PL 77: 1128–29.

13. Freedberg, *The Power of Images*, 162–66.

14. Hans Belting, *Likeness and Presence: A History of the Image before the Era of Art*, trans. Edmund Jephcott (Chicago and London: University of Chicago Press, 1994), *passim*.

15. Freedberg, *The Power of Images*, 82–160.

16. John Calvin, *Institutes of the Christian Religion*, trans. Henry Beveridge (Grand Rapids, Mich.: W. Eerdmans, 1989; repr. 1993), bk. 1, chap. 11, 90–103.

the word of justification and from the message of the simple signs of baptism and the Lord's Supper.

Calvin's claim was that for four centuries there were no images in places of worship. In his support of the visual primacy of the sacramental signs themselves, he could indeed have found support in Ambrose, and in the whole fifth-century mystagogical practice. This was an elaborate development of the signs and actions of the rites, against the background of scriptural words. On the other hand, while they did not have images of God nor crucifixes, representational art was placed quite early in Christian places of worship, as has been seen in the example of early baptistries. It was quite in keeping with this kind of representation that Calvin admitted the possibility of some images, but laid down clear limits. They were not to be of God, nor of saints, but could represent the majesty of God or historical events from the Bible. Such images could educate, and that was his reason for allowing them in moderation, but he preferred not to see them in church buildings where worship is held.

Martin Luther was more tolerant of images than Calvin. While he severely opposed what he saw as the veneration or worship of images, he grew to think that in themselves they were neutral. Given the priority of the word, and if the priority of the word were respected, images could even have some function in illustrating its meaning so that it could be better grasped by the illiterate. Thus he allowed for altar pieces in churches and of course was well served by Lucas Cranach. In these images, it is the crucifixion which has priority in keeping with the doctrine of justification. Even the subject matter could bring out the priority of word and faith. Thus Cranach in a painting for the predella at Wittenberg showed Christ crucified in the center, with Luther himself in the pulpit on the one side and on the other the congregation which his preaching draws to the Cross.[17] The issue is indeed that of recognizing the impact and focus of the visual, but relating it to the sacramental action of word and rite. The following considerations are addressed to this point.

The Design of Places of Worship

The earlier overview of the location of baptism illustrated what is involved in considering the visual elements in the sacramental tradition. This includes considering what the assembly saw done, the impact on the celebration of the disposition of the place in which they worshiped, and the role of iconography in enhancing celebration and drawing out sacramental meanings. The importance of place can here be considered in terms of the placement of buildings for worship and in terms of the marking off of spaces within the edifice.

---

17. See fig. 284 in Belting, *Likeness and Presence*, 469.

The Placement of Buildings

First there is the matter of where buildings are placed or situated. Mention has already been made of the difference between a baptism and a chrismation in a secluded baptistry and the same services carried out in full view of the congregation of the faithful. In early and medieval centuries, the baptistry was always outside the precincts of the main worship space, designated for the Eucharist. Its architectural relation to the main church differs from place to place, but it always meant a passage from the baptistry to join the eucharistic assembly. Excavations have even shown the existence of what is called the double cathedral, that is two worship spaces in separate buildings alongside one another, as well as a separate baptistry.[18] It is surmised that the second space may have served the catechumenate, though there is some dispute as to whether the purpose was the same in all instances. In some cases, as at Trèves (now Trier) and Milan, the baptistry was situated in between the two buildings, providing a passage from one to the other. This would have meant at the time of baptism quite literally passing from catechumenate to assembly through the baptistry, and the rites performed therein. The rebirth in the Spirit and the dying and rising with Christ would have taken place prior to joining the congregation. Today, when these rites are performed in the main church, in full view of the assembly, these become actions of the whole congregation and the candidates experience a different relation to it. In the two cases, the elect are brought to the communal table by two distinct processes, even though the material rites performed are the same in both instances.

Beyond this question of the relation within or between buildings in a worship complex there is the relation of these buildings to their environment. The Jewish synagogue and house church in Dura Europos fit into a line of dwelling houses and shops. This was also the case for some places of worship in early Rome. Others were outside the city, on the domain of wealthy members. Christians did not stand out by reason of their places of worship. Like the people themselves, the buildings were hidden within the cultural mass. It was what went on inside that made them distinctive.

In the world of medieval cathedrals, the main church and the baptistry belong within the complex of a special ecclesiastical geography, which in turn fits into the town or city. As well as the spaces for worship, there were the episcopal residence, the episcopal offices, the chancery, the canonical precincts, and the *hôtel Dieu*, or the place for hospitality and the care of the needy. The cathedral belonged with the town, surrounded by human habitations and other buildings of public use. This is the world to which

---

18. See P. Piva, *La cattedrale doppia* (Bologna, 1990). There is a survey of excavations that show a double cathedral, with reference to building accommodations for the present-day catechumenate, neocatechumenate, or evangelization program, in a new periodical in Italian and English, *Ecclesia: Arte, architettura e comunicazione/art, architecture and communication*, no. 4 (1996): 54–61. In a proposed plan, the baptismal fountain would be in a portico at the entrance to the main body of the church, but not in the church itself.

sacramental worship belongs, and the world into which people must enter in order to take part in it. In medieval cities, the cathedral and its adjacent buildings became architecturally and visually the center of the whole city. Churches in rural areas, placed atop a hill, but in the midst of dwellings, spoke to the surrounding countryside. These buildings had the effect of sanctifying the whole universe of living, and of including all human life and labor within the worship that with tower and pinnacle moved heavenward.[19]

In Washington, D.C., when the Episcopal Church chose a site for the National Cathedral and the Catholic Church one for the Shrine of the Immaculate Conception, they did so in what was the nineteenth-century view of the medieval perspective. They are situated with open spaces in front, set away from other buildings. The skyline of the city seen from its center on the Mall, or on an approach to it, is dominated by these buildings. They are of course perceived in a way different from what was common either in the Middle Ages or in the nineteenth century. In contemporary Washington, they are a curiosity or a puzzle. The storefront churches of evangelical groups may in fact be more significant of the place of Christianity in a contemporary Western world.

Interior Design

The marking off of space within the building where the sacrament is celebrated is also important to celebration and its meaning. Historians of eucharistic liturgy have pointed to the difference in symbolism between a rite enshrouded in spatial mystery and a rite of a common table of which all have full view and to which all have access. There are many variants to this. In the marking off of a holy space, there is the sanctuary space of Latin churches, where the altar and priest are physically separated but still visible, though not heard. There is also the holy space of Byzantine churches, where the *iconostasis* marks off the sanctuary from the body of the church. Where there is an open table, as with Protestant rites, there is still a difference between the one who stands at the table to proclaim the words of Christ and to invite to communion, and those who in humility and penance "creep" to the table. In some modern liturgies where all stand around, it is words and roles, not difference in location, that demarcate liturgical participation.

Some care and circumspection, however, need to be taken in considering the import of architecture and interior design for worship. Among historians of art and architecture, there are different approaches to this.[20] There is the functional approach, which asks what liturgical purpose was served and how

---

19. On the cathedral complex and the relation between cathedral and city, see Alain Erlande-Brandenburg, *The Cathedral: The Social and Architectural Dynamics of Construction*, trans. Martin Thom (New York: Cambridge University Press, 1994).

20. On these approaches to architecture, see Sible de Blaauw, "Architecture and Liturgy in Late Antiquity and the Middle Ages," *Archiv für Liturgiewissenschaft* 33 (1991): 1–34.

design related to the rites performed in the building. There is also an approach which begins with the consideration of form. That is to say, the first question asked is what the building represents. Only then can one ask how the rites were performed in this place. Thus, the Byzantine Church of Hagia Sophia is itself a representation of the divine mystery and its manifestation, in light and majesty. The liturgical rites then occur within a space that is itself manifestation and representation and are adapted to this space. The Byzantine church building itself was conceived as a place sanctified by the presence of God, but its form, ornamentation, and the placing of the *iconostasis* were over time given a cosmic, a human, and a salvific signification.[21] Cosmically, it signified the earth, the heavens, and what is above the heavens, that hierarchy by which the divine is manifested in creation and through which human beings ascend to the divine. The separation by the screen of the nave from the sanctuary, where the mysteries are celebrated, signified both the separation of the earthly from the heavenly, and the transition from the earthly to the heavenly. Humanly, the form of the building and the *iconostasis* expressed the ascent through sight and the visible to things invisible. Salvifically, the symbolism represented the mystery of the Word made flesh and the heavenly liturgy in which the earthly is a participation.

Comparably, the Roman basilica was conceived as a suitable place for the gathering of the *plebs Dei,* to whom much of the imagery of the city *plebs* was attached. The performance of some rites, for example, the grand entry procession, was the result of, not the reason for, the shape of the building. The old style of basilica was followed by the Romanesque, and this in turn by Gothic architecture. Each style expressed a particular vision of the divine and the earthly, and the liturgy which the building housed was in great part configured to the building.

This in effect leads to a third approach, which is more distinctly historical. Here the effort is to look for coordination or correspondence between buildings constructed at a given time and the prevailing symbolic and religious notions of the era. Thus Gothic cathedrals represent the upward heavenly thrust that faith gives to the entire cosmopolis, and beneath their arches and under the light of their windows the liturgy takes on this shape and meaning. Since its architecture is peculiarly suited to musical sound, such an edifice accommodates a liturgy that edifies through this medium of expression. There have been many studies which make the parallel between this type of building and the architectonic structure of the scholastic *summa* in theology.[22]

---

21. See Leonid Ouspensky, "The Meaning and Language of Icons," in *The Meaning of Icons* by Leonid Ouspensky and Vladimir Lossky (Crestwood, N.Y.: St. Vladimir's Seminary Press, 1982), 23–50.

22. See, for example, the essay "The Semiology of Space in the Middle Ages: On Manuscript Painting, Sacred Architecture, Scholasticism and Music," in Jesse M. Gellrich, *The Idea of the Book in the Middle Ages: Language Theory, Mythology, and Fiction* (Ithaca and London: Cornell University Press, 1985), 51–93.

A fourth approach is a more sociological and critical one. It addresses the influence of paradigms of the social upon church buildings, as, for example, the hierarchical separation of clergy and laity, or the marginalization of women in the C/church. This will be taken up together with other critical queries about sacrament in a later chapter.

None of these approaches can outrule the others, and they overlap and complement one another. It may be suggested that the approach which gives prevalence to the form of a building deserves primary attention. This is because it takes the building as a work in itself and allows it to express its own meaning, recognizing that architects and builders may have wanted to bring perceptions of the holy to the fore that were not related to the liturgy but stood by themselves as a suitable expression of the holy. The place did of course have its impact on the sense of the sacramental celebration, but in understanding this the point of departure is not functional. It is the consideration of the building itself as a work.

Interior Art

The four approaches taken to explaining architecture are likewise adopted in looking at images. Here we can first offer some historical perspectives on church art, and then say something about the power of images as this affects worship.

Historical Perspectives: Image and Worship

At the time of the Eastern controversy over the use of icons, the defense of images was that they were manifestations of divine mysteries and bore the power of what they represented.[23] Jaroslav Pelikan in *The Spirit of Eastern Christendom* remarks that at the time of these iconodulic controversies, both parties were agreed on one thing.[24] This was that images did have power. It was over the nature of the power that they fought. Did they, as John Damascene taught, make present the mysteries, or did they capture attention and promote idolatrous worship, as their opponents contended?

The use of figurative representations is widely known, whether these be figures of Christ, Mary and the saints, the Cross or later the Crucifix, and today these often serve to express the true intent and meaning of the iconic. However, these were not always incorporated into worship in the same way. The role that they had is known either through their actual placement or through the activity that surrounded them. Their varied placement can be illustrated by attending to their display on walls or in the apse of a church

23. For lengthy discussion of the image, very detailed illustration, and a collection of texts that show how they were viewed and considered in different periods of history, see Belting, *Likeness and Presence*.

24. Jaroslav Pelikan, *The Spirit of Eastern Christendom (600–1700)* (Chicago and London: University of Chicago Press, 1974), 117–33.

building, to their integration into the *iconostasis* of an Eastern church, or
to use as folding altarpieces in medieval Western buildings. Since they had
these varied positions, the relation to them of the sacramental action was
also varied.

Attention today to the figurative images helps us to retrieve a proper sense
of the iconic, as distinct from the more subjective role that is at times given
to the work of art. In art history, a work can be identified as the work of
a specific artist, and this is considered of great moment. The identity of the
artist enters the interpretation of the painting, and much attention is given
to its subjective appeal, to what it asks of the viewer by way of personal
engagement with the vision and perspectives of the artist. The iconic, on the
contrary, as it is attributed to the figurative images of early and medieval
worship, is almost "without an artist." Certainly, the painters of these icons
were not known, they were expected to conform to the rules of expression
in vogue, and the images were even in some cases thought to have had a
miraculous production. The best-known case of this latter perception is the
image of the face of Christ on the cloth known as the *Veronica,* or true image,
around which the legend of a holy woman of this name developed.[25] What
historians, such as Belting, or philosophers, such as Jean-Luc Marion,[26] now
point to is their representative quality; not in the sense of figurative imitation,
but in the sense of giving a presence to the person or mystery that is imaged,
and often to the power that is exercised through the medium of the icon.
The image is not looked upon as some artist's impression of the mystery,
but is looked to as to one who is gazing upon those who behold it. In other
words, the icon has a transparent quality, it brings the mystery of God, of
Christ, or of the Virgin, to the viewer or to the congregation that venerates
it. It does not attract attention to itself, but brings the mystery that is shown
through it into the presence of the viewers and draws them beyond itself to
this gracious and benevolent mystery.

There is then in images this sense of the divine mystery communicating
itself through the image, or exercising a power through it, or drawing to the
contemplation of itself by as it were drawing viewers through it to a higher
contemplation. However, in his work Belting points out that in the course
of history icons have not been static and unidimensional in form, but that
a variety of modes have been used to display the mystery. First, of course, it
has to be noted that in proximity to sacramental celebration not only images
of persons but also narrative images were displayed. Second, even the images
of the persons of Christ, Mary, and the saints were given different forms, so
that we can speak of iconic schools, even if the names of individual artists
are not known. The contrast between specific works helps to show how the
mystery revealed and celebrated could be diversely expressed.

---

25. See Belting, *Likeness and Presence,* 218–22.
26. Jean-Luc Marion, *La Croisée du visible et de l'invisible* (Paris: La Différence, 1985).

This contrast can be made by considering three prints of the Madonna and Child from Belting's *Likeness and Presence*. The first (fig. 8) is from the Pantheon in Rome, after it had been taken over as a church building and dedicated to Holy Mary at the site of the martyrs (*Sancta Maria ad Martyres*). This icon is a representation of mother and child, which is done in fact to resemble a portrait. This was a technique used to indicate that the picture can in fact be traced back to those whom it represents, not to suggest simply a memory of them but their actual presence. The second figure is found at Kiev, and is originally from a sixth-century building on Mount Sinai (fig. 22). In this both Mary and Christ gaze out at those who gaze upon them. Mary is holding the child in her arms, but there is no other interaction between them. In the third figure, from the thirteenth-century duomo in Siena (fig. 224), while Mary still gazes out at the viewer, the child is playing with the veil on his mother's head and his eyes are turned upward toward this veil, so that he does not at all look outward. As Belting comments, this kind of image gives considerable place to the emotive and seems to make both Mary and the child Christ more approachable. This does not mean that it is not iconic, that it is no longer a presentation of a mystery that is presenced, but rather that the human enactment of this mystery is given greater prominence.

In the history of the image, Belting points to two phases in depiction and use that changed its role in worship. The first of these is a phase in which public images were multiplied and reproduced for use in private devotions, and in the process the depictions often became more sensuous, more appealing to the affective, and lost touch with the force of the original as something unique. The second is the period during which, as he says, the image "encountered art."[27] This can be noted in Renaissance painting, or in Flemish and Dutch painters, and is marked by the fact that importance is now given to the artist, to his techniques, and indeed to his artistic vision. When painters such as Rubens or Raphael were commissioned to do works for places of worship (Rubens in the Chiesa Nuova, Raphael in the Sistine), on the one hand they had to respect the venerable tradition of the iconic image, whose origins are divine rather than human. On the other hand, they wanted to bring this into the life of those for whom they did their work, using the new techniques of painting which they developed. The solution was to paint the image of a venerable image and place it in a recognizable and more immediate context, by perhaps surrounding it with still life, indoor scenes, landscapes, or known personages. This made the image the recollection of a devotion, rather than itself the object of devotion. From this of course there followed a much freer approach to painting holy persons and biblical scenes, with little or no claim to actually representing the mystery, and more appeal to the imaginative, the affective, and the devotional.

---

27. See the essay "Religion and Art: The Crisis of the Image at the Beginning of the Modern Era," in Belting, *Likeness and Presence*, 458–90.

Quite interestingly, the hermeneutical approach to painting, such as that found in Gadamer's *Truth and Method,* calls attention even to such paintings in ways that distance them from the artist and from purely subjective responses. A larger awareness of the iconic emerges, relating the world of the picture to the world of the viewer, with the invitation to transcend one's personal impressions to respond to what is presented and enter that world. This is not achieved by empathy with the feelings of the artist, or by getting to know the artist's personal story, but by letting the subject matter enter one's own horizons, with the relation to being that emerges from the work of art.

The Power of Images

The history of religious devotion makes us appreciate Calvin's demurrals all too well. On the other hand, stripping down churches so that celebration can take place with total attention on word and action deprives a congregation of one medium of entering the mystery. At times of reform, this is the tendency. It happened in the sixteenth century, as it happened quite often in the renovation of Catholic churches after Vatican II. This went with a strongly functional approach to church architecture and interior design. It was fueled by a twofold reaction. The first was against the plaster statues and the banality of recent church decoration. The second was against the way in which statues and images and tabernacles could devour the attention of worshipers, to the detriment of sacramental participation. The intent was to alert the congregation more fully to the enactment of the ritual. The result may well be that the place as such is then made powerless.

Visiting a new church in Rome recently, the present writer met a woman who was acting as its custodian. Comment on the spaciousness of the interior and on the way in which the disposition of place made the rites of Mass and baptism visible to all, provoked the rejoinder, "ma non c'é niente qui," there is nothing here. The immediate sense of this response was that there were no paintings, no mosaics, no statues, nothing to catch and please the eye. The underlying meaning, however, was that without such things the place itself had no power, it had nothing to offer. People could indeed see the altar and all that was done there. Without the presence of depictions of Christ, Mary, the saints, and biblical scenes, there was nothing to speak to them of the great communion of saints at the table or of what is represented in the liturgical rites.

Some images have power for the precise reason that a ritual action or devotional use has invested them with this. Objects are consecrated, be this the vestments and vessels for Mass or the images of Mary and the saints that are displayed for veneration. Some have power because of the way in which they are located in the place of worship and integrated into the action. This is the case with the icons on the iconastasis of the Byzantine liturgy. It is also true of the *imago pietatis* placed in front of the altar table in some Western churches. This is the name given to the scene of the deposition of Christ from the Cross, being laid in the arms of his sorrowful mother.[28] To serve as the frontispiece for an altar, the central image of the deposition, that is the head and torso of Christ, was separated from the rest of the scene and placed facing the people. Sometimes the figure in this diminished presentation was supported on either side by angels. Thus it was, as it were, shown to the people below the altar, as the host and chalice were shown to them over or on the altar, indicating a correspondence between the mystery celebrated and the sorrowful death and burial of the Lord.

However, to even grasp the power that they have in sacramental action, we need to think about the power of images in themselves, precisely as works of art. The historical and contemporary examples mentioned above invite us to ask in a more theoretical and practical way about the power of images and their integration into the very form of sacrament. In his work entitled *The Power of Images*, David Freedberg quotes a sentence from Nelson Goodman to capture the effect which they have on those who read images as a work:

> [The] subsumption of aesthetic under cognitive excellence calls for one more reminder that the cognitive, while contrasted with both the practical and the passive, does not exclude the sensory or the emotive, that what we know through art is felt in our bones and nerves and muscles as well as grasped by our minds, that all the sensitivity and responsiveness of the organism participates in the interpretation of symbols.[29]

Goodman is not here writing only of painting but is concerned with all forms of artistic expression, including the written. Freedberg, however, is quite right in applying this to the visual arts. The response to them is total, and they draw persons into what they represent in mind, heart, and body.

This is better understood from Hans-Georg Gadamer's reflections on the work of visual art in *Truth and Method*.[30] He explains the work of visual art as an event of being. At the same time, he notes how it belongs in context. To be properly appreciated, it has to be viewed in its intended setting, not in an art gallery, where so many paintings and sculptures are viewed today. The relation to the setting is not often self-evident or totally transparent, but placed where they are images draw what surrounds them into the being of what is represented. It is there that the image brings to the fore the potentiality for being of what is represented, be it person, story, or mystery. It takes in the surroundings, captures them as it were in the communion of what it shows as coming to be.

---

28. Hans Belting, *The Image and Its Public in the Middle Ages: Form and Function of Early Paintings of the Passion*, trans. Mark Bartusis and Raymond Meyer (New Rochelle, N.Y.: Aristide D. Caratzas, 1990), 80–84.

29. Nelson Goodman, *Languages of Art*, cited by Freedberg, *The Power of Images*, 25.

30. Hans-George Gadamer, *Truth and Method*, trans. rev. Joel Weinsheimer and Donald G. Marshall, 2d rev. ed. (New York: Continuum, 1994), 101–64.

It would be a misunderstanding to see this as mere reproduction or image. Like the written text and the ritual, the work of art is distanciated from the thing, event, or person represented. It shows them coming to be, not in some static depiction of what they were, but in a new situation. It unveils the power to come to be of what is represented, both in themselves and in others.

While portraiture is not Gadamer's favored example of the visual arts, it serves to make the point of what is represented. In a good portrait, for example, that of Innocent XI in the Villa Doria Pamphili in Rome, the viewer is not simply given a good likeness. In the work, what is seen is the power of the man and his impact on history, as well as the imagination of what one might well expect of such a personage. Rembrandt's self-portraits are a rumination on his life at its different stages, on how he has been and on what might yet be in time to come. The effect is to carry the viewer beyond the images of Rembrandt himself to the thought of the seasons of life. Seen in the National Gallery of Art in Washington rather than in the Villa Doria Pamphili, the portrait of Innocent XI by Velásquez lost its relations to a family history and to the history of Rome, and so much of its impact. Placed in a museum rather than in a dwelling-place, the self-portraits of Rembrandt have not got the same appeal to human life in its unfolding.

These are important observations for what is offered through visual representations in a place of worship. They can be taken from there and put in a museum, as happens, for example, with the altar triptychs put in European art galleries. What they represent is much lost in that setting, since they belong with and to the altar. The problem surfaces in the write-up in brochures for an exhibition, which tend to be activities of conceptual understanding.

Emphasizing context is not to say, on the other hand, that every work of art found in a place of worship was produced with worship in mind. The religious art of this milieu is not to be treated as strictly functional. Sometimes indeed it appears to have been produced without any thought to liturgical function, but to express some other aspect of religious belief and tradition. The hagiographies of the stained-glass windows of Bourges or Chartres present models of holiness and the power of a saint's intercession. Giotto's frescoes of the life of Francis in Assisi are not ordered to enhancing the liturgical function of the place. Such representations have little direct connection with the mystery enacted in the memorial of Christ's Pasch, but that does not mean that they have no impact on participation in it.

Much imagery, however, whether in a baptistry or in a church, is intended to speak of, or to, the sacramental mysteries. We have already seen the purpose of icons in the Byzantine liturgy to make the word visible and to draw the congregation into the act of worship which unites heaven and earth. The Chi-Rho of San Giovanni *in fonte* or the scene of Christ's baptism in San Ponziano are about participation of the neophytes in this mystery. The representation of the Cross above the ark of the covenant and the milling of wheat in the medallions of the sanctuary of Saint-Denis in Paris are representations of the mystery of the Eucharist there celebrated. These representations are not, however, functional in the sense that they advance the celebration as a ritual act, but only in the sense that they are intended to represent what is going on to those at hand for the action.

A more functional work of art is one intended to be used in the celebration. This appears in objects used, as with the precious chalice of the Abbot Suger or the monstrances in which the Blessed Sacrament was to be displayed for veneration. To return to triptychs, one could say that scenes of the Last Supper are in some respect functional. In the collegiate church in Louvain, where, for example, one finds Dirc Bouts's *Institution of the Eucharist*, it is clear that this is about what takes place at the altar. Placed in a dining room of a religious community, as is the case with Leonardo da Vinci's famous painting of the Last Supper, the depiction of the Supper connects the meals of the fraternity with the action of Christ and his disciples. It may also make a connection between the meal of the friars and their own celebration of the Eucharist. Placed over the *banco del sacramento* in the Church of Santa Margherita in Venice, the Last Supper by Tintoretto acclaims that the work of the confraternity is centered on the Eucharist, while it also sanctifies the labors of its board in relation to both God and the sick whom they served.[31] In reproduction, none of these paintings have the power which they draw from, and give to, their respective settings.

It is a mistake to look at such pictures as simply representations of an idea or to connect them historically with ideas of the time in too narrow a way, granted that their historical setting helps to explain them. This is a problem with Barbara Lane's *The Altar and the Altarpiece*.[32] She connects fifteenth-century Netherlandish altar pieces with theological notions, such as real presence, transubstantiation, priesthood, and sacrifice. This sounds as though the painters were simply transposing to image the intellectual conceptions of the period. As a result, there is much for which she does not account, apart from losing sight of the particular import of art in itself. For example, while she notes that in Bouts's representation of the Supper there is an empty plate in front of the Christ who is holding wafer and chalice, she does not ask what this signifies. She is right to note the similarity to the priest at the altar, in that the bread and wine are given the shape and form of what was then used. It seems wrong to give all attention to this and see

---

31. See Thomas Worthen, "Tintoretto's Paintings for the *Banco del Sacramento* in S. Margherita," *Art Bulletin* 78, no. 4 (1996): 707–32. The *banco* was the bench, placed at the entrance to the Blessed Sacrament Chapel, at which the members of the board of the confraternity (all lay) presided at its meetings. On either side of the painting of the Last Supper there were paintings by Tintoretto of the Washing of the Apostles' Feet and of the Agony in the Garden. The first celebrated the confraternity's charitable work in devotion to the sick, the second the devotion to God in prayer, both done following the example of Christ.

32. Barbara Lane, *The Altar and the Altarpiece: Sacramental Themes in Early Netherlandish Painting* (New York: Harper & Row, 1984). See the review of the book by Carol J. Purtle, *Art Bulletin* 69, no. 4 (1987): 652–53.

in it a validation of priestly power to change wafer and wine into Christ's body and blood. One has to look more keenly at the plate. This plate is that on which the Paschal Lamb was served, and from which those at table had eaten it. When Christ blesses bread and wine, it is empty. By its absence, not by its presence, the Lamb prefigures the eucharistic sacrament and sacrifice.[33] The presence of twelve apostles around the table, without any singling out of Judas, represents discipleship and fellowship rather than the bitterness of betrayal in some of the Gospel accounts. Thus the painting does not simply image some ideas or simply reproduce the actions of the priest. It brings several things and actions into converse, such as Paschal Lamb and Last Supper, Supper and Eucharist, blessing and teaching, Eucharist and fellowship.

As anthropological foundation to the role of art or image, Freedberg's mention of the affective links the perception of a work with the work of the imagination. A viewer does not simply record or imbibe an image. Looking at an action or a representation is an act of communication between viewer and object. Viewers look at something out of the world to which they themselves belong. They are, as it were, a world in themselves, a universe of meanings and cultural expressions, a universe which takes in the domestic, the political, the ancestral, as well as the religious. In terms borrowed from Gadamer, they are wrought by their prejudgments in their acts of perceptions. In the interaction, the active imagination has a crucial role, for it brings the two worlds together into discourse.

The ritual action perceived, or the image displayed, opens an avenue to another world of being and meaning, a world that challenges and invites. In the world of celebration, these works speak of the religious, and in context they speak of what is going on in the sacrament. They bring some determinacy to the form of celebration. There is then a dialectic between the viewer and the work, two worlds of meaning that encounter each other, with the invitation to the viewer to engage with the world of being and of meaning represented and offered by the image.

Worshiping in churches built and furbished in a previous era necessitates a communication across time and cultures. The liturgical vessel, the fresco, or the mosaic is most likely to register cultural and time-bound perceptions peculiar to the period in which it was made, though one should never reduce an image to the generic of an era. Every work has its own individuality. Across time when the prejudgments of a people have changed within the context of social, political, and cultural perceptions, the imaginative communication between work and viewer comes less easily to act. There can even be a conflict of visions. The conjunction of the Eucharist with Mary and Child, for example, in the Netherlandish altarpieces mentioned above does not readily

---

33. This relation to the Old Covenant is more strongly brought out by reason of the fact that the side panels depict the story of Abraham and Melchisedech, the gathering of the Manna, the sleep of Elijah from which he was awoken to eat of the food God gave him, and the eating of the Paschal Lamb.

synchronize with current modes of participation or with the current theological and liturgical accent on the Pasch. Engaging with that vision is not to be discounted, but it requires more imaginative effort.

Kinds of Representation

Recognizing this role of the active imagination in perceiving and engaging with works of art in places of worship, it is useful to distinguish different kinds of representation. The meaning of the work, however, is not to be confused with readings of the work that are found in commentaries. In the history of interpretation, there are symbolic, moral, and anagogic readings of church art. These, however, generally proceed from some idea about their function, and do not attend to the form of the art work as we would today. In considering how different images enhance the power of sacramental worship, it is possible to consider the power inherent in the form itself rather than rely on these more conceptual interpretations.

The variety of imagery or types of work could be illustrated for different epochs, but one example will here suffice. Restricting himself to early Christian iconography, André Grabar distinguishes five kinds of biblical image that served in frescoes, sculptures, mosaics, and paintings.[34] First, there are image-signs, such as the peacock or the olive palm. Then there are representations of biblical personages, such as the ancestors of Jesus. Third, there are depictions of biblical scenes from Old and New Testament, particularly of those scenes which served as types of Christ, the Church, or the sacraments. Fourth, there are depictions of animals, which in places of worship represent the peace brought to the earth by the Messiah. Finally, there are theophanies from the Old Testament, such as the scene of the four creatures before the throne of God in Ezekiel or the worship in the temple described in Isaiah 6. Each of these is a genre of its own, and this factor belongs to its impact and interpretation.

When form and genre are taken into account, there is an analogy with the attention to genres in interpreting written work. Different kinds of image in fact appeal differently to observers and affect sacramental participation in different ways. The Byzantine icon represents the presence of the mysteries and of the saints. It is given a form which readily evokes such representation. The Western medieval display of the Madonna and Child over an altar link the Eucharist and the mystery of the incarnation. This is especially true when host and cup are evoked in the picture, as when Mary's breast is shaped like the host, which was the thing that was most clearly on display in the Mass

---

34. André Grabar, "Les sujets bibliques au service de l'iconographie chrétienne," in *La Bibbia nell'alto medioevo*, Settimane di studio del centro italiano di studi sull'alto medioevo (Spoleto: Presso la sede del centro, 1963), 384–412. For a more general survey, with copious illustrations, see André Grabar, *Les Voies de la création en iconographie chrétienne: Antiquité et moyen âge* (Paris: Flammarion, 1979).

and in eucharistic devotion, with the chalice placed somewhere close by.[35] It is also related to the Last Supper, as in the painting by Bouts.[36]

Narrative representation has a role in determining sacramental representation and participation. In the baptistry of San Giovanni, the paintings relate readily to prebaptismal catechesis. The moment of baptismal immersion and chrismation is drawn into the reality of which the stories illustrated speak and into the eschatological horizon of the figures from Ezekiel. The narrative sequence can be even more elaborate, comprising a larger galaxy of events. Such is the case with the ceiling of St. Martin, through which the mystery of the death and resurrection celebrated in the sanctuary is tied in with the Old Testament, the public ministry of Jesus, and the exemplary lives of the saints, in this case Martin of Tours.[37]

Narrative sequences can also be more obviously didactic. The stained-glass of the Saint-Denis belongs within this range. There is a choice of episodes to teach about the mystery of the Eucharist. The representation is more abstract, almost like a still life. A story is recalled (the bunch of grapes brought back to the Israel camp by the spies sent into Canaan), or a metaphor is put in an action setting (the milling of wheat), but what is shown is more a still image than a story.

In some images, the narrative is more clearly represented as type of sacrament. Such is the case when the baptism of Jesus in the Jordan is given primordial place. The fresco or mosaic can elaborate on this typology. When the river Jordan itself is personified, the event is given cosmological significance. When the angels are included in postures of veneration, with their hands covered with royal purple or green, the sense of theophany in the event of Jesus' baptism is heightened, with implications for the neophytes' participation in this type.

Folk art merits a place in the history of art's relation to worship. The poignancy of its recall of the suffering of Jesus and Mary, as well as its simplicity in figuring the presence of the saints, are not to be forgotten. The images of the suffering Christ or of the dead Christ in Italian, Spanish, Mexican, Filipino, and North American Hispanic churches are not considered great works of art. They have a vehemence, even a crudity, however, which draws the suffering of Christ close to the people. Moreover, they were given an active role in liturgical action, especially on Good Friday, and remained (still remain) the whole year in the church, within the space where the sacraments are celebrated.

---

35. Robert Campin, *Madonna and Child before a Fire Screen*, The National Gallery, London. Reproduced in Lane, *The Altar and the Altarpiece*, frontispiece.

36. See Lane, *The Altar and the Altarpiece*, 106.

37. See Ernst Murbach, *The Painted Romanesque Ceiling of St. Martin in Zillis*, edited and with photographs by Peter Heman, trans. Janet Seligman (New York and Washington, D.C.: Frederick A. Praeger Publisher, 1967).

The Visual and Appropriation

To grasp the import of imaginative representation for sacramental celebration, it is helpful to revert to the distinction between explanation,
understanding, and appropriation. Many questions are disputed in art history
as to the provenance and vision of particular images or periods of religious
art. However, by and large the effort is to see them within the world and
within the religious perspectives of the age to which they belonged.[38]

Thus in appreciating Byzantine icons, it is not enough to look at the
images. One has also to consider how they were integral to the liturgy in
their use and placement. The *iconostasis*, as Kessler puts it, served as a gate-
way between this world and the other world of divine mystery and glory. With
its images, it provided access to the mysteries celebrated behind the screen.
In earlier times, the screen was lower so that people could see the ritual, and
so it served as demarcation of space. When raised higher, to obscure the sight
of the celebration, it became a medium, taking the role of mediation. Within
such a setting the sacramental liturgy itself showed forth more clearly as a
participation in the heavenly liturgy of Christ, the angels, and the saints.

In the medieval Latin West, the adoption of the pseudo-Dionysian hierarchical cosmology had a strong bearing on the building and decoration of
places of worship. It took particular form through the influence of a light
metaphysics in directing the making and display of the visual in places of
worship. The things used in the liturgy, such as the vessels for the bread and
wine, were made from precious substances that radiated light or were orna-
mented to signify a certain magnificence. Windows let in multicolored light,
giving light to the place and its celebration without distracting by a view of
the exterior. The narrative sequence of wall frescoes, ceilings, and windows
was multiple and powerful. It included the *exemplum* of the saints alongside
the Old Testament and New Testament sequences. In them, the mystery was
made present in a special way, for it showed them as persons in whom the
power of Christ took form and in whom therefore this power was considered
to radiate. The representation of the seasons of the year, of the passages of
life, of crafts and trades added to the setting by relating them also to the
divine mysteries.

Protestant churches avoided such decor in order to focus primarily on the
word proclaimed. As far as the visual was concerned attention was to be
given to the elements themselves of water, bread, and wine. Older churches
were often stripped of their imagery, and new ones were built without it.

Everything thus suggested by art history, with its attention to form and
to use as well as to periods, belongs to the explanation of what is found in
places of worship and of their part in the making of sacrament. Understanding always goes hand in hand with explanation, so that we are faced with

---

38. See Herbert L. Kessler, "On the State of Medieval Art History," *Art Bulletin* 70 (1988):
166–87.

the issues raised by such representation. We grasp what world was being projected, what universe of meaning, and are compelled to ask how we ourselves in sacrament face questions that come out of such representation.

Appropriation is allowing one's mind and heart to be challenged by the representation. It is to take the offer made by the image of a gift offered, of a way of being that is opened up before one. It is to enter by this avenue into the mystery of Christ. This, however, raises particular issues in the present age and so deserves an appropriate reflection, which relates the question of image to post[-]modern concerns.

The Visual and the Post[-]Modern

The role of active imagination in communicating with what is presented in representations has been mentioned. It can be readily seen how difficult it may be for people today to resonate or engage with some of the works that past tradition has embodied in places of worship. In this post[-]modern era, appropriation is through engaging with dissonance.

This can be readily enough exemplified. In Catholic liturgies in Roman basilicas and Gothic and neo-Gothic churches, the setting is renovated to suit the liturgical reforms of the present. The altar table is brought forward. The baptismal font or pool is placed where it can be seen by an entire congregation. Sometimes these physical changes are discordant. An altar that is wheeled out every Sunday, so as to avoid using the altar at the back of the sanctuary, is quite simply "out of place." A lectern that is placed nearer the congregation is out of harmony with the majestic and ornate pulpit that stands behind it. In the liturgy itself, new music and a simplicity of ritual performance are introduced that do not go well with the place and its decor.

Protestant congregations have their own, rather different, experience of dissonance in the changed forms of liturgical revision. In places built and designed to set off the force of the word and the beauty of musical sound, they see a greater role given to ritual. Some pastors have even forsaken the simplicity of wonted vestments to adopt Gothic chasubles, drawing attention thereby to their cultic actions.

Experiencing this discordance, some Catholics wish, as was said in the first chapter of this work, to revive the sense of the holy of those more ancient times. In a more measured way, this also seems to have some appeal within Protestant communities. Others in their pure functional approach to liturgy appear to be blind to surroundings. In the age of the post[-]modern, the discordance cannot be missed. Retreat to an earlier sacred cosmology is not possible, or at least it is not something with which all liturgical communities can identify. The liturgy will therefore do well to admit the discordance, but in such a way that it points to where the roots of this lie, namely, in the divergent senses of the holy, the sacred, and the divine, and the relation of this to the remembrance of Christ and his Pasch.

Given this change and consequent diversity in verbal and ritual forms of memory, the role of the visual is hard to sustain or to adapt, and creative ventures will often breed dissonance. However, whatever is depicted needs to be aesthetically attractive and challenging. If the choice in celebration is to place the focus on the simple elements at the core of sacramental cele-bration, so that more attention is drawn to the location of the holy in the forms of bread, wine, oil, and water, these need to be presented in suitable fashion. Likewise, whatever is added to, or changed in, the decor of a place of worship, should have its own inherent artistic merits. Tawdry banners bearing dull symbols cannot supply for the great art works of history. Juxtaposition of well formed art may be the response. In other words, art works that represent Jesus Christ as artisan, preacher, suffering reprobate, have to be executed with artifice and visual appeal. The simpler vessels chosen for the liturgy cannot be kitchen utensils but need to have aesthetic quality. By drawing attention to the acts of eating and drinking, rather than to objects of veneration, they will indeed be dissonant with much of their setting. The dissonance, however, can be what draws into the celebration and raises the questions for partici-pants. It is not the dissonance between the magnificent and the tawdry, but between different worlds, different universes of meaning. In that, it has all the challenge of the Gospel within it.

The sense of the poetic employed in an earlier chapter helps in a reading of images. A poetic reading of the image attends to how it shows forth being and mystery and to how it invites entering into what is represented through imaginative play. When used of the visual, this can be called iconic. There is appeal to feeling and the affective, but this is not the ultimate power of the image. It is to connect realities, to draw humans into this connection. It is to point to something offered and to a way of being that opens up in front of this gift. When dissonance is inherent in what is seen, the poetic still functions, but by probing marrow and bone to raise the issue of what is the truly holy.

As the foregoing exemplifies, the post[-]modern affects the power to re-spond. What we now perceive are representations of life and mystery that do not dovetail and that taken together disturb our quiescence in representa-tions of mystery. This of itself awakens us to the sense of the particular and to the exploration of particular avenues of access to the mystery represented in the sacraments. Attending to the very diverse ways in which the visual be-longs to sacramental representation and celebration parallels the awareness in the verbal of the prevalence of *petits récits*, as over against grand narratives that claim universal appeal.

This is not, however, to say that interpretation is merely subjective. It is to draw attention to the perspectival in viewing a work of art. We come to images, as to stories, out of a background which does much to our vision. But the work of art can challenge this, invite into a fusion of horizons, explore in play new ways of living out the mystery represented.

Nonfigurative Images

Another question has to do with nonfigurative forms of art. There are modern and post[-]modern perceptions of the Christian mystery in works of art, but one does not often find them in places of worship. This could be done through what Jencks calls double coding, a deliberate creation of dissonance. In other words, can they not be given location there, as much a part of sacramental representation as the Ravenna mosaic or the medieval altarpieces?

In the lowest floor of the National Gallery in Washington, the *Stations of the Cross* by Barnett Newman are displayed. This is a way of the Cross that is abstract in form. There are no figures, but its power resides in a use of the tones of white, black, and gray, in the interaction of surfaces and of lines in black and white. The surfaces were painted over a period of time with different types of paint. Only at the end does a thin line of red disrupt the monotone of blacks, whites, and grays. The proportion and relation of lines and colors change from station to station. One cannot simply look at each frame individually, but one must follow through from station to station and be part of the power of the transposition in color and line formation. Newman himself called it a traversal and the expression of the cry of human neglect and dereliction. Through abstraction, Newman makes contact with the self of the human person and with the tragic of human existence. Through this perception and expression, he thought it possible to reach the sublime and the transcendental.

Overall, these stations as traversal convey a sense of formlessness seeking form, along with the confusion generated by shifting colors and line. The work is modern in its use of abstract form, but it is typically post[-]modern in expressing disillusionment with the ways in which art in its classical phase registers the human. It goes beyond previous art forms, yet relates to them. Though abstract, the placement of the lines relates to the shape and postures of the human figure. The work is displayed in a public gallery, whose isolated, subterranean hall provides a space that is not in any place. Yet it belongs among works that query the dominance of a cultural world that galleries and museums have appropriated. It is done on a surface within a frame as are all works of art, but the fourteen stations are painted on a variety of different kinds of surface. It uses paint, but not the same kind of materials for all the frames. It is one piece, but put together over a period of years, with each one in some sense standing on its own. Though breaking with it, it is done within a long tradition that precedes it. The title has no particular reference, yet draws from a whole religious tradition to give it reference.

The title indeed is not meant to refer directly to the Christ figure, but it is by its nature and the inbuilt cultural reference of the title open to this figure. If referred to Christian tradition, it is a novel play on the Cross of Christ as a self-emptying of form, both divine and human. This might be called anti-representational, being a journey into the formless, but every such journey is a descent that promises ascent, and the thin line of red promises something to those who traverse this journey. It contrasts starkly with the representation of the human in Byzantine icons. There too there is some deliberate disfigurement of the human body, but in order to suggest its divinization. Most of all, of course, this is important in the figures of Christ. In Newman, on the contrary, the abstract form given to the human figure displays travail and abasement, so that it could well serve to portray the self-emptying of Jesus Christ in the work of redemption.

There are also more recent representations which appear as deliberately dissonant. The images of Christ by Rouault portray the clown, the fool, the one without grace or beauty. The crucifixions of Chagall against a holocaust or a Jewish background belong in this range. George Segal's sculpture of Abraham and Isaac belongs within the same horizon.[39] It is suitably displayed on a university campus, though not on the one for which it was originally intended. The sculpture calls into question a quiet religious interpretation of that story, which fits it neatly into a divine design and covenant. It shows rather the conflict of generations, that conflict which came to a sorrowful tension point in the killing of students at Kent State University protesting the Vietnam War. This conflict belongs also within the religious. In a post[-]modern age, there is no easy unifying vision or divine cosmology which can speak to the experience of conflict and the questioning of institutions and traditions that marks the age. The traditional has been shown up for its failures, even for its cruelty. The point at issue is whether through a new play of forms something can be retrieved from the tradition. Beyond its broader possibilities for a state and a culture, Segal's sculpture offers not only Jews but all people who relate to the Bible and the power of tradition a new way of seeing God present in the human story. God, in his appeal to both Abraham and Isaac, enters into the conflict and embraces it as a mode of presence, wrestling with the horizons of the good, the true, and the faithful. This is, however, not a peace that smooths over it or suppresses it, but one that allows for an acknowledgment of difference and puzzlement. It does not have the power of easy resolution to conflict, but by appealing to an openness of spirit, openness to the other, it does have the power to render the conflict less vicious and ugly. For those that is, who allow their principles and prejudgments to be questioned.

Some attempts have been made to include more abstract forms of art in places of worship. When this is done, it is the use of art which deliberately departs from more traditional figurative styles, which are seen now to obscure the human and to be bearers of idealistic or ideological religious percep-

---

39. Jane Dillenberger, "George Segal's *Abraham and Isaac*: Some Iconographic Reflections," in *Art, Creativity and the Sacred*, ed. Diane Apostolos-Cappadona (New York: Crossroad, 1984), 105–24.

tions. There is an altar triptych of Willem de Kooning in St. Peter's Lutheran Church in New York, which includes an abstract representation of the crucifixion. On the outside of this same church, in the heart of the city, is a cross by Arnaldo Pomodoro. Dillenberger recounts that some of those who worship there thought that the images would distract from the sacramental act of worship. He himself opines that the triptych enhances it, since action and place belong together, and of course this is precisely the thesis of this chapter.[40]

To bring this kind of representation into sacrament would be to help locate the presence of Christ in the context of the sense of the tragic and of loss which Christians share today with others. It would relate this to the memory of Christ's self-emptying, in its conflict with the forms that humans endeavor to give to their societies and their religions. It would be to draw in those who experience this, and especially those who are its victims. It would be to identify a presence of Christ and of his sacramental self-gift in their stories. It would be a challenge to the entire ecclesiastical institution to be newly evangelized, in virtue of this potent memorial. Whenever unduly identified with sacred places, rites, and institutions, the memorial of Christ loses its power to evangelize. Christian memorial is always a wrestling with memories, with forms, and with horizons. Whatever underscores this enhances its power. This is the role of the visual in contemporary sacramental celebration.

When it is a matter of liturgical art and representation, of course, the issue is not simply that of the individual viewer. There are qualities of the active imagination that bring communities together in the act of communication.[41] The use of double coding invites the viewer to engage with others in the dissonance created by our current historical experience, just as in the past viewers engaged not only with the work but with others in affirming a certain worldview. Presently, since the collective world of meaning and symbols is not one of quiescent acceptance, even within a community there has to be an engagement across prejudgments and differing perceptions. Such interaction has to be empathic, as it requires an imaginative crossing over in attentiveness to worlds of imaged experience to which it is likely that one does not oneself belong. From this there arises the invitation to project future possibilities in which this conflictual encounter, this *différance*, to borrow from Derrida, is affirmed and yet crossed beyond, without the imposition of sameness. Were such approaches to art integrated into sacramental worship, the invitation would be to a memory and a representation of the mystery of Christ and of the Christ event which communicates across and within difference. The hope for the future, the hope for communion in Christ, has to arise out of this imaginative encounter and engagement.

---

40. Dillenberger, *The Visual Arts*, 205.
41. See Richard Kearney, *The Poetics of Imagining: From Husserl to Lyotard* (London: HarperCollinsAcademic, 1991), 210–28.

Architecture

In post[-]modern perspective, questions of the architecture for sacrament are even more complex than for art. The interplay with different historical facts of architecture and different perspectives needs to be admitted. With this in mind, it seems clear that the dominantly functional approach to designing space will not satisfy. This has two questionable suppositions. The first is that the rite gives shape and meaning to the building, whereas in fact buildings speak before rites do. The second is that there is a clear, functional map of ritual action.

The example of baptism may again illustrate this dilemma of the functional. In shape, the font is either octagonal, quadrilobe, circular, cruciform, or hexagonal. It is there, with its given shape and open referents before the rite is performed. The rite does not of itself determine which of these forms has priority. In position, the rite is either out of view of the congregation or in full view of the congregation. Either choice can be justified functionally, on condition that one has already made a choice between two perspectives. One is that the rite should be done in full view, the other that the rites of immersion and chrismation are numbered among liminal rites. Functional argument in regard to both shape and position are grounded in symbolic argument.

If we take it that the building speaks before it is used and is engaged in some kind of interaction with its usage, then we need to take note of the multiple interplay that occurs in designing worship spaces, when the present must interlock with the past. There is the interplay between historical forms that accommodated different kinds of celebration and the new heuristics of reaching out for modes of celebration. With regard to both baptism and Eucharist, there is the interplay between visibility and invisibility. There is the interplay between marked off spaces and common spaces. There is the interplay between an altar of sacrifice and a table of meal communion. There is the interplay between the table of commensality and the table to which the congregation "creeps" to receive from the table of the Lord. There is interplay too in the relation of the worship space to outside space. There is a kind of a space that captures the light that comes from outside into itself, taking the light but not permitting a view of the exterior. There is on the other hand the space that makes the place of congregation one with the surroundings. There is a kind of church that dominates its surroundings by its external design, and one that merges with the surrounding dwellings or public and commercial buildings. Both congregation and architect have to engage with these perspectives, and what is significantly post[-]modern is that no style can be said to impose itself. There are different approaches to architecture that now fall under the designation of post[-]modern. What they have in common is a move away from functional approaches to buildings. Churches, like any other kind of public edifice, are places for people to enter and live in, in a way that goes beyond the specific purpose for which they are built.

There is a present effort to allow people to find in church buildings a greater sense of the rhythms and the enigmas of human life, as well as a sense of belonging within a larger universe, and ultimately of being faced with the awe of transcendence. The building may embody some conversation with diverse cultural pasts, as well as the probing of new forms. In all of this, it would seem desirable to allow some play to elements of what is called post[-]modern in the sense of constructing places that create some feeling of disjunction and disorientation. Even if this is not the prevailing form of a space for worship, it does seem appropriate to allow for some sense of disorientation, since this in the nature of tradition belongs to an encounter both with the past and with the currently dominant cultural representations of faith.

Inculturated Forms

Though much of what is said here reflects Western experience, it is nonetheless pertinent to questions of sacramental inculturation on other continents. Symbol, representation, and sacrament are crucial to letting the Gospel take root in non-Western cultures. In the field of the visual, this might be taken as simply a matter of incorporating another culture's styles of art and architecture, so that representations of Christ and narrative sequences can bear the forms and faces of many peoples. In such perspective, there may even be place for embodying some of the ancestral, ritual, and cosmological imagery of peoples into Christian imagery.

For these peoples, however, engaging in the process of cultural transition is dissonant. Whether this is said or not, to raise the question of inculturation is to admit the breakdown of the symbol system introduced by a missionary presence, as well as the challenge of other traditional symbol systems. With the resultant effort to use African, Asian, or Latin American art forms, there is a juxtaposition of forms and a juxtaposition of worlds. This has to be experienced within the culture, as with the advent of the digital in the process of communication, and can hardly be spoken of outside it, but the reality of dissonance has to be acknowledged.

One example may make the point of art's role in the present phase of inculturation. For the Camerounais theologian, artist, and writer Engelbert Mveng, the key to an African hermeneutic of Christianity is the reality of the anthropological poverty of the African people.[42] By this, he did not mean that Africans have no cultural resources, but rather that with colonization and missionary evangelization these resources have been neglected and rendered marginal to the people's existence. They have been made humanly poor in order to take part in the progress of nations and in the life of the

---

42. Engelbert Mveng, *L'Afrique dans l'Église: Paroles d'un croyant* (Paris: Éditions L'Harmattan, 1985), 71–92. For his view of art, see *L'Art d'Afrique noire: Liturgie cosmique et langage religieux* (Paris: Mame, 1964).

Christian Churches. This human impoverishment is more deep-seated than the material poverty which inflicts much of the African continent. The work of art belongs to the retrieval of the peoples' cultural and human resources and, if they are Christian, within the expression of their faith. Mveng makes use of African motifs of color and of the role of the mask in ancestral rites. With these styles, he gives form to the experience of poverty and dereliction, and also the hope that arises within the conflict with external traditions that is inevitable in the inculturation of Christianity and the reevangelization of the Christian people.

It cannot be a question, however, of simply retrieving an African (or indeed Afro-Brazilian or Indian or Filipino or Vietnamese) religious view of the world that is precolonial or that supposedly continues to exist among the people and their artisans. Two things have happened to make this impossible. First, there has been the history of oppression and domination, and whole peoples have to find a creative way of moving out of this "postcolonial" situation. Second, modes of communication have changed also among African peoples (as among others). To suggest the retrieval from the past of an uncontaminated mode of expression and of an unsullied worldview is romantic. It is for this reason that another writer, Jean-Godefroy Bidima, challenges what he sees as Mveng's rather romantic view of traditional Africa, which indeed he thinks has undergone the influence of a Hegelian penchant for synthesis, so that it is not even traditionally African.[43] Bidima suggests that in artistic creation African peoples must recall their sorrow and their suffering and look for the projection of hope within this situation. The situation, he says, is one of an alienated art, the aspiration is that of becoming a society that can renew itself out of its own resources and find a place among other peoples, and the purpose and form has to be the remembrance of a history of suffering. Bidima writes of all artistic expression, not simply of religious. Many would claim that a genuine African art includes the religious. If this is so, the issue for Christian art would be how it can reclaim such a vision and incorporate it into a remembrance of suffering that gives rise to hope by being taken into the memory of the suffering of Christ.

Mveng himself in fact has raised an even more fundamental question. He asks how a religious language that shapes African existence and a vision of the world but which is itself mythical, or grounded in myths, can open the way to a hearing of the Gospel.[44] There is a tension between this religious vision and the eschatological vision of Christian belief which affirms salvation through the historical event of Jesus Christ. Mveng's concern is to allow this kind of religious language and belief create the space into which the Word of God may enter, and then to retain the symbols, rites, and artistic expressions of African cultures in giving form to the representation of this memory. In

---

43. Jean-Godefroy Bidima, *L'Art négro-africain* (Paris: Presses Universitaires de France, 1997).
44. See E. Mveng, "Christ, liturgie et culture," *Bulletin de théologie africaine* 4 (1980): 247–55.

this, he summarizes many of the questions of the inculturation of Gospel and liturgy, but adds the need, in his concept of anthropological poverty, to take account of the history that has relegated the cultural heritage of these peoples to a subordinate position in society.

In Western societies a different but comparable question arises. In recent centuries artistic and architectural forms have developed in nonreligious contexts, but they have expressed a sense of self, society, and world to which Western peoples relate. What can be expressed in these forms that opens the way to faith, and what elements that express the human, the social, the communal, and the cosmic can be drawn into the representation of Christian faith?

Conclusion

The purpose of this chapter has been to consider how the visual is integral to sacrament's form and meaning. The invitation into the sacramental action and the appropriation of what is liturgically celebrated are deeply affected by visual performance and the visual space or place in which the celebration occurs. Architecture and art can often be looked upon as accessories, important but not of the essence of sacrament. What has been contended here is that they are determinative of form, integral to the celebration and its meaning. This was illustrated from historical examples. The different kinds of impact of the visual were then discussed, namely, place, the visual of the rite itself, and the power of images. Finally, the question of the place of the visual in an era marked on the one hand by shifting perspectives and on another by questions of inculturation was considered.

Part III

Rendering an Account of Sacramental Action

— *Chapter Seven* —

Interpreting Doctrinal Formulations

While the gifts of Word and Spirit and of the living Christian faith are handed on actively through the scriptures, the sacraments, and practices of devotion, there are within traditions more precise and conceptual formulations of faith that explicate what is lived and believed. While the terms are not comprehensive or watertight, it is possible to distinguish between confessions of faith that belong within the liturgy, confessions of faith that summarize beliefs, magisterial teachings, formal condemnations of errors, and catechisms. To consider these kinds of formulation as they touch on sacraments and to place them within the sacramental traditions of the Church is the purpose of this chapter.

Whether these teachings were intended to resolve disputes, are found in confessions of faith promulgated by official bodies, or are the ordinary teachings of the Catholic magisterium of bishops and pope, they have to be looked at in their historical context and interpreted accordingly. When doctrines were stated in the midst of controversy, these controversies too have to be revisited. Hermeneutically, there is a twofold interest in this study. First, it allows us to see how the scriptures, traditions, and practices of the Church were interpreted at precise historical periods of time. Second, it allows us to consider the ways in which these past events and doctrines are to be interpreted today, and how they may still belong in the life of the Church.

As a prelude, it is helpful to explain how any *doctrine* is to be situated in the life of the Church and how it pertains to the transmission of faith. Then we can take the standard doctrinal formulations about sacraments and read them in their historical context, relating them thereby to present belief and practice. After the introduction, the chapter is divided according to specific periods in the life of the Church when sacramental issues were at stake.

What Is Doctrine?

The word *doctrine* in its early Christian and medieval meaning stands for the knowledge of the Christian faith as it was passed on through commentary on the scriptures and various forms of teaching. It is distinct from the transmission of faith through ritual, prayer, and devotion. Where we now use the word *theology* to refer to something distinct from doctrine, medieval writers used the words *sacra doctrina* as a comprehensive term.

The primary referent in presenting doctrine is sacred scripture, as contained in the canon of ecclesial writings attributed to divine inspiration and passed on as the Word of God. There are then the authorities who unfold and explain its meaning. It is within the competency of the tradition of the Church to recognize authorities, for the firmness and clarity with which they expound doctrine and faith. Many of these gain respect through their writings and the importance given to them by others, and subsequently their authors are referred to as Church Fathers. Later theologians in explaining the faith and the scripture look to these writers, either for exposition of the truth or for guidance in controversial matters. There is also the authority of the bishops, whose weight came more slowly to formulation. Bishops had the responsibility to teach and also to judge. Some of the principal Fathers of the Church were bishops, such as Ambrose, Augustine, Basil, and John Chrysostom, who expounded the faith in carrying out their responsibility as pastors. They are not, however, recognized as Fathers because they were bishops, but because they were good teachers and left behind a body of writings whose authority was later affirmed.

The role of bishops precisely as a body of bishops, with responsibility for the apostolic tradition, came to the fore in the context of Church councils called to address matters of controversy, such as disputes about the Trinity, about Christ, or about grace. Out of these there came formulas which had a judicial weight in matters of dispute and became a necessary referent for authentic teaching. They do not, and never did, constitute the entire teaching on a point, but they were a point of reference to assess teachings, where clarity and accuracy were required.

In the era of Protestant Reformation and Catholic Reformation, the Churches of the Protestant Reform issued their own confessions.[1] These were considered as compilations of standard beliefs for their members and authentic interpretations of the Word of God. Though not given the same authoritative weight as teachings of the magisterium in the Catholic Church, they are a necessary point of reference in the fields of doctrine, catechesis and theology. In the Anglican Communion, the *Book of Common Prayer* was considered the most reliable referent and norm in presenting the faith, since there it is expressed in the context of divine worship, but the thirty-nine articles of religion even today remain attached to it. In the post-Tridentine era, the word *doctrine* was applied in a special way in the Catholic Church to

---

1. See Philip Schaff, ed., *The Creeds of Christendom with a History and Critical Notes*, revised by David S. Schaff, vol. 3, *The Evangelical Protestant Creeds*, with translations, 6th ed. (Grand Rapids, Mich.: Baker Books, 1931; repr. 1993).

magisterial formulations, and at times indeed this application seemed to be given a monopoly in the use of the term.

Catechisms for the use of the faithful also have their place in passing on the faith. It is interesting to note the place given to Luther's Small and Large Catechisms in the Lutheran Confessions, *The Book of Concord*.[2] The Reformed Churches for their part have the *Heidelberg Catechism* (published in 1563) as a summary formulation of faith.[3] For Roman Catholics, catechisms, approved by the Holy See or by local councils, were added to magisterial formulations as pithy expressions of belief and were often honored with the name of *doctrine*.[4] In time teachings of the bishop of Rome, under his title as pope, were considered to be important formulations of doctrine for Catholics, and so there developed a theological practice of drawing up a list of criteria whereby to judge the weight of papal pronouncements, lest a Sunday homily or a letter to a local Church be given the same importance as magisterial teachings addressed to the universal Church.

Quite importantly, when magisterial teaching is given in an authoritative and definitive way, it is presented as the *belief* or creed of the Church, since it is as belief that the doctrine of revelation is passed on. The appeal to the *sensus fidelium* in expressing the belief of the Church is constant, even though there is not complete accord on how this ought to be done. Doctrine is intended to serve the faith to be lived by, and to know how essential it is to revelation it has to be seen as it has played out in lives of faith. Hence the criteria for doctrine in its broad sense are the teaching of the sacred scriptures, the life of faith in the Church, and the word of those whom tradition has come to recognize as authorities. Magisterial teaching fits within this complex, as a firm voice elucidating what is gleaned from the study of other expressions of faith. Even defined doctrines are to be put into the context of lived faith and other authorities, if they are to be properly understood and explained.

In considering the interpretation of doctrines, the most basic principle is to relate them to more fundamental confessions of faith. In fact, the profession of faith by articles of belief was the style given to the most basic formulations, which are the Creeds. A confession of faith is a response to God, who reveals and in revealing invites hearers into communion with the divine life. Hence it is that the most apt expression of faith is hymn or praise, proclaimed with the intent of entering into the communion to which revelation invites. This hymnic form, however, is to a great extent set aside by doctrinal formulations

---

2. *The Book of Concord: The Confessions of the Evangelical Lutheran Church*, trans. and ed. Theodore G. Tappert (Philadelphia: Fortress Press, 1959), 337–461.

3. Schaff, *The Creeds of Christendom*, 307–55. Also, *The Heidelberg Catechism* (Chambersburg, Pa., 1854).

4. The most important of these was *The Catechism of the Council of Trent for Parish Priests, issued by order of Pope Pius V*, and translated into various languages. Those of an older generation will remember how the teaching of the catechism in Catholic schools was entered into the curriculum under the rubric of Christian Doctrine.

so as to achieve propositional clarity, but it is useful to remember that they need to be related back to the confession of faith, since it is from this context that doctrine ought to arise and it is in it that it remains anchored. Doctrines when collected as a body of statements also serve communal identity. This became very clear in the sixteenth and seventeenth centuries, when confessions of faith or Catechisms were set over against one another to distinguish one Church or confession from others.

However, all of these doctrines and confessions can, and need to, appeal to a like context, as is becoming clearer in attempts at ecumenical communion.[5] To remember that their meaning relates to worship is a first helpful step, for this indicates that the conceptual formulation is set in relation to the hymnic and poetic expression of faith. Then it is important to clarify, as far as possible, what was at issue when the doctrine was formulated, lest doctrines be given some absolute status that outlives their historical and cultural context. Finally, the reference to the living memory of Jesus Christ as God's Word Incarnate is the deciding factor.

This last, however, is not that easily done. Some will see a historical reconstruction of the life, death, and word of Jesus as God's Word to be both possible and necessary. Others will take the Bible or canonical scripture as definitive and adequate statement of what is to be known about Jesus Christ in his relation to God and to the world. Still others will insist on the importance of canonical, historical, and literary exegesis of texts. The constrictions and the possibilities of expression inherent in language forms and cultural contexts are respected, as well the relation of any interpretation to the life of the Spirit in Christian communities.

Doctrines on the Sacraments

Within sacramental traditions, there are some formulas about sacraments that carry magisterial weight. For Catholics, this means doctrines passed on by the magisterium of councils, popes, and bishops. For the Churches of the Protestant Reformation, the writings of the leaders of the reform, especially Martin Luther and John Calvin, are always a necessary reference, but so are the Church confessions. In matters concerning the sacraments particularly, studies today give more attention to liturgical texts and practices, in recognition of the connection between the *lex orandi* and the *lex credendi*. This is especially important for the Churches of the Reformation, since leaders such as Zwingli, Luther, Calvin, and Cranmer considered liturgical reforms a vital and core part of the reformation of faith and life. The recent *Catechism of the Catholic Church* avoids a rigidly conceptual presentation of the doctrine

---

5. For an interesting proposal on how to deal with differing doctrines, see Yves Labbé, "Communication dans la foi et co-référence des doctrines," *Etudes théologiques et religieuses* 70 (1995): 31–46.

of sacraments by relating teachings to the actual celebration of sacraments and by drawing considerably on liturgical texts from both East and West.[6] In this chapter, attention is given primarily to these precise formulations, since these provide key problems of interpretation. However, the lead of the Catechism is followed by placing them within the larger context of that tradition, whereby faith and doctrine are passed on in the Church.

The best-known doctrinal formulations for the Catholic Church are those made by the Council of Trent, which for several centuries were even the basis of catechetical instruction on the sacraments, to the neglect of the rites themselves and of other authorities. Before the Tridentine teachings, there are the explanations given in the Decree for the Armenians appended to the Council of Florence, intended as an effort at reconciliation between the Churches of the East and the Roman Catholic Church. Even earlier than that, there are various decisions and formulations issued over time to meet particular questions and situations. These include definitions given at the Fourth Lateran Council and at the Council of Constance on one or other point of sacramental doctrine and practice. Although the manner of resolving disputes was quite different, it is impossible to understand these medieval controversies and doctrines without some reference to the disputes between the Donatist Church and St. Augustine. These concern the rebaptism of heretics, the formulas to be used in celebrating the sacraments, and the ecclesial context necessary for their worthy and efficacious celebration.

The controversies that gave rise to doctrinal formulation need to be revisited and the issues taken up again, in recognition that the Church now lives in a different context. What Alexandre Faivre says of the ingredients of theological disputes serves in the examination of issues at stake in doctrinal controversy.[7] Among the disputants, there is always a sway between tolerance and intransigence in face of contrary positions. There is the use of diplomatic maneuvers to resolve the conflict. Mixed with these, there is often the attempt to use the controversy to political and ecclesiastical ends. There is the call for historical research into past teachings and precedents. Coupled with this, there is the appeal to apostolic tradition as a means of justifying one's own position and condemning opposing views, but tenacity in one's own viewpoint can lead opponents to pass lightly over historical research. None of these factors can be ignored in examining the exact meaning and the continuing import of proposed doctrines. The relation to practice in these controversies is vital, since it is in the interest of some practice that doctrine on sacraments is formulated, and the issue is determined by what teaching does to practice.

---

6. *Catechism of the Catholic Church* (Vatican City and Mahwah, N.J.: Libreria Editrice Vaticana and Paulist Press, 1994), Part II.

7. Alexandre Faivre, *Ordonner la fraternité: Pouvoir d'innover et retour à l'ordre dans l'Église ancienne* (Paris: Éd. du Cerf, 1992), 331.

The interpretation can be guided by some reference both to Paul Ricoeur and to Hans-Georg Gadamer. While Ricoeur locates the ultimate stage of interpretation in the act of appropriation of the world put forward by a text, he makes it very clear in all his work that explanation is a necessary step on the way. In this light, it behooves us to explain texts as far as possible in context in order to understand their origins and see what they proffer. Gadamer for his part reminds his readers of the need to avert to prejudice. The prejudice, or presupposition, is first and foremost that of the reader, who needs to be free in this acknowledgment in order to be open to the world of a text. It is also true, however, that in reading texts we see what prejudices or presuppositions were at work at the time of their composition. From this double advertence to prejudice, the fusion of horizons becomes possible. That is to say, the issues and questions expressed in a text can enter the world of the reader or interpreter, asking for an enlargement of the horizons of this world in order to entertain what is of consequence in the horizon of the text.

With all this in mind, in interpreting doctrinal formulations about sacraments, four questions are kept in mind:

1. What are the outstanding doctrines of this nature in the past, and in what historical circumstances did they emerge?

2. Why were they important at the time, and to what practical matters did they relate, both sacramental and devotional?

3. How do they relate to institutional concerns, especially as these affect sacramental ministry?

4. What were the principal controversies involved, and can these now be revisited in relation to a broader and longer tradition, integrating the issues rather than just the formulas into this present moment of tradition?

Four historical disputes and their doctrinal resolutions will be considered. The first comes from the time of Augustine of Hippo. The second has to do with disputes with spirituals, where questions of faith, evangelical life, and ministry were intertwined. The third comes from efforts to reconcile East and West. The fourth has to do with differences on the sacraments at the time of the Protestant Reformation.

Augustine and the Donatists

In the earliest historical instance mentioned, there are no magisterial pronouncements as such, but the doctrinal formulations of St. Augustine were given authority throughout the Middle Ages in resolving comparable issues. Disputes on the question of baptism in schismatic Churches already arose in the time of Cyprian of Carthage, but the matter came to a head in North

Africa in the fourth century with the Donatist schism. The chief practical issue concerned was what should be done when a Christian passed from one Church to another. There were two questions at stake. Where a member of one Church joined another, was the ceremony of baptism to be repeated, or was the original baptism to be recognized? When a Catholic who had joined the Donatists sought reconciliation, was this person thought to have lost baptism through schism, or could reconciliation be given in a way that avoided repetition of the baptismal ceremony?

It was the concept of Church that was fundamentally at stake, but this showed up in practice in the way of treating baptism. The Donatists, as far as can be known from historical writings, held to the existence of a pure and spiritual Church. Only the just belonged to it, and sinners were excluded. As far as external institutions were concerned, only the followers of Donatus could be taken as members of this Church of the holy. Likewise, it was only among the holy that sacraments could be rightly celebrated. Hence any person coming from another Church was to be received as a sinner, and any baptism given in another Church was not to be recognized. The person could be received into the Church only through baptism celebrated within it.

Since persons who had been baptized by himself at Hippo were being baptized anew by the Donatists in their cathedral, this obviously hit home with Augustine.[8] At the same time, he did not want to retaliate, tit for tat, by baptizing those who sought reconciliation, coming from, or coming back from, the Donatist communion. Baptism as an external sign and ceremony, done in the name of the Triune God, deserved more respect than that. At the same time, the ecclesial context was necessary for baptism to have its full effect in communicating the life of the Spirit. Led as it were by the instinct of faith to recognize baptism when celebrated with the traditional action and formula, and also to affirm that it is given once and for all, Augustine gave this a consistent place in his doctrine of the Church. It is interesting that he relies on the Church's baptismal practice and liturgical profession of faith to establish right doctrine.

In his own way, Augustine in many of his teachings distinguished here on earth between the kingdom of the just and the kingdom of the wicked, between the Church of Christ and the followers of the devil. He did not, however, confuse this with the visible Church and its institutions and practices. Within the one body, the sinner and the just live side by side, in ways that leave it often indiscernible as to who is saved and who is not. For Augustine, the actions and institutions of the Church were not to be assessed in virtue of the sanctity of its members, and certainly not of its ministers, but by their orthodoxy and their fidelity to the apostolic tradition. If a sacrament is rightly performed within this tradition, it has the effect of aggregating to the

---

8. The principal work in this dispute is Augustine, *On Baptism against the Donatists*, NPNF 4, series 1. The Latin text is in PL 43: 116–50.

Church and to Christ. Within this context, Augustine formulated his understanding of sacraments as signs, signs which express true faith and which touch persons visibly, to signify something about them and their relation to Christ. As far as a minister is concerned, he is not to be thought to act in his own power. He acts in the name and the power of Christ, so that Augustine could say in his famous formula, "Whether Peter baptizes or Judas baptizes, it is Christ who baptizes."

Whether given within the Catholic Church or within schism, as long as it appeared as a sign of Christ's action, a sacrament was to be received and recognized. On the other hand, it did rightly belong to the communion of the Church in faith, charity, and the Holy Spirit, so that the life offered in the sacrament through these signs could flourish only within that true, apostolic, and orthodox communion. Thus Augustine would not acknowledge that grace and communion with Christ, or the life of the Spirit, was given in the Donatist Church. Hence forgiveness and reconciliation, though not baptism, had to be given to those who came over from, or returned from, this Church. Though they were formally members of Christ's body through baptism, the life of the body could flow in them only within the one true Church, his body on earth.

From this controversy, one understands better the nature of the Church as a visible body, which cannot be judged simply on the purity of its members. Having room within its visible self for both saint and sinner, it must minister to both within its life and practice. One also understands the importance of communion in love and in the Spirit, if the life offered in sacraments is to flow freely. One likewise comes to appreciate the nature of sacraments as signs of the action of God and of Christ, operating within the Church. Thus one learns to read the signs, and to rely on their signification as such, and not to look to the minister as a person to give them their power to sanctify.

While they raised the specter of a pure Church, the Donatists did rightly bring forward the question of the relation between holiness and sacramental ministry and participation. This in itself is an important issue, and one that raises much affective reaction. Augustine accepted the question, but resolved it by making a distinction between formal Church belonging and growing in grace within its communion. The institutional factor and the holiness factor are interconnected, but they are not to be collapsed one into the other. It is right faith and right practice, handed on from the apostles, as these are open to external evidence and observance, that constitute the visible boundaries of Church communion. On the other hand, sacramental practice does not of itself guarantee a part in the life of the Spirit, and is indeed useless outside a communion of charity. While generally Augustine did not believe that one could distinguish in visible terms between the holy and the sinner, he was more sure than we would be today that there are situations in which one can assume the absence of the Spirit. Because they had separated themselves from communion with the mother Church, Augustine would not credit the

Donatists with keeping communion in the Spirit, however exact and correct their formula of faith and their baptismal practice.

This raises an issue which had already emerged as important at the time and which became even more important in later times. This has to do with the communion between Churches that differ on expressions of faith, both propositional and practical. During the period of bitter christological and Trinitarian controversies, Churches were in the habit of excommunicating one another. This meant that they would not celebrate sacraments together. At what point did such lack of communion set a particular Church outside the communion in the Spirit and devoid of the grace to pass on to its members? One appreciates the very concrete situation in Hippo in which Augustine found himself, with a rival Church set up in opposition to his own community. Two communities in the same city calling for the allegiance of the faithful did not seem possible and led Augustine to his judgment on the absence of the Spirit among the Donatists. There was no room here for distinguishing between the subjective and the objective and no room for allowing that even in division two communions might recognize the truth and sincerity of the other.

Medieval Disputes

The desire for a Church of the pure surfaced repeatedly in the course of the Middle Ages, and along with this the tendency to relate the truth of sacraments to the holiness of their ministers or of the congregations celebrating them. This fascination with a perfect Church mingled with larger concerns about the need for evangelical reform and the revival of the evangelical life. Groups of Christians who felt dissatisfied with the vain life of the clergy, or the atrophy of Church institutions which failed to give testimony to Christ again and again, questioned the conditions for the ministry and celebration of sacraments. What needed to be true of the Church in order that it celebrate the sacraments? How much did it need to reflect the evangelical life in order to harbor and pass on the grace of the Spirit? Was it possible to rely on institutional factors, such as ordination within canonical procedures and the right external force of sacramental signs? Was more not needed to say that the sacraments of the Church were works of Christ and sanctified its members?

While monasticism had seen fit to reform Christian life by setting up communities to live the perfection of charity and communion, adopting the ideal of the evangelical life for its own members, these medieval groups wanted to see a Church that was evangelical through and through. This required right preaching and an evangelical way of life, as this was exemplified in the New Testament. For some of these evangelical groups, sacraments could not be celebrated within any other kind of body. As a result, some of them questioned the very need for ordination and thought that holiness of life was a better guarantee in a minister than ecclesiastical appointment. They also questioned the power of ordained ministers who were not holy, and hence the validity of sacraments performed by them.

These groups raised important and valid questions about the place of sacraments within the total reality of Church life and about the connection between the testimony of the Christian life and the celebration of sacraments.[9] Among certain followers of the ideal of the evangelical life, there seems to have been a measure of dualism in their perspectives, though for want of good historical information the validity of accusations made against them is not always certain. At least, however, we know what it was that the official Church wanted to exclude and condemn.

As with the Donatists, there was again the problem as to whether the true Church was only the Church of the pure. There was also a dualism between matter and spirit, arising from ideas about material and spiritual creation and affecting the role of visible signs and institutions in the Church. It was to this dualism and to the denial of priestly power in virtue of ordination, attributing sacramental power instead to holiness of life, that the Church officially responded. The practical implications of this are obvious. If communities had to assess the holiness of ministers to have faith in sacramental worship, much confusion and doubt would ensue. Similarly, if holiness of life were to be itself guarantee enough of right preaching and of sacramental action, without ordination, the role of ecclesiastical institutions in supporting, holding together, and guiding the Church is negated.

Teachings on the power of ordination and on the Eucharist were formulated by the Fourth Lateran Council and the Council of Constance.[10] First and foremost, these affirmed the power received through ordination and the sufficiency of this power to consecrate the eucharistic bread and wine. While the Fourth Lateran Council affirmed the transubstantiation of the elements, its chief concern was with the challenge to the power of the priest. The Council of Constance, in opposing the work of John Hus and the Hussites, condemned some propositions from the works of John Wyclif on the Eucharist. Here again, the council's major concern was to affirm the power given to the ordained minister to consecrate the Eucharist and to baptize. In upholding this, it affirmed the change of the substance of the bread and wine into the body and blood of Christ. Moreover, because of Wyclif's questioning of the origin of ecclesiastical institutions, the council also taught that the Mass stems from the action of Christ at the Last Supper.

The administration of penance was also a matter of division in this epoch. The Fourth Lateran Council affirmed the possibility of restoration through penance for those who sinned after baptism, stating this against the Cathars and Waldensians.[11] In combatting Wyclif and Hus, the Council of Constance

---

9. For a useful summary of these disputes, see M. D. Lambert, *Medieval Heresy: Popular Movements from Bogomil to Hus* (London: Edward Arnold Publishers, 1977).

10. See David N. Power, *The Eucharistic Mystery* (New York: Crossroad, 1992), 244–48.

11. Fourth Lateran Council, *De fide catholica,* in *Decrees of the Ecumenical Councils,* ed. Nor-

protected the practice of the confession of sins, which implied the power of the priest to absolve.[12] It is sufficient to recall that in these definitions the main concern was with the power of the minister given through ordination. This was affirmed to be both necessary and sufficient. Some ecclesiological implications were in mind within this context. The wish was to eliminate all desire for a Church of the pure, whose external institutions and actions were to be always subjected to purely spiritual criteria and judgment. There are no ontological explanations of this priestly power involved.

By isolating this issue, of course, other issues were not addressed, at least within that immediate context. The spiritualists, up to and including the Hussites condemned at Constance, certainly contended that institutions and institutional acts needed to be reformed and in some way subjected to judgment. They also saw the necessity, clearly exemplified in the writings of John Wyclif, to differentiate what has its origins in the scriptures and what comes from other concerns and sources in giving form to Church institutions and to sacramental practice and theory. In short, while the truth of the conciliar formulations can be accepted without demur, their judgment of those condemned and their adequacy to the issues at stake may be questioned. They do not fully address the problem of the relation between sacramental life and life lived in fidelity to the Gospel. They also privilege certain formulations of belief, especially about priesthood and about Eucharist, which are tied to a particular context and a particular controversy. From a hermeneutical perspective, it is necessary to consider the limitation of formulations and the questions or issues which lie hidden within them.

The Council of Florence

Theology manuals often cite the Decree for the Armenians on the doctrine of the sacraments. This is so because it clearly states the teaching on the seven sacraments, listing the matter and form as well as the effects for each and every one of the seven.

In terms of magisterial teaching and tradition, however, the document is quite unimportant. This Bull of Union with the Armenians, given at the eighth session of the Council of Florence and dated November 22, 1439, is in fact an appendage to the quest for union between Orthodox and Latin Christians.[13] Along with a document for union with the Copts, it was an attempt to include other non-Latin Churches with the Orthodox in the effort at the reunion of all Christians. There were, however, only three Armenian

---

man P. Tanner (London: Sheed & Ward and Washington, D.C.: Georgetown University Press, 1990), 1:231.

12. This is found in the condemnation of propositions 9, 10, and 11 of John Wyclif. Ibid., 422–23.

13. *Decrees of the Ecumenical Councils,* ed. Tanner, 1:534–59.

delegates at Florence, and the decree was really a Latin composition, done in scholastic style, and remained of little consequence.

The pertinence to sacraments of other issues discussed between Greeks and Latins at this council are of greater interest. The main points of dispute concerned the procession of the Holy Spirit and primacy of the bishop of Rome. As far as sacraments were concerned, the Greeks noted the absence of an *epiclesis* for the Spirit in the Latin eucharistic prayer, as well as the use of leavened bread by the East and of unleavened by the West. The question of purgatory was likewise a matter of dispute, and this involved differences over the Western practice of offering the Mass for the deceased. In the definition of the synod aimed at union, Greeks and Latins agreed to differ on these practical points, without imposing any uniform procedure.[14]

These points of debate, however, involve the pneumatological and es- chatological understanding of the Church and of its sacraments and are connected with the difference over the inclusion of the *Filioque* in the creed. In confessing the procession of the Spirit from the Father and the Son, Latins took this as the foundation of an ecclesiology which saw a direct relation of the ordained to the Son, both in sacrament and in jurisdiction. At the Mass, the priest was said to speak the words of Christ in Christ's own person (*in persona Christi*), thus effecting consecration and sacrifice. There was no in- clusion of the Spirit in the Roman Canon, but if pressed Latin theologians would say that the gift of the Spirit was one of the effects of Mass and sacra- ment. As Vicar of Christ, the pope also saw himself in direct relation with Christ, having from him the power of jurisdiction over other Churches in the service of the communion of universal Church.[15]

In including an invocation for the sending of the Spirit in the Eucharist and in other sacramental prayers, the Eastern Church expressed the belief that Christ operated in the Church and was united with it, through the action of the Holy Spirit. The Byzantine liturgical commentator Nicholas Cabasilas had offered an irenic resolution to the dispute between Greeks and Latins. He attributed the consecration of the bread and wine to the joint action of Word and Holy Spirit, through the words of Christ and the in- vocation of the Spirit.[16] The difference, however, remained. For Latins, the sanctification of gifts and the sanctification of the people are two distinct actions. Greek formulations express that the people are sanctified with and through the sanctification of their gifts. The invocation of the Spirit, more- over, reflects an ecclesiology which is centered in the Eucharist, where the Spirit is operative, and through which it is formed in the sacrament as the

14. Ibid., 527.

15. On the different ecclesiologies of East and West that played a part in the council, see Emmanuel Lanne, "Uniformité et pluralité," in *Christian Unity: The Council of Florence 1438/39,* ed. Giuseppe Alberigo (Leuven: University Press, 1991), 353–73.

16. Nicholas Cabasilas, *A Commentary on the Divine Liturgy,* trans. J. M. Hussey and P. A. McNulty (London: SPCK, 1966), nos. 27–30, 69–79.

body of Christ. Communion between Churches could not be attributed, as in the West, to the common submission to the one primatial jurisdiction. It has to come about as a communion between eucharistic communities, so that in some sense each local Church has its own independent, pneumatological, and sacramental center.

The connection between sacrament and institution is clear in these controversies over the missions of Son and Spirit and over their sacramental implications. Some kind of institutional authority is needed to assure unity and communion, but the issue is how closely related it can remain to sacramental ministry and how much imbedded in sacramental liturgy. Within the Latin Church, the governance of the episcopacy, and especially of the bishop of Rome, was too greatly cut off from sacramental ministry. Hence it lost much of its sacramental significance and reality and was expressed and administered in a rather one-sided juridical fashion.

The question of eschatology that surfaced in the dispute about making suffrages for the dead is also involved with a sacramental ecclesiology. To offer Mass for the dead is to attribute its efficacy for those departed this life to the power of the Church, and to extend ecclesiastical jurisdiction, in some manner, beyond life on this earth. This is more clearly the case when granting indulgences for the dead goes with offering Mass for them. For the East, however, the communion between the living and the dead also has to be seen as sacramental. When the departed are remembered in the Eucharist, it is as members of the communion in the Spirit which binds both the living and the dead, and the sacramental communion of the body of Christ includes them. If there were disagreements between the Greeks and the Latins over purgatory as a place or state of existence, it had very much to do with this conception of the extension of the authority and power of Church and priesthood. This is quite logical, since the very development of the idea and doctrine of purgatory is connected with those practices of prayer for the dead, whose extent and popularity we know from the *Dialogues* of Gregory the Great[17] and from medieval sacramental books. On the other hand, the practice of giving the sacrament to the dead, to give them peace, of which we read in Gregory, bizarre though it may seem to some, reflects an earlier, more sacramentally centered ecclesiology and eschatology. If the dead needed reconciliation with the living, as a young novice did with Benedict, it was in communion that this came about. This is no rank superstition, but a way of showing a sense of how the living and the dead remain united as the one body of Christ.

In the documents of the Second Vatican Council and in the subsequent liturgical reform, the Western Church revised its doctrine of Church and sacrament in such a way as to take account of the role of the Spirit. The

---

17. Gregory the Great, *Dialogi*, PL 77. This can be found in English translation: *Dialogues*, trans. Odo J. Zimmerman, The Fathers of the Church 39 (Washington, D.C.: Catholic University of America Press, 1959).

invocation of the Spirit has been introduced into new prayers. The solution, however, is a compromise, since the *epiclesis* is split, in order to retain a focus on the words of Christ and to differentiate between the sanctification of the gifts and the sanctification of the communicants. This in fact reflects an ecclesiology where the relation of bishop or minister to Christ is a direct one, and the Spirit is accounted for as a gift given, through the operation of ecclesiastical authority. Given a role in the sanctification of the gifts of bread and wine, the Spirit is effectively subordinated to the priestly power exercised in repeating the words of Christ.

A stronger retrieval of Eastern ecclesiology would better account for the twofold interactive mission of Word and Spirit. It would also allow for a more eucharistic ecclesiology, with more attention to the sacramental completeness, and thus in practice relative autonomy, of local Churches. This lays the way open for a more culturally rooted consideration of sacramental renewal and practice and a recognition of pluriformity in the communion between different eucharistic communities. With different sacramental perceptions and practices, the role of bishop or presbyter may also take a different institutional and juridical form in different local Churches. To grasp how this difference may come about, one needs to consider the paradigms that influenced the shape and power to the governance of the Church and to the link between sacramental ministry and governing authority. This will be done in the next chapter.

Reformation Controversies and Doctrinal Formulations

While Catholic theology is most concerned about the doctrinal teaching of the Council of Trent, to interpret the sixteenth-century divisions properly one has to take into account the confessional formulations of other bodies as well.[18] In like manner, one has to consider the sacramental practices that were defended or proposed on one side or the other. An ecumenical climate has certainly helped Churches to listen more accurately to what was said or proposed at that time, and indeed to learn from what for a long time was too readily condemned.

Sacraments in General

The very nature of sacrament was called into question by the Reformers, due to Protestant positions on the role of faith in justification. Luther strongly opposed the teaching of the efficacy of sacraments *ex opere operato*. This was because he associated this with an excessive reliance on sacraments, to the detriment of the exercise of faith, and with the primacy of priestly mediation

---

18. For a historical study of relevant teachings of the Council of Trent, see the collection of articles in André Duval, *Sacrements au concile de Trente* (Paris: Éd. du Cerf, 1993).

over the power of God's Word and of the Cross of Christ. As he taught, it is through faith in the promises of God given in Christ that one is justified, not through priestly mediation. Along with his concern over the role attributed to sacraments were his concerns with the proclamation of the Word and with the need for a clear mandate of the Lord in order to designate a rite as a sacrament. Since this could be found in the scriptures only for baptism and the Lord's Supper, the other five sacraments of Catholic dispensation were to be considered ecclesiastical institutions. This did not mean necessarily that they had no legitimacy, nor that they were unimportant, especially rites for confession, marriage, and ordination. Their contribution, however, was to be related to the power to arouse faith, to give some external mark of Christian profession, and they could not be allowed in any way to derogate from the role of faith and from the primacy of baptism and the Lord's Supper.

Both Calvin and Luther held to the importance of baptism and Lord's Supper, that is to say, of sacraments, as signs, but they placed this in relation to faith and God's promises given through the Word. The sign needed to be ordered to the role of the Word and of faith, but it did constitute a necessary part of the visible identity of the Church and acted as a seal on God's Word in giving the promise of justification. It is interesting that John Calvin revived the position of scholasticism that sacraments are God's concession to human weakness and that they have a pedagogical role. He defined a sacrament as "external symbol by which the Lord seals on our consciences his promises of good will toward us, in order to sustain the weakness of our faith."[19] Later, in 1563, to epitomize the position of the Reformed Churches, the *Heidelberg Catechism* stated:

> The sacraments are visible, holy signs and seals, appointed of God for this end, that by the use thereof he may the more fully declare and seal to us the promise of the Gospel; namely, that he grants us out of free grace the forgiveness of sins and everlasting life, for the sake of the one sacrifice of Christ accomplished on the Cross.[20]

Though it comes after the definitions and condemnations of the Council of Trent, this question pinpoints what was at issue. For Reformed doctrine, sacraments are indeed visible signs, pertaining to the identity of the Church of Christ. They are, however, the sign and the seal of the promise of the Gospel and their sole reference is to the Cross of Christ, not to the mediating power of the ordained priesthood.

Trent's response to the positions of Luther and Calvin had been a forthright reaffirmation of traditional medieval teaching. All seven sacraments are instituted by Christ. They are not simply for the nourishment of faith but

---

19. See *Institutes of the Christian Religion,* trans. Henry Beveridge (Grand Rapids: Eerdmans Publishing Company, 1989), Book IV, xiv, 491–92.

20. *Heidelberg Catechism,* q. 66, in Schaff, *The Creeds of Christendom,* 328.

contain the grace which they signify and confer it *ex opere operato* on those
who place no obstacle in its way. The council taught the necessity of faith for
justification and the fruitful reception of sacraments, but it read the teaching of the Reformers to make their efficacy as signs entirely dependent on
the faith of the recipient. Catholic teaching saw no proportion between this
faith and the power of Christ in the sacrament, as mediated through the
ministers of his Church. Of course, neither did the Reformers make faith an
instrument of justification, but took it to be the adherence to the promises of
Christ, without which there is no justification, and on which the sinner is totally dependent. Neither Catholic nor Reformer put any proportion between
faith and Christ's power to justify, but the issue was that of how this power,
forgiveness, and justification are received by the believer. It could indeed be
said to be the issue of the Church's mediatory role in relation to the power
of God's Word and the place of this mediation in the relation between God
and the sinner.

Eucharist

It was in the practice of the Mass and in the teaching on the Lord's Supper
that the key concerns of the Reformers emerged most strongly, and it is here
that the issues at stake are most evident. Both the attacks on the sacrifice of
the Mass and the eucharistic liturgies of Luther, Zwingli, and Calvin are well
known, as well as Trent's condemnations, affirmations, and teachings.[21] The
Augsburg Confession, art. XXIV, put the matter squarely and succinctly when
it condemned the multiplication of Masses and all practices attached to this
on the one hand, and on the other the notion that the offering of the Mass
was necessary above and beyond the one sacrifice of the Cross.[22] In response
to such accusations, it was very clearly stated by the Council of Trent that
there is but one sacrifice, offered in two ways, bloody and unbloody, and that
the Mass is the memorial and representation of the sacrifice of the Cross.
The council, however, did not wish to eliminate the offering of the Mass
by the priest, nor the stipendiary system, and taught that over and above
the principal means of taking part in it, which is sacramental communion,
benefit is to be had from the priest's offering, for the living and the dead.[23]
Though one could see some reconciliation between the doctrinal positions of
Trent and of the Reformers on the nature of the Eucharist as memorial of
the Cross, there remained a difference in the Catholic stress on offering over
against the Protestant stress on sacrament. The practical consequences that
resulted from the reform of the liturgies of the Lord's Supper were enough to
create what seemed at the time an unbridgeable gulf.

---

21. For a review of this debate, see Power, *The Eucharistic Mystery*, 257–63.
22. *Book of Concord*, 56–61.
23. *Decree on the Sacrifice of the Mass*, in *Decrees of the Ecumenical Councils*, ed. Tanner, 2:732–
36.

Among the Reformers themselves, it is perhaps the discussion of the presence of Christ in the Eucharist that shows very clearly what were their spiritual, doctrinal, and liturgical interests, as well as the difficulty in coming to a clear presentation of this when the importance of the response in faith is accentuated. Luther and Zwingli entered into acrimonious debate on the reality of the presence of the body and blood, Luther reading Zwingli to reduce this to something purely symbolic. It is unlikely that Calvin intended to mediate between them, but it is a fact that his formulation of the matter seems the most subtle and the most balanced.

In the *Institutes* he elaborates on the sacrament of the Lord's Supper at some length.[24] It is impossible to do justice to this in a few words, but these few points may be noted. Appealing to the power of the Spirit, he distinguished three aspects of the spiritual truth offered in the visible elements of the bread and wine. The first is the signification which has to do with the divine promises, offered in the Lord's words of institution, which remind the believer that Christ's body was broken for them, and his blood shed for them. The second is that in receiving the sign of the body and blood, through the power of the Spirit we are receiving the body and blood themselves, though in a communion which transcends all carnal consumption and union. The third is that the virtue or effect of the Eucharist lies in benefits won for the believer through the Cross of Christ. For Calvin, the communion with Christ and with his body is real, but it is a communion in the Spirit, not a physical bond, and it pertains to membership in the body of the Church.

The Fathers gathered at Trent wished to elaborate a teaching which upholds these devotions. As previously remarked, many of the concerns about eucharistic presence arose within the context of eucharistic devotions rather than in relation to eucharistic communion. This draws attention to another kind of ritual and ritualization. At times, people have given expression to their devotion to Christ through rituals that do not fit easily into the liturgy of the eucharistic commemoration. While the protective attitude toward these at the time of the Council of Trent may today seem excessive, it is true that they merit attention. In a larger way, they belong to the Church's ritual tradition, and one has to ask what such rituals expressed, and why they fitted more readily into the lives of many people much more readily than the Mass.

At the same time in looking at the writings of the Reformers, in the judgment of the members of the council what was said savored of a reduction of presence to a purely spiritual communion, or worse still to a sign of what is conveyed in promise and faith. The council therefore affirmed the mystery of real, true, and substantial presence, as well as the doctrine of the substantial change of the bread and wine into the body and blood of Christ, the species remaining for the sake of the sacrament.

In the decree on the sacraments in general, the conciliar Fathers wanted

---

24. *Institutes* IV, xvii.

to affirm the connection between sacrament and grace, lest the sacramental role be reduced to that of a sign of the recipient's faith.[25] But they did not choose to use the language of causality. Instead they employed the broader phrase "sacraments contain grace" (canon 6), along with the scholastic formula "confer *ex opere operato*" (canon 9). Repeating this formulation, even while affirming the necessity of faith in the one receiving the rite, they wished to attribute a power to the work of Christ in the sacrament which supersedes that of the faith of the recipient. In other words, rites have their inherent and special efficacy, even while recipients have to exercise their faith in receiving them.

In the same decree, the council wanted to affirm the role of the ordained minister, in face of what the members saw as a reduction of ordained priesthood to the common priesthood of all the baptized. This was done by reiterating the teaching that each of the three sacraments, baptism, confirmation, and order, gives its own distinctive character. This character was placed in the realm of the spiritual rather than in the purely external order. Apart from that, no particular explanation was adopted, though a number of theories were offered by theologians, with varying emphasis on the internal or on the external role of the sacramental character. With regard to the power of the ordained minister, to avoid any new form of medieval spiritualism the Fathers related the power of his action to the intention of the Church which he expresses, rather than to any personal intention or activity of his own. In line with this, in the canons on baptism the council affirmed the validity of any baptism conferred according to the intention of the Church, even if administered by heretics (canon 4). The same principle is adopted in regard to unworthy ministers in the decree on penance, where it is said that they too retain the power to absolve, since it is not in their own name that they perform this action (canons 9, 10).

In the two decrees on the Eucharist, that is, on sacrament and sacrifice, one finds not only the doctrine of the Eucharist itself but also foundations for more general sacramental doctrine.[26] While it was unfortunate that the two aspects of the Eucharist were addressed separately, there are parallels between the two decrees that are worth noting. The decree on the sacrament gives a fourfold reason for the institution of the sacrament by Christ. He wished to leave a memorial of himself to his disciples. In this memorial, he wanted his death proclaimed until he would return to judge the world. The sacrament gives food and nourishment, whose character is eschatological, that is, an anticipation and preparation for a share in Christ's glory. As a communal sacrament, it is also the symbol of the unity of the one body of Christ, which is the Church. To this, the decree on sacrifice adds that the Eucharist is a representation and memorial of the sacrifice of the Cross, to be immolated by

25. *Decrees of the Ecumenical Councils*, ed. Tanner, 2:684–86.
26. Ibid., 693–97, 732–35.

the Church down through the ages under the signs of bread and wine. While at one point it says *memoria crucis* (memory of the Cross), at another it says *in memoriam transitus sui* (in memory of his passage), thus interpreting the Cross as Christ's passage to the Father. To spell out the eschatological nature of the Eucharist, this can be placed alongside the proclamation of his death until his return. While this concept of memorial is spelled out in relation to the Eucharist in particular, it can be extended to other sacraments, inasmuch as they all relate to the Eucharist and share in its memorial character.

Penance

The debate about the sacrament of penance serves as another example of what it means to interpret the matter aright.[27] It is an interesting starting point to note that Martin Luther practiced confession to the end of his life and that he commended it in the Small Catechism.[28] Yet he roundly condemned Catholic practice and doctrine, and even came to deny it the designation of sacrament. From a study of confessional manuals and from his knowledge of confessional practice, Luther concluded from a practical point of view that the confessional generated scruple and anxiety and that priests pried too much into the lives of their penitents. From a theoretical point of view, he saw it as legalism and another example of works righteousness rather than an act of faith and confidence in divine mercy and in the Cross of Christ. Since, based on the example of baptism and Eucharist, sacrament was to be defined as proclamation of Word and sealing sign, confession fitted more readily into the category of devotion, though, done properly and without scruple, it did profess/confess the same deep faith in the power of the Cross as these two sacraments.

To uphold the practice of regular confession, that is, at least once a year, the Council of Trent developed its doctrine in terms of the power of the keys given to the Church to judge and absolve sinners and by way of analogy with the acts of a tribunal of judgment.[29] It also affirmed its divine origin, by way of reference to the giving of the keys to Peter and to the Apostles recorded in the Gospel of Matthew, or to the gift of the Spirit that unlooses mentioned in the Gospel of John.[30] Within the larger context, it made it clear that there is no forgiveness without faith and without true contrition, and that the analogy of judgment is subordinate to the understanding of sacrament as a gift of grace coming from Christ. In the controversy about penance, then, one can see that it was fuelled by an irate assessment of another's practice. One

---

27. Ibid., 703–9.

28. See Martin Luther, "The Small Catechism," VI, in *The Book of Concord*, 349–51.

29. Council of Trent, *Doctrina de sanctissimis poenitentiae et extremae unctionis sacramentis*, chapter 6 and canon 9, in *Decrees of the Ecumenical Councils*, ed. Tanner, 2:707, 712.

30. Canon 3 attributes institution of the sacrament "principally" to the words of Jesus in John 20:22–23. In *Decrees of the Ecumenical Councils*, ed. Tanner, 2:711.

can also see that at least theoretically there were misunderstandings of the other's doctrine.

On the other hand, there were clear differences in the understanding of ecclesiology and ministry in the teaching on sacraments. For Luther and other Reformers, the main task of the ordained minister is to proclaim the Word and the Cross, and so to let God's mercy work through the Word. It is the Word that counts, not the action of the minister as such, even though his ministry is needed and divinely ordained. For Trent, the ministry is a mediation of grace, done in virtue of the Word and of the power of Christ, but it is not a ministry that is totally caught up in the power of the Word. There is a listening, a discernment, and a judgment that has to take place over and above the Word and that is intrinsic to the sacrament. On the part of the penitent, likewise, faith is the ground of forgiveness, but in itself as an internal act it does not suffice. The sinner belongs to the Church and relies on its mediation in such a way that sins have to be confessed, just as the penitent must, as a member of Christ's body, be united with Christ in performing works of reparation, stipulated through the exercise of the power of the keys. On this ground, Luther's advocacy of confession looked like a devotional practice, and one that overlooked the sacramental conjunction between the acts of the minister and the acts of penitent sinner. What emerged in practice in the Tridentine era was a great stress on judgment and acts of satisfaction. Thus it is interesting to see that the current reform of rites of penance are intended precisely to underscore the sacramental nature of the process. Rather than being something that is added to, or corrects, Trent, this is in fact a more serious working out of what is seminally in Trent's own teaching and takes account of the Lutheran objections.

Ministry

Ministry in effect was at the core of much of the disputes about sacraments. Luther and others held that ministry was of divine origin and that the call to ministry comes from God. When Catholic apologists sometimes say that Lutheranism attributes the call to the community, this is a misreading. What Luther tried to retrieve was an ancient practice of giving the community a say in the approval and choice of ministers that was compatible with the notion of divine call. On the other hand, the Reformers objected to all theories that seemed to privilege priestly mediation. Thus they dissented from the theology of sacramental character. They also taught that in the absence of the ordinary ministry of the ordained, a community of Christians could still celebrate the Last Supper, because it was given to the Church and not to priests. It needs to be noted, however, that this applies to exceptional cases, not to the usual situation, and is an argument from redemptive economy. This is exactly what present-day Lutherans have in mind when they ask, not whether the historic episcopacy is to be restored, but whether it is to be restored in such a way as to privilege ecclesiastical mediation over Word and Sacrament and the role of the ordained over the gift to the Church.

The Council of Trent, on the other hand, taught the doctrine of the character as the fitting way to account for tradition and included the necessary mediation of the ordained in all matters concerning sacraments, with the sole exception of marriage. It is important to recall, however, that in condemning the celebration of the Eucharist by ministers of the Reformation Churches who had not been ordained within the line of succession, the council did not say that this celebration is invalid, but spoke rather of ministers not duly ordained as persons whose legitimacy cannot be affirmed.[31]

Hermeneutical Perspectives on These Controversies and Doctrines

From a hermeneutical point of view, when we consider these controversies about the nature of the sacrament or about the Eucharist, we can see how the interpretation of doctrine and practice in the sixteenth century was perspectival and that doctrine and practice were inseparably connected. It was the concern either of the Reformers or of Trent that dictated what was said about others and that inspired the interpretation of the past. The interpretation of the scriptures, of the practices of earlier times, and of the practices of other bodies at the time was done within the context of the believing community and related to its practice and religious experience. Though Protestantism is often said to signal the beginning of more subjective approaches to faith, practice, and doctrine, this is as true of Catholic interpretations at the time as it is of those of the Reformers. The Catholic Church was bent on upholding given and established devotional practices and devotional approaches to the offering of the Mass and the reserved sacrament. However objective and detached is the sound of Trent's language, the ground of what is condemned or what is taught lies in the practices and piety of the time, by which the council set so much store.

There is also a strongly institutional concern in the readings of scripture or tradition, both Catholic and Protestant. For both sides the visibility of the Church and its institutions was important, but they stated them differently. The Catholic defenders upheld a strong vision of priestly order and mediation, whereas Protestant formulations were more congregationalist and more centered on the priesthood of all believers and on the preaching of the Gospel. A further point to be noted is the difficulty shown in reading sacramental language and the subordination of this reading to theoretical and practical concerns. To illustrate this, it is enough to mention that few today would accept either Luther's interpretation of the Roman Canon or that

---

31. Canon 7 of the *Canones de sacramento ordinis* refers to those not duly ordained by bishops as ministers who are not "legitimate ministers of the word and sacraments" (*Decrees of the Ecumenical Councils,* ed. Tanner, 2:744).

of the theologians who intervened in the conciliar debates of the Council of Trent.[32]

Current Roman Catholic / Protestant Dialogue

It is impossible to survey the extensive discussions on sacrament that the Roman Catholic Church has held with different Protestant Churches over the last thirty years. It is enough to indicate the specific hermeneutical principles that have been at work and to pinpoint the issues important to the practice and understanding of the place of sacraments in the life of the Church. The example of the findings of the Ecumenical Study Group of Protestant and Catholic Theologians that met in Germany to probe the points of reconciliation and the points of difference between Roman Catholic, Lutheran, and Reformed positions on justification, the doctrine of the sacraments, the Eucharist, ministry, marriage, confirmation and anointing of the sick, is instructive.[33] These theologians pointed to the need to set the condemnations and teachings in their historical setting, to note the mutual misunderstandings at work, and to note the developments that have taken place in all Churches since the sixteenth century. When this is done, a considerable degree of agreement can be found, and while important differences still exist they do not warrant the continued application of anathemas. It is enough to quote the summing-up of the debate on sacraments in general.[34] This notes the misunderstandings of the past and the ways in which more modern developments have relativized the differences that did and do still exist. The differences are set down as follows:

> Both sides take as fundamental starting point the following essential marks of the sacrament: dominical institution, the external sign, the specific promise or communication of grace. But in particular instances they draw different conclusions from these things. The result is that there are two different "systems," in which the same statements take on different meaning, and apparently different statements mean something analogous.

While the report goes on to note considerable points of convergence on the Lord's Supper, it is of note that it gives little or no attention to the liturgical changes introduced into sacramental worship by the practice and books of Christian Churches today. This is, however, important in creating a new setting for convergence and puts a different tenor on differences.

We see then how current interpretation of the sixteenth-century positions is done within historical perspective and within a context where some mu-

---

32. See David N. Power, "The Priestly Prayer: The Tridentine Theologians and the Roman Canon," *Fountain of Life*, ed. Gerard Austin (Washington, D.C.: Pastoral Press, 1991), 131–64.

33. *The Condemnations of the Reformation Era: Do They Still Divide?* ed. Karl Lehmann and Wolfhart Pannenberg, trans. Margaret Kohl (Minneapolis: Fortress Press, 1989).

34. Ibid., 83.

tual recognition exists and the desire for communion. This makes a fusion of horizons between Christian Churches possible, without having to reduce differences to sameness. This results from a multiple retrieval: of the Word of God, of earlier liturgical practices, and of a sacramental practice that attends more sharply to the power of symbol and to the language of rite and prayer. This can be accompanied by a greater readiness for allowing diversity in the expression and practice of the faith, one that remains possible within a more fundamental communion.

Many of the early dialogues on baptism, Eucharist, and ministry, for example, tried to seek reconciliation and agreement on the specific points at issue in the sixteenth century. The Faith and Order document, commonly referred to as BEM, tried to go somewhat further and express positions on such matters as anamnesis, epiclesis, presence, sacrifice, eschaton, ministry, and apostolic succession to which all Christian communions could assent. Even with this, however, differences remained, possibly because the categories, though in some respects new, were quite closely related to earlier controversies. In some recent agreements, which deal with basic questions of justification, sanctification, and Church, a new image emerges within which sacramental communality and sacramental divergence may be considered. This is the image of *koinonia*.[35] The term expresses the communion of Christians among themselves, within their participation in the communion of Father, Son, and Spirit.

The issue of ministry is one that continues to posit great difficulties, as can be seen from two examples. First, in the last phase of the Lutheran/Roman Catholic International Dialogue it was noted that there is some agreement on the need for ordained ministry and on the exercise of the ministry of Word and Sacrament.[36] There are problems, however, on the mediating role of ministers. For Lutherans this is entirely related to the Word and Sacrament themselves, whereas for Catholics the ordained minister has himself a mediating role, at least through his prayer and representation of Jesus Christ, granted that this is totally in virtue of Christ's power and God's action. There are also problems on the exact nature of historical continuity in the ministry and in its apostolic forms. Because the Word and Sacrament are themselves the primary forms of God's action and presence, for Lutherans the exercise of these in the Church cannot be made totally dependent on a given in-

---

35. For helpful comment, see George Tavard, "Considerations on an Ecclesiology of *Koinonia*," *One in Christ* 30 (1994): 43–51; John S. Went, "*Koinonia: A Significant Milestone on the Road to Unity*," *One in Christ* 30 (1994): 22–39; Ola Tjorhom, "The Porvoo Statement — A Possible Ecumenical Breakthrough?" *One in Christ* 29 (1993): 302–9; Henrik Roelvink, "The Apostolic Succession in the Porvoo Statement," *One in Christ* 30 (1994): 344–54; A. Birmelé, "Status quaestionis de la théologie de la communion à travers les dialogues oecuméniques et l'évolution des différentes théologies confessionnelles." *Cristianesimo nella storia* 14 (1995): 245–84.

36. Lutheran/Roman Catholic International Dialogue, "Church and Justification: Understanding the Church in the Light of the Doctrine of Justification," section 4.5, *Information Service of the Pontifical Council for Promoting Christian Unity* 86 (1994/II–III), 159–64.

stitutional form of historical continuity. Catholic teaching, however, finds a
guarantee of this continuity in Christ's own institution and sees a breakdown
in Church life and membership where it disappears. This is because it invests
sacramental form in the institutional form of the historical episcopacy.

This problem has also emerged in a second example from current efforts
at ecumenical union. In the discussion on a proposed agreement between the
Lutheran Church and the Episcopal Church in the United States, *"Toward
Full Communion"* and *"Concordat of Agreement,"* the Lutherans asked whether
the recognition of the historical episcopacy meant giving precedence to institutions, and hence to ecclesiastical mediation over the ministry of Word and
Sacrament.[37] Even while recognizing the historical role of the episcopacy in
the apostolic tradition, and the pertinence of retrieving it as a common form
of Church government they did not want to see this done in such a way as
to obscure the precedence of Word and Sacrament.

The matter needs to be treated in reference to a living reality, and ultimately to life in the Trinity, rather than in reference to doctrines. Churches
may differ on doctrines, while still acknowledging the Churches with which
it thus differs as living realizations of this basic divinely given *koinonia*. It is
a very different ground on which to debate differences than that of doctrine
alone. When the discussion bears too narrowly on doctrine, or even on practices and rites, one can come too quickly to doubt the validity of ministry,
Eucharist, baptism, and the like in another communion. When the starting
point is an affirmation of the other's reality as a living communion in Christ
and in the Trinity, it is to this that their doctrines and practices are related,
rather than to some doctrinal norm which must transcend all differences and
become the criterion of judgment about ecclesial and sacramental realities.

Hermeneutical Perspectives

We can close this chapter by spelling out the hermeneutical perspectives at
work in formulating and in interpreting doctrines. To begin with, we can see
what was being done in this regard at key historical moments. Then we can
distinguish different kinds of proposition and their purpose.

Historical Examples

A good starting point to see the force of doctrinal propositions about the
sacraments is to see how much at the time of their formulation they were ex-
plicitly related to usage. This is very clear in the Donatist controversy, when
for Augustine all discussion had to respect the liturgical formulas used. It
was also clear in a different way in controversies with the spirituals. Then the
issue was the extent to which ritual and institutional factors sufficed and how

---

37. *"Toward Full Communion"* and *"Concordat of Agreement,"* Lutheran-Episcopal Dialogue,
Series III, ed. William A. Norgren and William G. Rusch (Minneapolis: Augsburg, 1991).

liturgical usage related to the evangelical life of the Church. In debates with the Orthodox Church at Florence, the role of the *epiclesis* and the eucharistic character of the local Church loomed large in ecclesiological differences.

The period of the Protestant Reformation and of the Council of Trent provides several examples. It is quite clear that the Reformers set all their sacramental explanations within the context of the preaching of the Word of God and of right piety. Their grand effort was to restore the word to the people, to relate the sacraments to this word, and to have rites that evoked true faith in the Cross of Christ and in God's promise of the forgiveness of sins. This is the context for catechetical and doctrinal explanation. The Council of Trent, however, also demonstrated its great concern to leave practice and piety intact, and indeed to protect it against invasions that the council saw detrimental.

Sometimes its decrees made more explicit reference to liturgical contexts in noting liturgical traditions that are to be respected. In the decree on extreme unction, the need for the blessing of the oil by the bishop is retained, so that the significance of the grace of the Spirit be kept in the anointing. In penance, while the council places the power of absolution in the words "Ego te absolvo," it notes the tradition of using various prayers alongside these words in the celebration of the sacrament. Likewise, in the case of marriage it instituted the celebration of the sacrament *in facie ecclesiae* as normative, acknowledging at one and the same time the significance of this form and the historical reality of entering marriage in other ways.[38]

There is one noteworthy point of liturgy and doctrine that is left quite open. This has to do with what is to be considered the efficacious action of the minister. In scholastic theology, it had become commonplace to attribute efficacy for consecration and sacrifice to the priest's repetition of Christ's words over the bread and wine. This of course left out any consideration of the power of the blessing prayer. The Tridentine decree on the sacrament of the Eucharist chooses a quite circumspect way of respecting both blessing prayer and christological words, though it does truncate the blessing in the process. It states that "after" the blessing of the bread and wine, Christ showed his disciples his body and blood, testifying to their presence by his words.[39] This includes the references in the account of the Supper to the actions of the blessing prayer, of showing (and giving) his body and blood, and of testifying by his words, "This is my body, this is my blood," that the gift is truly his body and blood. Beyond this, the decree did not choose to attribute efficacy to any one of these three actions in particular. Since the role of the ordained minister is to repeat what Christ did at the Supper, attention

---

38. *Decrees of the Ecumenical Councils*, ed. Tanner, 2:753–59.
39. "Post panis vinique benedictionem se suum ipsius corporis illis praebere ac suum sanguinem disertis ac perspicuis verbis testatus est" (chapter 1).

is thereby drawn to his threefold action in the Mass, rather than only to the repetition of Christ's words.

The Ecclesiological Context of Interpretation

Specific understandings of the nature of the Church are at issue when sacramental practice is debated. This has been made clear in relation to each of the controversies surveyed, and it is still today a key point. The spiritual movements of the Middle Ages avowed an evangelical ecclesiology. The Orthodox Church was committed to a eucharistic and pneumatological communion. The Protestant Churches fostered a reality centered around the Word of God. The Catholic Church in all these controversies stood for the institutional factors of Church life and for a spirituality of priestly mediation. Today, there is a growing recognition of bringing all of the considerations into conversation and harmony, and often it is the reality of *koinonia*, or communion in the life of the Trinity, that emerges as the ultimate point of reference.

The Nature of Doctrinal Propositions

In interpreting doctrines, however, and their impact on sacramental tradition, the crux of the matter is to locate propositional statements within the larger whole of faith expression, of lived faith, and of a living community. They are statements whose need derives first from practice, so that sacraments may be rightly celebrated, and then from the requirement of clarity on what is held in common. Their truth, however, does not stand in the propositions themselves, but in their adequacy to the whole body of what is affirmed in confessions and done in practice. In other words, their meaning and their truth are referential, so that they must remain bound to a corpus of beliefs and to a complexity of practices. It is within this whole that they function and render service.

Each proposition therefore has to be seen in its context and in its multiple references, asking with what other affirmations it belongs and to what practices it is attached. For example, the teaching of Lateran IV and of Constance on the sufficiency of ordination and on its need to guarantee the power to celebrate the sacraments has to be set over against the position of the spirituals that it is fidelity to the Gospel that does this, and that institutional factors have no adequate foundation in the Gospel. Similarly, Martin Luther's exclusion of the notion of propitiatory sacrifice from the Mass has to be seen in the context in which he believed that the Roman Canon and Mass offerings signaled a repetition of the offering of Christ by the Church that effectively eliminated the adequacy of the sacrifice of the Cross.

Propositions likewise emerge from and are bound to the semantics of symbolic and poetic language. In the case of the sacraments, this means the convergence in celebration of word, rite, and institutional authority. What propositions are intended to do is to clarify the meaning and the efficacy of this use of symbolic language and action. They do not add meaning to it, but spell out the meaning inherent in it. Specifically, they ought to illuminate the being in faith and in communion as a Church with God that is expressed in sacrament. They ought also to spell out the transcendental reference of all sacramental language and usage or, in other words, speak of that to which sacrament makes reference when it claims to be the action of God and the action of Christ.

At times, propositional affirmations lose touch with one semantic context to be imbedded in another. The case of the sixteenth century interpretation of the Roman Canon is a good example. Neither Luther nor the apologists whose voices were heard at Bologna and Trent were able to grasp the symbolic and metaphoric expression of the original composition. Instead, they both read it in the context of the symbolic and ritual highlighting of the priestly consecration and of the practice of making Mass offerings. Because the apologists referred this favorably to a symbolism of priestly mediation, they were ready to defend and affirm it. Because Luther read it in reference to the word of God and faith in Christ's satisfaction for sin, he roundly condemned it. Instead, he set up another symbolic and ritual context in which the words of Christ were heard as proclamation of forgiveness and the sacramental elements were received as a seal on this promise. The present-day reforms of liturgical books in both the Lutheran and the Roman Catholic Church attempt to retrieve a more complete and original sacramentary semantic, which allows a greater possibility of reconciling Catholic insistence on rite and Lutheran insistence on word. It is again the new semantic context which serves the possibility of discussion over propositions.

In the language and concepts that they employ, propositions are of mixed genre. In general one can distinguish several ploys, in the use respectively of negation, limit-concepts, and analogies.

Negations exclude what is inconsistent with the truth. Sacraments have no efficacy where the recipient is without faith. Neither do they confer grace outside the communion in the Spirit. The body of Christ is not present in the Eucharist in a way that allows it to be circumscribed by the place where this presence is affirmed and worshiped. Sacraments are not legitimately celebrated when the minister has not been ordained within the apostolic succession. There is a tendency to jump from these negations to positive affirmations, as though these were implied in the negation. However, it is important in interpreting such propositions to be clear on their exact intent and not to draw unwarranted conclusions. On the thorny issue of ministry, for example, to negate the legitimacy of a particular celebration is not to imply of necessity that there is no sacramental reality in this celebration.

Limit-concepts are such that set the boundaries of understanding. They are closely related to negations but have more affirmative content. They can be regulative of practice, as when it is said that the word of God is rightly preached within the communion of the Church, or that for Catholics a sacramental marriage is that celebrated before a properly designated ecclesiastical witness. Such propositions set the boundaries within which the meaning of sacraments can be spelled out. Limit-concepts may also set out the parameters of a more speculative understanding. Thus of Christ's presence in the Lord's Supper it is affirmed that the species of bread and wine do not change, that Christ is not physically located in the bread and wine, and yet he is truly present and offered when the species of bread and wine are offered. Any further explanation or speculation is done within these limits.

In this respect, negations and limit-concepts set the stage for some use of analogy in explaining sacraments. While this is to a great extent left to theology, doctrinal propositions put forward some analogies in the service of a common faith. Thus the Council of Trent in explaining the efficacy of sacraments used the analogy of *opus operatum,* that is, of a work that has its own inner impact and does not depend simply on the agility of the worker. Certain actions serve an end, however well or poorly performed, given their institutional and ritual context. A judge declares a sentence which holds, however well or poorly he put his mind to the decision, but it holds because of the weight of society behind it. In the case of the sacraments, it is Christ who has invested the word and rite with sanctifying power, and it is the body of the Church which gives it context. Hence, the efficacy of the rite requires only that minimal involvement of the minister which makes it clear that he is acting as a minister of the Church, though of course a better attention on his part and on the part of the congregation is needed to fit the holiness of what is done.

Similarly, Trent made some use, granted limited, of the analogy of the difference between substance and appearance to explain the presence of Christ in the Eucharist and the process of change. This made it possible to affirm some understanding of Christ's presence that reduced the Supper words of Christ, repeated in the sacrament, neither to physical presence nor to a simple exchange of signs about something else. John Calvin offered a different analogical understanding, which for him also satisfied the truth of the words. He spoke of a presence that belongs within a specific context and only there, in this case the context being Church. He also spoke of a presence in a nondimensional manner that grants true union between persons and a true communion in life, which in this case is the life of Christ mediated by the Spirit.[40]

One could go beyond these examples, but they should suffice to show how negation, the setting of limits, and the use of analogies go together in formulating doctrines, and how attention to this, as well as to historical context, is necessary when appropriating them into present belief and practice as part of tradition.

---

40. See B. A. Gerrish, *Grace and Gratitude: The Eucharistic Theology of John Calvin* (Minneapolis: Fortress Press, 1992), 182–83.

Conclusion: Church and Ministry

From the foregoing survey of doctrines on the sacraments, a number of things emerge that are pertinent to the interpretation of sacramental traditions. First, there is the need to place every teaching in its practical and historical context. This means looking at what the doctrine was intended to uphold in practice and what issues it addressed. It also means looking at the issues raised by those condemned and what alternate practices they wished to foster. Next, then, there is the present need to revisit these controversies and these issues and to see how they may be taken up in the present with both points of view in mind. The repetition of doctrines does not suffice, but a deeper and more pertinent consideration of the questions disputed is required.

With these two principles in mind, one can also note aspects of sacramental doctrine and practice that these historical disputes now call to our attention. To begin with, there is the ecclesial nature of sacrament and the need that sacramental celebration be grounded in an ecclesial context. Augustine's controversy with the Donatists and the medieval concern for the evangelical life were ultimately both about the nature of the Church and the place of sacraments in the life of the Church as a whole. The differences between East and West at Florence were in the first place about the procession of the Holy Spirit, but they were closely connected with ecclesiologies. In these ecclesiologies, the point of difference was whether the Eucharist or jurisdiction is the defining act of communion in the Church and whether communion between Churches needs to be centered in Eucharist or in common governance. The disagreements at the time of the Reformation also had deep ecclesiological implications. They were a matter of whether the power of the priesthood is the ground of Church life and sacramental celebration, or whether this is not Word and Sacrament in themselves, however they be given expression. In this, there are differing viewpoints on the relation between ordained ministry and sacrament in the life of the Church. As said before, what needs reconsideration at the present time is the notion and character of mediation within the Church. Neither the Reformation nor Trent seems to have dealt fully enough with this question.

In considering these questions, priority needs to be given to the sacramental reality of Church community. It is in the eucharistic sacrament that the Church is perfected as the body of Christ. This is done through that memorial which includes word, prayer, and rite. All forms of ministry and government have to relate to this priority and need to be adjusted and renewed in its service. The question of the Church's sacramental mediation therefore needs to be given further consideration. The issue was too starkly spelled out at the time of the Reformation. The Catholic position was formulated in terms of a power given through ordination to renew Christ's sacrifice in the Eucharist or to act with a power derived from him in the other sacraments. On the Protestant side, the priority of the proclamation of the Word of scripture was so strongly asserted that it seemed to overlook the Church's role in mediating this Word, not only in sacrament but also in interpretation. In face of both positions, the nature of ecclesial mediation needs to be more finely considered. It is neither purely a power to sanctify, nor purely an act of letting the Word speak of itself. The word of the scripture is always mediated through the living interpretation and appropriation of the Church, and the Word Incarnate and the Spirit act within the Church in bringing about the mediation of word and of grace. Moreover, as already explained, Word and Sacrament belong in conjunction with each other in this act of mediation. It is in appreciating the living mediation that takes place in sacramental action, in the appropriation of a tradition rooted in the scriptures, that we can pass beyond sixteenth-century controversies, without necessarily indeed having to achieve complete uniformity on what is taught or done.

At the present time, in an ecumenical climate, a way of addressing these issues that can allow them to be differently addressed is found in the accent on *koinonia*. This is not in the first place a juridical or sacramental unity, but it is a living communion which is served by word, sacrament, and governance, and which is given visible expression in these forms. This is a horizon within which to interpret the past and the sacramental reality and allows for a fusion of horizons, for a convergence within differences. With the accent on the living communion and its relation to the Trinity, the variability and flexibility of forms is more comprehensible and leaves room for the communion between Churches that allows for differences. This is not to say that any two theological or practical positions can be reduced to a common one, nor that there may not still be disputes as to the better way of celebrating sacraments. It is not even to deny that some positions may be irreconcilable and exclude communion. It is, however, to acknowledge the limitations and particularity of every position and to move toward a life of communion in the one faith and in the one baptism and Eucharist, even when these are given different shapes by different ecclesial communions. Differences can accommodate the fact that all seek to interpret and appropriate the one apostolic tradition and to live in the light of the gift given through the event of the Cross of Christ and its sacramental memorial.

A final comment must note the limits of this inquiry into doctrine. It has dealt with issues affecting Churches that are, as it were, in the mainstream. Faith, however, is sometimes expressed in living ways in other traditions, and these do have to be more carefully studied. With their insistence on believer's baptism, or on adult baptism, the Anabaptists connected this insistence with the relation of the Church to society and culture. Lutheran, Reformed, and Catholic Churches all found some accommodation with social and political forces. The Anabaptists were unwilling to accept these accommodations, and their insistence on believer's baptism was one way of bringing out the countercultural force of Christianity. This relativization of culture, if not always opposition to it, is one of the characteristics of bodies today which trace their roots to the Anabaptists.

On the North American continent, the frontier experience gave rise to new ways of giving expression to the relation between preaching of the word, conversion, and social bonding within the Christian faith. Expressions of bonding and of a common fidelity to the Gospel's social commitments were inherent in the eucharistic liturgies of John Calvin and Ulrich Zwingli. The desire to exclude the unworthy from the communion table remained a part of the norms of camp meetings. However, through the frontier experience, it also happened that these expressions of Christian fellowship were ritualized in different ways, with more attention simply to eating and celebrating together. In some Church communities today, the parish supper seems to be more effective in creating a sense of Christian bonding than eucharistic communion. Rather than decry this, the challenge is to see what is lacking in the rites of Eucharist and how the symbolism of commensality in Christ might be enhanced.

These are very sparse remarks on alternate experiences and expressions of faith and of their relation to sacrament. All that is intended is to draw attention to the need to incorporate these more fully into the understanding and revision of sacramental traditions and celebrations.

— Chapter Eight —

Conversion and Critique

It is commonplace to note that participation in sacramental worship brings about a conversion, as it is commonplace also to note that this will not happen without faith and a readiness to engage in what the Gospel calls *metanoia*. This is the readiness to hear God's word, to be challenged by it, and to turn to God from the heart in response to it. While this immediately concerns individual persons, it needs to be noted further that through their sacramental practice, communities as such constantly face the call to deeper conversion. They are moved to this by the work of the Word and the Spirit, operating in the rites. While this can be treated in terms of a theology of grace, it is helpful to look at it as the process in which participants engage when they are caught up in the language event of sacramental action.

The event of Word and Spirit necessarily occurs within the cultural, symbolic, and institutional structures of a community and necessarily reflects the cultural riches and perceptions of different peoples. Sometimes, however, this event of grace is almost identified with certain concepts that are supplied by particular cultures. What at first serves as a paradigm for understanding and guiding ritual development is allowed to claim a conceptual and commanding influence over the event of grace. This has sometimes been the way with, for example, the notion of sacrifice or the notion of efficient causality. Conversion to the wisdom of God and the wisdom of the Cross that is embodied in sacrament requires that such paradigms be modified when they are appropriated from a culture and also that they be broken open to the Word and Spirit even in their usage. Church communities are in a continuous process of communal conversion, both in their openness to grace and in their readiness to reappropriate this event through modifications in symbol, rite, and institution. This cannot be done without being open to a constructive critique of their existing forms.

Hence, in this chapter three things will be done. First, it will be asked how the nature of conversion appears in new ways when the questions raised by what are seen as post[-]modern issues are taken up. Second, it will be seen that sacramental celebration can impede the call to grace by reason of its rigidity and its appeal to time-restricted forms. This will constitute the bulk of the chapter and will be done by surveying various modes of this critique. Third, on this basis it will be possible to present important aspects of the

240

process of conversion that sacraments require and foster, when in openness to critique communities of faith are opened to the event of grace that comes in new settings.

Conversion in Crisis

The Church is constantly in the process of conversion, so as to conform more and more to Christ and the journey of his Pasch. As Paul VI said in his apostolic exhortation on evangelization, the Church not only evangelizes but must itself be evangelized.[1] In that same letter, he related this to what takes place in devotion and in the celebration of sacraments, since these need to be renewed in relation to the demands of the Gospel, as well as in relation to people's cultures.

While of course conversion is thought of primarily in terms of union with Christ and growth in the Spirit, it takes place within the realities of time, place, history, and culture. It is in living these out in communion with Christ that the Church is called to a conversion that allows the truth of the Gospel to appear more clearly in human forms and in the testimony of Christian life. In times of crisis and change, the conversion has particular and compelling demands, all the more difficult to discern and to navigate because sacramental change is tied in with changes in the culture itself, in the midst of which the Church in turn undergoes change. Facing the exigencies of this era and all that this requires of evangelization and inculturation is a work of conversion.

This does not mean that the Church simply conforms to new ways, but that in the light of the Gospel and its own sacramental heritage it wrestles with the issues raised. The conversion to the Pasch to which sacrament moves Christians is a conversion in form as well as in spirit. When society and Church are aware of the constrictions of the modern, as well as of the limits of the medieval and of the fragmentation of the present, there are new ways of looking at a tradition and of appropriating it. This is what has to guide the sacramental celebration of the language event, in communities more attentive to how an epoch relates to history and a people to the cultural fluidity of language.

Previous chapters have shown the variabilities of liturgical history and the different paradigms that can be used for the celebration of the same sacrament in different places and in different epochs. Present cultural appropriation cannot be innocent of this, nor innocent of its own rather fluid use of paradigms and of its choices from within traditions. This does not mean abandoning history or contending that we can live without reliance on traditions and on the institutions that serve their transmission. What it does mean

---

1. Paul VI, *Apostolic Exhortation, On Evangelization in the Modern World* (Washington, D.C.: USCC, 1976), no. 15, pp. 13f.

is that we need to be more conscious of how history is written, transmitted, and appropriated, and of the nature of our choices in mapping celebration.

Instead of thinking of history as the record of events, it is more truly considered as the writing of events, or in some cases their oral tradition. History is thus perspectival. It is brought to being by language, shaped in its reality by how it is recorded and made meaningful. This is not to say that events did not occur, but only that we are always distanced from them by the mediation of language. This language is in itself an interpretation. It subsumes certain ideals, it relates events to persons and institutions and to social and cultural patterns of how life should be modeled. Cultural forms, social identities, institutional composites, ethical ideals are all written into historical narrative and into the traces of history, whether in book or in monument, of what was once done or happened. When the record is read or heard today, or archeological sites examined, this too is a perspectival act. In other words, it involves an interpretation, which may well be done from a different viewpoint from that of those who originally narrated events or composed codices of ritual behavior or who built churches for worship. All of this leads us to recognize that pinning down the meaning of a word, a text, or a rite, once and for all, is not possible.

Interpretation, however, is not purely arbitrary, and hence we look for tools to aid us to be sensitive to what is said and what is transmitted of past events. That is why more thought is given to genres, why semiotics is used to help decipher codes, and why more attention is paid to social constructs and to their relation to lived reality. Though a Christian people, even in this crisis of language and transmission, has faith in sacrament as a language event of Word and Spirit, it is not ignorant of cultural determinations, of openness to meanings, of always moving forward out of a moment that is never totally in its grasp. In the process, as already noted, even while affirming its conditionality there is that in the post[-]modern which allows a different, but new, trust in the power of language.

Critique

Though we have faith in the tradition or transmission of God's Word and Sacrament across the ages, we cannot but be aware of the cultural limitations and at times even fallacies of this tradition. Critique and criticism are not of course to be confused, for critique is the effort to take some distance from a reality in order to gain insight into what is going on. Applied to liturgical history and celebration, the essence of this critique is to consider the cultural factors in sacramental development, to unveil any negative ideologies imbedded in ritual, and to recover possibilities of liturgical action that may suit a new cultural situation. It will uncover what is culturally bound and even perhaps point out ideological, nontheological, factors that have had a negative influence on ritual. The latent possibilities of renewal brought to light may come from some new insight into the tradition or may even lie at the margins of the symbolic and institutional forms generally embraced.

A community cannot be locked into its prevailing language code. It has to allow for critical reflection and a readiness to listen to variant points of view on how the rites are tailored and performed. This is vital in a period of pluriformity. In writing of ethical debates, Jean-Marc Ferry maps out the stages of exchange.[2] They are the stages of narration, interpretation, and argumentation. These can be adapted to the critique of sacramental tradition, opening the way to legitimate differences or to revisions of the code and its usage. First, there has to be the period of narration, of identifying the Christian stories that serve as matrix, of telling one's own stories openly, and of listening to the stories of others. Then there is the stage of interpretation, when participants in common discourse make clear what interpretations they give to their story or to the their language use, and in the case of the liturgy one would add to the common code and heritage. Third, there has to be discussion about the legitimacy of the stories, the interpretations, their social implications, and especially about the ethical consequences. In this third stage, all parties have to heed the challenge that comes from others, not just about consequences but about the language code itself. It is especially important to note how the code may exclude some, or even oppress them, by subjecting them to unwarranted domination. As this is noted, a critique can unearth what the tradition may offer by way of opening perceptions to new horizons or diverse perspectives.

There are tools which help this kind of discernment. What is taken into account here is fourfold. First, there is the use of semiotics and semantics to consider the grammar of a liturgy and its usage in specific situations. Second, there is the critique of the language used about the body in sacramental worship. Third, there is a critical reflection on the paradigms which guide the action and ordering of worship. Fourth, there is the process of ritualization, which has already been mentioned as something currently in process.

Semiotics

Semiotics by its examination of code, and semantics by its examination of performance, give us insight into a tradition in the act of its being passed on.[3] In advocating the use of Peirce's semiotics in the study of art, Mieke Bal recalls the major points of his understanding of sign. These are that a sign, or *representamen*, addresses somebody, that it creates in the mind of that somebody a more developed sign which functions as the sign's interpretant, and that the sign stands for an object on the ground of some particular way of

---

2. Jean-Marc Ferry, *L'Éthique reconstructive* (Paris: Éd. du Cerf, 1996), 69–73.
3. This approach is well exemplified in the collection of essays by Gerard Lukken, *Per Visibilia ad Invisibilia: Anthropological, Theological and Semiotic Studies on the Liturgy and the Sacraments*, ed. Louis van Tongeren and Charles Caspers (Kampen: Kok Pharos Publishing House, 1994).

considering the object.[4] This description of a sign can help in looking at any construct. It posits purpose and intent in the sign, it takes in the particular perspective of the sign-maker, but it also allows the room for the play of mind and imagination in the one who perceives it. The description allows room for both explanation and critique. It explains what the author, speaker, or artist was doing by examining the design and context of the sign. It also explains how and why it could be appropriated in different ways according to the perception of the receiver. On the basis of this explanation, it makes room for the critique of ideas and perspectives that belong either to the sign-maker or to the recipient.

When semiotics is applied to language, one of the chief fields of investigation is into narrative. The theory of Greimas was that stories have a deep grammar and a surface grammar.[5] The surface grammar is what is immediately apparent in the particular code of language in use. One finds the plot in the story, and in particular cultural traditions one can even see how certain figures continually recur, perhaps under different names, in its stories. Greimas's contention was, however, that written more deeply and more universally is another grammar that follows certain rules of interaction. Scriptural scholars have explored the fruit of such insight in studying parables. What is of interest is that they show how the normal functioning of such relations are actually reversed in parables of the kingdom. The narrative of the vineyard is an example of such reversal of the expectations of a narrative code.[6] When the owner sends his son, this would seem to be the moment when the laborers who have claimed the property and its fruits are undone, but the contrary proves to be the case. The sender, who supposedly has the power, is outwitted by the receivers, with no show of force on the side of the sender or his son. If the passion narrative, which is at the heart of sacramental memorial, is written according to the laws of the parables of the kingdom, then it too is a reversal of the usual characterizations of story's deep grammar. Reversal is then seen as the way to redemption adopted by a loving God.

The critical question for tradition is whether these reversals are always respected as the stories are passed on. At times, in fact, cultures or human tendencies turn the story back to the common deep grammar. The story of Christ's death becomes a story of domination of the greater, the victory of the hero, the punishment of the offender. The parabolic reversals of the Gospel's teaching on the kingdom and the parabolic reversal inherent in the passion

---

4. See Mieke Bal, "Signs in Painting," *Art Bulletin* 78, no. 1 (1996): 6–9. Peirce's description of sign is taken from "Logic as Semiotic: The Theory of Signs," in Robert E. Innis, ed., *Semiotics: An Anthology* (Bloomington: Indiana University Press, 1985), 5.

5. A. Greimas, *Sémantique structurale* (Paris: Larousse, 1966).

6. Paul Ricoeur gives an account of this in "The Bible and Imagination," in Paul Ricoeur, *Figuring the Sacred: Religion, Narrative, and Imagination*, trans. David Pellauer, ed. Mark I. Wallace (Minneapolis: Fortress Press, 1995), 151–56.

narrative have to be constantly reinstated, lest we slip back into prevailing cultural and social perceptions.

Semiotics also gives insight into bodily ritual. In examining the code of ritual behavior, as distinct from the code of verbal expression, semiotics looks into the relations expressed in movement. Structuralist semiotics serves up to a point in drawing attention to the repetition of certain kinds of binary movement, such as up/down, in/out, straight/circular. These have an inbuilt significance that is printed into the body itself and its relations to what is around it, so that some initial, even somewhat formless, meaning is found at the root of much liturgical action. The up/down movement is realized in baptismal immersion, the in/out in processions and in movement from one part of a church building to another. The straight/circular contrast draws attention to contrasting movements in the liturgy itself, such as the movement around the altar or the movement to the altar, or the coming to the front of the table for communion, where the place of the clergy stands in contrast with that of the laity. Trinomies such as those of subject/helper/opponent, sender/receiver/helper, often used in examining stories, also offer some insight into ritual actions, as do binomies of inside/outside, common/reserved. It is never the constant of the movement alone or in itself, however, which renders the meaning of the action, but the relations established through the action.

A careful semiotic study of the ritual code reveals how actions express relations. Gerard Lukken, for example, has remarked on the contrast in the ring ceremonial in marriage rites.[7] In one case, the groom gives the bride a ring. In the other, the two exchange rings. The husband/wife relation is diversely signified in these two ritual actions, so that the nature of the marriage contract and covenant is different. Within the same sacrament, Lukken also contrasts the action of hands. In one case, the bride places her hand in that of the groom, whereas in the other the two join hands.

Another example could be taken from the rites of communion to the sick. In these rites, the sick person (receiver) is either surrounded by family and friends (helpers), being given communion sent from the Eucharist of the community (sender), or alternately sent from the tabernacle by the priest (alternate sender), without reference to the community's participation. A comparable contrast can be shown in looking at communion rites in the Mass as they express the relation between people and clergy. In one case, clergy take communion first, from the table or at least within the sanctuary, while the people stand outside the sanctuary and away from the table. In the other case, all stand around the table in a place where there is no clear demarcation between nave and sanctuary and take communion together, from or close to the table. The first kind of action accentuates an ecclesial ideal of differentiated communion in Christ, while the second expresses that what-

---

7. Gerard Lukken, "Die Stellung der Frau im Trauungsritus des *Rituale Romanum* und nach Vaticanum II," in *Per Visibilia*, 317–20.

ever the different roles (which are not suppressed) all are one in grace within the body, without hierarchy of status.

These examples show how the examination of ritual space and its use sheds light on ritual action. In the course of history and in the Church today as allowed by the present ritual book, marriage rites take place in three different locations. In one case, they take place in the home of one of the partners, in that place which highlights kinship and family or, as in medieval blessings of the marriage bed, sexual converse. In another case, they take place in front of the church in an elaborate porch, entering only for the Eucharist. This accentuates the secular/sacral interaction of marriage, which is formed by secular customs and witness but is then placed under God's blessing in the Eucharist. The third ritual, now the most common in the West, is that the couple are in the sanctuary for the entire ritual. This gives a more sacral emphasis to the marriage covenant, but the position of the couple in the sanctuary betokens that they are the ministers of this rite and exercise their priesthood in it, before the community. In each case, the location and disposition of space is significant. Medieval churches created a space, the side-porch, to welcome this ritual and to place it in ready interaction with the rites inside the church. Modern churches adapt the sanctuary/nave distinction to this rite in a particular way. In homes, the festive table and the bridal chamber spell out the familial and social context of the contract.

Semiotics serves too in attending to the sexual aspects of sacramental place, word, and ritual. There are some studies of church buildings and their interior design which point to the buildings' sexual grammar, particularly to the location of the womb and the act of penetration which the use of the building allows or requires.[8] It is almost proverbial to speak of the baptismal font as a womb and of the act of immersion as a return to the womb, to be born again. Along with this, there is the sexual reference of blessing and ritual. For example, for a long time in the Roman Rite in the course of blessing the font, the priest placed the Paschal candle in the water in an obvious use of a phallic symbol to express penetration of this womb by the power of the Spirit.

There is no need for surprise to realize how much sexual symbolism there is in sacramental worship. This belongs as it were to the deep grammar of rite. However, its particular use is always culturally determined. What needs to be put to critique is the ideology of gender relations which may lie within the use of such language and rite. One of the things that needs particular attention is the tendency to consider the spousal and maternal role of the woman as passive and the male role as active. Hence the action of God or of the Spirit as a creative role is imaged by the action of male penetration, and the generative role of the woman is used to express the passive role

---

8. See Stephen de Staebler and Diane Apostolos-Cappadona, "Reflections on Art and the Spirit: A Conversation," in *Art, Creativity and the Sacred,* 24–33.

of thing or person blessed and sanctified. On the other hand, the maternal role of giving and nurturing life can be used to express divine action or the action of the Spirit as well as of the ministry of the Church. It can happen, however, that male roles are allowed to appropriate whatever is active in the female social role, and the women are given only passive part and their role expressed with passive sexual imagery, or the active feminine part made strictly interior, likened to the nurture in the womb of what is received from the male. It is never enough to say that we can use both male and female language of God, or use both kinds of images to express divine work. One has to look at how this is used, so as to assure that the grammar of active/passive or even active/receptive roles is not perpetuated, even in this adoption of names and images.

Language about Body

This thought leads readily to a consideration of the language of the body.[9] There are two aspects to the critique of this language usage. First, there is the social location of women's bodies in sacramental worship. Second, there is an image of the body as abject which has had a large place in Christian language.

The Social Location of Women's Bodies

In an article on feminist liturgy and the body, Teresa Berger comments that in liturgy women are subject to a double bodily taboo.[10] One surfaces in their exclusion from ordination, when their presence in ministering rites is thought to violate the order of creation and not simply the positive order of divine mandate. The second is the taboo of menstruation, the steps taken to keep woman's blood, maternal blood, out of liturgy.

Theological justification for the exclusion of women from ordained priesthood has varied over time.[11] Thomas Aquinas linked it to the difference between male and female nature in the power to lead and exercise social authority. Bonaventure related it to the relation between bridegroom and bride which reflects not just the relation of Christ to the Church but God's relation to the world, as embodied in the act of creation.

In all of this, it is the receptivity of women (some like to say that this is not passivity) which is emphasized, and this is given biological and affective roots in her nature. To have a woman as ordained minister would thus be

9. The work was not available to the author at the time of writing, but feminist critique and feminist reconstruction of sacramental theology are well supplied in the book by Susan Ross, *Extravagant Affections: A Feminist Sacramental Theology* (New York: Continuum, 1998).

10. Teresa Berger, "Women in Worship," in *Liturgy and the Body, Concilium* 1995/3, ed. Louis-Marie Chauvet and François Kabasele Lumbala, 112–20.

11. See Dennis M. Ferrara, "The Ordination of Women: Tradition and Meaning," *Theological Studies* 55 (1994): 706–19; John H. Wright, "Patristic Testimony on Women's Ordination in *Inter Insigniores*," *Theological Studies* 58 (1997): 516–26.

a violation of the divine order, and hence the presence of a woman's body in the sanctuary is taboo. Some push this even so far as to prohibit women from acting as servers at Mass or other liturgies, and there are always those who even query their presence at the lectern. If they speak in church at all, it must be outside the holy of holies. Pope John Paul II has attempted to remove all suggestion of inferiority from the principle,[12] relating it solely to a divine mandate, but nonetheless in taking sacrament to reflect the relation of Christ the bridegroom to his bride, the Church, he gives a justification rooted in his perception of the human, emotive, and bodily relations between man and woman.

The other taboo mentioned by Teresa Berger is that of menstruation. With all the emphasis of tradition on the blood of Christ and on the blood of sacrifice, the blood associated with the power of childbearing was deemed ritually defiling. For many centuries this was symbolized in the ceremony of "Churching," or cleansing of women after childbirth, which was required before rejoining the liturgical community.[13] Medieval rituals presented this as a need for purification before reentering the assembly for worship.[14] The *Rituale Romanum* of 1614 retained the welcome back to church after childbirth, or the element of "Churching," but replaced the notion of purification with thanksgiving. Local rituals unfortunately did not all follow the lead of the Roman Ritual.

This service has disappeared from the revised books of the Roman liturgy. Instead, the baptismal liturgy includes a special blessing of thanksgiving for the mother, and the new Catholic *Book of Blessings* has a ceremony of thanksgiving to be used when the mother has been unable to be present at the child's baptism. To this, there are parallels in the American Lutheran *Occasional Services* and the 1979 Episcopal *Book of Common Prayer*, where childbirth is seen as an occasion for thanksgiving, with all notions of purification removed. However, the memory of the tradition is not that easily obliterated and reflects how women have been seen by the Church and given place in its liturgical symbolism. Indeed, the metaphor of sacrifice is extended to include renunciation of bodily and affective realities associated with womanhood. Renouncing the enjoyment of sex in marriage is advanced as an ideal when virginity is lauded. Renunciation of the *jouissance* of motherhood is also privileged, the typical image being that of the Mother of Christ himself, who is extolled because of her renunciation of her Son in her communion in his sacrifice and her readiness to give up her child.

---

12. See, for example, John Paul II, *Post-synodal Exhortation on the Vocation and the Mission of the Lay Faithful in the Church and in the World* (Washington, D.C.: USCC, 1988), 143–60.

13. For details on this, see Walter von Arx, "The Churching of Women after Childbirth," *Concilium* 112 (1979/2): 63–71.

14. This fits with Julia Kristeva's suggestion that woman is excluded, made absent, or indeed sacrificed in Christian ritual in order to enable men to free themselves from dependency and from their terror of nonbeing. On this, see Ross, *Extravagant Affections*, 152–55.

This part of Western cultural and religious tradition is taken into account by Julia Kristeva in her distinction between the semiotic and the symbolic and in her desire to let free woman's aesthetic capacity as contribution to a new socio-symbolic order.[15] The semiotic, in her distinction, is expression that is corporeal in its roots, that is imaginatively associative and drive-patterned, and so less socially calculating. The symbolic is found in expressions that are overtly rational, socially conscious, and related to the organization of society or community. In the Western tradition, where the religious has played a significant part, women and their power of symbolic expression have been largely excluded. In exploring the ways in which women may find their own aesthetic expression and a place in the symbolic code of society and its ordering, Kristeva asks whether religion can play any part in this, given its dubious history. Obviously to Christians, and especially to those concerned about the centrality of sacrament, this is a great challenge.

The Abject Body

Associated with this sense of man/woman relations in the symbolic order is Kristeva's notion of the abject body.[16] This relates to the dilemma of simultaneously affirming God's initiatives and lordship and the human creativity which is grounded in the realization of the self's potential. Religion is all too prone to ask for renunciation of the self and its potential in order to allow it place in a symbolic order which treats the bodily human self as abject, so that all creativity is located in the spiritual realm, or perhaps in the arts of the spiritually beautiful. Bodily postures and exclusions contribute to this sense of abjection, but most of all it is the language of self and of sin that casts the body in a dubious role within the Christian mystery. As Kristeva states the matter, the abject "is not lack of cleanliness or health," but "whatever disturbs identity, system, order." Since on the one hand the Judeo-Christian tradition affirms the good of the human person, but on the other treats certain kinds of person or certain bodily experiences as unclean, this gives rise to the phenomenon of the "split self."

In her reading of the New Testament and the attitudes of Jesus to the law and to sin, Kristeva acknowledges the importance of relating sin to human act and human responsibility rather than locating it simply in transgressions of the law. In this way, sin and the capacity to sin are interiorized. She also points out that the price of this in Judeo-Christian religious history has been some errant ways of treating desire. Desires located in the body are too readily seen as sinful, and the body itself is designated as something abject. The "abject" in her vocabulary is that which is opposed to the "I," or the self, that is legitimated by cultural norms. Bodily desire or the body itself are thus all too

---

15. See Julia Kristeva, *The Kristeva Reader*, ed. Toril Moi (New York: Columbia University Press, 1986), 34–88.

16. Julia Kristeva, *Powers of Horror: An Essay on Abjection*, trans. Leon S. Roudiez (New York: Columbia University Press, 1982), 1–132.

readily dubbed sinful, unclean, unlawful, to the extent that their fulfillment would disturb the right order and the quest of the approved spiritual ideals. Sexual desire and the love of earthly things are very readily cast as contrary to God's order, as in those prayers which request that we may despise the things of earth and love those of heaven.

In tandem with this language about the body, Kristeva points to the confession of sin as an ambiguous ritual which has the potential for either greater guilt or for an affirmation of the self. To confess to God and to receive God's forgiveness is ritually enacted through the medium of Christ's representative. This can enhance the sense of the abjection of the body/self when unsanctioned desires are interiorized and their guiltiness affirmed. On the other hand, a new freedom can be won through this rite if the power of the Spirit and God's affirmation of the self as self are underscored. Freed from anxiety about the body and from internal guilt, the person is given the power to affirm the self, affirmed as it is by the love of God and the gift of the Spirit. Thus one can come to own the inner power to act freely and to act creatively through the action of the body and its motivations.

The role of the priest/confessor is quite ambiguous and needs keen spiritual insight. Exercised in one way, it can communicate an image of God as Lawgiver and Judge and confirm the feelings of internal abjection associated with the body. Exercised in another way, it can introduce the confessor as mediator, who mediates a relation between God and the sinner which is affirmative, dwelling on God's love of the person and on the affirmation by this love of the person's internal power for good and for creative action. It can help the person to interiorize desire in a positive way, as intrinsic to human being and the capacity to be human, and thus to overcome abjection.

What this means to sacramental understanding is first the need to take note of the negative ways in which liturgy often speaks of the body. Then there has to be the effort to draw from the Christian tradition itself more positive ways of signaling the place of the body in redemption. In the interiorization that comes with the grace of the Spirit, there needs to be a healthy and affirmative interiorization of bodily desires. These have a place in a life of grace and in an economy that makes all things new. Third, the appreciative use of body language and material things can convey a much better sense of being graced in body as in spirit. The core elements and rituals of sacramental action deserve and require great respect, which they are not always given. As long as the realities of bread, wine, oil,[17] and water are rendered unnoticeable the body itself is subjected to the same treatment. As long as bodily pleasure, in movement, in touching, in washing, in smelling, in chewing and sipping,

---

17. The use of oil in anointing may be particularly forceful in giving a renewed sense of self and of self-worth to the sick or the elderly whom society treats as incomplete persons because of their bodily debility or lessening of mental agility.

is banished, so too is the reality of being in the body submerged in the order of grace, which is given a dematerialized face.

Kristeva's studies highlight the need for feminine and maternal image within the symbolic order, in a way that incorporates women's experience and expression. The Virgin Mother, Mary, occupies a large place in many of the devotions that in peoples' religions complement the liturgy, or even prevail over it. Much of the imagery and power associated with this figure are in effect symbols of the divine, especially those having to do with mercy and love or those that illustrate the co-presence of mercy and suffering. They are attributed to Mary in popular religiosity, where they have a serious religious role, because they are not given adequate place in the imagery of God or of Christ within the formal public liturgy.

While Kristeva points to the presence of feminine and maternal imagery in what she calls the semiotic and wants to find it expressed in symbolic orders that regulate the social life of communities, this does not mean the elimination of the paternal and masculine, but a renewed expression of it. She holds that in the semiotic there is in fact expression of the masculine and paternal that fits well with the maternal and with love. Love is the interplay of the masculine and the feminine in its fecundity.

Following out the order of *agapé* that is the heart of Christian revelation, one does not have to destroy the union with the mother, nor negate the mother's pleasure in offspring, to be united with God as Father.[18] The body of the Son is surrendered in sacrifice and given to be eaten. In this a communion is given with the Father in virtue of the totally gratuitous divine love.[19] It is a union given through death, but not destruction. It is the Word of God renouncing its omnipotence and domination by being "crossed out," crucified in the flesh, that is offered to humans. Through this gift, we are united with God in a movement whereby the maternal and the paternal are joined in mutuality, and which takes the gifted into a communion that transforms human existence. This is a communion with the Other of God, and it opens to a communion with the other of the stranger, who in and through it becomes neighbor.

As Kristeva marvelously puts it, Christian baptism is an immersion into the name of God revealed in love,[20] in gift, in gratuity, without any demand for a prior reciprocity. Other biblical studies, for example, that of Paul Ricoeur, have shown how calling God "Abba" is in a sense a crossing out of

---

18. See Julia Kristeva, *Histoires d'amour* (Paris: Éditions Denoël, 1983), especially the essays "Eloge de l'amour," "Freud et l'amour," "Dieu est agapé," and "Stabat Mater." What follows does not pretend to give Kristeva's thought exactly, but it is inspired by it.

19. See especially the essay "Dieu est agapé," in ibid., 177: "agapé est gratuite, moins élection que générosité bienveillante, paternité non pas sévère mais domestiquée et éclairante. L'amour pour les impies est la meilleure démonstration de cette primauté sans réciprocité de l'amour divin."

20. "Immersion nominale. Baptême chrétien," in ibid., 175.

the name of God as Father, transforming the address into a new kind of relationship.[21] The name is transformed from the way in which it is used in prevailing socio-symbolic orders in which it signifies the law-giver, the protector of order, the other with whom a reciprocal relationship is denied, the one to whom the child is always a rival. The Christian naming in Christ and in the sacrament of baptism is the naming of God as the loving source of gratuitous gift who invites into loving communion. This is a communion in which *agapé* prevails. As Kristeva expresses it, the paternity thus acknowledged is not one of severity but one that is "domesticated," one that illuminates and brightens life. It is the naming of God as a communion in which fatherhood and motherhood are one, not in the otherness of opposition but in the otherness of mutuality, that is fecund and outpouring. The Christian naming of God as "abba" includes the symbolism of God as Father and Mother, not passing over the otherness in this relationship but affirming it as a communion, as a One that transcends the otherness.

It is also a naming that transcends the difference between God and creatures, again without a suppression of otherness but in a communion with the other that becomes a one-ness, an at-one-ment. It is a communion in the Spirit who unites. It opens the heart to God and so to the other of the stranger, who becomes neighbor in the communion at the table in the Word made flesh.

What has happened in Christian social and symbolic ordering is that the figure of the Father has been given the role of law-giver and judge, the preserver of the good order needed for the social coherence of societies. It is opposed to that of Mother, and feminine and maternal images are attributed largely to Mary, who in popular devotion, and indeed in some theologies, crosses the boundaries between the divine and the human in a rather ambiguous way. Within a more spontaneous imagery that derives from nature and the heart, the Father figure is one of love and tenderness, who unites with the feminine in a truly mutual, reciprocal, and covenantal love. In the transformation of sacramental symbolism to which feminist theologies and liturgies may give rise, the Father figure would be given this kind of placement within an imagery of the divine that allows for the mutuality of the feminine and the masculine in love.

Rebecca Chopp's presentation of the Word as the perfect open sign allows for the inclusion of women's experience, discourse, and imaginative play with traditional Christian symbols. The Word handed on by tradition functions as open sign when it is opened to the inclusion of alternative experiences and images. The signifying process of language works through this openness and inclusion. In this, Chopp adopts Peirce's understanding of signification, which moves between past significations and present reality, thus generating new

---

21. I have summarized this in *Unsearchable Riches: The Symbolic Nature of Liturgy* (New York: Pueblo, 1984), 158–69.

signification. On this account, it can be emancipatory. It frees people from time-encompassed meanings and constructs and opens the symbol system to the inclusion of those excluded, or brings to the center those who have been merely recipients, or subordinates, of what is presented to them and of those who do the presenting.[22]

Socio-Critical Interpretation

The interaction between worshipers is essential to sacrament, for its purpose is to establish communion in Christ between believers and disciples. It can happen, however, that in the process of interaction certain paradigms and forms of communication occur or are standardized in a way that hinders communion. As Anthony Thiselton puts it, "socio-critical hermeneutics may be defined as an approach to texts (or to traditions and institutions) which seeks to penetrate beneath their surface-function to expose their role as instruments of power, domination, or social manipulation."[23] If this is brought to light, it makes room for an intersubjectivity which is emancipatory and for a fuller participation in the goals of community as a being-together, rather than simply being part of an organization. Socio-critical interpretation looks at the process of communication and the way in which this affects relations between peoples and power structures in communities and societies. It looks for ideologies that enter the process of communication, whether consciously or unconsciously. When this is applied to Church institution and ecclesial sacrament, the purpose is to free the rites so that they may bring about intersubjective communion without imposing domination or division.

In keeping memorial of the passion of Christ, albeit in a plurality of forms, sacrament instills an openness to the other which is evoked by the memory of Christ's self-giving and self-emptying love. This is the transcendental reference of Christian memorial, which can never be reduced to a set of laws and concepts, but which calls for a constant practical ethic that is always open to self-critique. It is in the power of sacrament to engage its participants in this kind of mutual loving and in loving beyond the boundaries of community. To allow this to happen requires a review and a critique of rites, institutions, and paradigms that emerge in the course of tradition.

A critical approach has serious implications for bodily codes and ritual ordering, as well as for texts. For one thing, it examines the possibilities of communication in which all are party to the exchange. This is possible only if all know the code and all are given a positive part in its exercise and in its shaping. It is in placement, actions, and attitudes of body that ideologies affirming hierarchies of lower and higher are given power. It is because

---

22. See Rebecca S. Chopp, *The Power to Speak: Feminism, Language, God* (New York: Crossroad, 1991), 30–39.

23. Anthony C. Thiselton, *New Horizons in Hermeneutics: The Theory and Practice of Transforming Biblical Reading* (Grand Rapids, Mich.: Zondervan Publishing House, 1992), 379.

of practical paradigms of sacrifice, hierarchy, and instrumentality that much ritual ordering is done as it is done. Instead of affirming these paradigms without question, sacramental theology has to look to evangelical origins of order and sacrament and there recover other insights and possibilities.

A critical sacramental theology renders three services. First, it makes a critique of prevailing paradigms, pointing to the ideals or ideologies that affect order. Second, it investigates the cultural, religious, and philosophical sources of this ideology. Third, it looks into Christian tradition for alternatives. In this it opens up the possibilities of that process of ritualization discussed earlier. Rather than examine these points separately, they may here be considered together, focusing on the role of order and authority in Church and sacramental celebration.

Ritual development includes a process whereby office and its roles are legitimated, without of course being reducible to that. This is especially true of the relation between ritual and power structures.[24] The original rite for installation in ecclesial ministry and office was the laying on of hands. As far as New Testament evidence of this rite is concerned, it seems to have been a gesture, made with prayer, asking that the Holy Spirit come upon some person whose gifts and mission the community acknowledges. On the one hand, it was a recognition of gifts bestowed. On the other, it gave a role and place in the community, confirmed by ritual and associated with social and institutional ordering. This ritual legitimation is needed for the coherence and continuity of a community, and is indeed confirmed by divine blessing.

Three things, however, then happened which need critical attention. In the first place, the rite as such was taken to be the conferring of grace and power, even where there was no acknowledgment of previous activity and gifts. Some evidence of personal holiness continued to be expected, but the ritual was often enacted without discernment of the person's gifts of leadership and prayer. In the second place, bishops began to claim an authority over factors in ecclesial life which of themselves are not totally dependent on their authority. In particular, these were the canon of the scriptures and charisms of the Spirit. In the case of the scriptures, they asserted a magisterium of interpretation and control which asserted itself over all gifts of preaching and teaching. The hagiography of early Christian centuries, for example, the lives of Martin and Gregory of Tours, show how important it was to attribute gifts of teaching, monastic foundation, and healing to bishops, since this confirmed their authority and leadership. Not only was this variety of charisms attributed to bishops, but the charismatically gifted who were not ordained began to have a smaller role in the life of Christian communities. In the third place, the bishop in person rather than the Eucharist became the center of community life and apostolic continuity in the faith. The final

---

24. See David I. Kertzer, *Ritual, Politics and Power* (New Haven and London: Yale University Press, 1988).

split between Eucharist and bishop as community center came with the appointment of bishops to jurisdictional office, leaving eucharistic ministry for the most part to presbyters.

In the course of this process of legitimation, the ritual itself became more and more a process of conferring authority and power. Rites emerged which accentuated this, such as the giving of a book, the giving of instruments of office, vesting, and the handing over of an instrument of appointment by some higher authority. Even the presbyterate emerged in its own quasi-independence as a rite conferring the power to consecrate and offer sacrifice instead of being a rite conferring a sacramental and institutional role within a eucharistic community. That the candidate possess some gifts of prayer, teaching, and leadership remained a requirement in decrees and synodal instructions. Those ordained had to be able to explain the Creed and the Lord's Prayer and to know enough Latin not to deform the form of Mass and sacraments. This, however, seems little enough when considered in the light of the power given to the ordained.

Various paradigms and symbolic constructs were used to confirm the power of the ordained. The paradigms which need some critique are those of hierarchy, priesthood and sacrifice, ritual reenactment, and historical continuity. While these are given voice in words, they deeply affect the bodily action of rite and how it is seen, understood and performed.

Hierarchy

This term in itself simply means sacred or holy power. In this, it can stand for the source of ecclesial power in God or for the role which it has in mediating holiness. In the course of history, however, it was associated with specific roles in the Church, to the exclusion of others, and it was used to express the idea that, according to divine design, ecclesial relations are between some who are higher and others who are lower. During the Middle Ages, this was given rational confirmation by the theory that God ordered all human relations deliberately in this way, according to a providential design to rule the lesser by the greater. Along with this, theories of gender differentiation ranked woman of her nature in the category of lesser or lower. All of this has been thoroughly examined and is simply recalled here because of its importance to sacramental liturgy and theology.[25]

As Alexandre Faivre has shown, the distinction within the body of the Church between clergy and laity does not originate in the New Testament era.[26] In that time, there are differences in charism and service, with appropriate but diversified structures of order. The designation of some as clergy and others as laity comes not from the originary condition of membership in

---

25. See Mary Collins, "The Public Language of Ministry," in *Official Ministry in a New Age*, ed. James H. Provost (Washington, D.C.: Canon Law Society of America, 1981), 9–26.

26. Alexandre Faivre, *Ordonner la fraternité: Pouvoir d'innover et retour à l'ordre dans l'Église ancienne* (Paris: Éd. du Cerf, 1992), 85–117.

the body of Christ, but from the need in face of given situations to secure constancy in order and distribution of services. It was confirmed by the evocation of apostolic norms that go back to the time of the Lord and that are found in the canon of the scriptures. The service of worship and the maintenance of the faith of the tradition were prime needs, and for this purpose the distinct body of the clergy emerged, though not with uniform timing or shape in all local Churches. The word *lay* was not at first synonymous with being a member of the people or of the Church. It was used to designate some, who though not clergy, carried a function in the Church, perhaps that of teacher or of sponsor to catechumens. Later it was more commonly used to mean those who helped to secure the position of the clergy, first of all by supporting them monetarily, and secondly by upholding their leadership of the community in lesser orderings, such as that of teacher, readers, and acolytes, or by attending to the initiation of the order of catechumens, or even by functioning as teachers. Faivre has pointed out that this ordering between clergy and laity was initially an exclusively male ordering.[27] Not all males, however, were of the order of the laity, but only those who were given the roles proper to this order. Women were not among the laity, until widows and virgins were included in the listing of orders in the Church.

We need to recognize today that baptized and lay were not always synonymous, but that the term *lay* itself was adopted in function of an ordering among the baptized. It was when most roles fell to clergy, so that there remained few lay roles, that being lay became synonymous with being counted among the baptized. This indeed divided the Church into clergy and laity. The image of hierarchy is then appended on to this ordering as a way of sacralizing the order and role of clergy. The exclusion of women from all ordering, and then from the order of clergy, was never a simple matter of a divine ordinance that all knew about from the beginning. It was tied up with the public roles taken by clergy, usually seen as inappropriate for women, with specifically conceived social and family values, with ritual actions sometimes exercised by women and then in practice judged deviant, and with the appeal to some works in the canonical scriptures that spoke of women as lesser, at least in public life. All that remained for women with the precision of ecclesial ordering was to belong to the order of widows or the order of virgins, and these were ways of life devoted to prayer and devotion rather than ministries. To assign some function to a widow in the liturgy was more the exception than the rule.

If the language and reality of ministry is examined in early Christian tradition before the emergence of this ordered distinction, alternatives to hierarchy emerge. The language of power in the New Testament, and especially that associated with Jesus in the Gospels, is that of *pneuma, charisma, diakonia, exousia.* None of this has anything to do with social ordering, but reflects

---

27. Ibid., 205–12.

the source of spiritual, reconciling, and healing power in God. It can be located anywhere in the body, but ordering the celebration and distributing roles constitutes it as the action of the body of the Church as a social reality, with the appropriate symbolism to express its origin and meaning. In the Eucharist, the primary symbolism of the body and of order is that of the shared table, of the one loaf and the one cup, of which all equally partake. To this is attached the ideal of presiding as serving, the one who presides being as the one who waits in service. The symbol of Christ as servant, in his gift of self and in his self emptying, was the key symbol for service, order, and ministry in the Church.

Roles, preaching, praying, are gifted by the power of the Spirit, and are to be recognized there where they emerge. The community may confirm them by a laying on of hands, and thus give the social status and power in the life and liturgy of the Church which accompanies such symbolic action. The testimony given to Christ in how one lives or is prepared to die is important in one exercising authority, and it too comes as a gift of the Spirit. This was often the foundation on which one was given a place in Church ordering, but in fact it could be given by anyone in the body, either man or woman, or indeed by a group, as with the women who stood by the Cross or received the message of the angel at the empty tomb. The diverse communities of New Testament times, as, for example, examined by Raymond Brown,[28] are evidence of the tensions existent and the choices made in different congregations about the exercise of power and the acknowledgment of leadership. They are not uniform or identical and of themselves therefore point to the need to be critical and open to change in the orderings adopted for community life and for liturgy.

One of the consequences of such critical examination of order is that it points to the common identity of all the baptized, diversified only in their gifts, and then to the need to attend to the power of the word and of other charisms. It is not correct to invest all power and authority in the ritual actions or in the word of those whose position is socially and symbolically ratified by ecclesiastical process, though of course some special authority does necessarily come with occupying a special role. Liturgical history makes us all too aware of the fact that priests could be silent in their sacramental action, and that this only served to surround their ministry with mystique. Their hands, their use of things, body postures, and sacred vestments were what marked them as agents of divine power. In fact, however, these bodily realities have to go together with word, and much more attention needs to be given to the inner efficacy of the word spoken and prayed. Ministry requires the gifts to speak, to preach, and to pray, and these gifts do not come automatically with ordination. They are rather a condition for ordination. The significance of ordination is that it expresses the relation of a community to

---

28. Raymond Brown, *The Churches the Apostles Left Behind* (New York: Paulist, 1984).

the apostolic tradition and to the communion of all Churches in the one faith and tradition. The grace of ordination is that of service and to use well in service what are its preconditions in terms of personal and spiritual qualities.

Priesthood and Sacrifice

The language of priesthood and sacrifice has been present in the Christian sacramental tradition from very early times.[29] Its use in relation to the community of disciples in the New Testament is primarily ethical, transferring the language of rite to the community itself, whose living reality is the glory of God. In very early documents, as in the *Didache* and the writings of Justin Martyr, it is used of the Eucharist through a reading of Malachi 1:11 that says that it is in this act of *eucaristia*, or thanksgiving, that Malachi's prophecy is realized. The metaphorical intent of such language is clear, and it does not impinge on a celebration which highlights the proclamation of the Word, the blessing of God's name with thanks in memory of Christ, and the communion in the gift of his body and blood.

It was primarily with the Carolingians, in the last few centuries of the first millennium, that the paradigm of the Aaronic priesthood came to the fore in imaging ministry.[30] In conjunction with this, the sacrificial character of the Eucharist was given a much more ritual understanding. It was ritualized more frequently as an act of propitiatory offering, and this lay behind its considerable use in the commemoration of the dead. Though the eucharistic prayers of Western liturgies were voiced in the language of community offering, the ritual performance, as exemplified in the Romano-Frankish *Ordines Romani*, separated the action of the bishop or other celebrant from that of the congregation and highlights the moment after the Sanctus when he prayed the Supper narrative and the prayers surrounding it in the silence of the Holy of Holies. Ordination was thus seen more and more as priestly consecration, and this was given visible form in rites of anointing and vesting.

The primary critique of this paradigm is in fact practical. It derives from the retrieval of the nature of the eucharistic prayer and other blessings as community actions, even if pronounced in the name of the people by the community presider. Second, it is located in the centrality of community rather than ministerial ritual, for example, in the return to the table of the Eucharist as the central moment in its celebration, or to the exercise of the many ministries necessary to the adult catechumenate and its rites. As far as the use of language is concerned, critique points to the ethical purpose in the origin of the language of sacrifice and priesthood when it is used to

---

29. On what follows, see David N. Power, *The Eucharistic Mystery: Revitalizing the Tradition* (New York: Crossroad, 1992), 114–18, 320–24.

30. Reference to Aaron, his sons, and the levites is already made in the ordination prayers of early Roman rites, but it is to accentuate the design of ordering and ranking the clergy. See *Sacramentarium Veronense*, ed. L. C. Mohlberg (Rome: Herder, 1956), nos. 942–54.

underscore sanctification through the death of Christ and the holiness of Christians in the Spirit.[31]

The second critique has to do with the kind of social order promoted by the symbolism of propitiatory cultic sacrifice. In this conception of sacrifice, the sacrificial act of consecration and propitiatory offering is given more importance than the communion rite and has more to do with ordering the society than does the communion at the one table in the body and blood of Christ. As a result, it highlights and undergirds a distinction among the members of the Church between priests and the baptized. Retrieval of the origins of the sacrificial imagery attached to Eucharist, however, shows that it is connected with communion sacrifice and with thanksgiving, not with propitiation. In more traditional terms, it is as food and drink that the Eucharist is the forgiveness of sin and the antidote to death, not as the offering of a victim.

Further critique points to the controlled acceptance of violence that is inherent in the prominence of this ritual paradigm.[32] When the death of Christ is remembered as a sacrifice of propitiation, or the Eucharist is thought to be a continued offering of this sacrifice, the ethical consequence is to support the notion of offering lives in propitiation. This may be as simple as the self-sacrifice couched in the denial of the body, to make reparation, or as complex as the support of the death penalty as the enactment of a divinely sanctioned *lex talionis*. To counteract this tendency in sacramental language, the Church has to speak more and more consistently of the divine gift given in sacrament, and of the communion in love and forgiveness to which Christians are invited. Ethically, in countering evil, acts of reconciliation need to replace acts of propitiation.

The alternative paradigm is that of covenant. In sacramental and eucharistic language, when sacrifice is adopted as a comprehensive term the model is that of *communion sacrifice*. This is a ritual of covenant and is expressed in a table communion, into which members are initiated by appropriate ritual. The image of covenant has a complex background in the Hebrew scriptures, but it is always grounded in God's initiatives and in God's promises. Martin Luther gave importance to the word *testament* in his comment on the words of Jesus at the Supper, because for him this underlined both divine grace in taking initiative and divine promise. Lutherans have preferred the word *testament* because in certain contexts *covenant* appears to savor of the legalistic. However, when laws and institutions are part of the covenant and of keeping the covenant, this is subordinate to promise and

---

31. For an interesting study that shows also how this conception of sacrifice supports the exclusion of women from order, see Nancy Jay, *Throughout Your Generations Forever: Sacrifice, Religion and Paternity* (Chicago and London: University of Chicago Press, 1992).

32. For an application of the theory of René Girard to biblical interpretation, see Raymund Schwager, *Must There Be Scapegoats? Violence and Redemption in the Bible*, trans. Maria L. Assad (San Francisco: Harper & Row, 1987).

living from the promise. Seeing them within the covenant is both a reminder that life among God's chosen cannot be upheld without a legal and ritual system, without attention to moral obligations, and that they are servants of the covenant rather than that which gives it its essence as a relationship and as a guarantor of God's fidelity. This is guaranteed by the word that proclaims God's gracious initiative and by the table communion in which memory is kept of the striking of the covenant. Of its nature, this keeps life according to the covenant open to the future and open to change in the human factors of covenant life, when fidelity to God's word requires it. In the New Testament, this is accredited to the act of the Holy Spirit within the covenant people. The language of priesthood or of sacrifice can be retained in speaking of Church and of ministry, but this is best done within the context of the language of the covenant.

Reenactment

Some of the new paradigms introduced as a result of appeal to ritual studies are not without serious limitations. The idea of re-presentation or re-enactment of Christ's Pasch has done some good service in overcoming sixteenth-century controversies. However, the weak side of the paradigm is that it fosters in some cases an idea of rite as mimetic action, in which the death and burial of Christ are acted out. This can take from the power of the Word heard in the Spirit, by which the salvific action of Christ is present in the liturgy. As noted earlier, one may not simply identify sacrament with rite, recognizing that this can undo the role of the Word in Christian gathering and celebration.

Historical Continuity

The clearest expression of the paradigm of historical continuity is that of the unbroken succession in the laying on of hands in the ordination of bishops. This is believed to express a transmission of power that originates in Jesus Christ and his mandate to the apostles. This already needs to be modified when we look to Christian writers in early centuries to see what episcopacy signified.[33] In Irenaeus, Cyprian, Augustine, and even as late as Isidore of Seville, the succession in ministry has to do with the transmission of the apostolic teaching, which is the ground of the life of the Church. Cyprian, Augustine, and Isidore all relate the commission given to bishops to teach to the words of Jesus to Peter at Caesarea Philippi. They interpret these as a confirmation of Peter's faith in Christ, on the ground of which Christ gave him the mission to pass on this faith, as its custodian and defender. In the words to Peter, they read the mandate to all the apostles and to the bishops who receive this mission from Christ through them. None of this is an exact

---

33. On this see Faivre, *Ordonner la fraternité*, 107–36.

reading of historical fact. It is a legitimation, by appealing to Christian origins, of what has come to pass. The question for readers today is not whether such use of scriptural texts in fact points to a historical continuity, which is too evidently absent. It is whether the sense of teaching and leadership ministry practiced at a later time is faithful to the foundational narratives and their horizon of purpose and meaning.

In recent efforts to establish communion between the Lutheran Churches and Churches in the Anglican Communion, the paradigm of historical continuity has been modified to exclude the idea of an exact succession going back to an ordinance by Christ. There is, however, an effort to maintain the idea of a moderate historical continuity in the form of episcopal government, once it was established and claimed to be divinely ordered.[34] This is put forward, as it was put forward by the Faith and Order Commission of the World Council of Churches, as sign of unity and apostolic succession which is known from early stages of Christian history.[35] The Faith and Order Commission made it clear that the apostolic continuity in ministry is grounded in, and at the service of, the apostolic continuity or succession of the communities of faith. What is at the heart of the Church is the faith and its transmission. Orthodox theology and practice would relate this to a continuity in eucharistic celebration, since for them the Church is present in its proper reality in the eucharistic memorial, where it is united in Christ and the Spirit, as the body of Christ. It is in the celebration of the Eucharist that the faith is active, that the mystery of faith is contemplated, and the sure grounding of the faith is in the Eucharist.

From all of these discussions it becomes clearer that historical continuity needs to be located in communities of faith. It also seems to be clearer that what is to be guaranteed is indeed the transmission of the faith and sacramental life and that institutional forms are there only to serve this. It is likewise clear that God has continued to gift the Church with a ministry of Word and Sacrament, in one form of another, and that the role of the episcopacy is certainly historically important in this. What is still unclear is the exact way in which ministry and institution interrelate and the extent to which forms of order and government can be flexible.

Local Church

In the documents of the Second Vatican Council and in subsequent theological and liturgical developments, renewed attention has been given to the link between local Church and Eucharist. One description of a local Church is that it is a eucharistic community, gathered in a particular place. The

---

34. See *"Toward Full Communion"* and *"Concordat of Agreement,"* Lutheran-Episcopal Dialogue, Series III, ed. William A. Norgren and William G. Rusch (Minneapolis: Augsburg, 1991).

35. *Baptism, Eucharist, Ministry,* Report of the Faith and Order Commission (Geneva: WCC, 1982), nos. 34–38.

Constitution on the Liturgy of Vatican II (no. 41) gave the rather idealistic principle that the local Church expresses and realizes its reality most fully when gathered for the Eucharist with the bishop. More commonly the eucharistic community is a group of persons gathered under the presidency of a presbyter. Usually, this is determined by geographical location, though with greater mobility and the development of suburbia, it is increasingly common to find a strong intentional element of free choice in community membership. The link between Eucharist and local Church is built on a retrieval of early Christian sources, and it has always remained a lively part of Orthodox theology and practice.

A critical perspective, however, needs to be introduced into its use today when this comparison is made. The local eucharistic Church in early times was constituted by the coming together on the Lord's Day of all Christians living in a given vicinity. It included rich and poor and even slaves and free. In conjunction with the common meal and later with the practice of *diakonia,* this meant that the eucharistic gathering had to take note of fulfilling the justice of God in caring for the poor and establishing among themselves an economy of sharing. With suburbanization, those who come together for Sunday liturgy are people of similar economic standing. There can be, and often is, some connection with social concerns through the collection. Without the face-to-face encounter, the question of a divine justice that links care with the eucharistic table is less tangible.

Today, the issues of justice have fortunately gone beyond the feeding and clothing of the poor, but the connection between Eucharist and God's prophetic justice may lack expression and focus. Instead of a simple resort to the ideal of the equation between local and eucharistic community, it is necessary to ask how the eucharistic table, how the sharing of the one loaf and the one cup, expresses the communion between participants and the communion with the "other" that belong within divine and eucharistic justice. This of itself raises questions of a social and ministerial ordering of the local Church that is not too stringently bound to prevailing geographic, financial, and ethnic divisions. The risk of this paradigm of local eucharistic community, in short, is that it may fail to integrate the elements of social justice that are inherent in what the Eucharist symbolizes of the reign of God and God's justice.

Heuristic

What has been suggested at an earlier stage of this work is the use of the paradigm of language event. This is not presented as some archetypal or theologically all-sufficient theory. It is better seen as a heuristic which allows due place to all the elements of memorial celebration and which is adequate to the history and symbolism of covenant. The ritual is constituted by the interaction between proclamation of Word, hearing of Word, blessing prayer, ritual actions in general and gift in particular, all situated within the communion in Word and Spirit which is the outcome of the divine gift coming forth from the eternal Trinity as God's covenant with humanity.

A community cannot function without social models for its institutions. The concern is to find one that allows best for all the data of history that we seek to interpret and that serves the growth of life that fits a covenant relationship. It has been suggested in the secular sphere that the rhizome provides a model that is alternative to models of cosmological hierarchy. Its use is intended to avoid a simplistic model of intercommunication or of a circle of communication. The rhizome is described in the dictionary as a prostrate or subterranean root-like stem emitting both roots and shoots. Its usefulness in a sociological heuristic of institutional forms is that it conveys the image of a life that is always at work and giving forth new life. It has a stability about it, since it is always subterranean and present, but it is active and gives forth what is new as well as old.

This could help as a model for developing the necessary institutional leadership in the Church, respectful of God's covenant initiative, of the life of the Spirit within the Church, and of what has been passed on by traditions. In adopting it for a sacramental Church community, the rhizome images the presence of Christ, alive and active in the power of the Spirit, and through the ministry of Word as well as through the contribution of institutions. It allows for a history, it allows for continuity between epochs, and it allows for the growth of new shoots and of new life forms. It is an alternative to the model of institution as foundation to a concept of ministry, yet allows for institutions and for continuity in changing historical forms. Employing this heuristic, there is room to take account of the Lutheran concern about the primacy of Word and Sacrament over institutional form which surfaces today in discussion of the restoration of the historical episcopacy. There is also room to accommodate the attention of spiritual groups to the way in which the charismatic as the work of the Spirit is root to institution, keeping the Church faithful to the evangelical word. The paradigm speaks also to the Catholic concern with a constancy of sacramental forms within change and for the relation of these forms to the life of the Church community within which sacraments are celebrated, since the life-force which engenders institutional forms is ever constant.

Ritualization

As feminist writers point out, ritualization is integral to a hermeneutic of sacramental tradition and action. As Mary Collins puts it, in addressing the marginalization of women to the symbolic code, the foundational principle of feminist liturgy is "the ritualization of relationships that emancipate and empower women."[36] What such celebration allows for is the exploration of

36. Mary Collins, "Principles of Feminist Liturgy," in *Women at Worship: Interpretation of North American Diversity*, ed. Marjorie Procter-Smith and Janet R. Walton (Louisville: Westminster/John Knox, 1993), 9–26.

symbols, language, and rites that draw on traditions and on creativity in giving voice to the suppressed or the undernourished of sacramental action. Within this ritualization, important is a forceful remembering of those whose lives or experience has been discounted in their own time or in history. While feminist ritualization is of unique importance in these insights and contributions, the principle applies beyond the issues of feminism.

The kind of critique that has been surveyed forms the basis and indeed the insight for much of the ritualization of which there was a discussion in the first chapter of the book. New directions and ritual performance do not emerge merely from new ideas. Though critique and ideas enter into the process, the recovery of sacramental forms relies heavily on ritualization, in greater or lesser measure. Even the revised liturgical books recognize this to some extent in allowing for conversation with cultural rituals and periods of experimentation with new rites.

Summary of Critique

The critique suggested may be summarized as follows, together with the path toward resolution proposed. First, it was noted how we need to examine the use of space and ritual for the ways in which they may include and exclude, or set one thing or one person in opposition to another. Second, the language of the self and of the body was considered for the reduction of the body and of the self to the abject, even within a process of needed interiorization. Third, a look at the language of ordering showed how it may allow some to dominate others in inappropriate ways. The response to the critique is likewise in essence threefold. First, what is marginal to the symbolic code needs to be heard and integrated, especially in what has to do with women's experience and expression. How this surfaces may be learned from greater attention to feminist or womanist ritualization. Second, the abjection of the self may be overcome by a reconciliation of the split self, in receiving from God the affirmation of the graced self and of the wellness of fundamental instincts and desires that in the tradition have often been discountenanced. Third, new metaphors and paradigms of ordering may be retrieved from within the tradition, beginning with the New Testament, by looking at orderings grounded in the vocabulary of service and of charism.

Conversion / Conversions

Clearly, a community cannot accept this critique without being faced by a need for conversion, for the commitment to a challenging Christian horizon. In understanding sacramental action, a great contribution of the critique outlined is that it gives insight into the practical, visible, and communal aspects of the process of conversion that sacrament induces and effects. By the same token, it shows how absence of conversion can block sacramental exchange and sacramental communion.

The fundamental point in sacramental conversion is the readiness to let oneself be invited into the world of the sacrament, to hear the word, to enter into the prayer and ritual, and to let oneself and one's world be called into question. Today, this applies to the Church community as such, and not only to individuals, as it continues to initiate its members into sacramental celebration. This readiness to be vulnerable to the Word is not a simple thing, since peoples have appropriated the Word and sacramental actions into their culture to good effect in the past, and hence tend to reaffirm what in the past has been found gracious. In a period of change, many have resort to ritual to confirm, not to question, their beliefs, outlook, and moral values. This is true not only of those who wish to reaffirm the more immediate forms of tradition, but it can also be true of some who find a comforting experience through ritualization and new forms of celebration which meet their perspectives. It is of course one of the functions of rite to maintain a link with tradition and confirm community cohesion. Some rituals within sacrament serve this in a particular way, such as the profession of faith or the use of well-known sacramental formulas and materials. This collective identity in a given religious and cultural pattern, however, is not the main point of sacrament. The main purpose is conversion in Christ and the Spirit, even when this requires changes in form and practice as well as in the heart. Sacramental memorial is a constant hearing and wrestling with memory, such as is called forth by listening to the Word of God and obeying the movements of the Spirit, through the response that the advent of the Gospel to a culture and a society inspires.

Given this fundamental acknowledgment, one may not confuse sacramental conversion with a process of human maturation. The laws of human change within social belonging do not account for the change that sacrament invokes, when a whole people begin to see reality in a totally new way under the sign of the divine event of Word and Spirit. Provided that this is kept in mind, some further insight may be had into the process of conversion by considering its religious, affective, ethical, and intellectual aspects. There are, as it were, different kinds of conversion within the one conversion. They are not to be located only in individual persons, but by analogy apply to the ongoing conversion of communities.

Religious

The religious has to do with the horizons of the ultimate within which a person or a community lives and to which the personal and social self is committed. This does not mean adopting existing religious paradigms without reserve. Evangelical conversion in effect asks for the breaking with religious and philosophical paradigms that prevail in human societies and cultures. As Paul put it, living by the Cross cannot be assimilated either into the religion of the temple or into the wisdom of the Greeks. In the process of sacramental conversion, how do we account for the scandal and folly of the Cross? In listening to the word and engaging in the memorial of the Pasch, the

Church has to break with the religious paradigms that tend to surface in religious communities and in its own history. It has to enter time and time
again into what Hans Urs von Balthasar calls the theodrama of Christ's self-
giving, opening itself to a freedom that breaks with the wisdom of religious
institution or of philosophy. There are three diverse insights into this process.

The first comes from sacramental history itself. From it we know that when
the Church adopted known paradigms of religious rite and of social order, it
broke with them even as it adopted them. When some talk of metaphoric
use, this is in part what they are expressing. A clear example is always that
of sacrifice. Theology has often been tempted to explain both the death of
Christ and the celebration of the Eucharist as a ritual of sacrifice in which
something is offered to God, primarily to propitiate sin. Rite itself has sometimes given itself the form of such offering, as when the table is given the
shape of an altar, bread and wine are ceremonially offered, and the minister speaks direct sacrificial language. In fact, in the New Testament, in early
theology, and in early rites, to name either Christ's Pasch or the Eucharist a
sacrifice was to say that they are not a sacrifice, but that their power may be
revealed by the odd application of sacrificial memory to this action of self-gift
in death and to this rite of breaking bread and sharing cup. The same holds
for the terminology of priesthood, applied to people of faith and evangelical
ethic, or to the Christ who gave himself in death for the sins of the world.

Even the later theology of sacrifice is testimony to the breaking of forms
in order to allow something to speak out of the metaphor. Aquinas in his
treatment of the mode of redemption says that the sacrifice of Christ is no
mere matter of sufficient retribution.[37] It is rather a mystery of excess, in
love and in suffering. Neither is sacrifice the ritual of a victim offered. It is
rather the communion of all in deeds of grace and mercy to which they are
moved by the identification of Christ with his body and by the memorial of
his passion, done in faith and Eucharist.

Another example of metaphoric usage is that of order. The comparison of
salvific action, in Christ's relation to the world, and in the life of the Church,
to cosmological order was taken up in the letter to the Colossians. It would
seem that the Christians of this city used some known religious hymns to
express the power of Christ and of his body in these terms. The writer of
the letter, even in accommodating the hymn, broke with this pattern. It is
not by having contact with Christ as though with some superior cosmic body
that believers are saved. He is rather taken up into the glory of the Father,
having assumed the flesh of humanity. Hence it is through contact with his
humanity, even being made one with him in his passion and death, that his
followers find salvation. The metaphor of cosmic order serves, but only in the
process of its subversion.

We have noted the use of concepts and styles of order in mediating the

---

37. *Summa Theologiae* III, q. 48, art. 3.

grace of Christ and the Spirit in the Church. Perhaps, however, people point more to their abuse than to the often difficult, and indeed mystical, perceptions of theologians and communities who resorted to this paradigm. The legal becomes the dominant model for power in the Church only when the Church is pastorally weak, but unfortunately it took on too strong a role in teaching and theology. This went even to the point of defining the Church as a *societas perfecta*, whose hierarchies are endowed with power.

Much that is attributed to order in the Church is derived in one fashion or another from the Pseudo-Dionysius. However, in transmission it is often simplified, almost caricatured, so in this case one needs to go back and work through his thought to see what was this writer's concern.[38] It is not a pure and simple application of a notion of hierarchical order to the Church. It is the manifestation of God's glory in the incarnation and in the Church, and the mystical and liturgical response to it, that is the monk-writer's concern. There is an aesthetic to this manifestation, but not a human aesthetic. This aesthetic is shown in the process of coming forth from, and of return to, God of all creatures. God is not imaged, though named. The manifestation is imaged, but always subordinate to the Word. What is served primarily in sacraments is the spiritual ascent, which gives rise to a spiritual hierarchy among the faithful. The ascent is through the purification of the catechumenate, through the stage of illumination in baptism and Eucharist, to the union which the Eucharist symbolizes. Hence within the Church, there are catechumens, the faithful, and the mystics, a state which the monk-writer tended to identify with the monastic life. There is room also, however, for the half-converted in the order of penitents, which can redeem the wayward path of the baptized.

The ecclesiastical hierarchy serves this spiritual ascent in the orders of episcopacy, presbyterate, and diaconate. For the Pseudo-Dionysius there was a fitting correspondence between one's place in the spiritual hierarchy and one's place in the ecclesiastical hierarchy, so that it was from monasteries that candidates for episcopacy came. Aspects of the charismatic are in fact kept in this theology of order, since for this writer an ordained minister did not truly act as such who did not act out of a personal spiritual life and grace. One could not really expect such a person to be heeded or to do much for the Church. Sacramental celebration for this writer means a contemplation of divine mystery, but this can happen only if through the ritual and what it symbolizes the community ascends to union with Christ and the Father. This meant some pastoral judgment about participation in rites, whether of the faithful or of the ordained. Exclusion was a matter of truth. This is provided first in the dismissal of penitents from the divine liturgy. It is provided very

---

38. See "The Ecclesiastical Hierarchy," in *Pseudo-Dionysius: The Complete Works,* trans. Colm Luibheid (New York: Paulist, 1987), 193–260.

starkly in the refusal of the rites of burial to one who manifestly lived outside the spiritual communion of the Church.

Elements of this theology of order remain in medieval scholasticism, especially in St. Thomas Aquinas where he writes of the episcopacy as the state of perfection.[39] This is not something that comes about automatically with ordination, but has to do with candidature for pastoral office. While Thomas derived the charge to pastoral care from jurisdiction, he related this to a theology of the spiritual life in writing of the states of life. The power of jurisdiction is rightly for those who have the power of the spirit. The other great scholastic, Bonaventure, also related sacramental order and spiritual order.[40] The power of sacramental dispensation, which is the work of the Word who is the principle of redemption, fits within the dispensation of spiritual order. A candidate begins with being tonsured, since this is a sign of total dedication to God. He is then ordained as a psalmist, for a psalmist learns to give God praise. The ascent through the minor and higher orders is a way of purification and illumination that readies candidates for priestly and episcopal service.

This theology of order had a strong impact on sacramental dispensation. It is here briefly rehearsed only to show what issues were at stake and how paradigms were always applied and modified in order to attempt to do justice to the wonder of an order of grace. Whenever it was legalized or yielded in practice to the authoritarian exercise of pastoral office, it was jeopardized. Today, similar issues are at hand, in situations different from those of the past. There is no purely given of order. It is always subject to its efficacious service of the work of Word and Spirit, whose power in the end can be known only from the living testimony of communities of faith. Legal criteria are useful and indeed necessary, for without them the symbolic and the institutional support of community falls apart. They need at the same time to be subjected to criteria of life and testimony, which is what is intended when we talk of ministry as service. Tradition gives enduring insights into the sacramental role of order, but not permanent and unshakeable institutional forms.

This is where von Balthasar's narrative of theodrama can serve, even for those who find his canonization of specific ecclesial forms of order and his gender theories difficult to accept.[41] This is the drama of the Word's *commercium* with the world in his incarnate life, ministry, and ultimate self-giving. It is the drama of an exercise of freedom that comes only in the act of self-giving, which recognizes the freedom and dignity of others and the origin of all things in a divine self-giving. It is a drama of free self-giving lived out

---

39. See David N. Power, "Theologies of Religious Life and Priesthood," in *A Concert of Charisms: Ordained Ministry in the Religious Life*, ed. Paul K. Hennessy (New York: Paulist Press, 1997), 71–73.

40. Ibid, 74–75.

41. See Hans Urs von Balthasar, *Theo-Drama: Theological Dramatic Theory*, vol. 4, *The Action*, trans. Graham Harrison (San Francisco: Ignatius Press, 1994), 317–423.

in a world of sin, engaging with the sinner and the sin itself and with the sufferings of those on whom its burden falls. When the Church of the disciples is made one with Jesus at the Supper and in the communion table of the Eucharist, it is drawn by the Spirit into this theodrama. As the body of the Christ, like Christ himself, it enters into this drama of sin, freedom, and salvation. No reflection on sacramental grace can endure without attention to this gift of freedom to act in suffering for others. Likewise, no reflection on sacramental grace is adequate which is dehistoricized, and this is what happens if the community which keeps memorial is not aware of its ethical involvement with the society and culture of its place and time.

In gauging the depth and manner of this *commercium* in Christ and Spirit the community of faith does not forge its own way, out of some rational ordering. It can enter the drama only if inundated with Word and Spirit. Paul Ricoeur's reflection on the stripping of self-consciousness asked of Christians in listening to the scriptures is quite pertinent to sacramental memorial and engagement.[42] Here in Christ and in the outflow of the Spirit the community of believers receives this testimony, in word and sign, of God's own presence in self-communication, a self-communication which in the theodrama of the incarnation is given through the sign of the Cross. Faced with this testimony, believers have to let go of all claims to a personally and socially attained consciousness of self. They have to be enlightened and judged by this event of the Cross alone. Human powers of self-making and self-healing are inadequate to the *mysterium iniquitatis*. Only the mystery of crucified self-giving responds to it.

What has been said earlier about the place that parable and wisdom have in sacramental celebration, as the language of reversal, is pertinent. As explained before, it is the fitting of the narrative of the Cross to the reversals of parable that enable us to see how the Cross belongs to living the human in the faith of God's presence. This is very important in an age which involves us in reversals, not only in society but in the Church.

Affective

Religious conversion involves a deep affective commitment. The affective is that which enables a person to connect with others in mutuality, to develop a sense of belonging, to pledge oneself heart and soul to persons, to values, and to a sphere of action. Our emotions and our emotive tendencies are allied with the power to do and the power to act. They relate to those with whom we wish to live, or whom we wish to follow. They come into play in the religious commitment to God and God's kingdom. They are intimately bound with the values which we hold important and which we endeavor to realize in our personal actions and in consort with others.

---

42. See Paul Ricoeur, "The Hermeneutics of Testimony," in *Essays on Biblical Interpretation*, ed. Lewis S. Mudge (Philadelphia: Fortress Press, 1980), 142–53.

The affective is closely tied in with the symbolic. Indeed, the primary impact of the symbol, of the signs that express communal identity and societal horizons, is not to make known, but to engage the person and the society affectively. This is where the role of the symbolic differs from that of indicative signs, which are simply intended to communicate knowledge or to remind.

In the Lonerganian school of thought affective conversion is presented as a matter of bringing the emotive into line with the intention of knowledge and action. To a great extent, it is cast as a growth in personal and spiritual maturity. Lonergan himself describes self-transcendence as a falling in love, a gift of oneself to another where personal interest yields to the other whom one loves.[43] Others bring out the affective dimension of this religious conversion.[44] When that is allied with religious conversion, it means loving God about all and loving the neighbor with the same love.

From this point of view, Christian symbol and sacrament serve to engage persons and communities wholeheartedly in the love of God, made known in Jesus Christ, and in the power of the Spirit who dwells within as a dynamic force of self-giving. In light of what has been said above about the language which sacramental traditions have been wont to use of the body, we can see how a mature affective conversion will integrate body and spirit and relate bodily and emotive drives to the end pursued, rather than reject them as prone to sin, or even sinful. From what has been said about the woman/man relationship, it can also be appreciated how this can be distorted by the affective, through a strong symbolic attachment to male symbols for Christ. The affective must integrate a balanced relationship into sacramental and ecclesial practice, and this cannot be done except through revisiting the symbolic ordering of male and female relations and actions.

This is helpful and necessary, but it is not the whole story, for it is easy in a concern for maturity to by pass the singular character of conversion to Christ and the way of the Cross. The postulate of the call of Word and of the impulse of Spirit in Christian sacrament is to reverse human orientations and values, though without distorting them or despising the human. Christian conversion is not purely a transcendent realization of native impulses to the good, in fulfillment as it were of what scholasticism called obediential potency. As a divine revelation, it even contradicts what personal and societal tendencies may be in the pursuit of the common good.

Thomas Aquinas himself offers an insight into this when he contrasts the order of divine justice with the order of human justice in his treatment of the redemptive act of Christ.[45] The common good of human justice would be distributive justice, the concerted effort to ensure that everyone has what is needed for life with dignity. Some laws of proportion between act and reward

---

43. Bernard Lonergan, *Method in Theology* (London: Darton, Longman & Todd, 1972), 107.
44. For example, Walter Conn, *Christian Conversion* (New York: Paulist, 1986), 134–53.
45. *Summa Theologiae* III, q. 48, art. 2.

would be promoted as the means to this. Reconciliation within such a society would mean some process of retribution. The order of divine justice on the contrary is an order founded on mercy, even on an excess of mercy and love. It does not obey the laws of distributive justice, though for the sake of social order it can find some room for these within the greater order of mercy and excess giving. If one relates these thoughts of Aquinas to a reading of the scriptures, this would be to the sayings of Jesus about the least being the greatest in the kingdom of God, or to the parables about divine excess in forgiving and in giving. At the heart of this is the law of the Cross, the example of the self-emptying of Christ, which means acting for others without personal concern and the readiness to yield even one's life.

This postulates considerable affective conversion and an attachment to these values. This is brought about through identification with what is represented in the symbolic and parabolic of Christian sacrament. It is more than a matter of shifting "the loyalty of one's sensibilities" from "self to family, nation, and planet, even to the point of generously giving oneself for a cause well beyond one's personal means."[46] While indeed the process of affective conversion within sacrament can be helpfully illustrated by comparison with the norms of psychological and personal development, it needs to be seen to go beyond that. The attachments, the feeling of being community, the communal élan, is identification with Jesus Christ in the totality of his self-gift, which is a revelation of divine *agapé* for which human reason cannot account. It means involvement in the *theodrama* of the ministry and death of Jesus. It means identification with the needy and the sinful, facing the postulate and the urge of the Spirit to give oneself without reserve, and to do so indeed in the solidarity of a community committed to this. It means also a oneness with earth and creatures, even they being granted a precedence over the glories of human achievement. It means transforming, in Christ, the meaning and the process of death/dying itself. Entering into the initiation of Christian sacrament, into the way of Christ's self-giving by reason of the gift received, means deep affective conversion which cuts across even that which humanly may seem proper and mature affective growth. The testimony which corroborates the sacramental symbolism is that of the martyr, or of the fool for Christ, such as Francis of Assisi or Ignatius of Loyola or Edith Stein. All mature and intelligent people, it was not their human maturity that witnessed to Christ and his love but the going beyond, even outside of, human wisdom in their giving and in their identification with Christ.

Ethical

Ethical or moral conversion is closely allied to affective, because it means living by this identification in movement and intentionality with the Cross.

---

46. Stephen Happel, "Speaking from Experience: Worship and the Social Sciences," in *Alternative Futures for Worship*, vol. 2, *Baptism and Confirmation*, ed. Mark Searle (Collegeville, Minn.: Liturgical Press, 1987), 182–83.

The key insight in the philosophy of Emmanuel Levinas is that the ethical is actually the first step in philosophy.[47] This can be said also for theology, inasmuch as theology is a reflection upon living by mystery, and so on the mystery lived.

The ethical turns of the post[-]modern, as identified by Richard Kearney, readily find hospitality within the post[-]modern turn of sacramental action.[48] Like the post[-]modern way of looking at texts, at philosophy, at literature, the post[-]modern turn of sacramental action allows for considerable diversity, a readiness to review personal and social positions, and a prior interest in the other, especially the excluded other. Kearney points to the interest in the other, to hearing the other and allowing place to the other, as a key characteristic of post[-]modern writers and movements. Grounded in this, he maps out an ethical imagination which is empathic, testimonial, and utopian. The empathic is the feel for the other to whose word and interest one opens oneself. The testimonial is the heeding of testimonies of action and suffering. The utopian is the hope beyond hope for a conversion of society from the ways of modernity.

This can serve to fill out the ethical interest of Christian sacrament, or "the way" to which Christians are called by sacramental participation in the mystery of Word and Spirit. The way of Christ calls for listening to the testimony of the other, even of Christianity's own victims. In asking forgiveness of African and Indian peoples in Santo Domingo, in asking forgiveness of women, in asking forgiveness before the ovens of Mauthausen, John Paul II has given public voice to the Church's need to listen to the interests and the voice of those to whose sacrifices it has at least contributed, and in many ways ideologically served. The table of the Eucharist, the center and end of all sacramental celebration, sets one down beside this "other." There has to be a heeding and a listening if the communion in the one body and the one cup is genuine, is really felt and acted upon.

From such sacramental communion, a new ethical urge ensues. The utopian of the Christian Gospel and sacrament is the eschatological, the hope of the kingdom to come in Christ, the constant openness to the future, in the expectation of what is yet to come out of God's generous and loving self-giving. It is as a community, as a people, as a people one with victims and one with abused earth, that Christians voice this expectation in sacrament, urged to ethical action from within the language of their sacramental encounter.

Intellectual

Affective and ethical conversion, this identification of oneself in intentionality and action with the way of the Cross, is the ground for the intellectual

---

47. For a summary statement of this position, see "Ethics as First Philosophy," in *The Levinas Reader*, ed. Seán Hand (Oxford: Blackwell, 1989; repr. 1996), 75–87.

48. Richard Kearney, *The Poetics of Imagining: From Husserl to Lyotard* (London: Harper-CollinsAcademic, 1991), 225–27.

conversion postulated by sacramental participation. This has to do with the way we see, consider, understand, and judge. It means surrendering one's own conceits and judgments, one's own individual and societal efforts at control - ling self-consciousness and human progress, to the word of God, to the Cross of Christ. It is the affective impulse of grace that turns one to the sacramental symbols, that opens one to entering the sacramental language. From within this house of being, a community can ponder its meaning in intellectual terms that guide action.

Postulates of this intellectual conversion have already been made clear in the discussion of sacrament's critique. There are clearly pitfalls to be avoided, if the pursuit of understanding of the gift given in sacrament is to be genuine. I have described these elsewhere as naive realism, turning symbols to allegorical purposes in simple support of already existing convictions, rationalizing symbols so that they are held to some conceptual definition, distorting symbol systems to support ideologies, and the breaking down of communication within the symbolic world which is built on the exclusion of some from being truly partners in Church life.[49] This is in effect a way of summarizing much that has been said about taking a critical stance in a reading and appropriation of sacramental traditions. Pursuit of this understanding is taken up in the following chapter.

Conclusion

The concern in this chapter has been with the conversion that sacramental participation both asks for and fosters. What is intended is not simply how persons are converted by receiving the sacrament, but how the Christian community as a whole, as an entity, is converted to the Gospel and to living by the Gospel. At any time, social and communal change belong to sacramental celebration, as a people enter more fully into its language and its symbols in a self-critical way. Changes in sacramental liturgy can indeed express this communal conversion. Today, however, the crisis of the post[-]modern and the call to live this moment of crisis as Christians calls for epochal change within the Christian Churches and in their Gospel stance in human society. Hence, the first part of the chapter took a critical look at developments in the sacramental tradition, considering what in this tradition may impede con - version. After that, it was possible to describe the conversion that may ensue, in its religious, affective, ethical, and intellectual dimensions. The key, it was said, is to enter fully and without reserve into the sacramental process, to be taken up into the language and the rite, allowing the individual and the communal self to be emptied of the hubris of contained self-consciousness, so as to receive the gifts of Word and Spirit that come through the celebration and renew all who take part in it.

---

49. See David N. Power, *Unsearchable Riches,* 174–80.

Chapter Nine

The Event of Gift: Systematic Reflections

In writing of sacraments, even with the turn to language, is it possible to avoid ontotheology, that is, that type of discourse which treats of God in the language of being and first cause and of sacraments in terms of causality. If this is not done, does all speculative theology cease, with a retreat into either fideism or language games? With the turn to language, what are the demands of speculative thought?

Responding to this question, speculative thought can start with the speculative thrust that is already present in daily speech and in poetic language. Daily speech realizes potentialities there present, the poetic projects a world in which newly disclosed potentiality would be realized. As Richard Palmer writes:

> Speculativity involves that movement, suspension, and openness which wills to let new possible relationships in being speak to us and address our understanding. For the poet, it is openness to being coming to language; for the interpreter, it is openness to place one's horizon in the balance and be willing to subject it to modification, in the light of the new understanding of being that may emerge from an encounter with the meaning of the text. Ultimately, speculativity is grounded in a creative negativity, in the nature of being, which forms the background of every positive assertion. A speculative hermeneutics is alive to the significance of this negativity as source of every new disclosure of being and as a continuous antidote to dogmatism.[1]

In short, there is what Paul Ricoeur calls an "ontological vehemence" inherent in daily and poetic language. It emerges there through the use of metaphors, the interplay of genres, and the convergence of word and ritual, that express the contours of being and its openness to mystery.

As noted in the chapter on doctrine, propositional discourse uses negation, limit-concept, and analogy. While this serves specific and often concrete

---

1. Richard E. Palmer, *Hermeneutics* (Evanston: Northwestern University Press, 1969), 212.

purposes and is effective in addressing conflicts, speculation carries this endeavor forward. Its aim is to give a coordinated expression to all factors that are pertinent to the whole. It brings negations, limit-concepts, and analogies together, into a relationship with one another, and gives them a role within the vision of the whole, and not just the parts.

In sacramental theology, the quest is for a systematic reflection that is not grounded in the thought and language of being and that does not resort to theorems of causality. Taking a point of departure in the language of gift makes this possible. The word proclaimed, the language spoken, the gifts shared, come from God, but the Godself is outside the range of human speech and human thought, even though the gift given is a share in the divine mystery. All consideration of sacrament is consideration of how God approaches and gifts creatures, who stand in wonder before the divine and ineffable mystery to which they cannot give a name but from which they receive life, a life which draws them up into the mystery. Silence precedes all thought about the sacramental mystery, and all thought ends in silence. This is thinking that is more circumspect than metaphysical thought and that finds its limits drawn by doxology. Theology does not simply end in doxology but begins there, in the awe and wonder of sacramental gift.

The Gift, as it emerges through gifts, has to be related to event, both to the event of Jesus Christ and to the language event of sacrament. The Gift given is spoken of in words that are metaphorical, but that evoke the use of analogies of gift-giving among ourselves. What this actually discloses about the divine mystery is a matter approached in different ways, which will be briefly considered, but the focus here is on sacramental expressions and realities. To pursue such thinking, the following points are taken up in this chapter.

1. Some further reflection is offered on gift and gift-giving and on the limits and possibilities of using this as the key insight into the Christian sacramental economy.

2. To pursue further the way in which gift appears and is given, use will be made of the paradigm of the iconic.

3. To explain how the sacramental gift transforms the lives of participants and of the Church, the language of being will serve as a limit-concept, and the limits of self-consciousness will be set within the economy of sacrament. In this way, the contribution of two common paradigms, namely, sacramental causality and symbolic causality, will be both respected and set within due boundaries.

4. Various analogies will be explored for their contribution to a fuller understanding of an economy of sacramental gift.

5. On these grounds, it will then be asked how we may reflect on what is revealed and communicated of the mystery of the Trinity in the sacramental economy.

An Economy of Gift

The metaphor of gift has been consistently used throughout this work to express what is given and done in sacramental worship. Some further reflection is offered here to show how it "gathers and scatters" all reflections on sacraments by designating sacramental dispensation as an *economy of gift*.

The metaphor is in fact suggested by liturgical history. The English word *economy* is taken in the sense of exchange, or sharing in what is communal possession. It roughly corresponds to the French *échange*, the Italian *scambio*, the Spanish *intercambio*, or the German *Wirtschaft*. If *economy* is here preferred to *exchange*, this is by way of a play on words which points to an entire order which is built up on an exchange or a sharing in gift. It is an attempt to translate the Greek *oikonomia*, or the Latin *commercium*.

An example of the use of this metaphor can be found in the *Sacramentarium Veronense*, whose texts originate in the Roman Church.[2] The Mass orders of this collection indicate clearly enough that the congregation of the time brought gifts, probably both the bread and wine for the Eucharist and offerings for the needs of the poor and of the clergy. Using the vocabulary of offering, whether this be *oblatio* or *munus*, the texts include these things brought, and also the offerings of prayers and thanksgiving, in the act of celebration. Along with this, there was an illuminating use of the term *commercium* to name the mystery being celebrated. The term is taken from the world of commerce, where trade and exchange are practiced, in order to refer to the redemptive mysteries enacted in sacrament. It is used of the exchange between the divine and the human that originates in the Word made flesh and is celebrated in the sacrament, to the benefit of humanity and in the liturgy of those who participate therein. This is the true exchange, or economy, of sacrament. From the earth, the Word takes human nature, but brings it into an exchange with the divine, and so sanctifies it by the gifts of grace. The exchange therefore is not rooted in the bringing of gifts by the community, but in the gift that comes forth from God in the incarnation and that constitutes an exchange, or a *commercium*, between the divine and the human.

In worship, Christians "engage in this glorious exchange,"[3] which greatly exceeds even that which has its origin in creation. Contemplating in the Word become flesh a wondrous exchange of divine and human natures, the

---

2. *Sacramentarium Veronense*, ed. L. C. Mohlberg (Rome: Herder, 1956). Referred to henceforth as *Ver.*

3. "Exercemus, domine, gloriosa commercia: offerimus quae dedisti, ut te ipsum mereamur accipere" (*Ver* 69).

people are moved to pray: "even though immense is the wonder of what is given in the beginning with the gift of human nature, much more wonderful are the works by which not only have you brought back to life that earthly and mortal thing which had been extinguished, but have made it divine."[4]

A Christmas postcommunion prayer crowns this imagery of exchange by reversing the use of the language of gift employed in prayers over what the people have brought: "God, who touch us by this participation in your sacrament, work the effects of its power within our hearts, so that we may be made fit to receive your gift through the gift itself."[5] It is God's gift and giving which makes the sacrament, not the people's. The gift given by God is not a return for what the people have brought or offered, but a reversal of the order of giving, placing it totally, like the incarnation, in the gratuitous initiative of God. The *commercium* initiated by the taking on of flesh by the Word is celebrated in thanksgiving and communicated in sacramental reception.

Such examples, which could be multiplied, are in keeping with what has been pointed out before about the anaphora of Basil of Caesarea. In it, the self-emptying of the Word in taking on human flesh and the blessings thus brought to humankind, is the commanding metaphor used to voice the dispensation of redemption celebrated in the sacraments of baptism and Eucharist. Whatever gifts the people may bring, they are taken up into the celebration of the wonderful exchange between God and humans enacted in the fleshly mysteries of the Word. They do not so much bring gifts as lift up that which is to be transformed into the symbol of the one wondrous gift that stems from God. The fundamental reason, befitting this economy of exchange, why the Church brings its gifts is not to offer something to God, but to present them to God so that they might be taken up into the celebration of what God has given, and gives, in the Word made flesh. The economy of redemption is initiated by the assumption of fragile human nature by the Word, endowing it with the grace that comes from its union with the divine. The setting forth of the elements of human exchange is incorporated in the Spirit into the communion in the flesh and blood of the Word Incarnate.

The use of the word *gift* is so marked by its use in human orders of friendship and society that it is not easy to grasp the meaning of what scripture and sacrament say of divine gift. So burdened is gift-giving with impositions on others and so bound is it to certain expectations from the receiver that some recent writers have questioned the possibility of true giving and see it more as the "impossible" to which we may aspire in aspiring to the good and to openness to the other. In the context of sacrament, we can fail to do jus-

---

4. This is how this is expressed: "Quondam licet inmensa sint omnia, quae initiis humanae sunt conlata substantiae . . . longe tamen mirabiliora sunt opera, ut terrenam mortalemque materiam non solum vivificaris extinctam, sed efficeris et divinam" (*Ver* 90).

5. "Deus, qui nos sacramenti tui participatione contingis, virtutis eius effectus in nostris cordibus operare, ut suscipiendo muneri tuo per ipsum munus aptemur" (*Ver* 1256).

tice to the superabundance of divine gift unless we are quite careful in using this analogy.

Phenomenological and philosophical writing on gift look back to the work of anthropologists, especially Mauss and Malinowski, who supplied data on gift economies in what are called archaic societies.[6] These are presented by them as barter economies, where there is an exchange of goods, or even persons such as slaves and women, rather than the use of money to guarantee the social and economic ordering of life together. A person achieves high status by much gift-giving, for his contribution to the order is high. The gift is hardly totally gratuitous, however generous. What the gift-receiver owes back is not so clear, but smaller gifts and recognition of status are expected. Among those of equal social status, there is some equality in gift-giving. It feeds the relationship and the sharing in life, but it too implies some expectations in the giving of gifts. It is the sense of relationship, not the value of goods or production, which determines what is given, but this form of exchange has served to maintain the public order and economy, that is, the distribution of goods, within some societies.

When gift-giving is transposed from archaic societies into societies of monetary and production economies, it is not essential to the economy but has another place in ordering human relations. There has been an odd change in the use of money, however, since its introduction. At first, when given as a gift, instead of some good, money actually freed the recipient from certain obligations or impositions. When a good is given, it has to be used in a certain way and for certain purposes, since it fits no other. As a gift, money allowed the recipient a choice of the goods or purposes to which it was to be put. Of itself, it carries no intrinsic imposition on action. In today's market economy, however, money is given in return for work or is put as a price tag on goods. In today's global economy, gifts or loans of money are used to impose certain ideals of productivity and democracy. Gifts are then not free.

Feminist writers have suggested that the problem of turning gifts into barter and loading them with expectations is a peculiarly male one. Women, it is contended, are much more free in living out of gift, and in living gift-giving as a free, unencumbered act. Possibly this is because they are so vitally connected with the primordial gift, which is the gift of life, of life to be lived, to be lived in plenitude and generously. Hélène Cixous expresses this pithily in the following paragraph:

> How does she give? What are her dealings with saving or squandering, reserve, life, death? She too gives *for.* She, too, with open hands, gives herself — pleasure, happiness, increased value, enhanced self-image.

---

6. For a collection of essays, see *The Logic of the Gift: Toward an Ethic of Generosity,* ed. Alan D. Schrift (New York and London: Routledge, 1997). For an essay on its use in Christian context, see John Milbank, "Can a Gift Be Given? Prolegomena to a Future Trinitarian Metaphysic," *Modern Theology* 11 (1995): 119–61.

But she doesn't try to "recover her expenses." She is able not to return to herself, never settling down, pouring out, going everywhere to the other. She does not flee extremes; she is not the being-of-the-end (the goal), but she is how-far-being-reaches.[7]

As far as other writers are concerned, Robert Bernasconi has noted the difference between Jacques Derrida and Emmanuel Levinas on the possibility of gratuity in gift-giving.[8] Derrida accentuates more the aporia which leads him to speak of the "impossible" gift, even while taking such free and unself-centered giving as an inspiration. Levinas contends that it may become possible when we learn to give primacy to the other, to attend to the face of the other, and not to ourselves. However, he does speak of this as "an eschatology of liberation from my own time," thus in his own way placing it always in the future, as something to be hoped for.[9] In gift/giving the giving is not reducible to the gift/given, nor is the giver represented (either figuratively or as totally present) in the gift. The problem with humans in giving gifts is that it is hard for them to recognize this distance and this irreducibility. The giver would like to be fully known and acknowledged in the gift, would like to build a bridge that overcomes distance between the giver and the gifted, the lover and the loved. But both gifted and giver need to recognize in gift-giving the otherness of the other, the fact that the two are not and cannot be the same. When the one to whom the gift is given is given the due of being other, then the gift/giving is a giving in freedom. In turn, the gifted is free when in the enjoyment, the living out of the gift, the distance and otherness of the giver are affirmed. Gifts are spoiled when either the one giving or the one receiving wants to objectify the other person in the exchange, to represent the other person in a way that belies the distance.

What Derrida and Levinas see as difficult to come by, Cixous sees as already central to a woman's world. The "impossible" gift, or the "eschatological" gift, or the "womanly" gift, is one that gives the gift of freedom. That is, it opens up possibilities of free action for the recipient, who is impaired neither by the nature of the gift nor by the expectations of the giver, nor by the need to try to be the same as the other, but acts purely out of an appreciation of the gift in itself and out of what it opens up as possible. Nonetheless, there is a relationship between giver and recipient, some exchange or participation in the gift, for it is the passage from one to another, without loss to the giver and in a mutual living from the gift. The gift of life may indeed best exemplify this, even though in the pettiness of our humanity at times it is given with strings attached. When a mother gives birth to a child, she gives it life.

---

7. Hélène Cixous, "Sorties: Out and Out: Attacks/Ways Out/Forays," in *The Logic of the Gift*, 159.

8. Robert Bernasconi, "What Goes Around Comes Around: Derrida and Levinas on the Economy of the Gift and the Gift of Genealogy," in *The Logic of the Gift*, 256–73.

9. As quoted by Bernasconi, ibid., 258.

When parents care for a child, they open up the gift of life to it. The ideal reception is for the child to value life as the parents do and to live freely from this gift, not out of a sense of indebtedness to the parents. The child's living leads to life's enhancement and moves it to give to others out of this gift. There is a flow to true gift, that means it is not consumed but passed on and given increase in this very passage.

Some aspects of the analogy can be clarified further.[10] The accent in the analogy of sacrament with gift is on the giving. We are making a comparison with gifts that are in the giving, with a giving that never ceases. The analogy with motherhood serves, once we recognize that this is a constant giving of life and is not reducible to a biological fact. Another feature of gift that is brought to the fore is that there is no fusion between giver and gifted, that the giving gives rise to participation and mutuality, but never means total identification with one another and does not require a representation of the giver to the given which obscures the distance between them, or their otherness. The response of the gifted to the giver is one of drawing from the source and finding union, but not one of giving back. A fusion of giver and receiver would mean that gift-giving ceases in the merging of the two into one, in the common and undifferentiated possession of one thing.

Furthermore, gratuitous giving moves toward and into the future. A purely gratuitous gift cannot be a "present." At Christmas people give presents, which have as their purpose to enhance the moment, to spell out good cheer for the hour. Gift-giving, as distinct from presents, is such that it is ordered to the future. The best gift will continue to enhance life with its giving, with the expectation that its fullness will be realized only in the future. To give somebody a dividend in stocks, without expecting a return on it oneself, might be an example, even if a necessarily weak one. The value of this continues to increase, in a measure not known at the time when the giving starts.

Gift-giving and gift given can be paralleled with saying and said, where the former is never reducible to the latter. The one giving the gift addresses the one on whom the gift is bestowed, calling forth a response. However, here too the sayer and saying cannot be represented by the said, either figuratively or as though totally present.

These qualities of giving provide an analogy for what is done in the sacraments, with the giving of Word and Spirit, and with the divine address thereby speaking. The gifts of life, of forgiveness, of communion with the Word, of the inner grace of the Holy Spirit, are truly a share in God's own life and love, but even in giving God remains unpossessed in the sense that there is no fusion of the divine with the human and that the divine remains mystery. Attempts to categorize God, to represent God through thematizing giver and gift, are a block to the giving. Furthermore, the sacramental gift

---

10. Compare Jean-Luc Marion, *Prolégomènes à la charité* (Paris: Éditions de la Difference, 1986), 147–81.

is not a "present," it is not consumed in the present passing moment, nor indeed fully possessable in that moment, but is eschatologically oriented. The gift/giving continues to increase, being at any one moment beyond measure.

If we can use the language of the "exchange of gifts," or in Latin the *divinum commercium,* this is to underline that what is given is the seed of participation and mutuality. It is a being together, a loving together, a covenantal relation by which both God and people pledge and work for the enhancement of the same gift. It does not mean that the beneficiaries are giving something back to God. When those who celebrate sacraments in faith receive the gift of the life given in Christ, of the divine *agapé,* they enter into its flow. The self-giving love of God shows forth in the self-giving love of Christ. The self-giving love of Christ shows forth in his giving of himself for sinners on the Cross and in the self-giving of the table of his body and blood in the sacrament of the Eucharist. This self-giving love of Christ shows forth further when through the Spirit it is embodied in the Church, which in turn gives that life, pours out that love from within itself, so that others may share in it. Bestowed upon, Christians are in turn bestowers. The communion established through sacramental giving is totally from God and not in any way given back to God and is a communion with the Father through Christ and the Spirit.

It is to this gift of divine *agapé* that the testimony of Christ and Spirit spoken in sacrament witness, and it is this gift that is brought to life anew when the Church brings the Gospel and the sacraments into the lives and cultures of peoples. It is this which sets up the order of divine justice, where human relations, being in the world, the hope for the transcendent, and the naming of God are vivified by gift and its flow. It is in the bestowal of this gift that humans are given the freedom to love and to live. It is with this gift in their hearts that they enter the drama of redemption, seeking to give witness to God's love in the following of Christ and in the power of the Spirit, so that the world may be transformed. It is through this gift that they break through and enlarge the boundaries and limits of human being in the world.

Analogy of Being

Some writers suggest that the analogy of gift needs to be complemented by the analogy of being in order to adequately express the relation of the world to God and to keep the distance between God and creatures, without any confusion. If it is the analogy of being as a concept that is intended, this is unacceptable. However, the analogy of being as presented by Thomas Aquinas may have some place, since for him the being of God is not conceptualized but affirmed as the pure *actus essendi,* irreducible to any set of concepts or any metaphysical system.

In wanting to retrieve the analogy of being from Thomas Aquinas, Ghislain Lafont locates its use in relation to a principle of narrativity, that is, he locates it within the narrative of God's action for our redemption, so that it becomes clear that it serves a better grasp of what this divine action and initiative bestows on creatures.[11] In this sense, the analogy of being starts with the divine initiative rather than with a concept of being derived from understanding creatures. It says that though they participate in God's gift and in God's life, creatures do not provide concepts for thinking the being of God. It says that God is inconceivable within the range of concepts that belong within metaphysical systems, but that all created beings have their being as gift from God and that this does in fact open them to a participation in God's own life. In this respect, the analogy of being, whereby God is affirmed as the pure and unlimited *actus essendi* and humans are said to have their being as gift from God serves an appreciation of the mystery of God's giving.

The Iconic

If we do not wish to speak of the cause of this gift, or of this gift being produced by sacramental action, nor explain it in terms of the human subject, and yet allow for its advent through sacrament, an alternative way of thinking is furnished by the use of the term *iconic*. This is indeed somewhat favored of late, though it is employed in various, quite diverse, ways, so we need to be careful about the sense in which it is used.

Icon is not to be confused with representational image. Such confusion arises when, for example, the term is used to emphasize the real presence of Christ in the Eucharist or to explain the restriction of ordination to males. It is the imaged likeness which is then accentuated. There is the likeness of the body of Christ in the exposed sacrament and the likeness of the human and historical Christ in the male celebrant of sacraments. It is true that such use of the imagination was exploited in mystagogical catechesis, when going into the pool was said to be a likeness of Christ's descent into the tomb, or the preparation of the table with white cloths was described as the likeness of laying Christ in the tomb. That, however, is not what is intended by reference to the iconic.

The term is appropriated from the Eastern use of icons in worship by post[-]modern thinkers to overcome ontotheology and to avoid speaking of God in terms of being and of cause. The great defender of icons, John of Damascus, explained their veneration and their power to sanctify by their relation to the prototype, who is the Word Incarnate, and by linking them with the scriptures. The salvific events imaged in icons are those of the Word made flesh, and they are those recorded in the scriptures.[12] Their advantage is their appeal to sight, their making visible what has been done for human salvation through the Word Incarnate. The Damascene, however, is careful

---

11. Ghislain Lafont, *God, Time, and Being*, trans. Leonard Maluf (Petersham, Mass.: St. Bede's Publications, 1992), 297–324. More will be said about this later.

12. St. John of Damascus, *On the Divine Images: Three Apologies against Those Who Attack the Divine Images*, trans. David Anderson (Crestwood, N.Y.: St. Vladimir's Seminary Press, 1980).

to note the distance between the image and the imaged. The image partakes of the reality of the imaged, makes it indeed present as communicable, but it does not reproduce it. Indeed, in its very visibility it points to the invisibility of the mystery, at once revealed and concealed.

In this, John is faithful to the thought of the Pseudo-Dionysius. For this fifth-century monk, the use of symbols to lead into the contemplation of the mystery of the Word made Flesh both merged with and overcame the need for hierarchy in bridging the distance between God and humans. The symbol or image expresses God's descent to creatures, it is "a procession of the light which spreads itself generously toward us, and in its power to unify, it stirs us by lifting us up. It returns us back to the oneness and deifying simplicity of the Father who gathers us in."[13] It is necessary to the role of the image in letting the light descend and illumine that it conceal the likeness in the unlike. Paradoxically, by bringing the reality of God and the Incarnate Word to the community and its worship, the icon draws the viewer away from what is seen to what is unseen. Setting aside the neoplatonist suppositions of these writers, this insight into symbol and icon serves today to suggest a way of thinking about sacramental gift different from that which depends on the language of sacramental causality.

If the primordial reference is to Christ, the icon or image and likeness of the Father, who as the eternal Word was made manifest in the flesh, it has to be remembered that this likeness is hidden in unlike, in the self-emptying of all glory that would reflect the glory of the Father. At its core the power of sacrament to reveal lies in the unlike, in the concealment needed to make known what is revealed. An icon is a coming to presence of the divine, without it being present as knowable in "it"self. The sacraments do not in and of themselves image the event kept in memorial. Jesus availed of the giving of bread and wine to his disciples to represent the event of his self-giving, but in this there is no reproductive image of the gift made through his giving himself over to death, which is now remembered in this ritual action. Bread, wine, oil, and water are images which first express human and cosmic life. It is in and through such images that the event and reality of redemption is shown forth, so that it can be known in how it enters in the power of the Spirit into human living.

Giving it a phenomenological meaning, Jean-Luc Marion calls the iconic the visible mirror of the invisible, a visible reality suffused with divine light while leaving the divine itself incomprehensible. The icon can be painting, sculpture, sacrament, or even concept, provided it does not draw attention to itself but keeps its role as medium. The ultimate reference is to the Word Incarnate as image of the invisible God, whose role is to bring

---

13. "The Celestial Hierarchy," 1,1. Eng. trans. *Pseudo-Dionysius: The Complete Works*, trans. Colm Luibheid (New York: Paulist, 1987), 145.

the divine into the world and deify creatures, without ever gainsaying the incomprehensibility of the divine.

In using the word in *God without Being*, Jean-Luc Marion contrasts its service with adherence to an idol.[14] He points out that one and the same thing can be either idol or icon, according to how the thing is welcomed. In Marion's use of the term, it is what shows through the icon that matters, or rather that to which the gaze is drawn by passing beyond the image and which is in no way imaged. Even the human acts of Christ which are remembered must only draw us to the contemplation of the love which is poured forth in the complete self-giving of self-emptying. *Icon* is thus used to counter images of representation, physical, metaphysical, and epistemological. All of these seem to draw the power of divine being into themselves, draw attention to themselves as acts of divine presencing, and place God within the confines of either the language of the physical or the language and structures of being. By contrast, through the iconic, one passes through affirmation and negation, not to the knowledge of some more eminent way of being, but to the contemplation of what is "nonbeing," or nothing of anything that is shown to us and known to us, either physically or in intelligence.

To pinpoint the difference between idol and icon, Marion writes that in approaching a sign as icon the beholder does so in the sentiment of being gazed upon rather than gazing. What it does is to place us in the presence of the God who pours forth a love which takes a hold on the community, without, however, allowing us to then use analogies which capture God's own being.[15] In brief, following the line of though suggested by Marion's elaboration of the iconic, one can see a way of addressing the issues of presence that have always been raised in sacramental theology. It helps to see that to which sacramental presence cannot be reduced. It is not a matter of the investment of the ritual actions and words of the priest with God's power, though asking how God acts through these is legitimate. Neither is it a matter of how the minister or any ritual action images what or who is represented. Nor is divine presence, or the presence of grace, a matter of the presence of the sign's clear meaning to the mind of those who see the sacramental actions, as though they could be given clear conceptual formulation. Nor indeed can the central sacrament presence, which is that of the presence of Christ in the gift of the ritual action of eating and drinking, be adequately explained by explanations of how the bread and wine are changed into his body and blood.

These insights taken from Marion can be amplified by looking to what

---

14. Jean-Luc Marion, *God without Being*, trans. Thomas A. Carlson (Chicago: University of Chicago Press, 1991), 7–26.

15. There is some affinity with the distinction made by Aquinas between presence in place and substantial presence to avoid identifying Christ with the signs or the act remembered with what is imagined. However, he still explained this unique presence of Christ and of his action in metaphysical terms, whereas post[-]modern thinking sets the limits to human comprehension more consciously.

some call *iconic augmentation*, in a particular casting of image or language. To refer to painting, ritual, or word usage as iconic is to recognize how through these images, actions, and words, a meaning and truth are given to life that is gift to it, some greater force and power and hope that appears, advents, in the moment of the iconic.

In sacramental action, all three kinds of expression converge, each crossing with the other, giving the whole a cumulative significance and offering a gift that is not of human making. The simple things of bread, wine, oil, and water are saturated with the sense of the holy when they are embodied in ritual action. The action invites to a washing, consuming, anointing that brings the recipient/agent into the presence of cosmic power and of communal acts that come with all the life-force of a tradition that makes for communion between the living and the dead. The rite is such that even prior to their use these things of earth take on an appearance; they are brought into vision in such a way that they appear as awesome, full of enormous forces of life and death. The candidate for baptism can only tremble on entering into this tomblike womb, filled with all the hopes, fears, and loves that have been poured for generations into the act of keeping safe and providing water as a cleansing and life-giving force. The table participants see in what is laid before them all the wonder and energy of the cosmic seasons and all the shared lives of their forebears and all the toil of those who provide meat and drink. And so they dare not eat and drink unless with hands soiled by labor, and yet stretched out with purified and stainless reverence.

But it is to the word of the sacramental celebration that we must look for the greatest augmentation of the reality of thing and act, and so of the world of being together. Image is spoken before being seen, as Ricoeur puts it,[16] so that a grasp of the power of poetic language coincides with the appeal to the iconic. It is through the word event, linked indeed to something happening in history, that the visible icon becomes possible. The word itself can be said to be icon, in Marion's sense of the term, because something comes to us through word that does not emerge from the world of being and cannot be conceived in the language of being. It brings us something "from before" and brings us "toward beyond," but can never be figuratively represented or conceptually contained.

The blessings of the things of earth set them and the ritual actions into which they are encompassed into a world of God's gracious, forgiving, liberating, and life-giving activity. They make of them signs and actions given in the memorial of Jesus Christ, who in taking on human nature restored it to immortality, and in giving himself in his self-emptying filled his disciples with the power of the Spirit. The reference to Jesus' own words and com-

---

16. See, for example, "The Function of Fiction in Shaping Reality," in *A Ricoeur Reader: Reflection and Imagination*, ed. Mario J. Valdés (Toronto: University of Toronto Press, 1991), 117–36.

mands augments the power of thing and action, so that the gifts of life that God gives in him and the very gift of himself shine through. In the sacramental words, however, their iconic power appears properly only if the words of gift encompass all other words. Words of gift of course are manifold, and herein lies the importance of seeing how the prayer of thanksgiving or of confident intercession is the setting for the recall of all other words and stories. It is in and through an act of receiving that the Church appears before God, in a readiness to be filled with the life that God gives through Christ and the Spirit. The words of blessing augment all the actions with meaning and power, and they augment the significance and power of all the other words spoken and proclaimed.

For example, in the eucharistic prayer it is said that we give thanks or make intercession, commanded to do as Jesus did at the Supper and to receive the gift that he offered to his disciple at the Supper. The words of Jesus in the setting of blessing cannot be heard only as words of transformation of bread and word, but they are heard by a community which is open to gift, as words of gift, where the gift is the self of the self-emptying of the Cross and the self raised up by God as the firstborn from the dead. Such gift is given in the appearances of bread and wine, and so in the appearances of the life that these embody in themselves. It is given in "comfortable words" that promise forgiveness and immortality. It is given in words of hope that look forward to a fullness yet to come.

As icon, sacraments are thus the eventing of the mysteries of Christ's flesh, as these are remembered in words and related to signs that express the continuation of coming and of giving. A sacramental action is the showing forth of the gift given by God through Word and Spirit, present/ing now through the medium of the signs, that is, rites and language. In the remembrance of the Church, in all its appropriation of what has been said and revealed, the original event of the Pasch, in all its complexity of passion, act, and proclamation, keeps showing forth and eventing. In this showing forth, there is the continued outflow, the continued giving of the Word and the Spirit, in whose power the gift of God takes form among peoples of different times, places, and cultures. By the same token, the Church's sacramental action is the place where word and tradition are interpreted, and where they take on new form, as this is called forth by historical events or encounters with new cultures or with changes in culture.

Iconic Forms

It is in this sense that Marion refers to the Eucharist as hermeneutic site for interpretation of words and practices, since they are there related to the gift of Christ that is manifested and offered in the eucharistic bread and wine. In so locating the interpretation of scripture and traditions, however, Marion gives special importance to the word of the bishop who presides. In the word and ritual action of the bishop, the present/gift of Christ, Word made flesh, is conveyed. One certainly sees the importance of the word being interpreted within the actuality of giving that appears in the offer of the body and the blood of Christ and of seeing this as Christ's own offer and gift, through and within the Church. However, it does not necessarily seem to follow that this gives such a role to the homily and interpretation of the minister. Relating the power of the bishop to act *in persona Christi*[17] to the iconic seems to take from what is more central, for it is the ministry of the presider to let the word and the sacrament serve the gift and appearance of the Word and of divine love, so that he is more the servant of the iconic than an integral part of it.

One might ask how much Marion is indebted at this point to Hans Urs von Balthasar and to what the Swiss theologian has written of Seeing the Form.[18] With the Cross as center-piece, von Balthasar finds an aesthetic completeness in the interaction of scriptures, Church ministry, sacraments, and spirituality. This is not confused with common ideas of beauty, but the notion of the aesthetic is associated with coordination and completeness. This is to say, that by an act of divine order, the Form has an integrity and a validity which endures, even within some passing change and inculturation. This, however, supposes a continuity and a harmony that is not verified in the origins and history of Christianity.

A better sense of the discontinuous character of the Church's form and of the need to constantly reinterpret can be found in the work of Stanislas Breton, which meshes well with the accent given to gift and to the iconic as the channel of gift/giving. The appeal of this thinking is that in writing of revelation and of sacrament it makes it possible to complement the notion of the iconic with that of *trace* and of *fragment*, which he uses in helping us to move through and beyond metaphysical thinking.

This French philosopher in the evening of his life has devoted three volumes to developing a theology of revelation which comes from his insight into the neoplatonist philosophy of Plotinus and into the metaphysics of Thomas Aquinas about the correlation between *esse in* and *esse ad*. Together, these currents of thinking pave the way to the deconstructionist and reconstructionist moves of post[-]modern inquiry. In the first of these books, *Écriture et révélation*,[19] Breton set forth an understanding of revelation, and in the second, *Le Verbe et la croix*,[20] he showed how the proclamation of the Cross of Christ fits this notion. What he does in these volumes is to move through ontotheology, or the thought of revelation in the language of being, to "me-

17. Doctrinally, this term refers merely to the power that is at work in the sacrament, contrasting that of Christ with that of a human agent.

18. See Hans Urs von Balthasar, *The Glory of the Lord: A Theological Aesthetics*, vol. 1, *Seeing the Form*, trans. Erasmo Leiva-Merkakis (San Francisco: Ignatius Press; New York: Crossroad, 1982), 429–683.

19. Stanislas Breton, *Écriture et révélation* (Paris: Éd. du Cerf, 1979). For an introduction to Breton, see Jacquelyn Porter, "Stanislas Breton's Use of Neoplatonism to Interpret the Cross in a Postmodern Setting," *Heythrop Journal* 39, no. 3 (1998): 264–79.

20. Stanislas Breton, *Le Verbe et la croix* (Paris: Desclée, 1981).

ontology" or the thought of God beyond being, and to "henology." This relates all things to the One, in essence unknowable and incomprehensible, from whom they come forth by the passage of the signs left by the passage of his self-giving love through human history.

There are four steps to the notion of revelation which are pertinent to understanding the movement of sacrament as it reveals the movement of revelation. God is named "beyond being" as the One from whom all things come by an act of freedom. In terms taken from Plotinus, Breton speaks of this One as being nothing of anything that proceeds forth. The One is source and principle of all that is, and there is nothing in creation that can provide an adequate analogy or an image. No created thing in its being provides an analogy that allows us conceive of the essence of this One, supreme giver, and no religious ritual provides an image. Second, this beneficent One, whose naming cancels itself out, chose in an act of self-emptying to enter human history by an act of covenant. Since this was a historical event and had to be recorded and passed on in writing, rites, and institutions, we may speak of its traces in human memory, action, and story, rather than of its representation. In recalling the event through its traces, Christ's disciples seek to be open to God's giving and to set themselves on the path to union with the One. Third, in this passage of the divine and in the traces in which it is passed on, a gift is given to humans and specifically to the people of Israel and then to the followers of Jesus, which calls on them to write themselves as testimony to the visitation and to the gift, in the freedom of the self-creation thus made possible. Fourth, both the divine advent of self-giving and the ecclesial action of self-creation constitute a being within (*esse in*) history and within the forms of thought, institution and rite that constitute a community, and a being in relationship (*esse ad*) with the world and with the One to whom they turn/return in all that they are and do.

Applied to institution, to the writing of the scriptures, and to rite, this working out of the gift of revelation shows how the Church, its institutions, and its sacraments come forth from God, through Word and Spirit. It also shows how these are never adequate to an appropriation of the passage/passing of the One God, how they do involve human choice and creativity, and how they are historically conditioned. It is this historical conditioning which constitutes their openness to the creation of new forms. New forms must indeed emerge if the Church is to be faithful to its call to be living testimony to the self-giving love of the God who has come, passed through, remains present in the traces of his coming and will come until the end of time. Breton's perspective fits with the sense of the icon as the manifestation and gifting of what is gifted in the marks left by the events of God's coming, and so indeed of the gift-giver who is beyond being and beyond naming. It also satisfies the inadequacy of the icon to the gift and the need for a constant "rewriting" and "reshaping" of the Church as God's people.

It is in the volume on the Word and the Cross that it appears how the soteriological, institutional, and ritual implications of keeping memorial of the Cross fit into this concept of revelation. The Cross manifests the extent of God's love and self-emptying in his covenant with his people. It also manifests the conflict that ensues between this generosity and all attempts to hold to the provisions of religion and of thought for expressing the presence and action of God and response to God. In looking especially at Paul's proclamation in 1 Corinthians 1:23, Breton finds nothing essentially wrong in the religious practices of the Jewish people in their fidelity to Yahweh, nor in the efforts of philosophers (and theologians) to think about God. What is wrong is to raise either religion or thought to a comprehensive, rigid, and immovable system. In seeking to give form to God's action in history, or to the presence of Christ and of the Spirit in the Church, we need to be engaged in a continuous process of "crossing out." By this play on words, much as Marion does in writing God "crossed out," Breton contends that in fidelity to the self-giving of Christ for our salvation on the Cross, all ecclesial enterprises have to be crossed over and perhaps crossed out, in order to allow this gift to be communicated to others who have not received it or to bring it into a new moment on the stage of human history.

In the biblical image and story of covenant, Breton has found a symbol that can gather these perspectives into a unity, but a unity that is open to appropriating new forms of God's presence. God, imaged as the ineffable and invisible One, enters human reality by free choice, forging a covenant relationship with the people of Israel, and then with the disciples of Jesus Christ. This covenant comes from the divine initiative, an initiative that is marked in all the instances of covenant, from Abraham to Jesus, by a gratuitous self-emptying. It is promise and the guarantee of abiding presence, but it is also an *apocalypsis*, a moving forward in expectation and in the readiness to accept judgment on the forms of remembrance and religious practice that represent this advent and event. Hence in keeping remembrance, in appropriating the traces of divine passage, the Church continues to "write itself" as the people of the covenant. Living by the covenant means faith in the divine initiative and promise, but it includes the rites of memorial and of initiation into the covenant community. It also means assuming the covenantal obligations that flow from fidelity to the promise, so that even in keeping memory the Church embraces the twin commandment of love of God and neighbor, and with this the readiness to promote the legal institutions that carry and that forward a regime of divine justice.

Breton's understanding of the Word and of the Cross as gift and trace of God's love can be complemented by more attention to the gift of the Spirit. The power of the Spirit that indwells the Church and its members makes possible the remembrance and the creativity that brings what has been revealed to further and new expression in different historical and cultural situations. The "crossing out" of forms in fidelity to the Cross of Christ and in openness to the culturally and existentially other is more faithful to the manifestation of God that makes it impossible to assimilate the divine into any particular form of rite or thought than Marion's apparent canonization of the role of the bishop, which leaves little room for the emergence and development of culturally adapted forms of eucharistic remembrance. The Christian sacrament is a remembrance of the covenant given in Jesus Christ, even as it is a remembrance of the action and event of his self-emptying love. God's own testimony remains living in the Church through the remembrance of the event of the Word made flesh and through the inner power of the Spirit. Thus in sacramental memorial the Church celebrates the *esse in* of divine trace, presence, and gift, as well as the *esse ad* of relationship to the One who is uncontainable in any form, and the *esse ad* of relationship to the world in all its immense human, historical, and cultural diversity.

Being in Sacrament

The language of being is used in writing of sacraments in order to relate the event and gift of grace and their manifestation to human existence and the horizons of human perception and hope. It is human life which is described through the language of being, not the divine *agapé* which appears and is given through sacrament, to augment our being.

In a very particular way, rituality awakens participants to the reality of human being in its facticity. By sharing in common ritual, persons are one with each other, called to be one with the neighbor who seeks initiation or reconciliation or who is invited to the same table. By reason of the things used in rite, they are alerted to their being with the things of the earth and to the cosmic character of being human and earthbound. By the relation to cosmic time, rites reveal the tension between individual existence, historical existence as a people, and the belonging within a time that escapes human measure and yet configures human existence.

By being called to the future through memorial, those who take part in sacrament are invited to enter consciously into human mortality, to face being as being toward death. At the same time, they are given hope beyond death, through the communion of rite and word. Poetic language opens human understanding and willing to this participatory being, so that it is in communion with others and with the world of which they are a part, that the grace and revealing word of God come to Christian believers.

Though the gift itself that is offered in sacrament cannot be thought in the terms of human being, acting, and suffering, nor within the time frame of human existence, from the side of the human it can be thought as a way of being that is given. The gift is addressed to participants with the possibilities of living and loving in a way that transcends the boundaries that circumscribe being in this world, even if on condition that one consents to these boundaries as the conditions of life. If the sacramental dispensation is ever abstracted from these conditions and structures of being, it divorces the order of grace from the order of being in the world. When it does tie in with these conditions of being, it brings the divine gift into the lives of Christian people as they share the limits, the alienations, the oppressions of others, as well as entertain with others the hopes and possibilities, the bounty and the wonder of being on earth and being with others on earth.

The being that is gift given is best thought of in terms of act. A practical theology is needed that can heuristically grasp the structures of human action, in its openness to gift. In the first place, this means looking to the narrative through which the contours of act are made known. This narrative is the narrative to which sacrament invites configuration, the narrative(s) of the Pasch, of Christ's self-giving in self-emptying. The narrative(s) is also the narrative of how persons and communities act when acting out of Christian love, so that hagiography and other testimonies of action belong to an understanding of being.

In the second place, thinking of human being as act means thinking it according to the relation between action and suffering, the relation of *actio* to *passio*. The Latin word *passio* serves here because it can be translated both as "being acted upon" and as "suffering," relating the two without making them synonymous. Humans never proceed to action without being gifted with the power to act. They pass from the potency to act to act itself when moved to do so. This being moved by another in no way destroys inner movement of the self, but it sets its conditions. Narrative, however, also shows us how people and whole communities suffer, suffer the violence of nature and in a singularly cruel way human violence. It is a paradox of the human that in this suffering, persons and communities learn to act, are moved to action, both taking responsibility for themselves and responsibility for others. It is the tragedy of history that in some events and episodes persons and communities appear to be dehumanized by violence to the extent of being rendered incapable of human action. The narrative of Christ's passion is a narrative which bespeaks the power to act within suffering, to act for others, to love others without reserve. Whatever dehumanizing tragedy the world encounters and even while taking on the duty of its memory, the passage through the baptism of water and to the table of the Lord's action/passion proclaims the gift of act even within suffering, and indeed of an act that emerges with particular intensity and love out of suffering.

This conceptualization of being from within sacramental celebration is to think it as a limit-concept. It posits the limits to human being and action, but it also opens to what is given by divine grace beyond these limits. Such a limit-concept of human being allows us to perceive the boundaries and openings of the human situation in life, to grasp the gratuity and superabundance of the grace that is offered in God's self-communication through Christ and Spirit. It introduces participants into the world where loving does not cease and where it is unlimited in its embrace, often reversing the values and aspirations of human order.[21] Brought into the world of limited being, love is often in conflict with the limitations that people choose as boundaries, but it keeps alive and hopeful, as long as the assurance of divine gift and presence are renewed.

In earlier chapters, the meaning of sacramental praise and thanksgiving has been explored, and these kinds of prayer were related to the facticity and the openness of human existence. Some words are added here about incorporating the genre of lamentation into sacramental remembrance. Lamentation is actually given little place in traditions of sacramental celebration, as though it were somehow a refusal of God's saving action and grace. It may, however, prove a fecund place from which to know the mystery of gift and to proceed to praise and thanksgiving. Laments are abundant in the Hebrew Psalter, and in other parts of the Old Testament, such as the Book of Job, the Book of Wisdom, and the Servant Songs of Isaiah. We can learn from these what lament's place may be in Christian prayer, with relation to being in the world and in history.

One kind of lament expresses the anguish of an individual or the people when overcome by enemies and God's covenant seems to be in question. This is exemplified in the Psalms. Another kind, largely exemplified in the Book of Job, is lament in face of the limits of human mortality, the grief over suffering or over death. A third kind is the expression of anguish over the suffering or death of another. This is found, for example, in the lament of David over the death of Absalom, in the laments of the Book of Wisdom over the sufferings of the just, or in the Servant Songs of Isaiah when others lament his uncomeliness. Typical of these laments, however, is that they give rise in the end to some expression of hope and even of thanksgiving.

From the first kind of lament, the Jewish people learned of the future orientation of God's covenant and promise and in the process learned to recast the narrative of the making of the covenant. What God promises in the Law and the Prophets or in Jesus Christ is not something in hand once and for all. It is for a people who live in virtue of the future as the reign of God, proclaimed in the parables, comes day by day, life by life, into being. This indicates what the orientation toward the future means in living within the conditions of present being. It has to extend to lamentation over the failure of institutions and leaders that can claim divine appointment when these pretend to too much and fail to guide toward the future by concentrating on the exercise of their power over the immediate. We know this readily enough from the acknowledged failure of judges, kings, and priests under the covenant of Sinai. We have to dare to bring such lament to our experience of ecclesial institutions lest they lock us into their power structures, even in the celebration of sacraments. Hope returns to the persons who suffer violent in-

---

21. As mentioned before, the parables serve well to bring out this aspect of reversal prompted by acknowledgment of divine gift/giving.

roads on their expectations when they learn to look to the resurrection of Christ as the promise of the future and come to know the limits of all the present forms of ecclesial configurations of the kingdom.

The second kind of lament expresses the confines of existence imposed by mortality and suffering, and here too lament meets ritual experience. The effort within ritual to transcend worldly limitations, to reach into some transcendent form of existence that limits limits themselves, is frustrated by its own necessary rhythms. Lament is an acknowledgment of this reality, but it too opens the way to another hope, to the hope of overcoming death given in the Pasch of Christ.

The third kind of lament is lament over the suffering of the just and the innocent. It is perhaps the most difficult, for this kind of experience strikes us as most inconsistent and unjustified. Not even God can justify it as necessary or meaningful. It is imposed, it comes without sense, it cuts lives and hopes short, not just for individuals but for families, generations, cultures, and peoples. Yet, it is only when we enter into, live within, the memory of such suffering that the promise of God's loving gift in Christ can truly be heard and received. It is not received on the pretense that it gives this suffering a meaning that can be explained, but rather as a love and a life that maintains itself even within such confines and destructiveness. Within Christian traditions, this sort of lament has been given life in the Byzantine liturgies of Good Friday and in the *laude* of Western medieval confraternities that accompany the deposition of the Cross or of the Blessed Sacrament in the tomb. It is likewise found in the popular passion narratives that narrate or act out the passion of Christ and the sufferings of his mother. In these texts, voice is given to Christ's own laments over his suffering and his repudiation by others or to lament over these sufferings by the faithful.

All of these laments, in one way or another, can find a place in the celebration of Christian sacrament. In revealing to the participants the limits of human being in time, place, and history, they invite entry into this reality without illusion or false hope. By that very fact, they invite into the drama of the passion of Christ and open eyes and ears to a better grasp in faith of what is promised in and through his Pasch. They also invite with fresh eyes into the communion of sacrament, into the kind of communion that is offered and celebrated therein, and of course they make participants attend to its ethical implications of being for others, beyond the limits imposed by the facticity of being.

Lament opens even wider the horizons of praise and thanksgiving. It is wondrous to see that love remains alive and potent in such circumstances, that the love of self-emptying and giving can be more powerful than the constraints put on it by suffering, mortality, and finitude. It is only through the wonder aroused by this mystery that the Church can properly proceed to thanksgiving. The act of thanksgiving is to acknowledge that what is wondrous in such love has been given to those who come to the communion of sacrament and to all those with whom this community enters into communion.

Possibilities and Limits of Self-Presence

These reflections on being and sacrament raise the question of the present, presence, and presence to the self. Being is possessed only through language, beginning with narrative. Humans live not in virtue of what is already possessed or realized of the self, but in virtue of what is to come. This coming is not in virtue of human action and potency, but in virtue of what is gratuitously given, what is to come to, rather than what is to come from, the self.

There is no pure and complete self-consciousness, either of a person or a group. In fact, it is only through language, through the detour of story and other genres, that consciousness of the self is given. The same is true of consciousness of events. No past event can be immediately present to us but is there only through language. The language of the self and the language of the event converge, but both involve an equally passing sense of reality or a sense of reality passing into what it is not yet. The appeal that is sometimes made to some transtemporal quality in the acts of Christ that escapes both time and narrative seems to be based on the idea that we can be present to ourselves in the essence of our being, even within change. This is what is projected into the idea of the presence of the Christ event beyond time. There can then be the thought of the essential salvific act and the essential self converging in one sacramental moment. When we think about it, however, we may well see that there is nothing of ourselves that we are not constantly trying to come to grips with. Who knows what intelligence she or he has except in knowing and judging, and who knows how one may judge tomorrow about today? Who knows the depths and potentialities of feeling that life may bring forth, above and beyond, and perhaps even contrary to, what has already been brought forth?

Having an identity means finding it in a narrative that draws facts and event together into a plot. The plot, however, is open-ended, always pointing to the future. The story changes as episodes are recast for their future potentiality. When a new event has to be taken into the narrative, the narrative is readjusted. The self of a person or of a people is in this sense precarious. There is a feeling of being always the same and yet never wholly oneself. Things of the past slip the memory, but when recalled have to be taken into the narrative, and this affects the inner plot of the narrative as it affects the expectations to which narrative gives rise. If I ask who I am, I cannot rightly say, yet I try to say it by telling stories, and maybe even the story of my life. At the same time, I wonder what will come tomorrow and how this will affect my being and the way in which I remember my past. The other genres, alongside narrative, have to come into play precisely because story is so precarious. We want to speak of the things that narrative does not seem to accommodate, yet which strike us as true. Lament, lyric poetry, sheer wonder at what is in front of us but not accounted for, the wisdom sayings of how to live day to day, all complete narrative identity even as they eat into it.

Who can say that it is really the self who has forged whatever one is. One has had a part in it, but is it not rather the result of what has come across our tracks, of the persons and situations into whose company we have been projected? Is it not something given to us rather than made by us? That is why all humans hope for a beneficent future. They fear being cast into situations that are harmful and crush the power to act and to be. They aspire to a care that will take care of them, trusting that they can respond. Action is grounded in being done onto, in being given the power to do something or to love. Humans are recipients of being and life, before being doers and creators. Even in the midst of a suffering without exit, of a suffering within which we cannot act responsibly but only endure, the Christian story tells us that love and life keep coming to us. This is the apocalyptic sting of Christian narrative. It cannot be apprehended in terms of the future that it promises, as though this were clear and predictable. It has to be open to what is to come and, in judgment on what has been, will often be the unpredicted.

These considerations are a reminder of the need to shed the illusions of self-consciousness and culture-consciousness, if the Word is to be received in the grace of the Spirit. The effort to create a whole, to subject all things to an overarching consideration and meaning, whether for oneself, for one's family, for one's people, for one's Church, is spontaneous, persistent, and even intelligent. It absorbs, however, so much human ambition, even to the point of subjecting others and closing situations into themselves, that it is pierced through by the wisdom of the Cross and its parabolic reversals. The way of the Cross can be unhappily practiced as an abjection which demeans the self, as an abnegation of some part of the self, but in truth it is a call to the opening to a new wisdom, to bringing all the parts of self into that way. It is a response to the testimony of divine love, whose height and depth come to us, as in a mirror or under a veil, in the stories and ritual memories of Christ's Pasch. It is this that sacrament is constantly offering, giving, and giving forth in the body-self, within tradition, within place, within time, within history.

Thus one's being is re-created. We are in our own bodies, and in the body of Church, within the body of culture and society. With the being given to us in sacrament, we are open to the advent of the other and the Other, to the coming of the Other to this body. We are called to receive and to act out of what is received, while always receiving anew. We are being in love, even in the midst of suffering ourselves and of suffering with others.

Analogies

There are a number of analogies that may further the insight into the nature and action of sacrament as gift and about how this enters human being and action through the modes of iconic manifestation. These are the analogies of event, testimony, justice, freedom, and communion, which coalesce as it were around the analogy of gift. They illuminate the action of God, revelation and sacrament, but are not dominated by knowledge that brings God within the range of reason and human understanding. They are of a God who remains hidden, who is mystery, and is yet present to us, not in representations but through traces. The intensity, or density, of any analogy derives from being grounded in the language of scripture, sacrament, and mysticism. With that in mind, we can consider the ones listed above.

Event

This analogy does not need great elaboration here. It has already been presented in chapter 2 of this work and retrieved above in the discussion of the iconic quality of sacrament. It was said that it is by looking to the Pasch of Jesus Christ as foundational event that we can interpret its manifold sacramental memorial and celebration. This is because a community of faith comes together through its faith in the Cross and in the gift of love that God bestows therein upon the world. It was also said, however, that it enters into a world that is shaped by the bread, the wine, the oil, and the water, in the cultural shapes that these symbols take among peoples. By these means, the event takes form according to the structures and realities of humanity's being in the world and in time.

The analogy was with the way in which past events of any community or tradition are appropriated through the event of language itself, in a world circumscribed in symbol and rite. Events take on their historic importance and are woven into rites and institutions through language. That is how they enter a tradition. Having entered it, they continue to be interpreted, appropriated, and even recast, in conjunction with the events and the lives of communities. A ritual enactment can be seen itself as an event, because it is where the community brings the past event through language into its own present, and through this opens up a perspective on the future. The memorial of the past, enacted through language, offers possibilities for acting and suffering in the future. As memorial, expressed in the many forms of language examined throughout this work, the Cross of Christ events anew in the life and history of the Church, worked into the many histories and cultures of the peoples called to be the body of Christ. The two words that were used in chapter 2 to express this were *mimesis* and *anamnesis*. On the one hand, *anamnesis* expresses the remembrance of the past event that in language and rite is effectively represented, but in forms that are distanced from the event and in openness to the future given in the promise given body in the event. On the other hand, *mimesis* expresses a participation in the here and the now in the divine mystery of love and gift that showed itself in the event of the Pasch, a being in time and the world that is also a participation in a way of being that transcends world and time.

Covenant / Testimony

Testimony, testament, promise, is closely allied with the biblical image of covenant.[22] The event which is remembered and appropriated is known to the Church through the testimony of Christ, of the Spirit, and of those who have preceded us in the faith. As a testimony affirmed and appropriated, it occurs as an event in the life of the Church or indeed brings the Church to event anew among peoples.

The phenomenon of having faith in something on the evidence of another rather than on the basis of personal knowledge is well known to us. This takes on sharper focus when the evidence is set in a court of law, and there is witness and counterwitness. Judgment has to be made by those who hear the evidence, and judgment will be pronounced by another between the litigants. This is an analogy that is amply used in the Gospels to present the work of Jesus and to depict his conflicts with those who oppose and reject him. He is giving the testimony of his works, testimony that is not simply his but that of his Father. It is on this evidence or witness that he asks for faith in his messianic mission and in what he offers as God's gift of life. He presents this evidence to the court of human opinion, but he counters the judgment made against him through pronouncing the divine judgment that is inherent in the works he does and will be made apparent in his being raised from the dead.

As already said, ritual brings the conditions of human existence to the fore. In face of limit, there is a human aspiration to the absolute that will transcend these limits and assume all being into itself. Philosophies and societies endeavor to portray and achieve this ideal condition. Even ritual can express such a claim, especially when it is hierarchically ordered and demands submission to ritual ordering at any cost. Jesus addresses this in the Gospel on many occasions, especially in face of rituals of the Sabbath or ablutions. Indeed, he even specifically uses the image of men of law who bind others with the burdens of observing these rituals by their judicial decisions while they themselves will not lift a finger to help.

The testimony of Christ given in his works and ratified on the Cross is a testimony against such aspirations and efforts, and in the end is a judgment on them. It is given, however, not in the mode of prescribing burdens to carry, but of giving life, and not in the mode of human authority but through self-emptying love. The absolute is shown not in systems of order, but only in the self-emptying of the Cross. Paul spells this out in his letter to the Corinthians when he says that this is neither the Law of the Jews nor the wisdom of the gentiles, that is, neither a religion of ritual nor a philosophy, but a new wisdom which is that of the Cross and a new religion which is that of life poured out for the other. The response to this witness or testimony is faith,

---

22. Jean Greisch summarizes the positions of Ricoeur in relation to Heidegger, Nabert, and Levinas. See Jean Greisch, "Témoignage et attestation," in *Paul Ricoeur: L'herméneutique à l'école de la phénoménologie* (Paris: Beauchesne, 1995), 305–26.

and a faith which involves self-abnegation, in the sense of recognizing that human effort to achieve the absolute is overthrown in this court of divine justice.

Being open to the testimony of Christ means furthermore attending to the testimony of multiple others, given in their lives and in their works. In the first place, there is the testimony of believers, of those who act for others in their faith and hope in Jesus Christ. His testimony is continued in his Church, in the works of those who live their belief in the Cross. This is the testimony of individuals and of communities. It is essential to the taking root of the Gospel in many cultures that the evidence of these cultures be heard, as of those who live faith in Christ within the expressions proper to particular cultures. The testimony has to extend further to include the testimony of the suffering. Indeed it will not be heard unless it extends to include those who have been put down by others to the rawest limits of existence. In 1988, standing before the gas ovens of the extermination camp of Mauthausen, Pope John Paul II spoke to those who had died there, asking them to allow us to hear their voices, to attend to their witness to suffering and against cruelty and injustice.[23]

In a very special way, Christians have to hear the testimony of the Jewish people at this high point of their suffering. This is a witness that calls God into question, and not only humans. It asks of the God of the covenant what it means that the chosen people should not only be killed, but that they were attacked at the roots of all that made them a people, so that even their memory might be wiped out. The anti-Semitic strains of Christian centuries impose upon the Jews a Christ who denies and judges them. Churches must dare to ask how the witness of Christ's self-emptying may sound when heard with the lament that goes up from the Jewish people, as a lament over the Nazi attempt to annihilate them.

There is nothing comparable to this witness, because of its specific religious dimension. This, however, cannot be allowed to prevent us from hearing a testimony which is so very important in these days where there is much talk of inculturation of Gospel, Church, and sacrament. This is the testimony, which needs to be heard even within sacramental memorial, of all those peoples who were stripped of their humanity in the process of colonization. These voices rise up on the African, Asian, and Latin American continents. They are the voices of people who have been, in the words of African theologian Engelbert Mveng, deprived of their very humanity, even as the Gospel of Christ was implanted on their soil.[24] They are the voices of the dead and of the living. In what Mveng calls their anthropological poverty, they are, he says, deprived of all, of their language, of their history, of their

---

23. John Paul II, "Address at Mauthausen," *Origins* 18(1988): 124.

24. Engelbert Mveng, "A la recherche d'un nouveau dialogue entre Christianisme et traditions africaines," in *L'Afrique dans l'Église: Paroles d'un croyant* (Paris: Éditions L'Harmattan, 1985), 71–92.

traditions, of their arts, of their kinships, of their own religious and spiritual resources. One cannot today be serious about inculturation without recognizing that what is now acclaimed as a cultural richness is addressed to peoples who have had these riches beaten down, so that they have to be reclaimed as it were from the grave, or out of an ancient past which they had been expected to discard. It is a new point of departure for the self-emptying of Christ in his Church to stand stripped among these peoples, awaiting for what may rise up out of these emptied selves when at length they find their voices.

To accompany the outer testimony of Christ's word and of the suffering of the "other," there is the gift of the inner testimony of the Spirit, which is precisely what makes it possible to join with the emptied Christ among those emptied of their humanity by force and oppression and by contempt and neglect. The work of the Spirit is the testimony of grace that hearers experience in the movement of their own hearts and in their consciences, which themselves prompt judgment. Like the disciples on the way to Emmaus, those who hear this testimony feel their hearts burning within them. They can judge between the economy of system and institution and the economy of love that comes to the aid of those burdened and suffering. They adjudicate between good order and a love that reaches to the very fringes of the order. They attend in the Spirit to the voices of the suffering and their cries against those who impose suffering, or who have simply kept silent, or who did not even "know" what was taking place. The analogy of the court of judgment and of the evidence heard in it needs to be retained, lest we forget that the words of Christ from the scriptures and from the ones silenced through history ask for judgment. They do not simply ask us to be open to a greater infusion of cultural and religious riches. They ask us to hear again the narrative of Christ's passion as a narrative of judgment, where witness is pitted against witness, and the ultimate appeal is to God's witness/judgment in the divine pouring out of love within the deepest human distress.

Justice

Justice also relates to divine covenant. It is the assurance of divine righteousness, but by that same token it makes human systems of justice that are related to God's justice necessary and possible. The testimony to the absolute that is given through the Cross of Christ is not given as an order of things that is here and now implemented and imposed. It is a testimony, passed on in the writing of the traces, in sacramental proclamation, in action on behalf of the poor, and in sufferings. It is of its nature prophetic and eschatological. In its many forms, it is given as a word from God, a word indeed of God. It does not come from human perceptions. It is about what is to come when divine justice prevails. In this sense it is eschatological through and through, not an order of law or of rite that places all its trust in the present, or in the present presence of divine justice. Indeed, the testimony of Christ and the Spirit are still being given. They have not been heard out. They are embodied in the Church, in the word spoken, in the gifts proffered, in the actions done out of faith in Christ and Spirit, and in the sufferings of those in whom Christ suffers. They are embodied in the poor who are the privileged of God's judgment, those who give evidence in their own bodies to what others have or have not done in the name of Christ, as well as to depths of humanity in themselves.

The analogy of justice must therefore complement the analogy of testimony. Distributive justice is an ordering that allows each and all their rights and their needs for a dignified human existence. It has its *quid pro quo,* however, and citizens are expected to make their contribution and deserve their place in the order. Those who fail are punished, denied full participation, or even expelled. In the scriptures, divine justice is sometimes portrayed in these terms to bring home that to which those who enter this kingdom are called. However, it is placed within a prevailing order of mercy and covenant. Hence, divine justice is distanced from human justice. Its judgments are totally different. It is more future oriented than caught up in the present ordering of things, though of course how things are done now opens to what is to come. It is an order of free gift and of forgiveness, not one based on contributory services. It does not focus on judgment as to how well public order is kept, but on how well the afflicted are served.

All this is proclaimed in the word of sacramental celebration, but it is embodied in rites. These rites are such that they bring participants into a divine ordering of sharing gift, and of being akin to all persons, and especially to the other who is alien. This other may be of another race, may be poor, or may need to be given forgiveness or to be asked for forgiveness. Sacramental ritual is one that brings with it the face-to-face encounter and the hand-to-hand communion which signifies the order of divine justice to which the testimony of Jesus speaks and that of the Spirit prompts.

The remembrance of injustice spurred by the hope of divine justice calls for the confession of sin, which is an integral part of the sacramental prayer of commemoration. While due to the trends that gave shape to past Church discipline we may think too readily of the one-to-one encounter in the confessional, new light is cast on the confession of sin when Church leaders and Church communities make confession of past actions and dominations. Since all are bound together in communities of tradition, the freedom to act now means some corporate as well as personal judgment on the past and solidarity in confessing the wrong done, the violation of the order of divine justice. Whether it be in front of the ovens of Nazi camps or on the streets of Prague where John Hus was committed to flames or on the plains of the Indian and African peoples of the Americas or in a synod of African bishops or in a letter addressed to women or in the academic halls where Galileo's truth was silenced, the Church has to confess the sin which it brings into its present. The lamentation of the victims has to be joined by the confession of the body corporate which acted against them.

Not to confess is to accept solidarity, to make the sin one's own, to be oneself privy to this pride and domination, to refuse to listen and to hear Christ's testimony, to harden the heart against the Spirit. The voice of human justice will of course protest and say that only the perpetrators carry the burden of the sin, or excuse it by avowing that at the time this action was necessary and justified. If the doctrine of original sin is allowed its word in the setting, it is that we are bound together in sin and death and that only a divine gift will free us from this solidarity in evil, from the mystery of iniquity symbolized in this story and doctrine of corporate human sin. Rather than burden the conscience, however, and possibly it is this which is feared, such confession frees because it acknowledges and praises another order, a reversal of human orderings, and a divine forgiveness which is rebirth and recreation.

This is why confession of sin and praise go together. Indeed, the traditional terminology joins them together, for we talk in one breath of *confessio fidei, confessio peccatorum,* and *confessio laudis.* Praise is the wonder in face of this mystery of divine justice, forgiveness, and remaking. It is the wonder that in this justice, based in self-giving and the forgiving of self-giving, the mystery of God's own self-gift is revealed and communicated. To this there follows thanksgiving, the acknowledgment that this is given to us here gathered, that we personally and corporately are beneficiaries of God's justice. The somewhat cumbersome reform of the prayer of forgiveness in the sacramental ritual of penance points in this direction, but needs to take its own genre more seriously. It praises God for the mystery of reconciliation testified in the Pasch of Christ and the gift of the Spirit. It thanks God for making this gift here and now available. It pronounces a word of freedom, by which the penitent people are set free from sin's burdens and opened in heart and mind to the gift of divine justice, so that they may be free to live from this new freedom.

Freedom

Freedom cannot be reduced to the capacity to perform either one action or another, nor to the will to do right or wrong, nor to the right to act as one chooses. Freedom consists in acting out of a consciousness of the self, or what may be called self-possession, and in acting consistently with this self-possession. This means taking reflective cognizance of one's powers, one's capacities, and one's inclinations, but doing so in context, that is, over against one's place with others and in the world in which action is called forth and rendered possible. In this, some notion of and desire for the absolute is inherent in human consciousness, but it takes accessible form only when seen in this-worldly context as an end to which to strive, with others and with respect for others. Conceived as the limits of existence to which humans strive, and as the good which will complete or perfect desire, this instinct is both erotic and outgoing. It seeks self-completeness, but also communion with others, persons and things.[25]

As already noted, the consciousness of self is incomplete and often faulty. Hence, tensions are inherent in the effort to be and act in true freedom. There is the tension between self-interest and being for others. There is the tension between the erotic and the outgoing nature of loving. The history of human action makes it clear that a harmony is difficult, and often fails. It may be that something is lacking in self-possession or in self-cognizance. The illusions of power, domination, self-gratification, on the one hand, and of the ability to better the lives of others on the other, are all too obvious. Human history is also a history of sin, of human enterprise marked by the evil that is done in the pursuit of self-interest or in closing self off to the exigencies of the other person, or in the self-centeredness that is an obstacle to and even a rejection of the presence and entry of the divine. Hence in remembrance of Christ, there is the forgiveness that reconciles the sinner and reconstitutes freedom of Spirit. In freedom, the Church is invited to embrace the way of reconciliation that is the way of the Cross.

In Christian proclamation and sacramental encounter, an alternate vision and power of freedom is offered, but one that is not based on self-possession and consciousness. This is the freedom exemplified in Jesus Christ in his giving of himself for others, even to the point of self-emptying. There is nothing, however, that is lacking in self-fulfillment in this freedom, for it was through it that Jesus was perfected as God's Son and as the Christ in reaching for communion with others. Betrayal did not stem the will to love, nor did its refusal. The sacrament of the Lord's table, of the gift of the body and blood in bread and wine, is not simply a way of ritualizing something already done. To leave this gift was to act freely toward the future. It was to go to death, leaving the word and the rite and the promise around which the gift of his life would continue to exercise its force. The openness to communion in his love would continue to grow and to find new this-worldly situations in which to show itself.

There is no conflict between the freedom that comes with the gift of love and the freedom that is the desire of human self-consciousness when the latter recognizes its limits and is open to gifted freedom. The gift given in Jesus Christ suggests a trajectory and offers a potentiality which humanity of its own initiatives has not, and cannot, conceive or attain. It is spoken to us in the language that comes from God and made possible to us within the communion that is celebrated in the Eucharist and to which access is given through the other sacraments.

---

25. The reflections on freedom found in the theology of Hans Urs von Balthasar are helpful in appreciating the freedom which divine justice gives. See, for example, *Theo-Drama: Theological Dramatic Theory,* vol. 4, *The Action,* trans. Graham Harrison (San Francisco: Ignatius Press, 1994), 137–48.

Communion

The covenant of God is a call to communion in the gift that is given and a call to an exchange in which this gift is received and shared. In appreciation of this gift of divine love that is given in the mission of the Word and of the Spirit, it is of interest to note the image of the Church that is emerging in ecumenical conversations as a guide to relations between Churches. This is the image of *koinonia*.[26] The term expresses the communion of Christians among themselves, within their common participation in the communion of Father, Son, and Spirit. It is a communion in the love given as gift, even within historical, ecclesial, and paradigmatic diversity.

The gift of divine love is an embodied gift. As sacrament of Christ's self-gift and self-emptying, it takes on specific community and historical forms through the action of the Spirit. The twofold mission of Word and Spirit is ever working in the Church to bring believers and disciples together in the one communion of love. The gift is embodied, the communion takes on cultural and historical shapes. Thus it is a communion in diversity.

To take account of this gift as it is embodied, love and service are the activities and the images which come to the fore, activated in the ethical commitments undertaken. The description of the Church of Jerusalem in Acts 2:42–46 has always had a fascination for Christians, especially in times when reform seemed necessary. It depicts the necessary, communion in the faith of the apostles, communion in prayer, and the communion of goods whereby none care only for themselves but always have the need of the other at heart. Alongside this most fundamental communion, to have a living picture we have to think of exchange and sharing in material goods, the care of the needy, mutual relations within communities and between communities, exchange of letters, hospitality, common stances on social issues, living within a shared vision of the future, and a sense of common identity. It is through Word and Sacrament that this communion is formed, as a realization and sacrament of the divine *koinonia* of Father, Son, and Spirit.

The sacramental images of communion are at the same time images of the gift given. At the heart of the matter is the common table in the one loaf and the one cup, gift given by Christ in the Spirit, gift shared by all in fellowship and hospitality. Putting this in context, the words of Ignatius of Antioch are ever pertinent: one faith, one baptism, one table, one altar, one assembly, one bishop. The imagery of baptism is imagery of access to this table, namely, forgiveness and rebirth through the passage through the water and sealing with the Spirit. Within this common assembly, forgiveness and reconciliation are offered to the vagrant and healing and strength to the sick and suffering. Within it, some are appointed and ordained to ministry, others

---

26. See above, chapter 7 on doctrines. Compare Gordon W. Lathrop, "*Koinonia* and the Shape of the Liturgy," *Studia Liturgica* 26 (1996): 65–81, and Albert Gerhards, "A Response," ibid., 82–91.

in marriage witness to the communion of the love of God with humanity, in sacrament and in action.

The gift of communion in divine love is also one that is shared by different communities, even across unhappy schisms. On the one hand, all may recognize that their own fidelity to the word and their sacramental practice, their reception and embodiment of the gift, brings them into this Trinitarian communion. On the other hand, they can affirm that the preaching and sacramental practices of other traditions and bodies do likewise for their members. This image of an ecclesial and historically realized communion in the divine communion is open to the recognition that there can be different ways in which this communion is both expressed and shared. Furthermore, when it is the wonder of the gift of love that is shared in communion that is to the fore in the life of the Church, its ethical action as a body is given priority over all liturgical, doctrinal, and institutional forms, and this is a basis for sharing among Churches. All else exists for the sake of the outpouring of love in the action of loving. Word, sacrament, doctrine, and order serve a tradition which is the passing on of the gift of love.

This is to treat the matter of communion in reference to a living reality, and ultimately to life in the Trinity, rather than exclusively in reference to liturgical rites, doctrines, and institutions. Churches may differ in these matters while still affirming participation with one another in the divine communion that is the embodiment of the gift of self-giving love. This image of *koinonia* is a ground on which to consider relations between the members of a Church and between Churches. Sometimes this ideal of communion is put forward as a way of legitimating specific ecclesiastical structures and hierarchical ordering. If we see structure rather as emerging with the gift, given within historically and culturally diversified embodiments, the fundamental communion in the gift of love is better appreciated. Structures formed in charity are rather embodiments of and service to the tradition of this gift. Within this perspective, diversity is more readily allowed and affirmed. A community cannot function without social models for its institutions. The concern is to find one that allows best for all to share in the communion of life as one body of mutually loving members.

The Liturgical Mystery of the Triune God

With these analogies in mind, it can be asked again what naming of God takes place in sacrament and what knowledge of God goes with that naming.[27] The liturgical accent of sacramental tradition is on the gift of love, the ineffable holiness of the name revealed through this gift, and on the glory which is communion in the eternal communion of Father, Word, and Spirit.

---

27. This is to pursue what has already been said about naming in chapter 2.

With regard to what sacraments reveal of this ineffable mystery, Western theology has begun to give more attention to the long tradition of apophatic theology in the East. The heart of this theology is located within the Eucharist as the locus of participation in the divine. One more recent example of this approach is found in the work of Vladimir Lossky. While insisting that knowledge of the Trinity is generated within the liturgy, when together with its participation there is the practice of *ascesis*, Lossky stresses the apophatic character of *teologia* and of all discourse about the Trinity, which cannot allow of cosmological analogies. Thus he rejects the Western emphasis on the opposition of relations in theology of the Trinity, since this brings the idea of distinction to the fore instead of the contemplation of undivided unity, as he also rejects any equation between the transcendent One and Being. At the end of a long essay in which he examines different modes of apophatic theology in early Fathers of the Church, Lossky concludes:

> The apophasis of *Mystical Theology* [i.e., of the Pseudo-Dionysius] is not determined by the principle of absolute identity of the transcendent One to Being. The dialectic of affirmations and nonopposed negations, applied to Trinitarian dogma, makes it necessary to go beyond the One opposed to the Other. It is not the impersonal Monad, but the "superessential and more-than-divine Triad" that the author of *Mystical Theology* invokes at the beginning of his treatise, in order that it direct even beyond unknowing and towards the way of union with triune Divinity, the theologian in search of the God of Christian revelation, who transcends the opposition between the transcendent and the immanent, since He is beyond all affirmation and negation.[28]

By way of some contrast, while Jürgen Moltmann appeals to Eastern theology and the importance of liturgy in theology, he believes that this opens the way to incorporating the event of the Cross into the inner mystery of God.[29] This can be done within the limits set on concepts by the return to doxology. Thus he speaks not only of God in action in the world, but of God "in passion," not only of God giving, but of God suffering and coming to be among us in and through suffering.[30] In the passion of Christ and in the sharing of that passion by his members, the bliss and joy of the Spirit of hope is also experienced and known. This leaves the way open to some appropriation of the analogy of passion, of being acted upon, into the inner life of the ineffable God in the Trinity of the processions of Word and Love.

Some contemporary theologies in the West are closer to the apophatic approach when they write of God beyond being, that is, of a God who within

28. Vladimir Lossky, *In the Image and Likeness of God* (Crestwood, N.Y.: St. Vladimir's Seminary Press, 1974), 29.

29. Jürgen Moltmann, *The Spirit of Life: A Universal Affirmation*, trans. Margaret Kohl (Minneapolis: Fortress Press, 1992), 298–306.

30. Ibid., 298–301.

Rendering an Account of Sacramental Action

the Trinity is beyond all conceptualizations with which philosophy treats of being and its manifestations. Thus Jean-Luc Marion finds in Christ and in his eucharistic presence the icon of God as *agapé*.[31] In sacramental liturgy, participants experience that love as a beneficence which gazes upon us and calls us to worship God beyond all visible elements or human concepts. The Holy Spirit as an inner force makes it possible for us to be free of attachment to the text itself of the scripture or to the sacrament itself to affirm in faith the God of Love whom Christ, the Word which speaks of him, and the sacrament which is his icon reveal.

As already seen, Marion follows von Balthasar in the role which he gives to Church order. To connect Word and sacramental rite and gift, Marion highlights the action of the bishop in proclaiming the Word, praying the blessing, and offering the gifts to the people, as icon of the Word made flesh. The community joins with the Word in the Holy Spirit in returning love to the Father. Marion does not allow any language of representation or the language of being in explicating the mystery of the Eucharist. The iconic, in which the Father's gaze of love settles on the community, transgresses the language of being. Gift, goodness, and love cannot be expressed in representational forms, nor in the language of being. Neither is presence expressed in images or concepts of fixed presence, for the presence of the Word made flesh in the sacrament is a presence in time, which can never be a moment of being, but is always suspended between the past which is remembered and the future which is hoped. While the love of the Father is shown and given in the icon of the Word made flesh and returns to the Father in the Spirit through communion with the Word, this does not allow any explanation of the mystery of the Trinity in concepts of being. Communion with the Trinity is rendered possible to those who yield to the trinity of transgression, excess, and gift. In the icon of divine love, the forms of being which humans can image or conceive are transgressed. The love itself poured out in the flesh of the Word is a love of excess, exceeding the norms of rationality. The love abiding in the heart is totally gift and a response to gift, not something that arises from human sensibility.

Marion locates the icon of divine love in the Eucharist and particularly in the action of the bishop in the Eucharist. For others who agree with that there is no legitimate resort to the concepts of being in explaining the eucharistic mystery, there has to be some appropriation of the hermeneutic of deconstruction in face of ecclesial forms. This is suggested by Breton's image of the Cross crossing out all representations of the One and of God's love in order to leave the freedom to the Church to "write" itself afresh within different settings.

---

31. Jean-Luc Marion, *God without Being*, trans. Thomas A. Carlson (Chicago: University of Chicago Press, 1991), especially 139–58.

The positive power of this hermeneutic lies in its openness to the possibilities of language and of the insights provided by language beyond any conceptual limitation. This is not to be confounded with negative theology, but allows for a nondetermined or open hermeneutic of eucharistic language and ritual, which is attentive to the insights into God's presence and action in the world, which the very diversity of eucharistic expression offers. Appropriating the approach of deconstruction into eucharistic theology through the process of critiquing the claims of representation does not embrace the definitive forms of iconicity sponsored by Marion or von Balthasar. While allowing for a tradition of eucharistic action, within this tradition it opens the way for newly emerging insights and expressions of divine acting and being in the world, as the Eucharist finds expression in the language of diverse communities.

Louis-Marie Chauvet, in a sacramental and indeed eucharistic reading of Christian existence, espouses Breton's way of meontology, but then looks for a word about God not in the language of being, nor even of the one and triune, but as the totally Other.[32] It is in Christ crucified that God is revealed as such, and the Spirit is the indwelling of God which allows us to see beyond both conceptual representations and the visible forms of Christ and of his Church to this totally Other God of love.[33] Quoting Stanislas Breton, Chauvet follows his thought that the Cross means the crossing out of religious ritual and the crossing out of the being of Greek philosophy as ways to God. He also quotes Eberhard Jüngel to the effect that it is in God's own *esse* that when coming into the world it was divinely necessary to appear in a form which abrogates all human ideas and religious constructs of God. This is similar to Breton's thought that the Cross is the crossing out of what human mind and affect calls God. The gift of the Holy Spirit, the inner presence of God as other, is precisely that inner vitality which makes it possible to take body in this form of negation. It also renders it possible for the Church to embody this difference, in its discipleship of Christ, within a symbolic and ethical communion, built on the remembrance of the Cross. By that same token, it is open to diverse forms, which in the memorial of the Cross of Christ and the inner freedom of the Spirit is free within, and even from, the forms of bodiliness assumed.

What is accentuated in this approach is the affirmation of God, even in the love sent forth, as Other. This Other is not simply the beyond-being of apophatic theology, which we contemplate beyond all negation and affirmation of what is thought. It is instead the surprising Other of a God who is revealed in self-emptying love. This comes among us in all those forms which

---

32. Louis-Marie Chauvet, *Symbole et sacrement: Une relecture sacramentelle de l'existence chrétienne* (Paris: Éd. du Cerf, 1987). On the Holy Spirit, see 520–41.

33. It is a reading of Jacques Derrida that keeps one mindful of the refusal to privilege any form of representation which smacks of logocentrism or of an inner word that is formed by concept or image to render the Other present.

come upon us as other to what we commonly hold firm. It is other to the instinctively religious, other to whatever we expect as outcome of human effort. It is revealed as other also in the faces of the ones who meet us with new ethical exigencies of love. The memorial of Christ in the Eucharist is precisely the memorial of God appearing in that Otherness, other even to the religious expressions and sentiments of religious traditions. The epiclesis of the Spirit to make that memorial possible is the appeal to the inner power of God indwelling as the Other of Spirit. This inner force enables a stripping of representational self-consciousness so as to appropriate and recognize, first the icon of Christ, and then the icons of the Other in the sacramental and ecclesial communion of the body of Christ. Such sacramental communion however, is unrealized without the welcome of those others who are alien to us by reason of common human standards. A communion in sacrament is a communion, that is held open to welcome all who wish to pass through the water and the oil and share the common bread and cup.

Not all of those who take the concerns of post[-]modern rejection of ontotheology seriously wish to discard all language of Being in speaking of God through the metaphor and analogy of gift. Ghislain Lafont and John Milbank can be given special mention in this regard.[34]

Lafont considers that the real problem in ontotheology's use of the language of Being in speaking of God lies in its use of the categories of the necessary, the absolute, and *causa sui*, as well as the notion of divine presence. These do indeed put God into the categories and limits of common being, if only by way of eminent comparison. The comparative language starts with creatures, not with God. Aquinas, however, had pointed out that if an analogy holds, it has to have its starting point, its analogatum in God, not in the finite. This lies not in any concept of being, but in the affirmation of God as pure *actus essendi*.

On the other hand, Lafont thinks that writers such as Jüngel and Chauvet in the very effort to avoid analogy and use biblical language cede too much to ontotheology. Particularly when they talk of a God who becomes through suffering or wish to integrate the mystery of suffering into the Godhead, they continue to speak in human terms, by way of human comparisons. For Lafont, as for Milbank, the primary analogy, which is biblically based, is gift, or donation as the act of giving. This, however, needs to be thought as Being in Act if we are to avoid anthropomorphism. Moreover, to be considered as truly from God, while the act enters the world within the framework of time, the primary act of divine donation is transcendent to time.

Finite being is given, and is act inasmuch as it is given. Gift as predicated of God is giving, donation. This does not mean that God is to be taken as giver and the gift given, but as the very act of giving. This donation is

---

34. Lafont, *God, Time, and Being*, esp. 257–324; John Milbank, "Can a Gift be Given? Prolegomena to a Future Trinitarian Metaphysic," *Modern Theology* 11 (1995): 119–61.

made historically real in creation, in the missions of Word and Spirit. In these missions, it appears more than just giving to be; it is the giving of love, of self-giving, and it is this which animates the beloved, the "being given" of those who are in the communion of gift, of donation. In grasping the meaning of donation, Lafont thinks that the act of Being is the hermeneutical key.[35] Placed within the founding narratives of creation and redemption through the Cross of Christ, as one must do in speaking of God, the being of finite creatures, in its act, is totally gift, even in its capacity to be in turn donation, whereas God is totally donation. Lafont indeed claims that it is precisely the doxology of sacramental liturgy which frees the possibility of this analogy.

Milbank ties such thought about the divine act of Being/donation with von Balthasar's way of seeing the eternal relation between the Father and the Son. There may be some familiarity among readers with Hans Urs von Balthasar's eucharistic reading of the relation between the Son and the Father, where the self-emptying of the death and the surrender made in the eucharistic action of the Supper is taken as an expression, a showing forth, of what is eternally true of the divine processions and relations.[36] It is in the self-giving unto self-emptying that the Father and the Son are united in the love of the Spirit, which itself proceeds as this communion between the two. There is room here for some resolution of the diverse formulas of East and West for the procession of the Spirit, since within this analogy it is possible to speak without contradiction of the Spirit proceeding as the relational Love of the Father and the Son, as it is also possible to say that the Love with which the Father empties himself in bearing forth the Son reposes on the Son, who in turn is totally gift to the Father.

Milbank too would see human relations as participating in the relation of giving between Father and Son. If the divine being, which we know through revelation is Trinitarian, it is there before all creative act. If this is not kept in mind, then theology ends up with a God who is only "on the way" to Being. At the same time, Milbank believes that biblical images and language have to prevail in reflecting upon the mystery of the Trinity. Here it is the aesthetics of intersubjective communion which is uppermost.[37] Even while the communion is foremost, an accent needs to be kept on the difference in order to respect the dynamic between Father and Son. Though the Holy Spirit may be rightly termed the love in which Father and Son are united, it is also the Spirit which keeps the difference and the relationship between them, making way for the continued dynamic of an eternal, nontemporal relationship. Milbank then relates this to the twofold mission, in which the dynamic of an open temporal relationship has to be kept. Though the Word Incarnate is the express image of the Father, the presence of God in the

---

35. Ibid., 307.

36. Von Balthasar, *Theo-Drama*, 4:389–406.

37. Though Milbank does not mention worship and liturgy, it is there that the biblical language is kept alive in the prayer of the Church.

world cannot be limited to any particular earthly expression. It is the gift of the Spirit which guarantees the necessary openness to critique and new poetic expression. As Milbank states it, the Spirit in an aesthetic model of the Trinity is necessary to the irreducibility of the interpretative moment, either to formal structures or to subjective aesthetic categories.[38]

While these theologies differ on the use of the language of Being or on the extent to which we can have some knowledge of the inner life of the Trinity, they all appeal in the final analysis to the analogies of gift and love. It is this which sacramental tradition and practice bring to the fore in proclaiming God. All likewise retain the importance of the role of doxology, as praise and wonder and silence. Sacrament perfects our being in the world, making of it a revelation of love, but it also leads us to the door of contemplation. Doxology, in which liturgy is consummated, places us in the horizon of mystery and praise, where we look to the founding narratives of creation, Cross, and resurrection for orientation and cease speaking in contemplation of what is given. Whether one prefers the more apophatic approach or this postmodern retrieval of the language of Being, theological inquiry certainly needs to cease in doxology and refresh itself in that act of wonder in face of the gift of love that is given through Word and Spirit.

Conclusion

The endeavor in this chapter has been to pursue some deeper reflection on the mystery celebrated in sacrament, which takes the postmodern critique and the need for sacramental interpretation seriously. It noted that all speculative thought on sacraments centers around gift-giving and the language of sacrament. Within this hermeneutic, it spoke of the pertinence of the category of the icon and of the limits on the language of being. It also noted the limits of the turn to the subject that does not fully follow the path of the turn to language. It also proffered some analogies that enable us to speak of sacrament, of what is given in sacrament, and of the revelation of the divine in sacrament. Relating them always to gift and language event, it took up analogies of justice, testimony, and freedom to explore the meaning and reality of sacrament. Finally, it considered some approaches to the knowledge of God that comes with the sacramental naming of God. However far these may be pursued, however, theological discourse must find its peace in doxology.

---

38. John Milbank, *The Word Made Strange: Theology, Language, Culture* (Oxford: Blackwell Publishers, 1997), 186–89.

— Chapter Ten —

Sacramental Catechesis and Praxis

The best test of a theological study on sacrament is how it connects with celebration and how its insights affect this. Linked with this is whether or not it can translate into homily and catechesis. Hence, a way to summarize and test all that precedes about sacrament as a language event is to ask how it may contribute to celebration and a sacramental catechesis that is rooted in celebration. This could provide a contemporary mystagogy.[1] The attention to language evokes thought on what is seen, heard, and acted in ritual. Reflection draws primarily on an appreciation of gift and event as these terms express God's action in the Church, among different peoples, through the Word and the Spirit. What is brought to the fore is not simply the idea of a gift given, but more importantly all that is expressed in the word *donation* or act of giving.[2]

In any catechesis and sacramental practice, due attention has to be given to culture and history. Since sacramental celebration itself is in flux and is an act of interpretation, its catechesis has to include a sense of history, open to both past and future. The history and customs of a people pass on their cultural perceptions and values, which shape the world in which they live. Cultural studies can give weight to the historical past as a set of events that contribute to the shaping of culture, or to its disruption. For example, in current examination of the popular religion of Christian practitioners among peoples of Latin American countries, the Philippines, or African countries, it is possible to distinguish what is prechristian, what comes from the missionary activity of those who brought the Gospel, and what has been the people's own blend of the two. It is also possible to point to this popular blend as a way of refusing to be totally dominated by the vision of foreigners. People

---

1. For some orientations, see Richard N. Fragomeni, "Wounded in Extraordinary Depths: Towards a Contemporary Mystagogia," in *A Promise of Presence,* ed. Michael Downey and Richard N. Fragomeni (Washington, D.C.: Pastoral Press, 1992), 115–37. For an outline of how sacraments can be presented by following the dynamic of celebration, see David N. Power, "Sacrament," in *The New Dictionary of Catholic Spirituality,* ed. Michael Downey (Collegeville, Minn.: Liturgical Press, 1993), 840–44.

2. The interplay between *don* and *donation,* works better in French. In English, donation sounds too much like money into the basket or a check in the mail.

discover ways themselves to welcome Christ, Mary, and the saints into their cultures.

Alongside this, however, one has to note how historical events have marked the people and their way of transmitting Christian faith, and how the people may now wish to give shape in freedom to their own future, overcoming much that is historically present. It is often impossible to overlook the fact that they are a people subjugated by foreign powers, political, military, economic, and religious. It is part of this domination that foreign religious standards and expressions have been imposed upon them, often to the neglect of the cultural expressions which a previous history had transmitted. In catechesis it is necessary to connect with the people's language, as shaped by the historical complexity of their past, if Gospel and sacrament are to be appropriated within their lives and cultural realities. Any people's own religious language provides stories and symbols of the holy, of links with the past, of bodily time and wholeness, or of cosmic and social harmony. Christian mission and sacramental worship may not have respected this language in the past, but may now draw on it in celebrating Christ.

Needless to say, what is suggested here is only an outline. It is intended to show how the material presented in the work can serve practice and be the foundation of a sacramental catechesis. First, some points are noted about elements that need rethinking in sacramental practice. The catechetical section starts with some considerations on gathering for worship, and then moves on to the motives for assembly and to reflection on the language of the place itself in which people gather. It then considers catechesis on the word, on ritual action, and on blessing. With the context thus established, the concluding thoughts have to do with taking gift as the central motif and with the meaning of mission, first the mission of Word and Spirit from the Father, and then with the mission of the people as Christ's Church.

Liturgical Practice

From what has been presented in this work, it follows that many areas of liturgical celebration are in flux, and that this needs to be acknowledged. This touches on all the factors of celebration treated, namely, the ritual action and elements, the oral, the use of scriptures, the resonance of language, prayer, and the attitude to space and place. Four things are singled out here, however, as matters of urgency for a poetics and praxis of sacramental celebration. These are the form and use of sacramental elements, the forms of prayer, the appeal to the scriptural tradition in a sacramental gathering, and the character of the congregation which gathers.

If there is one aspect of sacramental practice that needs attention more than anything else, it is the respect for the elements of bread, wine, oil, and water. Celebrations should find their focus and their climax in the communal action which shows reception to the revelation given in these elements, when prayed over in blessing God's name. Too often, the ritual shows little regard for their authenticity and little regard for the expression of communion in bringing them forward and then in accessing them when they have been blessed. Furthermore, the issue of their place in a culture and of the appropriate forms which they take in a culture cannot be avoided or set aside. In virtue of the incarnation, and of the sacramental dispensation, the gift of God's love is given people in the flesh and is even ingested into their bellies. This touching and consumption, moreover, best occurs in a gathering which transgresses social boundaries, brings together Christians of all ages and status, and opens their minds and imaginations not only to one another's presence, but also to the presence of the absent. When sacramental things and actions fail to touch both the body physical and the body corporate, the sound and feel of this love is silenced.

Along with this, prayers of blessing need composition which highlights the elements and which invokes God and the remembrance of Christ in images and metaphors that find resonance in the culture of the gathered community. The interplay of the different kinds of praying includes many forms, such as praise, thanksgiving, intercession, exorcism, and lamentation, within this one prayer. This may be highlighted by intonation, music, and response, so that congregations are invited into the movement of prayer, concluding in the doxology that opens their eyes to what is given in the sacramental action. Furthermore, in the composition of blessings due place has to be given to the forms of orality that prevail in any given culture and to the changing relations to orality in the present age.

Accompanying concern for the cohesion of prayer and action, there has to be respect for their common link to scriptural proclamation. Ongoing lectionary revision has to be more attentive to a choice of readings which relies less on traditions of typological explanation and is more attuned to contemporary insights into the genres and forms of scriptures. This may mean a more discordant intertextuality, but is not to be avoided on that account. Most of all, the place given to Old Testament readings in Christian sacramental celebration cries out for serious reconsideration.

Finally, the congregation for keeping sacramental memorial is fittingly composed of a social diversity of persons. Under the conditions of urban living, assemblies are often homogenous in character. In multicultural or multiethnic societies, cultural and ethnic groups worship separately. In cities and suburbs, housing divisions are usually according to class and as a result Church assemblies do not reflect a great social diversity. Furthermore, one of the consequences of the flawed efforts at liturgical renewal in the past thirty years is that those who come together for Sunday worship tend to be like-minded on religious and ritual matters. None of this kind of division can be entirely avoided, but for this very reason congregations need to make efforts to gather the unlike, to represent other to other. It can be rather romantic to point to early Christian communities as ones that brought all the Christians of a place together for worship, since there is early enough evidence pointing to distinctions within these gatherings marked by dispositions of space and rite. However, they at least reflected the fact that belief in the reign of God celebrated in worship involved concern for the material and spiritual welfare of all community members, however socially diverse the membership may have been. It behooves communities today to be more attentive to the bringing together of the diverse when memorial is kept of Christ's Pasch and to the ethical implications of this being together as one in Christ and the Spirit.

Sacramental Catechesis

If the preceding chapters were taken as a guide to sacramental catechesis, this would lead to a reflection on the different factors of celebration discussed, attending to what they mean for involving people in the memorial of Christ as a Church. The reflection might appropriately begin with the act of assembling itself, and then consider place, exchange in the word, ritual actions, blessing prayers, the sacramental gift, and the mission of the Church that is inspired and guided by the same Word and Spirit that are operative in acts of worship.

Gathering for Worship

The first thing to be done in catechesis is to draw attention to the last of the four points mentioned for practice, that is, to the act of gathering. What is it that calls people to assemble and worship? What is to be said of the act itself and to the circumstances of coming together?

The day calls. Each week, communities gather as one week ends and another begins. Apart from the Sunday gathering, sometimes it is the passage of life for members of the community that is being marked. A child has been born and is brought for christening. People marry and testify to their covenant before the Christian community. Some have died and are to be buried, while their part in the communion of faith and love celebrated in worship is still recognized. None of this happens without a call to come together and to ask that lives be taken into God's care. So people are called by the rhythm of life and of time itself to mark the sense of these transitions, to seek direction, to ask what God's beneficence gives to them in giving life, what there is to lead them on, stopping for a while from their own efforts to drive themselves and others forward. Yet, though a rhythm of time has been established, the act of coming together for worship, to hear God's Word, ask God's blessing, remember the divine saving action, breaks the rhythm. It is God who calls, and time is interrupted/disrupted by an extraordinary intervention of grace and promise.

Neighbors call on one another to gather, either by explicit invitation or just by being there, but their very presence asks for a deepening of what is communal in the venture of living. People meet one another constantly in the work place, along the streets, on public transport, in the markets. It is time to meet in some place and in some way, where they can together be given the reason for the hope that brings them on from day to day, from season to season, from year to year. It is time to meet those who are neighbors, to meet some who are left out of one's daily routine, but may more rightly belong there. People have to meet as humans, as God's children, not just as workers and transients on the roads and highways.

There are sounds that convey the call to come together. The church bell rings, or in some parts of the world the drum resounds. This is a call perhaps breaking the stillness, or breaking into and across the noises of living and doing, of telephone and radio and television set. There is an urgency and an invitation in this sound. It is a sound that in its waves gathers in the voice of the atmosphere in which people move, of the earth on which they dwell. It is heard by many, across the streets of a city, across the fields of countryside, across valleys and rivers. Many hear it at the same time, from places distant and separated. It is an invitation to people to respond together, to come together, to let themselves be joined as dwellers on this earth, to move with the rhythm of this sound along the paths of life.

There is movement toward the place of communal worship. As those convoked walk the ways and come closer to the place of assembly, they encounter others. They meet on streets, in parking lots, before the door of the church. They converge from different places, belong maybe to different races, but here they encounter each other, seeing in the face of the other one who beckons them into communion and challenges their vision of themselves. All converge and enter the place of worship as a people gathered and gathering.

Time calls; past and future call. These are people who belong to "their times," but also to their history. Gathering together they "gather in" the past and shape their outlook on the future. What events, past and present, it may be asked, give shape to their existence and expectations at this time. Time itself is constantly interrupted and reshaped by divine event and by divine grace. Something happens in worship that brings something new into the living of time, which alters it and our way of living in "our times." In connection with what memories and what perspectives, then, do people come together to assemble around the words and rites of Christian worship and to think differently of their future and of the future that God promises to those who are now in need and in pain.

People may of course in fact come out of nostalgia for an era that is passing away, when certain kinds of religious expression still seemed to evoke the holy for them. They may come because they want something deeper to their lives than "earning a living." They may come looking for a community that respects their being as humans and saves them from dehumanizing forces. They may come prompted by the presence of evil of one sort or another, quite literally expecting redemption. They may come because they see being Christian part of their national and cultural heritage, or they may be looking for a fullness and a holiness that the culture seems to deny. Celebration has to resonate with all this. Catechesis has to touch on all these motivations in order to find the point at which the Gospel and its sacramental promise address people, confirming, disrupting, or changing these motivations and the outlook on life that they express.

Reasons to Assemble

The next point, therefore, would be to draw out the religious reasons for assembly and to relate these to the call that comes from Christ. It is one thing to touch on why people assemble and another to ask why God calls them to do so. Then one has to ask what may move them to respond to this call that they have heard in such different ways? For all who hear the bell or the drum or meet their neighbors along the way, a voice speaks, but often it is heard indistinctly, wonderingly, or even inattentively. For believers, there is a divine voice revealed and concealed within the sound that summons. It says to come. It says to come to hear a word from God. It says to come to receive the gifts of life and spirit that are set forth. It says to come, to be one in Jesus Christ, the Savior of the world.

It is a voice that those who gather have heard before, a voice that has promised life, a voice that says that there is urgency in remembering Jesus Christ and all that God is and speaks through him. They are called as Church, to heed God's call and offer, to remember and proclaim Christ, to receive a gift, to strengthen themselves as disciples. Assembly is a response to God's call, to the covenant with God that Christ offers in his body and blood, and in the gift of his Spirit. To gather is to respond in the Spirit, to let the Spirit who dwells within break through all the noise and anxiety of scattered lives, to bring people to the very center of their existence and there be renewed, to still time's passage and to find a vector toward a life consummated in the exchange offered by God's giving and gift. To assemble is to be Christian together, to gather as a people of God, as Church, as the body of Christ. They are called as a people, with the past present to them and the future yet to be discovered, yet located in the acknowledgment of God's gifts.

Gift-Bringing

Assembling, people bring gifts, in gratitude for what they are and have, in a sense of communion with others, and especially to bring into the assembly the richness of their lives and the depth of their need They bring gifts that express themselves, the urges and the needs of life, expecting to encounter the urges and the needs of others. Though gathering to receive from God, they obey the urge to bring something of their own, even if only in this way to bring themselves more fully. They place their gifts in the basket, putting them there, alongside those of others, confiding them to the caring Church. What they bring will be blessed, shared, and increased by God's own giving. In the blessing of the gifts, it is life itself that is given increase. An exchange, an economy, is opened up in which God's initiative outstrips humanity's and brings about a new order.

The Place of Sacramental Action

Entering the place of worship is an important moment in sacramental action and deserves attention in catechesis and practice, lest the visual aspects of sacramental life be passed over or merely glanced over. The place for gathering is a place that welcomes and gathers. How the place is disposed intertwines with the mystagogy. There is a table at the center, laid out for all to access, a pool through which to pass, oil to heal and anoint, porches for penitents to approach reconciliation, a chapel in which to wake the dead and keep their memory. It may be an ancient building, rich in history and in artefacts of the past. It may be a very simple space, and ad hoc gathering spot for a pilgrim people. In older buildings, practice and catechesis are faced with the jolt occasioned by the juxtaposition of present liturgy and past aesthetic. In improvised gathering places, it will highlight the drama of God's incarnational presence, leaving its traces on people's lives without need of majestic splendor, but giving a divine glory even to the provisional, the tent, in which Christian people find themselves assembled.

The Cross, caught maybe in the light from the windows or receding into the shadows, is the axis of the place. There are the saints and their stories to gather into a history of being a people. There are the mementos of the dead. The living and the dead are together a community, invited and gathered by what is offered by the Cross of Jesus Christ, a community that has lasted many generations, eager now to transmit truth and life as they have been transmitted in the past. This is a community that will continue with new memories to pass on, with fresh witness to God's love and Christ's covenant, and the power of the Spirit to make all things new.

Often in church buildings, there is a place for quiet prayer, and in Catholic churches it is often the place to keep the reserved eucharistic sacrament, and maybe the holy oils. Its role in relation to celebration of the liturgy needs care, in its placement, its physical disposition, and in catechesis, lest it draw people away from this, instead of drawing them into it. The spot is one that is connected with the gathering, a spot where people may prolong its reflection in silence, in the depths of their hearts, before God and his Christ, or even come together in quieter moments, a few at a time.

Within this disposition of place, there are things to see and to be given thought. There are bread, wine, oil, water. Making these visible is a necessary preliminary to catechesis and blessing. They are the elements in which the Church celebrates, keeps memory, transforms life. This is no gaudy and rich banquet, but it is more full of life than any festal gathering. These elements give focus to human existence in the world, their oneness with each other and their place within the universe. They are the gifts of creation and life and the heart of communion. They are what life on the earth produces

and gives, when human beings live with it in harmony. Too often, their possession and production are contaminated by sin, for they are not always given
generously, not always shared, or perhaps they have to be won by hard sweat,
against many odds. They are simple things that bring joy, yet they are often
won through struggle and suffering and amid grief. Many memories may be
connected with these simple realities and can be catechetically evoked. Good
celebration honors them and lets them speak.

As people settle into place, they hear the call to gather in Christ's name,
a call proclaimed by the priest and ministers who serve this gathering. Opening words and song, the music of instruments, maybe even dance, engender
harmony with one another and with the universe. All this is essential to right
worship. United thus in memory, gratitude, jubilation, sorrow, hope, and contrition, the community gathers itself into a holy silence. To let the silence
make people catch their breath at the beginning of liturgy brings them into
God's space and time. The priest prays and all pray as one with him and with
one another to bring themselves all together before God in his holy place.

Hearing the Word

The hearing of the word needs good homilies and ample catechesis, words
that enable people to hear the Word in all its richness and plenty. It is presented as the Word of the Lord addressed to the congregation, with the oft
repeated phrase, I am the Lord, to bring out this prophetic quality. Though
people are aware that as originally formed it was not directed to them, they
can appreciate how it comes to them from God, across time, within a community, through the constant hearing, reading, and reflecting upon the dealings
of God with the people of Israel, of Jesus with his disciples, of the preachers
and writers of the New Testament with their communities. Along with attention to the prophecy of the Hebrew heritage there has to be attention to
the prophetic elements in Jesus' discourse, as he calls on people to heed the
kingdom and speaks to its eschatological future.

It is by a good understanding of the different genres of scripture that
people can grasp what it is to keep memory of an event in the past. It is
when the word is related to symbol and ritual action that the link to human
life, within the cosmos, comes to the fore. The word prophetically addressed
is a word that is alive within a people, within the Church, and transmitted
through these mediators as God's own call and promise to the people of their
own time and place. Noting the place and character of prophecy in the work
of salvation, a congregation is also brought to better appreciate the nature of
covenant and the kind of relationship God has with the Church. Its members
will be attentive as a result to both the eschatological nature of their call
and the ethical commitments of being God's people in the societies taking
shape around them. The eschatological tone inherent in prophecy touches
on their sense of being part of the world and of all creation, of living out of

God's promise and advent, and out of hope for the future. Ethically, this is to challenge the oft assumed modes and manners of society and history making.

Thus through a catechesis on prophecy, a congregation is readied to hear the stories and narratives of God's saving deeds. In the memory of Jesus Christ, all these stories that draw people converge around the story of Christ's Pasch. Preaching and catechizing on these stories, one can be mindful of the threefold path of *mimesis*. The narratives are heard but need to be recast in terms of the stories, rites, symbols, and images that constitute people's own daily and cultural identity. In this transposition, however, the plot of the story has to be kept intact, and this will differ somewhat from story to story, given the diversity of plot in each of the Gospel narratives. Attention to this diversity is important in contemporary catechesis, given the cultural and historical flux of the era. This very diversity can draw the congregation into the story, challenged as it is to bring what they hear into their own remembrance. In this way, the hearers of the word move to concrete insight into the gifts of forgiveness and redemption given through Christ, the promises made, and the way of discipleship opened up as a way of witnessing to God's kingdom in the world. Invocation of the Holy Spirit in guiding the hearing of tradition and engaging in faith with God and the Church is a supplement to the hearing of the story itself.

Among the narratives that deserve explanation, due attention has to be given to the episodes from the Hebrew scriptures and to parables. As explained earlier, a good hearing of the Hebrew scriptures draws attention to the various ways in which in the midst of life faith in the God of covenant grows, even within challenge. The parables are the stories that enable people to grasp how faith and hope in Christ are lived out, through a daily wisdom and often through a reversal of accustomed suppositions and values.

In a sacramental catechesis on memorial that is suited to this present age in the life of the Church, the plot needs to underline the central imagery of divine love and divine gift. In this it will show the role of the Word made flesh and of the Spirit in giving God's love to the world. As a striking image of this love, there is the self-emptying of Christ, the pouring out of his life, on the Cross and at the Supper into his sacraments. A catechesis on the baptism in the Jordan highlights his relation to the Father and to his mission, and the gift of the Holy Spirit that anoints him. The gift of the Spirit is further appreciated through the recall of the stories of Pentecost and of the life of the early Christian Churches. The inner freedom that comes in the gift of the Spirit is what enables people to hear anew and to shape their lives anew as they appropriate the word.

Teaching and preaching wisdom literature is one of the more effective ways of relating faith, both to the daily and to the mystery of creation. This literature expresses the wonder of God's guidance and love present in created things, and in the daily round of activities shaped by living in harmony with earth and the passage of seasons and of time. It also offers a model of the just person as one who respects the earth and neighbor, who knows God's loving and just presence, and who is willing to suffer in testimony to the goodness of God and to the divine justice that guides human relations.

Ritual Action

Attention is already drawn to this by highlighting the presence and the meaning of the elements of ritual celebration, bread, wine, oil, and water, connected with gathering. Both their link with the cosmic and their link with human living can be brought out. This goes with a reflection on living in time, with a sense of the daily blended with an openness to history, to cosmic time, and to the transcendent of God which is outside of all measurements.

What is vital to good exercise of the body and to catechesis on bodily movement could follow out the lines pursued in chapter 4 of this book, on rituality. This means being alert to what is experienced through the body, in humanity's being one with earth, in being marked by traditions, and in being together a social body. All this is then related to the being Church, being on this earth the body of Christ, and so sharing in the oneness of the triune God manifested in love and self-emptying. The postures of prayer are those of gratitude, supplication, wonder, and receiving. They need to be learned for all the key moments of sacramental action. In Western congregations today joining hands at the Lord's Prayer and hearty embrace at the kiss of peace often exhaust the bodily repertory of a congregation. African and African American congregations are more responsive in their body and movement to the Lord's presence and giving.

This ritual catechesis will differ somewhat according to the participants in the rites. One kind of catechesis is needed, for example, for adult candidates for baptism, and another for infants and small children. In the former case, more notice is given to images of pilgrimage, process and conversion, to the journey that is followed to the pool and the anointing, and through them to the eucharistic table. Even here, openness to gift has to be the central motif. It is this openness which is fostered by the path of conversion. In the case of children, it is the faith and responsibility of parents and of the Church community in marking the beginning of life with this rite which has to be explained and made conscious, as well as the gifts given to the child that will guide and direct its progress through life, within the body of the believing Church. In talking of the journey to be taken in faith or of the grace given to a child through parents and community, the situation of time and place is necessarily addressed, as the promise of grace and of the gift of life and love is inserted into the realities of human life.

Congregations share in the ritual actions and blessings of the anointing of the sick, penance, marriage, and order. When two people exchange consent and gift before a community, with hands and face as well as with words, there is a radiance which draws into the light of Christ. In the anointing of the sick, those present may be asked to touch or lay hands on the sick person. In penance, people prostrate themselves and rise from the ground in welcoming the renewal of the grace of the Spirit. Within the celebration of the sacrament of order, there is room for rites that witness to the candidate's readiness to serve and to the congregation's presentation of this person to God.

A eucharistic catechesis attends to the actions of the common table. Eucharistic practice still has to let the rites of celebration converge toward the central act of communion. To serve these aims, it is possible to draw on Gospel images and stories, such as the washing of the feet at the Last Supper, the meals shared by Jesus during his lifetime, the feeding of the crowds as narrated in several places, and the meals with the disciples after the resurrection. People themselves enjoy various experiences of sharing a meal, in plenty and in poverty, and know what it is to toil for food and to share food with others, even with people unknown to them, but whom they are called to meet at table. Finally, there is the imagery of the eschatological banquet, which locates hope and promise in the eucharistic sharing in the bread and wine, in the body and blood of Christ.

Blessing Prayers

The primary blessings of Christian rite are proclaimed over the things of the earth, in recognition of the wonder of God's revelation and gift that come to us within them and over the actions of members of the community in anointing, marriage, order, and penance. The blessing prayer itself is enhanced by good voice, good posture, good song. Otherwise its proclamation and its catechesis will fall flat.

The first thing in the catechesis of blessing is to explain that it is a proclamation, that is, in hymnic form the Church takes up the wonder of God's grace and proclaims it in the voice given her by the Spirit. If a proper appreciation of the things of earth and their significance has emerged in the practices and in the catechesis of gathering and ritual, it will be evident that this proclamation is one that in the first place shows forth the love and self-gift of God in the act of creation. It is in the acknowledgment of this gift that the Church is led to proclaim the gift of redemption, the restoration of all things in Christ, and the love of God poured forth in Christ and in the gift of the Spirit. Proclaiming and thanking God over the things of earth and for the gift of creation, is not properly speaking a sacrifice or a return of things received. It is rather to acknowledge the presence of God's love and self-communication in this act of creation. It is to acknowledge likewise that in the harmony of creation and redemption in the gift of Christ offered in the incarnation and now in sacrament, God continues to bless the world and to reconcile it to himself through the things of earth, and through humanity's oneness with these things. Sacramental spirituality is incarnational, terrestrial. When blessing is pronounced over persons, their lives and their testimony of faith are assumed into the congregation's memorial of the actions and gifts of Jesus Christ, in which God events again among this covenant people.

The two primary forms of proclamation are praise and thanksgiving. In thanksgiving, the Church recalls all the works of creation and salvation, which find their apex in Christ and in the expectation of the peace and justice of God to which the mysteries of his flesh give rise. There is no break between offering the things of earth and making thanks for redemption, but the thanksgiving is one extended acknowledgment of what is given through earthly realities, first the love and life of creation itself, and then the reconciliation of a world disrupted by evil through the Word made flesh and through the sacraments of blessed earthly realities which he has given to the Church. In this thanksgiving, she recognizes that the gifts given in Christ and the Spirit have joined her with Father, Son, and Spirit in a communion of love and of mission. The doxology of blessing draws people into the center of God's own triune mystery. It is from that center, that people are sent forth with the mission to extend God's gifts of love and reconciliation to the world.

It is quite often intercession that joins congregations more directly in their own lives with the sacramental blessings. In making intercession, people touch on those things in their lives and remember the persons for whom they are grateful or who stand in need of God's grace. Intercession can paradoxically open minds and hearts to the blessing already shared, and thus it can lead people from need to thanksgiving. In face of trial and stress, catechesis can also make use of the genre of lament to lead to intercession and to a deeper insight into the nature of God's love and blessing. Exorcism is another form which if rightly explained can point to those things in human life where evil enters and which need to be opened up to receive the peace and reconciliation of God.

A catechesis of blessing prayers is a good place to explain the nature of sacrament as memorial and the role of the Holy Spirit. Memorial takes in present, past, and future. As an *anamnesis* it looks to God's actions in Christ and in the sending of the Spirit and finds in these a continued promise and assurance of gift and of life to come. As a *mimesis*, it draws this promise and gift into the living reality of the congregation, opens it to God's love, and draws it into the divine mystery revealed. It highlights both the grace of what is possessed and lived and the need for forgiveness and reconciliation. It looks to the past and the promises held forth in the deeds of God, and especially in the works of Christ. This opens forth the hope for the future that can embrace present reality and insert that hope for the future into it. In this memorial, it is the one loving act of God that is active in past and present and that gives hope for the future of gracious blessing. The presence of Christ in this sacramental memorial emerges from the act of giving which he made at the Supper, from his blessing of the water through descending into it, which are ways in which he gave concrete and communicable shape to the gift of himself in his death on the Cross and at his Supper with his disciples.

The role of the Spirit is tied to the Church's act of memorial. It is the inner action of the Spirit which enables her to see Christ's gift in every and any moment and human reality and to express this in a prayerful and creative way and out of an act of love which abides in the heart. It is in the communion of this love, and only in the communion of this love, that Christ is remembered and that hope is engendered.

The transformation of the things of earth, bread, wine, oil, and water, which is ascribed to blessing, needs to be inserted into the memorial of creation and redemption. They are no "ordinary" things when thanksgiving has been made over them in the name of Christ, because they have been made transparent to the love and grace of God that is shown forth in them and in their participation. It is their being within human life which is changed, for they now take on sacramental reality, not only as signs but as gifts of grace and, in the Eucharist, of Christ's self-gift.

Gifts Given

Gift is the pivot of the sacramental action and catechesis. Catechesis would highlight the nature of the Church as the place and the assembly in which God's gift is received and its presence recognized in life and in things of earth. What the ritual, the word, and the prayers do is to open up the space for the reception of this gift and for the recognition of its presence. The sacrament names this gift, names it as God's self-gift, and as the gift which forms and shapes the Church. In the sacramental action, the faithful receive the gifts of Christ, Word Incarnate, and the Spirit, gifts of God's own Love. These gifts touch people within the ritual action and prayer, at the point of human living signified by the ritual action. The bodily rites bring to the fore the relation to daily time, historical time, cosmic time, and beyond time. The gifts, Word and Spirit, given through sacrament insert themselves into human life in the space opened up by these rites, in the struggle with mortality, evil, and sin. A sacramental catechesis of these gifts may draw on the story of Christ's baptism in the Jordan, on the healing stories of Christ's ministry, on the story of the Last Supper, in its intrinsic relation to the Cross, and on the story of the Supper at Emmaus, with its promise of what is to come in the light of the resurrection. There is room likewise to draw on the parables of the kingdom, relating them to sacramental action and sacramental wisdom. Elaborating on sacramental gift points to communion with Christ in his Paschal mystery, the gift of the Holy Spirit, the gift of eschatological hope, and the gift of communion in the Church. Furthermore, this communion cannot be lived except in communion with the things of earth, as gifts of God's love in creation, and gifts that share in the redemptive promises of Jesus Christ.

Mission

At the end of each sacramental liturgy, the congregation is sent forth in Christ's peace, with a mission to witness to him, to the power of his Spirit, and to the gift of God's love. A catechesis on this mission has to complete sacramental catechesis, for it tells of what people become through receiving the gift of divine love, in the varying ways in which this enters their lives, through each of the sacraments. As they go forth, in the fullness of the gift received, the congregation expect their faith to be tested and their words challenged. They will also expect to be met by the other who awaits them finding in them the Christ who awaits. When these opportunities and challenges are met in the love and hope generated through sacramental worship, the Church in all its members and as a community gives witness to the sending into the world of the love of God, embodied in Christ and in his disciples, and active through the power and gift of the indwelling Spirit. With due presentation of the relation of mission to gift, catechesis can incorporate reflection on the ethical commitment asked of those who celebrate God's love.

Conclusion

This final chapter is skeletal. The intention has been simply to show how the lines of reflection pursued throughout the work can affect practice and be retrieved in sacramental catechesis. If there are two key words to this, they are *celebration* and *gift*. Good celebration and good catechesis open hearts to the dynamic of celebration. In so doing, they open them to the gift of God, to the gift of life and of love, given in the giving of Word and Spirit.

Selected Bibliography
in English

The purpose of this bibliography, restricted to titles published in English, is to present key works that help to incorporate contemporary studies of language and ritual into the theology of sacrament. Some carry extensive bibliographies that allow for further research.

Hermeneutics and Language

Bleicher, Josef, ed. *Contemporary Hermeneutics: Hermeneutics as Method, Philosophy and Critique*. London: Routledge & Kegan Paul, 1980. This is a selection of texts, with introduction to each, from key writers in the field.

Eco, Umberto. *Semiotics and the Philosophy of Language*. Bloomington: Indiana University Press, 1986. This is a good introduction to the field of semiotics, with explanations of other writers such as C. Peirce and A. Greimas and an ample bibliography.

Gadamer, Hans-Georg. *Truth and Method*. Trans. Joel Weinsheimer and Donald G. Marshall. 2d rev. ed. New York: Continuum; repr. 1994. This remains the most fundamental contemporary work in the field of hermeneutics.

Grondin, Jean. *Introduction to Philosophical Hermeneutics*. Trans. Joel Weinsheimer. New Haven and London: Yale University Press, 1994. This is a good introduction to the history of hermeneutics and to leading contemporary authors and trends.

Kristeva, Julia. *The Kristeva Reader*. Ed. Toril Moi. New York: Columbia University Press, 1986.

———. *Powers of Horror: An Essay on Abjection*. Trans. Leon S. Roudiez. New York: Columbia University Press, 1982. These two titles provide insight into Kristeva's feminist hermeneutics and her way of looking at symbolic systems.

Ricoeur, Paul. *A Ricoeur Reader: Reflection and Imagination*. Ed. Mario J. Valdés. Toronto: University of Toronto Press, 1991.

———. *Figuring the Sacred: Religion, Narrative, and Imagination*. Trans. David Pellauer. Ed. Mark I. Wallace. Minneapolis: Fortress Press, 1995. Of the abundant works of Paul Ricoeur, these two collections of essays seem to be the most directly helpful to reflection on sacraments and sacramental liturgy.

Hermeneutics and Theology

Chopp, Rebecca. *The Power to Speak: Feminism, Language, God*. New York: Crossroad, 1991. In this work, Chopp is in dialogue with French feminism to work out an understanding of the Bible as Word of God and of its interpretation by feminist theologians who are looking for a transformation from patriarchy for Church and society.

Schüssler Fiorenza, Elisabeth. *Bread Not Stone: The Challenge of Feminist Biblical Interpretation.* Boston: Beacon Press, 1984. In this collection of essays, Schüssler Fiorenza presents the hermeneutical principles which she has developed in her major works in feminist theology.

Thiselton, Anthony. *New Horizons in Hermeneutics: The Theory and Practice of Transforming Biblical Reading.* Grand Rapids, Mich.: Zondervan Publishing House, 1992. Thiselton surveys the major trends in the study of language in relation to their influence on the interpretation of the scriptures, and hence on the theological implications of such readings.

Tracy, David. *The Analogical Imagination.* New York: Crossroad, 1985. With abundant reference to the work of Gadamer, Ricoeur, and Mircea Eliade, Tracy looks at the nature of the religious classic, at the New Testament as the Christian classic, at the dialectic between proclamation and manifestation, and at the sacramental imagination.

Postmodernity, Postmodernism

Hutcheon, Linda. *A Poetics of Postmodernism: History, Theory, Fiction.* New York and London: Routledge, 1988.

Jencks, Charles. *What Is Post-Modernism?* London: Academy Editions, 1986. Rev. ed., 1996.

Kearney, Richard. *Poetics of Imagining: From Husserl to Lyotard.* London: HarperCollins-Academic, 1991.

Madison, G. B. *The Hermeneutics of Postmodernity.* Bloomington and Indianapolis: Indiana University Press, 1990.

Tracy, David. *Plurality and Ambiguity: Hermeneutics, Religion, Hope.* San Francisco: Harper & Row, 1987.

Hermeneutics, Postmodernism, and Theology

Lafont, Ghislain. *God, Time, and Being.* Trans. Leonard Maluf. Petersham, Mass.: St. Bede's Publications, 1992. Lafont weaves hermeneutics, an interest in the postmodern, and Thomistic metaphysics into a theology of God. Sections of the book treat of the Eucharist in the context of biblical interpretation and naming God.

Marion, Jean-Luc. *God without Being.* Trans. Thomas Carlson. Chicago: University of Chicago Press, 1991. Though this is a work of philosophy/phenomenology, it does in part treat theology, and specifically eucharistic theology. It has proved important to writers who want to develop a postmodern sacramental theology.

Tilley, Terrence W., et al. *Postmodern Theologies: The Challenge of Religious Diversity.* Maryknoll, N.Y.: Orbis Books, 1995. This is a simple but useful survey of the various types of theological writings and of the principal theological writers who tend to be connected under the label of postmodern.

Ritual Studies

Bell, Catherine. *Ritual Theory, Ritual Practice.* New York and Oxford: Oxford University Press, 1992.

Fenn, Richard K. *Liturgies and Trials: The Secularization of Religious Language.* New York: Pilgrim Press, 1982.

Grimes, Ronald J. *Beginnings in Ritual Studies.* Washington, D.C.: University Press of America, 1982.

————. *Research in Ritual Studies.* Metuchen, N.J.: Scarecrow Press, 1985.

Kertzer, David I. *Ritual, Politics and Power.* New Haven and London: Yale University Press, 1988.

Sacrament, Language, and Ritual Studies

Chauvet, Louis-Marie. *Symbol and Sacrament.* Trans. P. Madigan and M. Beaumont. Collegeville, Minn.: Liturgical Press, 1995. This is currently the most influential work in the field developing a postmodern approach to the theology of sacramentality. Most critical reviews have been written in French and Italian, but there is a summary and critique of the book by Vincent J. Miller: "An Abyss at the Heart of Mediation: Louis-Marie Chauvet's Fundamental Theology of Sacramentality," *Horizons* 24, no. 2 (1997): 230–47.

Cooke, Bernard. *The Distancing of God: The Ambiguity of Symbol in History and Theology.* Minneapolis: Fortress Press, 1990. In the light of contemporary studies on symbolics, Cooke treats of the ambivalence of organized religion in its patterns of worship, structuring, and theological reflection.

Irwin, Kevin W. *Context and Text: Method in Liturgical Theology.* Collegeville, Minn.: Liturgical Press, 1994. In the light of his interpretation of the principle *lex orandi lex credendi*, Irwin sets out the principles for a theological interpretation of liturgical texts, rites, and symbols.

Joncas, Michael. "Giorgio Bonaccorso's Semiotic Approach to Liturgical Studies: A Review of *Introduzione allo Studio della Liturgia*," *Questions Liturgiques* 73 (1992): 161–69. In this review article Joncas introduces English-speaking readers to the use of semiotics by one of the leading figures in the Pastoral Liturgical Institute attached to the Abbey of S. Giustina in Padua, Italy.

Lukken, Gerard. "Liturgy and Language: An Approach from Semiotics," *Questions Liturgiques* 73 (1992): 36–52. A very helpful introduction by this Dutch author to the use of the semiotics of A. Greimas in the field of liturgical studies.

————. *Per Visibilia ad Invisibilia: Anthropological, Theological and Semiotic Studies on the Liturgy and the Sacraments.* Ed. Louis van Tongeren and Charles Caspers. Kampen, The Netherlands: Pharos, 1994. Though only some of the articles in this collection are in English, they exemplify the use of semiotics in different areas of liturgical studies.

Power, David N. *Unsearchable Riches: The Symbolic Nature of Liturgy.* New York: Pueblo, 1984.

————. "Liturgy as an Act of Communication and Communion: Cultural and Practical Implications in an Age Becoming Digital," *Mission* 3, no. 1 (1996): 43–62.

Procter-Smith, Marjorie, and Janet R. Walton, eds. *Women at Worship: Interpretations of North American Diversity.* Louisville: Westminster/John Knox Press, 1993. With an introductory article by Mary Collins on feminist principles of worship, this book includes other specific studies of North American diversity.

Saliers, Don E. *Worship as Theology: Foretaste of Glory Divine.* Nashville: Abingdon
    Press, 1994. In this highly readable book, Saliers develops a theology of worship
    from a hermeneutical reading of the texts that belong in the liturgical canon.

In addition to these works, there are several helpful articles in the *New Dictionary of
Sacramental Worship.* Ed. Peter E. Fink. Collegeville, Minn.: Liturgical Press, 1990:

Collins, Mary. "Liturgical Language," 651–60.
Fink, Peter, "Imagination and Worship," 587–94.
Happel, Stephen. "Symbol," 1237–45.
Martos, Joseph. "Sacraments and the Human Sciences," 576–86.
Saliers, Don E. "Hermeneutics and Worship," 523–26.
————. "Liturgical Aesthetics," 31–39.
Zimmerman, Joyce. "Language and Human Experience," 644–51.

The following issues of the international periodical *Concilium* are pertinent:

Liturgy and Human Passage. Ed. Luis Maldonado and David Power, no. 112, 1978.
Symbol and Art in Worship. Ed. Luis Maldonado and David Power, no. 132, 1980.
Liturgy: A Creative Tradition. Ed. Mary Collins and David Power, no. 162, 1983.
Liturgical Experience of Faith. Ed. David Power and Herman Schmidt, no. 72, 1992.
Liturgy and the Body. Ed. Louis-Marie Chauvet and François Kabasele Lumbala,
    1995/3.

Sacraments, Liturgy, and Culture

Chupungco, Anscar J. *Liturgical Inculturation, Sacramentals, Religiosity and Catechesis.*
    Collegeville, Minn.: Liturgical Press, 1992.
Egbulem, Nwaka Chris. *The Power of Afrocentric Celebrations: Inspirations from the
    Zairean Liturgy.* New York: Crossroad, 1996.
Kabasele Lumbala, F. *Celebrating Jesus Christ in Africa.* Translated from the French.
    With a Foreword by David N. Power. Maryknoll, N.Y.: Orbis Books, 1998.
Power, David, and Herman Schmidt, eds. *Liturgy and Cultural Religious Traditions.*
    Concilium 102 (1977).
Senn, Frank C. *Christian Worship and Its Cultural Setting.* Philadelphia: Fortress Press,
    1983.
Stauffer, S. Anita, ed. *Worship and Culture in Dialogue.* Geneva: Lutheran World
    Federation, 1994. This book carries an extensive bibliography.
Uzukwu, Elochukwu E. *Worship as Body Language: Introduction to Christian Worship:
    An African Orientation.* Collegeville, Minn.: Liturgical Press, 1997.

Art, Architecture, and the Religious Imagination

These titles have been chosen because they focus on interpretation and not simply on history.

Apostolos-Cappadona, Diane, ed. *Art, Creativity and the Sacred.* New York: Crossroad,
    1984.
Belting, Hans. *Likeness and Presence: A History of the Image before the Era of Art.* Trans.
    Edmund Jephcott. Chicago and London: University of Chicago Press, 1994.

Blaauw, Sible de. "Architecture and Liturgy in Late Antiquity and the Middle Ages. Traditions and Trends in Modern Scholarship," *Archiv für Liturgiewissenschaft* 33 (1991): 1–34. This article gives numerous references in the footnotes.

Dillenberger, John. *A Theology of Artistic Sensibilities: The Visual Arts and the Church*. New York: Crossroad, 1986.

Freedberg, David. *The Power of Images: Studies in the History and Theory of Response*. Chicago and London: University of Chicago Press, 1989.

Kessler, Herbert L. "On the State of Medieval Art History," *Art Bulletin* 70 (1988): 166–87.

Miles, Margaret R. *Image as Insight: Visual Understanding in Western Christianity and Secular Culture*. Boston: Beacon Press, 1985.

Walton, Janet R. *Art and Worship: A Vital Connection*. Wilmington, Del.: Michael Glazier, 1988.

Index of Proper Names

Index of Subjects